Communism and the Politics of Inequalities

Communism and the Politics of Inequalities

Edited by
Daniel N. Nelson
University of Kentucky

LexingtonBooks
D.C. Heath and Company
Lexington, Massachusetts
Toronto

Library of Congress Cataloging in Publication Data
Main entry under title:

Communism and the politics of inequalities.

Includes index.
1. Equality–Communist countries. 2. Social classes–Communist countries. 3. Elite (Social sciences)–Communist countries. 4. Equality of states. 5. Communism. I. Nelson, Daniel N., 1948–   .
JC575.C65 1983   305.5'2'091717   81–48525
ISBN 0–669–05415–1

Copyright © 1983 by D.C. Heath and Company

Published simultaneously in Canada   86–4875

Printed in the United States of America

International Standard Book Number: 0–669–05415–1

Library of Congress Catalog Card Number: 81–48525

Contents

Introduction

Daniel N. Nelson

Most governments and the citizens they rule accept differences regarding skills, intelligence, interests, and desires as givens and therefore irrelevant to politics. Likewise, specialization and differentiation of occupations and organizations are understood generally as unavoidable consequences of socioeconomic development. Some differences, however, are regarded as inequalities—differences in access to socioeconomic or political goods among classes, nationalities, regions, and sexes that ought not exist. Inequality, then, is not a neutral concept. Instead, it is value laden, implying a judgment that certain dimensions of difference should be combated via governmental decisions affecting the allocation of resources.

Most governments promise to mitigate inequalities but fail. Communist systems are unique neither in their rhetorical commitment to combating inequalities nor in their mediocre performance. But communist systems *are* distinct insofar as their legitimacy is linked inextricably to egalitarian values.[1] Communist party governments are identified strongly with efforts to diminish and, at some point, eliminate inequalities. Their raison d'être, indeed, is to eliminate old, and prevent new, inequalities that arise from economically based class distinctions. For Marxists, inequalities have but one origin; as long as the means of production are owned privately and the labor of others exploited to produce for the profit of those owners, many dimensions of inequalities will follow. Marx did not claim that the initial stage of communist society would be cleansed of all inequalities, but that standards by which workers are rewarded would be equal; classes would cease to exist, although more productive individuals would receive proportionately greater benefits. As the remnants of bourgeois society were uprooted, however, the principle of need would increasingly guide the distribution of resources.

Ironically, for communist regimes, their Leninist roots stress hierarchy and elitism while their Stalinist pasts emphasize power and coercion.[2] These are not regime characteristics from which egalitarian policies implied by Marx can easily emanate. This book concerns such an irony—of regimes speaking the rhetoric of equity while maintaining elitist, coercive, and in-egalitarian systems. Within these contrasts among promises, policy, and performance in communist systems lies the politics of socioeconomic inequalities. My intention in assembling this book has been to address the political antecedents, consequences, and correlates of socioeconomic inequity in communist states. I have asked nine other scholars known for their research on communist politics and the distribution of resources within them to examine these issues from either comparative or nation-specific perspectives. (The content of the chapters and their relationship to one another will be considered in detail via introductions to Parts I and II.)

Whether in comparative or case-study selections, the reader will become aware that a core debate turns on whether or not communist systems, vis-à-vis noncommunist ones or in comparison with their own pasts, have made significant headway in combating socioeconomic inequalities. Participating in that debate, the contributors to this book are in less than total accord regarding the most appropriate indexes by which to test such a proposition; they also focus on different levels of analysis and employ varying definitions of certain dimensions of inequalities, such as class or nationality, or different notions of how such terms are interwoven. Ultimately this book's contributors are not unanimous in their views about communist states' performance in combating inequalities or the consequences of such performance.

Contributors also point to variations among communist systems regarding the degree to which inequalities remain, the reasons for or origins of such inequalities, and their systemic impact. In the broad comparative chapters of Part I, by Bunce, Nelson, Robertson, and Clark, the system of communist states, the patterns of inequalities among them, and politics by which inequalities are combated, are considered. In six case studies, by Bahry, Lampton, Woodward, Fischer, Bielasiak, and Wolchik, specific dimensions of inequalities and their impact on communist systems are examined.

The diversity of views and approaches is critical because it represents the debate among scholars and practitioners about the politics of inequalities in communist states. For some observers, especially those in governmental posts concerned about communist regimes' stability and their consequent diplomatic or military reliability, attention must be nation-specific and focused on immediate and policy-related issues. (Do inequalities motivate workers in a particular strike? Will their demands be met? What will be the outcome of such a crisis regarding that nation's economy or political leadership?) For another set of observers, testing theoretically relevant propositions, probing the utility of concepts, and challenging existing paradigms are the principal tasks of inquiry. Because it was written by scholars, the orientation of this book is toward the latter tasks. But the mix of analytical tools and perspectives means that the practitioner will find guidance here too.

The debate about the politics of inequalities in communist systems in the West could be misconstrued as scholarly smirking about the failures of socialism. The gaps among promises, policy, and performance, however, are universal, as suggested in several of the chapters in Part I. Moreover, the desire to combat inequalities may be dimmed by a limited capacity to effect significant change in the way resources are distributed. None of the contributors argues that the state socialism of Communist party regimes has failed where Western capitalism has been a model of success in the promotion of equality. It is nevertheless fair to say that Communist party governments have, more than Western capitalism, put all of their eggs in one basket—that of system performance in an effort to derive legitimacy from growth while reducing inequalities. When growth slows or evaporates while inequalities persist, communist systems have little else on which to lean for their legitimacy. The consequences of such tenuous legitimacy can be seen in the course of Polish politics not only in the 1980s but in prior decades as well. Perhaps it goes without saying that Poland is not a typical case of Communist party regimes. Yet, the need to foster an image of growth and egalitarian extractive and distributive policies is evident in all communist systems through rhetoric devoted to such topics and the socialization efforts that insist that these policies are being pursued and achieved. Enormous political capital is invested by Communist party regimes in their reputation as opponents of inequality. To their publics and each other, European Communist party leaders allege that they have reached a stage of developed socialism in which expanding participatory opportunities are coupled with an increasingly equal distribution of wealth in an environment of economic growth.

In systems so linked to the concept of equality, then, Western political analysis cannot ignore the conflicting implications of economic integration with the USSR, heavy military and industrial investments, political repression by regimes against dissident citizens, and other decisions that limit capacity to pursue egalitarian values. The contributors to this book examine these conflicting implications and other aspects of inequality in communist systems. My concluding remarks will return to the themes developed by the authors, offering an assessment regarding the political futures of communist states given findings presented in this book.

Notes

1. Steven Lukes, "Socialism and Equality," in Leszek Kolakowski and Stuart Hampshire, eds., *The Socialist Idea* (London: Wiedenfeld and Nicholson, 1975), p. 74.

2. Far more forcefully than Djilas's *The New Class,* Felipe Garcia Casals indicts Communist party states and their Stalinism for becoming a system that rests on power and coercion not theory. See Casals's *The Syncretic Society* (White Plains, N.Y.: M.E. Sharp, 1980).

3. John Echols, "Racial and Ethnic Equality: The Comparative Impact of Socialism," *Comparative Political Studies* 13, no. 4 (January 1981):404-407.

Part I
Comparative Analyses

Inequalities in communist systems are (1) not confined within nation-states or caused by domestic variables alone, (2) not divorced from the political control of the Party and, (3) not resolved by the policies of Communist party governments. Such findings are elaborated in Part I by Valerie Bunce, Daniel Nelson, John Robertson, and Cal Clark. They focus on the relations among socioeconomic and political variables from comparative and international perspectives. The authors seek to respond to questions such as the following:

How do international inequalities shape domestic inequalities in communist states?

To what extent do inequalities have political functions in communist states?

Are the policies pursued by a communist system guided by a welfare ideology that, as in the West, limits the effect such policies will have on inequalities?

How do communist systems compare (with each other or with the West) regarding the distribution of resources among regions or among segments of the population?

Valerie Bunce assesses the link between domestic political economies of European communist systems and the regional system of dependency established after World War II. She argues that our understanding of inequalities in Eastern Europe, and the political correlates of them, must incorporate a sense of how dependency on a regional hegemon (the USSR) has produced policy dilemmas for these regimes. Bunce finds that inequalities in Soviet bloc economic interactions, in conjunction with the move from extensive to intensive development in the early 1970s, led to structural imbalance with all of these economies—imbalances with important consequences for rising mass expectations, inequalities by class, and domestic unrest. The party's response was various political and economic reforms that failed to solve the problems while furthering economic dependence on the West, a decline in party legitimacy, rising mass frustrations, and contradictions between Soviet foreign and domestic interests as well as East European political versus economic interests. Inequalities within CMEA (the Council on Mutual Economic Assistance), then, led to contradictions that undermined Soviet control and economic growth at home and in the bloc while weakening the political and economic viability of Eastern Europe qua one-party states.

1

In the second chapter, it is posited that participatory and resource inequalities that remain pronounced in communist states are not disassociated from the party's grasp on political control. It is argued that Leninists engage in practices similar to those adopted by all political leaders insofar as they preserve political inequalities: a differentiation of access to power in policymaking. The reasons for the preservation of political inequalities in Leninist regimes and the systemic consequences of such nonrevolutionary politics are examined. The chapter concludes with an assessment of the role of political inequalities in impeding or promoting political change in communist systems.

As the political dimension of such stratification and inequalities in the distribution of power is discussed, a model of the linkage between access to power and the combination of resource availability and political activism is offered. The key to maintaining political inequalities in communist systems (or in any authoritarian policy), it is argued, is the separation of resources from political activism and vice versa. The degree to which those factors are combined helps determine a ruling party's political control.

John Robertson compares the substance of distributive policies, East and West, in chapter 3. The USSR's welfare ideology is presumed to be based on significantly different allocative principles than the American and British models. Robertson tests for the effect of welfare ideology—the justification for the welfare effort in society—using time series data for social security and public assistance disbursements in these three cases. He finds that inequalities persist because a welfare ideology and its related policy style limit the redistributive effect of social security and public assistance policies. He concludes that the political costs of removing such limits may imply a difficult path toward greater equality.

Cal Clark, in chapter 4, explores empirically the performance of communist systems in combating inequality. Drawing data from many countries' reports on public expenditures and state budgets as well as from prior analyses of inequality by other scholars, Clark is able to offer judgments regarding the relative performance of communist states. Differences among various regimes are highlighted, particularly with regard to the redistribution of wealth among regions. Overall Clark finds that ruling Communist parties have done no better than noncommunist developed states in the redistribution of wealth; these same regimes, however, have pursued policies of welfarism (my word, not Clark's) whereby the public services available in poorer areas have been increased.

Conclusions offered in these four chapters do not coalesce neatly into a composite view of inequalities in communist states. Nevertheless the authors argue that inequity will not soon fade in communist systems. Bunce denies, by implication, that a specific regime has the capacity to extract itself from an international milieu in which inequality is endemic. Nelson adds that the existing inequalities are not without political costs and benefits for the Party's internal control. The very welfare ideology of a communist system, Robertson concludes, may limit the effect of any redistributive politices, while Clark points out that these states have performed better in the provision of public services than in equalizing per capita incomes across regions or population segments.

The comparative and international frameworks within which these authors have viewed the inequalities of communist systems suggest, then, the intractability of those inequalities. Because domestic socioeconomic inequalities are linked to international relationships and have utility for the Party's political control, it is unlikely that communist systems would be able to confront the origins of inequity within societies they rule without risking external and internal political dangers. The degree to which communist states' performance in mitigating inequalities is thus limited is amply discussed by Robertson and Clark.

The irony of regimes committed to egalitarian values being unable (and in some ways unwilling) to achieve them has political consequences. Comparative and international chapters in Part I are meant to offer generalizations about such relationships. The case studies, by contrast, are meant to examine certain dimensions of inequality in specific nation-states and to focus on the politics of those kinds of inequality.

1

Neither Equality nor Efficiency: International and Domestic Inequalities in the Soviet Bloc

Valerie J. Bunce

Nothing happens the way it is first imagined.   —Janos Kadar[1]

When the talk turns to incentives, you can assume that some people are going to get very rich.   —John Kenneth Galbraith[2]

When social scientists think about inequality, they tend to think in terms of who gets what *within* nation-states. Analyses of the distribution of income and wealth tend to focus on how economic well-being, however defined, varies by class, gender, ethnicity, or region within the borders of a nation-state. These are the emphases of subsequent chapters, for example. Similarly, if one's concern is the distribution of power, the terrain of study tends to be hierarchy within the factory, the polity, or the local community. Even studies of the origins and im- pact of inequalities tend to be confined to the mapping of domestic and not international forces—for example, the role of capitalism or socialism in generat- ing certain inequalities within the United States, Great Britain, or the Soviet Union, the impact of unequal land-holdings on agrarian unrest, and the like. Thus for most social scientists, the concept of social inequality immediately brings to mind the idea of differences among individuals within a particular state in their access to certain values and items, differences that originate in forces operating at the national or subnational level and that in turn have primarily intranational effects. Social inequality therefore appears to respect national sovereignty.

In an interdependent world marked by large and growing gaps between rich and poor states, between influential states and their respective clientele, such an assumption makes less and less sense. Inequalities among states affect not only what happens in the global system but also as a result of international inequal- ities, how much money, status, and power are effectively available for domestic distribution; global inequalities also help shape the very structure of domestic inequalities. The burden of defense outlays in response to perceived military inequalities, for example, seems to be borne disproportionately by the poor East and West, while Third World economies heavily dependent on foreign capital tend, not accidentally, to feature a more inequitable distribution of power and income by class than less dependent economies at a similar level of economic

5

development.[3] Global inequalities are therefore important not just in their own right in shaping the character and frequency of international transactions. They are also important in shaping what happens in the domestic sphere: the rate of economic growth, the prospects for political stability, and even in some cases the distribution of burdens and benefits, power and privilege among various social groupings. Indeed global inequalities may even shape the very structure of the polity and the economy. This, at least, is the thrust of both the dependency literature and the arguments underlining the notion of the Soviet bloc as a regional hierarchical system.[4]

In this chapter I examine the impact of international inequalities on the domestic distribution of power and economic well-being in the Soviet bloc. More specifically I look at how the unequal and changing division of power and economic resources between Eastern Europe on the one hand and the Soviet Union on the other have affected (1) the structure of the economy and polity throughout the bloc since World War II; (2) the power and authority of Eastern European elites, their changing agenda of concerns over time, and the varying constellations of interests that have been represented in these political economies; (3) the distribution of privilege and income by class within Eastern Europe; and (4) the resulting political stability and economic growth over time in the bloc and the changing political and economic relationships between the Soviet Union and its clientele states.

I selected the Soviet bloc as the terrain of study because this region represents both a relatively uncharted *and* an intensively analyzed area of study with respect to the issue of social inequality. Numerous studies have been done in recent years on inequality by class, gender, ethnicity, and region within various Soviet bloc nations,[5] and a few studies have been done on inequalities in the distribution of power and economic resources among these socialist states.[6] However, the connections between these two spheres of inequality—the domestic and the international—have been overlooked by most analysts, not because such connections seem untenable but, rather, because of the artificial division in the social sciences between scholars who study domestic affairs and those who study interactions among nation-states. Indeed, the case for examining links between domestic and international inequalities in the Soviet bloc is a compelling one. Literature on both dependency and the nature of regional hierarchical systems argues that the relationship of a powerful, resource-rich, and large hegemon with its small, resource-poor, derivative client states facilitates an interaction between external and internal distributive arenas, which exacerbates domestic *and* international political and economic inequalities over time. When one adds the ideological importance of the equality issue to socialist states[7] and the capacity of such systems to manipulate the distribution of power and privilege, then it becomes evident, to paraphrase Walt Connor, that socialism is about certain inequalities abroad as well as at home.[8] In fact one can argue that the failure of the centrally planned party-states in the Soviet bloc to reduce significantly the gap between the haves and the have-nots discussed comparatively in the chapters by Nelson, Robertson, and Clark, and the changing size of these gaps over time have as much to do with international as with domestic forces. The combination of dependency relations and a regional hierarchical system in the Soviet bloc has meant in practice the sacrifice of *both* equality and efficiency, the very real possibility in some cases of political and economic bankruptcy, and for the Soviet Union a "yawning height"[9] between the goal of Empire and the goal of domestic economic growth.

Inequality, Dependency, and Dependency Relations: Some Theoretical Considerations

It would be useful to define more clearly the terms social inequality, dependence, and dependency relations. The first concept, social inequality, refers to an asymmetrical distribution of some highly esteemed and therefore scarce value or item. Social inequality is ubiquitous almost by definition,[10] and is *not* synonymous with differentiation, in that only some differences are socially created, recognized, and reflective of what society chooses to hold dear. People may vary in hair color, for example, and this would not ordinarily be called social inequality. Differences in power, income, and wealth, access to social services, or status—that is, variations in what most societies value—would, by contrast, constitute social inequalities.

Two points are important about social inequalities. First, analyses of inequality must specify the "who" and the "what"; that is, what tangible or intangible item is being distributed—money, power, or whatever—and the cleavage along which those items are being distributed—for instance, inequality by class, gender, ethnicity, or among states. Thus, to argue that socialist states are more "equal" than capitalist nations is to make a meaningless, or at least an altogether too poorly specified statement, since we do not know to which dimensions of inequality such an argument is referring. One can imagine, for example, situations in which political power is more equally distributed by class than is economic well-being, the common argument in descriptions of capitalist polyarchies —or where there is greater income equality but less equality in the level of political influence by class, the trade-off purportedly made in state socialist systems.[11] Thus, close attention to the dimensions of inequality is critical, especially when trying to disentangle questions such as who is exploiting whom politically and economically in the Soviet bloc and within each Soviet bloc nation as well.

The second requirement for understanding social inequality is sensitivity to changes over time in the distribution of power and economic well-being, as well as to the complex origins and ramifications of those changing distributions. For example, it is evident in theory and more so in practice (hindsight tends to refine theory!) that the Soviet bloc states have undergone since World War II several stages in their drive for equality *and* growth. First, there is the destruction of the capitalist system and the creation of a new distribution of power and a new political economy—that is, Stalinism. In this stage, greater economic equality occurs through the elimination of the capitalist class and the introduction of social ownership of the means of production—a form of ownership communism claims leads to greater equality by class in access to the means of production.[12] The second stage, so-called postmobilization involves a greater emphasis on reducing certain economic disparities, such as mean income by occupation (one is tempted to say by class) and the distribution of the social wage, while maintaining large power differentials and significant differences in access to less basic consumer items. The third stage, which I would call the immobilization stage, involves a growing contradiction between the short-term needs of these states and their long-term goals, a contradiction that works against economic equality, growth, and political stability, linkages among which are seen in many of the following contributions (see Woodward on the Yugoslav case, for example).

These domestic stages reflect in some measure parallel stages in the evolution of international inequalities in power and economic resources—between the Soviet Union and her satellites and increasingly between East and West. The main question regarding inequality within and among socialist states is not why some have more than others, but rather, why different periods have featured different distributions, and what impact these changes have had. Socialism has entailed different inequalities at different times, and these shifts are neither necessarily inconsistent with ideology nor are they a simple reflection of a trade-off between equality and growth.

Dependence, a second key concept, is a specific type of inequality; that is, "an asymmetric control of one state by another."[13] Dependent countries are those in which external constraints are imposed by another state, a regional system, or a global system on the political and economic opportunities and behaviors effectively available to these countries and to their political and economic elites. A regional hierarchical system, such as the Soviet bloc, is thus an example of dependence. The regional hegemon (the Soviet Union) has set to a large extent the domestic and foreign policy agenda and behavior of all of its client states (Eastern Europe) and has limited as well their interaction with one another and their economic and political transactions outside the regional system. There are degrees and types of dependence, moreover. The more a state's external *and* internal opportunities and behaviors—the agenda of what is possible and likely and what is done—are shaped by another state, the more dependent it is. The dependence can be measured by the degree to which external dependence takes on political, economic, military, and even cultural forms and the extent to which these transfers of values are unidirectional in their effects. The more dependent a country is, the more its structure and the values and interests of its

elites are an extension of the interests and values of the dominant state. Moreover, the more dependent relations in which a state is engaged, the less control
that state has over its domestic and foreign decisions, and the less power each
dominant state has relative to that of the other dominant states. In other words
dependency can become quite complex and layered with a hierarchy among
dominant as well as among dependent states.

The importance of dependency relations has to do with how the power of
the "core"—the term dependency theorists use for late capitalist states, a term
applicable to the role of the Soviet Union—translates into not just certain international inequalities but also into economic and political inequalities within the
periphery, or Third World states drawn into the world capitalist system. The
position of Eastern Europe vis-à-vis the Soviet Union and the West is likewise
within the periphery.[14] The argument is that late capitalism, in monopolizing
capital and internal markets, in seeking profits, cheap labor, and raw materials,
and in overproducing for domestic markets, exploits Third World economies that
are beholden to the core for capital, technology, expertise, and therefore for
economic growth and improvements in domestic economic well-being. This affects the distribution of income and power within the peripheral nations and
may have ambiguous returns as well for economic growth and for the quality of
life of the poorest of the poor. An alliance with external capital can work to
strengthen Third World elites politically and economically and can create, as a
result, severe economic and political gaps between those who profit from foreign
capital—the political and managerial elite, the coopted internal bourgeoisie, and
others who depend on foreign political, economic, and military support—and
those who are most vulnerable to oscillating demand and employment and who
have the least access to imported goods and imported sources of power. The
latter are, of course, the newly formed and small working class and the peasantry.

Thus in terms of political economy, dependency relations inevitably present
Third World policymakers with severe dilemmas reminiscent of those Eastern
European elites have faced in their dealings with the Soviet Union and the West.
For example, should indigenous elites ally with external capital, given its promise
of jobs, investment, growth, and entry into the global trade network but with its
decided economic and political liabilities? The liabilities derive from (1) needing
to provide optimal investment conditions (cheap infrastructure costs, low taxes,
and low wages); (2) diverting public funds, as a result, away from basic human
needs and toward the needs of the world market, capital, the landed aristocracy
(whose support elites need), and the internal bourgeoisie, thereby risking a
worsening distribution of income and wealth, oppression in the countryside,
and cumulative pressures on the state to maintain certain class alliances while
ignoring others, pressures that mount, once such alliances are set and once the
state becomes externally dependent and increasingly internally repressive;
(3) squeezing the poor rather than the well-to-do or multinational corporations
by focusing on the supposedly more productive sectors and on groups on which

the state depends for capital investment for growth and for political support; (4) setting up entrenched cosmopolitan expectations among indigenous elites that cut into external trade advantages as cooptation of these groups becomes more politically necessary, and therefore harder to break without serious injury to the legitimacy of the state; (5) reinforcing certain economic problems by basing the economy on the production of export items targeted for investment by capitalist states and their coopted groups in the periphery, thereby exposing the periphery to fluctuations in the global economy; and (6) generating certain political problems, given the deterioration in the distribution of economic and political power that follows from trade dependence, mounting external debt, and domestic economic austerity measures.

Would it be better for Third World states to try to go it alone? Choosing this course entails risking political instability, a decline in public consumption, at least short-term economic deterioration, the loss of certain primary products and finished goods, and alienation of certain domestic interests that had benefited from prior capitalist penetration. Thus in opting out of the capitalist world system, peripheral economies face import controls and therefore scarce capital, lagging internal demands for what is produced and great demands for what is not, in some cases reprisals from the capitalist world in the form of stiffer debt negotiations and trade embargoes (as did Cuba after the revolution), and certainly domestic economic austerity policies aimed in most cases at the least productive sectors: the poor in the city and in the countryside.

Dependency arguments and the data that buttress them thus suggest that international inequalities in power and economic well-being might generate parallel domestic inequalities. These arguments are relevant to understanding not only North-South relations but also the linkage between domestic and external inequalities in the Soviet bloc. It can be argued first, that the external political and economic dependence of Eastern European elites on the Soviet Union, and the contradictions this has engendered in terms of their coalition of support at home, are not dissimilar from the position of many Third World elites. More specifically their connections with the Soviet Union in the 1950s and the 1960s meant that they were torn between domestic and foreign pressures. On the one hand they needed to establish authority relations with intellectuals, the workers, the peasants, and home-grown communists. They needed to prime public consumption, meet certain ideological goals, and deal with the legacy of history as well as the standards set by the proximate Western example of consumer societies with what they deemed bourgeois civil liberties. On the other hand there were Soviet pressures to move in a different direction. They had to respond to Soviet demands in foreign policy, economic specialization within Comecon, bilateral trade relations, and the reproduction of the Soviet political and economic model—policies that worked to alienate domestic clienteles. In this sense the inequalities in intrabloc relations built into a regional power system and the political economy of dependency relations led to a vicious circle of dependency and political and economic instability for Eastern European elites, a dilemma that resonates clearly with the Third World experience as it is captured in analyses by dependency theorists.

The parallels are not perfect, however.[15] For example, the considerably smaller gap between the Soviet Union and Eastern Europe in terms of economic development, the structure of internal markets, the peculiar combination in the Soviet case of general economic strength and strength in primary products, the degree to which the Soviet Union functions for political reasons as a captive consumer *and* producer within the bloc and, finally, the costs to the Soviets of maintaining political control and regional defense while pursuing global power status all differentiate Soviet bloc relations from those between the capitalist core and the Third World periphery. Dependency relations in the bloc, then, are *very* complex, reflecting the existence of both a regional hierarchical system and core-periphery dynamics. To paraphrase William Zimmerman, one woman's exploitation in such circumstances becomes "another's mutually advantageous sharing of resources, know-how, and capital."[16] Indeed by the 1970s one could argue that the Soviets were, in an economic and political sense, hoisted by their own petard, as Eastern Europe placed increasing demands on the Soviets and became, at the same time, the newest recruit to the periphery in the world capitalist system. It is to that evolving contradiction that I now turn.

To the Periphery: Evolving Contradictions of Soviet-East European Inequality

Setting the Context, 1948-1956: Opportunity More than Equality

The political and economic inequalities between the Soviet Union and Eastern Europe were, of course, very large in the early post-World War II, period when socialism was being constructed in the People's Democracies. As regional hegemon, the Soviet Union dominated the external as well as the internal politics and economics of its satellites, in some cases being the prime mover in the liberation struggle and in *all* cases dictating (especially after 1948) the form of their new political economies, the priorities within domestic and foreign policy agendas, the distribution of political and economic power, and even the very composition of their ruling strata. During the "revolutionary breakthrough,"[17] whatever the Soviets said, the Eastern Europeans did. Especially in those cases where indigenous support for communism was weak, historically tied to Moscow, or, finally, intermixed with social democratic support—in Hungary, Poland, and Czechoslovakia—Eastern European elites followed Soviet precedents and Soviet orders. Sealed off from any contact with capitalism, these elites centralized political and economic power in the hands of the Communist Party, and adopted the Soviet definition of socialist democracy; that is, democracy through enforced social consensus with serious reprisals against pluralist demands and deviance, and socialism through centralized planning and party-state ownership of the means of production. They also emulated, to varying degrees, and over a shorter span of time, the entire array of policies known as Stalinism.[18] They adopted for example, with some reluctance or at least modification, Stalin's version (or rather distortion[19]) of primitive socialist accumulation.[20]

Thus, if dependency means asymmetrical external control by state A over the opportunities and policy options available to state B, and if this impact is defined as including the domestic as well as foreign policy agenda of state B, then Soviet bloc relations in the early 1950s were clearly an example of dependency relations. Indeed in some ways the power of the core over the periphery was perhaps even greater in this case than it is in the more familiar terrain of North-South relations.

However, such large international inequalities should not be equated too quickly with the concept of exploitation or "unfair exchange."[21] After the initial transfer of capital eastward after the war—a transfer similar in size to the Marshall Plan and perhaps not without similar justifications given Soviet wartime damage and the long-term economic viability of the region[22]—and after the establishment of derivative and dependent political economies, Soviet economic exploitation dwindled after 1949. More important, the Eastern Europeans began to receive at that time some benefits from the empire as well. Economic autarky was a reality in Eastern Europe and the Soviet Union. The Soviets did not use the economic levers they might have used, and they freed the Eastern Europeans from imported business cycles and price changes in the world market, an appealing outcome especially in Hungary, Poland, and Czechoslovakia, given their experience between the two world wars. Second, imports from the USSR emphasized raw materials and energy, items they would have had to import from somewhere. These items were, moreover, at least of unvarying price and amount when bought from the Soviets. Thus the Soviets offered predictable supplies and costs and a guaranteed, albeit very small, market for Eastern European goods.

Finally, economic duties went along with the job of regional hegemon. In 1953 the Soviets bailed out the East Germans, as they were to do later for the Poles, the Hungarians, and the Czechoslovaks, not to mention the entire bloc after 1956 and the Cubans.[23] Thus the deal was not as lopsided as might be assumed, precisely because of what Eastern Europe got for dependency in those years and what the Soviets lost in the pursuit of empire.[24] Indeed on the Soviet side, buttressing regimes in trouble (or even those in trouble by association, as throughout the bloc 1948-49 and after 1956), creating identical political economies in Eastern Europe that repeated rather than shored up Soviet weaknesses, and setting a precedent in being stuck with Eastern European goods that were all the Eastern European states had to exchange for Soviet primary products, were costly sacrifices for what amounted to only partial socialist encirclement.

The question then becomes: What were the *domestic* effects in Eastern Europe of dependency relations and the creation of a regional hierarchical system? First was the reproduction of the Soviet experience, the creation of a mono-organizational society in each Eastern European state in a matter of only five years.[25] This meant that the large international political and economic inequalities were recreated in the domestic sphere *within* each Eastern European state. Alec Nove's description of planner and party sovereignty in the Soviet Union, that the "political and the economic merge, become undistinguishable,[26] captures the fusion that evolved between political and economic power in all of the People's Democracies. Nove implies that inequalities of power and access to economic resources resulted within these societies. In such systems economic control begets, necessitates, and is expressed through political control, and political power is based on control over what is to be produced and how those items are to be distributed. Just as the Soviet Politburo became by the 1930s "the board of directors of the great firm, USSR, Ltd."[27] so in Eastern Europe the Politburos took on a similar role after World War II.

The fusion of political and economic spheres and the interdependence between political and economic power had a number of similar and important practical effects on the domestic political economies of Eastern Europe by the first half of the 1950s. Those economies featured all the trade-offs of Soviet industrialization, specifically rapid growth, large economic inequalities by class and production sector, and the tensions and the strengths induced by what Charles Lindblom has termed specialization in "thumbs," or brute strength, and weaknesses in "fingers."[28] Second, the policy agenda of the Eastern European party elite was severely constrained and kept relatively simple. Growth was to occur by plowing money into heavy industry and its elite corps while holding down the cost of agriculture as well as popular consumption through investment decisions and repression. In other words Stalinism widened the income and power gap between rural and urban areas, white collar and blue collar workers, and certainly between party members and all others. The role of the Communist party in the Stalinist system was important. To draw upon dependency arguments, the party in Eastern Europe was a coopted elite, dependent upon the Soviet Union for political survival and the effective exercise of political power at home. The powerlessness and dependence of Eastern European elites externally, therefore, necessitated the development of an authoritarian state at home. To use Marxist terms, external inequalities reproduced domestic inequalities.

Thus the power of Eastern European elites in the early 1950s was primarily externally based, amplified at home by their position in a one-party, economically planned, autarkic, and centralized repressive state, yet severely limited abroad. This meant that their claims to domestic legitimacy were based *not* on a social contract so much as on the guarantee of employment and a minimal but stable standard of living, on the multiplication of political and economic elite posts, and therefore on the mobility offered to peasants, the working class, and the small middle class. As Paul Johnson and Wlodzimierz Brus have noted, the appeals of Stalinism were hardly negligible. Rapid change created its own unique coalition of support—not for economic equality, but for mobility and change:

> What is less commonly given due weight in Western analyses is that even during these most trying of times very large numbers of workers could reasonably evaluate their material possessions as improved either because they no longer had to face periodic lay-offs or unemployment . . . or simply because the gap between rural and urban incomes and living standards was historically so very large that mobility from the former to the latter could almost completely over-shadow the effects of near stagnant wages for those newly arrived from the country.[29]

> around 1948 the Polish Party leadership could feel a glimpse of hope breaking through the blank wall of hostility and non-recognition by the people as a legitimate Polish government. . . . The plans for the future promised a dynamic development unknown in the inter-war period, with exciting prospects not only for the technical and economic intelligentsia but also for the large strata of former social underdogs. . . . Socialism as such could become genuinely acceptable and even attractive for increasing numbers of the population.[30]

The relationship between Eastern European elites and their societies in this early period, then, was based on growth, with equality of opportunity interpreted primarily as the expansion of opportunities rather than the provision of economic and political equality. It was a delicate deal, because rapid growth could slow down, the number of opportunities in the new political economy could eventually stabilize, and the utility of the past as a favorable point of comparison would necessarily fade as new generations based their expectations on what had been done for them lately. This was the irony of rapid economic change. It created a society of hopefuls and a large cadre of opportunists. Moreover, just as the party could take the credit for creating the good or at least the better economic life, so it would have to take the blame when things got worse. This was the irony of creating a strong state monopolizing the distribution of political and economic resources and social opportunities. Who was to blame, just as who was to be thanked, was readily apparent, especially to those who were sacrificing now for pay-offs later and in whose name the party ruled—the working class. This meant that when growth slowed, the issue would have to turn to more equality or at least to the provision of greater economic security. If the party could not promise new positions or new status levels, it had to deliver on improvements in the quality of life *within* one's status level for all sectors. This was the irony of creating working class consciousness in a worker's state, and creating at the same time a new and privileged class that expected special access to certain perks in exchange for its support and the risks it had incurred.

Thus international inequalities in the Stalinist phase generated and indeed depended upon certain domestic inequalities in the distribution of power and income within Eastern Europe. These inequalities strengthened the power of the party elite in Eastern Europe, given their monopoly of political power, capital, and labor and their coalition with the ambitious, while making them, at least potentially, highly vulnerable. Like many of their Third World counterparts, external dependence in Eastern European states led to large gaps at home between those who had power and capital and who stood to benefit by dependence, and those who did not. At this time, however, the strategy at home meshed with the demands imposed from abroad. Serving domestic clienteles did not conflict with Soviet hegemony; indeed, these were interdependent processes of alliance formation. But this would never happen again.

The Krushchev Period: From Opportunity to Equality

The effect of the Khrushchev regime on intrabloc relationships and on the domestic political economies of Eastern Europe was dramatic both by intent and by accident. Khrushchev imposed significant changes in Soviet economic and political relations with the satellites, pushing for less autarky and more economic integration within the recently created CMEA while trying to solidify the political base of Moscow and Eastern European regimes through more positive ties between the party-states and their societies. Soviet domestic reforms, however, also spilled over into Eastern Europe, both because of the peculiar dynamics of a regional hierarchical system—that is, highly permeable borders within the system and relatively impermeable frontiers around the region—and because these derivative states shared certain domestic pressures for reform with their regional hegemon.

The key concept was de-Stalinization—decompression at home and in the satellites as the masses were trusted more and the Party and the bureacracy less.[31] This was combined with a new theory of the state, a new basis for regime-society relations, and, finally, a new version of what constituted a progressive socialist political economy. Khrushchev pushed at home for greater equality by class of opportunity *and* result, more mass participation in the polity and the economy, more stress on labor productivity over infusions of more and more capital investment and labor, and, finally, a greater balance between normative and material incentives within the party through *Partiinost* and within the economy as a whole. Externally Khrushchev tried to regularize and institutionalize politcal and economic relations within the bloc, expand external economic linkages, and encourage Eastern European elites to follow his precedent in terms of decompression and of the creation of new and positive political and economic linkages between the party and the society. To use Khrushchev's favorite metaphor, his vision of regime-society relations and intrabloc relations was that of an orchestra, with the party serving in both cases as the conductor.

In practice Soviet domestic shifts and a renewed concern with the bloc as a system allowing regional division of economic labor increased Eastern European economic dependency on the Soviet Union. Such dependency was furthered as bilateral trade increased, which locked the small economies of Eastern Europe into certain economic priorities. That Soviet exports to Eastern Europe were focused on primary products that only the USSR could provide, also promoted dependency. The export of these products to Eastern Europe grew over time because of their undervalued cost in domestic production, their growing role in the production process (in lieu of an expanding labor supply), and their obvious importance to the development of heavy industry. Emphasizing the Soviet role as *the* market in the bloc (and a large, stable, and captive one at that), creating universal standards and parts within the bloc, and expanding coordination of plans and essentially pegging unconvertible currency to the ruble were all additional factors contributing to East European dependency.

The movement away from autarky led to greater economic dependency, but not to greater exploitation. The Eastern Europeans and the Soviets seemed to do well by each other in the late 1950s and early 1960s. The issue of who was exploiting whom, at this time "was at least an open question."[32] As Paul Marer has summarized:

> Since the mid-1950's, there is no clear evidence that the Soviet Union gains unrequited resource transfers from Eastern Europe; in fact, evidence suggests that the USSR might be paying an increasingly steep price for the political benefit it derives from the continued economic dependence of the Eastern European countries on the Soviet Union.[33]

Political dependency, however, was another story. Here the Khrushchev reforms ended up having an effect precisely opposite to what was intended. De-Stalinization, in combination with the structurally induced slowdown in socio-economic transformation (given finite supplies of labor and capital and the diminishing returns of repression and heavy industrial investment), made Eastern European elites *more* politically vulnerable at home and therefore more dependent on the Soviets for their political survival. De-Stalinization was a problem, because Eastern European elites were guilty by direct and recent association with these alleged excesses, and they were highly vulnerable because they were not, in most cases, home-grown communists with a supportive constituency. They were, instead, Soviet-picked and Soviet-trained and had led the attack in the destruction of national communism. Nor had they been in power long enough to become accepted, at least passively, or to have developed an image of endurance and autonomy. Instead, after selling out national communism, compressing Stalinism into a few years, and showing their clear dependence on Soviet power in many cases for a number of years, these elites could hardly claim that they had been wrong without risking losing support both from the ambitious and from a public expecting immediate reparations for their seemingly unnecessary suffering. Newness, complicity, external dependence, very short term expansions of mobility, a more ambigious historical tradition, and a weak mandate, then, separated the Eastern Europeans from the Soviets. These distinctions meant that de-Stalinization was far more traumatic in Eastern Europe, especially in Hungary and Poland, and where politically possible, was resisted, as with Czechoslovakia and the German Democratic Republic.

This was particiularly problematic because economic slowdown endangered the precarious hold on legitimacy of Eastern European regimes. During the Stalinist stage the ability of the party to generate change, to foster a dynamic, new economic system with new economic, social, and political roles, was critical for its legitimacy. The state, then, had a double and pressing economic burden. Its power grew from economic growth *and* so did its very claims for authority:

> Every state and social order has its development and structure determined to a large extent by economic processes. This is particularly true of the countries of Eastern Europe. The very ideological foundation of Eastern European socialism . . . attributes unequivocal priority to the economy over other determinant factors. . . . Furthermore, it has been postulated again and again since Lenin that the economic-ideological legitimation of socialist planned economic systems is closely linked to economic success. . . . Thus, the targets of economic growth policies take pride of place amongst political objectives.[34]

The problem was that, as the Soviets pressured for reform through liberalization, more political participation, more *Partiinost* and less reliance on economic incentives, the most readily available source of popular support—growth and hence mobility—begain to dry up. This meant pressure for political and economic reforms at the same time, which would spell the loss of the party's political and economic preeminence. Reform, in short, would be difficult to contain, especially given the flood of demands that had been created yet blocked by Stalinism. More growth depended on decentralizing the planning process, and more legitimacy depended upon decentralizing the polity.

The price for all this was too high, as Hungary and Poland revealed in 1956, and Eastern Europe elites searched for an alternative strategy that would somehow win support, expand productivity, *and* maintain their political power and control over the distribution of capital and labor. The problem was that the options were limited. External dependence and the Soviet occupation of Hungary canceled out the possibility of an appeal to patriotism or social cohesion in response to a common enemy. Indeed they had met the enemy and, to paraphrase Pogo, it was their patron. Expansion of political participation, at least at this time, was also problematic, given the declining legitimacy of the Party and the dangerous relevance of the Yugoslav experiment in self-management to the working class. Nor were economic reforms very palatable or clearly necessary; they would have served only to complicate the move toward regional interdependence, which appeared at that time as potentially beneficial to Eastern

Europe. What was possible, however, was greater income equality among classes. This could expand class support and give credence to ideological claims without forfeiting political power. Such an approach, called by Bogdan Mieczkowski "the courtship of the population,"[35] was at least in the mid to late 1950s a stopgap measure, which combined fortuitously the short-term needs of politicians to win some support with their longer term desire to maintain political and economic hegemony. Indeed, "the secularization of legitimacy claims"[36] was increasingly characterized as a boon to productivity as well; that is, consumption outlays were increasingly redefined in the mid 1950s as productive, rather than unproductive investment.

As a result, the mid to late 1950s in Eastern Europe was a time of more concern with equality in income by class. For example, a huge jump occurred in budgetary outlays designated for social consumption from 1955 to 1957 in Czechoslovakia and a similar expansion occurred in Hungary in 1957-58. Indeed, the correlation in shifts in public consumption versus productive investment between the Soviet Union and Eastern Europe during the 1950s was very high, averaging 0.92, precisely because of the parallel expansions in 1956-1958 throughout the bloc and because these improvements formed the new base for the rest of the decade.[37] One cost of empire, then, was the development not just of similar problems but also of anticipatory reactions. Unrest in Poland and Hungary was contained by priming public consumption *throughout* the bloc, at times with substantial economic aid from the Soviet Union.

These shifts in favoring public consumption over industrial investment were matched in the mid-1950s by other economic measures that lifted up the standard of living of the poor. Focusing on agricultural investment, social wage transfers (pension, housing starts and outlays, family allowances, and the like), and the distribution of average wages by class and economic sector, one finds that throughout the Soviet bloc from 1955 to 1959 (1) agriculture received more funding than previously, the thrust of the increased funding being to improve the standard of living in the countryside; (2) the minimum wage increased faster than other wage categories; (3) expenditures by the state on housing grew faster than the budget as a whole; and (4) the costs of government subsidies of basic items—in particular, foodstuffs—began to rise, reflecting the fact that farmers received more for their goods and the state apparently was reluctant to pass these costs on to consumers.

So 1956-1959 seems to have been a time of some equalization in economic well-being throughout the bloc.[38] This trend toward equalization was more pronounced in the northern tier of Eastern Europe, especially Poland and Czechoslovakia, because of the slowdown in economic growth and declining productivity. In those countries where the party-state had most clearly lost the ability to offer mobility and growth with all of its positive spin-offs for the mass public, and where economic reforms were avoided, the "revolution in income"[39] seems to have been more dramatic. Indeed the strategy appears to have been to seek equality in income instead of pursuing economic reforms. This explains why greater income equality in Eastern Europe correlates with less efficiency *and* why equalization in income went further in systems with circumvented serious economic or political reforms, for example Czechoslovakia.[40] Thus the often noted, though never empirically verified, trade-off between equality and efficiency may in this case, at least, be misspecified. When the appeal of growth is gone, given failure to decentralize the economy and when the stick of Stalinism is denied to the party-state, economic equalization through budgetary and social wage policies may be the only policy lever left that binds government with governed.[41]

All of this suggests connections between international and domestic inequalities from 1956 to 1960 in the Soviet bloc. There appeared to be a spillover from the Soviet domestic political economy to the Eastern European political economies that reflects several axioms of Moscow's relationship with its empire. First, like systems respond in like ways to changing pressures and demands (compare the similar role in Hungary and Czechoslovakia, Poland, and the Soviet Union of the succession connection). Second, there is the influence of Soviet policy dictates to the Eastern European satellites. Although it is difficult to gauge how these two effects should be weighted, they both reflected the tremendous impact of the regional hegemon and dependency relations. Greater income equality by class had a great deal to do with the relationship of Eastern Europe to the Soviet Union and the need of Eastern European elites as a result to buy support from their publics. This indeed is the ironic outcome of combining centralized and economic power with external political dependence in a time of lower growth and little authority.

The Mid-1960s to the Present: The Janus-Faced State[42]

By the mid-1960s, several trends began to develop that severely complicated intrabloc relations and that led Eastern European regimes to the position of sacrificing *both* equality and efficiency and becoming in the progress more and not less externally dependent. First, the costs of drive toward equalization throughout the bloc began to mount. In an expanding economy redistribution can always be sold as essentially distribution; everyone's economic lot can improve, so that conflict between winners and losers is muted since one group's gain does not have to be seen as subsidized by another. If growth slows, however, as it clearly did by the mid-1960s, conflict over income distribution and access to valued goods grows, and the pressure of interests more vital to the functioning of the economy—to paraphrase Charles Lindblom,[43] the reassertion of the privileged role of planners and managers when times get tough—grows as well. The problem by the mid-1960, was not that greater income equality had led to less efficiency—which was how the argument was usually made, especially in

Czechoslovakia,[44] but, rather, that mature socialist economies, for structural reasons, acquire more and more demands and less and less surplus over time. The line drawn between what constitutes productive and unproductive investment, as a result, becomes much sharper and much more politically explosive.[45]

A second problem had to do with the growing need of the state to devise some scheme that would soak up all the money the state had transferred to various less-privileged groups. Giving poor people money, providing greater economic security through an expanding social wage, and improving as well the access that more privileged groups have to desirable consumer items and certain perks, such as travel abroad and superior housing and medical care, depends upon two things. First, basic goods such as food, rent, and consumer durables must cost more, thereby reducing the state subsidy of these items. Second, a consumer goods industry must be created that would simultaneously meet basic as well as more exotic needs. The problems involved in dealing with the first task were revealed in Poland in 1970, 1975-76, and 1980-1982. Having created a large, cohesive working class in whose name the party rules, having bettered their lot for ten years, and facing a generation that was more cosmopolitan and less assuaged by favorable comparisons with the bad old days, the Polish party-state found it increasingly difficult to take the gains away by charging more for what they had presented to the public as basic rights, not privileges to be withdrawn at will. Caught between peasant expectations for higher pay for goods delivered and worker demands for low-cost basic goods, more representation, and more consumer goods, the Polish state was locked into a "public consumption cycle."[46] In the state's need to respond quickly to public pressure without little recourse to introducing cost increases in basic items, funds dried up for investment, subsidies increased, and shortages became commonplace. This in turn slowed economic growth and fed into further demands from what had become "the decreasingly malleable publics."[47]

The second need, the provision of numerous and high-quality consumer goods, was also a problem. Industries producing such goods are labor intensive (a problem, given labor shortages), and they are dependent upon both high capital start-up costs and the creation of strong fingers in the economy. Nor do these industries generate spin-offs for greater productivity and a surplus for reinvestment, especially in the short run. The evident difficulties of such an economic decision were exacerbated by greater pressures for plan coordination in the bloc during the 1960s and the resulting pressures against economic decentralization.

On the political side lie further problems. The longer a transition toward a consumer-oriented society is put off, the more likely it is that economic resentments will become political resentments. Pent-up demand places greater and greater pressures on the distribution system, and this leads to higher prices and serious shortages, both of which affect the poorer level of society.[48] Privilege in consumer-deficit society is expressed increasingly not just in terms of income but also in terms of more clearly defined class-stratified access to goods *and* services.[49] When one adds to this the growing knowledge that upper status groups in these societies had about Western consumption levels (and the knowledge Soviet elite groups increasingly gained about consumption in Eastern Europe),[50] then it becomes clear that a stalled consumer revolution eventually generates political discontent among *all* classes. To decentralize the economy is, however, to take away power and resources from all those who benefit from planning: party and planning elites, who would lose the rationale and the very basis of their privileged position; lower level party prefects, who are the expediters in helping enterprises meet their targets; factory managers, who revel in power without responsibility for failure; and the workers, who want to maintain economic and job security.

Thus the costs of a consumer-oriented society and decentralization are high, especially in a time of shortages of energy and capital. To combat these shortages, the state needs both to channel investment into productive areas and to control what is to be produced and the mode of production. It is a time when centralization also makes sense.[51] Pressures existed, then, to reindustrialize, to move from extensive to intensive economic development. Blunt additions of labor and capital were no longer plausible strategies for generating growth, and technological innovation and more sophisticated microeconomic strategies became the only option for mature socialist economies. However, both required massive investment in human and material capital and time, both of which were in short supply. Thus just as equality had generated pressures for economic decentralization that would in turn have undercut the gains in economic equality, further growth likewise depended upon contradictory pressures—for more and for less centralization.

The resolution of this dilemma of needing simultaneously economic equality, intensive growth, efficiency, and consumer goods while wanting to maintain Party hegemony was to adopt the strategy embodied in the concept of developed socialism, an exercise in wish fulfillment that promised equality and efficiency without any major change in the system's distribution of economic or political power.[52] Developed socialism, as a theory, promised greater growth and efficiency through the scientific-technical revolution and greater worker participation in the policy and the economy.[53] It also promised greater productivity, because participatory and economically secure workers, being satisfied, would presumably work harder. In this way a certain level of economic security and the use of graded economic incentives would beget productivity, and more capital and better micromanagerial techniques would beget more efficiency and growth that would allow a surplus for redistribution. It was strategy combining trickle up and trickle down economics. The strategy signaled, in the short-term at least, the end to the drive for equality:

> The gradual, cautious, partial replacement of administrative controls . . .
> by concepts including economic rationality and efficiency and relatively
> more economic responsibility for managers signaled . . . an attack on

socialist egalitarianism. . . . The introduction of material incentives, wage differentiation according to contribution to production, a system of bonuses, standardization of work norms, and other rewards favored the white collar staff . . . over the workers.[54]

The linchpin for all this was the scientific-technical revolution, the key to which became détente, or what the Soviets call *razriadka*, the lessening of tensions. This became the central concern in the early 1970s throughout the Soviet bloc. Several considerations motivated the concern. Arms reductions meant lower defense outlays and the potential channeling of that money into productive investment and public consumption, an outcome particularly appealing to the Soviets, given their sizable defense burden. Such reductions would allow closer economic relations between East and West, thereby mitigating problems in technology and consumer goods. Planners and party officials would be allowed greater security and flexibility to order economic priorities, an outcome desirable in Eastern Europe, where public pressure was and is considerable for consumer goods and high technology. Cultural and scientific relations would expand as well—a third consideration, particularly for the scientific, technical, and managerial elites who would benefit most. Finally, the possibility of increased travel, access to high quality consumption items, and the recognition of political equality with the West held definite appeal to insecure party elites, operating within a consumer-deficit society.[55]

Thus détente was an optimal strategy. As economic holes were plugged in the short run, medium- and long-run domestic group pressures and needs for economic growth and intensive development were addressed. It was a way to maintain inequalities in power with some equality in income distribution and access to goods and services and to allow certain inequalities in access to those perks desired by the upper strata and the party elite. It was a Pareto optimal strategy, allowing Eastern Europe to maximize its advantages in its external linkages to the Soviet Union while maintaining class alliances at home. It freed the Soviets of the growing disadvantages of semiautarky and entrapment within Comecon. They could meet their domestic economic needs without pressuring the Eastern Europeans to disturb their class alliances at home through the diversion of consumer goods and scarce capital to the Soviet Union. This meant political stability in the empire, continued Soviet control over the empire, and Soviet domestic stability as well. At the same time, in meeting the needs of Western markets and using Western not Soviet capital, the Eastern European economies would become more efficient, less draining on the Soviets, and more capable of producing high-quality items. *Razriadka* contained within it, therefore, the fortuitous resolution of internal and external pressures reminiscent of the early 1950s, that is, a symmetry among Soviet and Eastern European needs, regarding economic growth and domestic political stability with the maintenance of the Empire in the bargain.

By the end of the 1970s, however, the empire was in trouble. Economic growth was stalled throughout most of the bloc, the drive toward equality was halted, and Eastern European dependence increased, falling on *both* the West and the Soviet Union. In short, *none* of the goals envisioned in the theory of developed socialism were met. International and domestic inequality grew, as did economic inefficiency and political instability. The Eastern European party elites found themselves more vulnerable than they had ever been, and the Soviets found themselves exploited by their clientele states, on the verge of risking both empire *and* domestic economic growth.

What went wrong? To put the matter succinctly, the impact of international inequalities in the 1950s, in combination with capitalist business cycles in the 1970s, led to a situation wherein the Soviets and their Eastern European client states increasingly paid a very heavy political and economic price for creating like, interdependent states with parallel political and economic distortions. Translating this into more concrete arguments, the Soviets created systems that could not shore up Soviet problems and that increasingly depended on the Soviets for economic and political support in terms of basic raw materials and energy, the provision of a large, captive domestic market, and aid in generating strong economic performance and sizable social wage transfers as a way to bind the masses to the state.

Because of the liberation, the brevity of the Stalinist period, higher mass expectations given the proximity in geography and culture to the West, and the glaring fact of Soviet dominance, Eastern European elites were much more pressured than Soviet elites to meet quickly mass economic and political demands. As a consequence the same Eastern European parties began to build up heavy economic and political debts in the process. They were highly vulnerable and used the state to buy support, especially in cases where the working class was large and economic reforms were avoided, as in Poland and in Czechoslovakia. It was also in these countries where succession and popular unrest worked to expand these debts in geometric fashion. Hence the revolution of rising entitlements converged with lower growth and a delicate governing formula, which led in turn to short-term rationality in political and economic decision and longer term irrationality. Gierek's alliance between Polish housewives and Western bankers demonstrated the short-term horizons of a planned economy responding to past external economic and political dependence and current internal demands for economic and political equality. As Jan Triska has argued, the ironic outcome by the 1970s of Soviet power in the 1950s was the veto power of domestic groups within Eastern Europe.[56] Thus in the northern tier of Eastern Europe popular demands undermined economic rationality through investment strategies that encouraged further demands on the state and more short-term responses and long-term economic dislocations.

The rising expectations of the public and the short-term needs of Eastern European politicans to win over that public combined with Western economic dislocations due to the energy crisis and global recession, to expand trade with the West and, more important, debt to the West. The Eastern Europeans were hit severely by the downturn of the Western economies, drawn into debt by high expectations and a surfeit of petrodollars in Western banks in the mid-1970s. Yet they were denied easy access to Western markets and capital later on because of recession, protective tariffs and high interest rates. As Zvi Gitelman has summarized:

> The initial smugness of Soviet and Eastern European observers of sky-rocketing energy prices, Western recession, unemployment and inflation was replaced by a realization, admitted publicly, that economic advers-ity in the West could have a harmful influence on the East.[57]

The "debt trap"[58] became a serious problem in Eastern Europe because (1) the debt-servicing charges began to accumulate in a geometric fashion, such that growth merely met these at best and did not even help with paying off the principal; (2) ability to borrow in the future was hampered, and this spilled over to other socialist states as well, breeding resentment, recession, and parallel problems throughout the interdependent bloc; (3) growth slowed due to the hiving off of crucial funds to pay off the debt, and investment was pulled out of the less productive—read, public consumption—areas of the economy; (4) state pressures increased to exploit labor in lieu of capital and to encourage productive workers and sectors; (5) imports were cut back as well to finance debt and protect hard currency, thereby leading in these small, narrowly specialized economies to class-based deprivation, resentment by elites as well, and spiraling costs for basic but scarce goods. The responses to the debt trap led to outcomes opposed to those which originally had encouraged the termination of autarky and greater economic ties with capitalism. That is, the trap led to *less*, not more economic equality by class; less, not more economic security; a smaller and a *more* class-stratified consumer goods sector; less flexibility in planning; less control over income distribution because of the growing impact of world market, not internal prices; greater economic dependence on the Soviet Union and the West; and, finally, increased political instability reflecting the class impact of low growth and domestic economic austerity policies. Moreover, pressures for economic reforms increased, rather than decreased, as was originally planned and this meant serious inroads into planner and party sovereignty.

> The governments of many Eastern European countries believe that they can increase the effectiveness of their economies . . . without having to go the way of economic reforms. . . . Empirical studies have shown, however, that East–West cooperation has better chances for success in the Eastern countries in which economic reforms have been made. . . . East–West cooperation does not appear to be an alternative to economic reform, on the contrary, the further development of cooperative agree-ments would be promoted if some far-reaching improvements would be

made in the functioning of the economy, the rights and duties of enterprises . . . were expanded, and a rational price system and a sensible
credit and exchange rates were established.[59]

Thus the short-term solution of incurring external debts, which was to facilitate
productivity and equality and to circumvent an economic reform that would
lead to more political equality, created the worst case scenario: less equality, less
growth, political instability, and a more precarious grip by the party elite on the
economy and the polity.

Nor did the Soviets gain much. Indeed they paid a great price for their empire during the 1970s and its flirtation with capitalism. There was the problem
of having generated their toughest competition for Western capital, high technology, consumer goods, and Western markets by creating derivative, rather than
complementary political economies in their empire. Another problem was having
responsibility for their satellites in their economic dealings with the West. A
regional hegemon bats last, establishing credit-worthiness and standing behind
any debts incurred. Being a bloc was a problem in itself. When one state went
bad, the others had to pay the price—in their ability to procure loans and in the
diversion of their resources to the state in trouble. This meant, as the events of
1981 demonstrated, that the Soviets had to deliver the bad news and pressure
their allies as well as the domestic Soviet populace to float the Polish economy.
Finally there was the problem of dependency. The Eastern European states depended on the Soviets for raw materials and energy, a dependence only exacerbated by the decades-long disincentives in these planned economies to use
energy efficiently, by the movement toward intensive economic growth, and
finally by the declining possibilities for growth through an expanding, hard-
working labor force.

Because of this dependence and the spiraling costs of energy on the world
market, the Soviets were stuck. If they asked for more money (which they did in
the early 1970s through a new indexing scheme), they risked higher Eastern
European debt to the Soviet Union and further class-based austerity policies,
recession in Eastern Europe and hence more dependency East *and* West with a
reinvigorated political consumption cycle, and further pressures on the Soviet
market to absorb Eastern European goods regardless of quality and higher prices.
If they kept prices low (which they did, at below world market prices), they
incurred several risks. Satellites would be encouraged to use energy inefficiently
and to expand their dependence on the Soviets. Such expanded dependence
would accelerate depletion of Soviet energy sources, thereby putting more pressure on the Soviets to import Western technology to exploit resources and increasing the possibility in the process of more debt and more pressure on the
Soviet economy to penetrate Western markets. Low prices would also deny the
Soviet Union one of its major trump cards in gaining access to Western markets
and capital: a large energy stock.

In other words, the Soviets faced a real dilemma. A trade-off between empire and domestic economic growth was in the making. The politics of a regional hierarchical system came up against the economics of growing Eastern European dependency and the political ramifications in the satellites of less equality and imported economic business cycles. The result was a high correlation in the pattern over time of growing Eastern European debt to the West and to the East.[60]

None of this was made any easier by the unraveling of *razriadka*. The pursuit of global power status, in combination with the political economy of the succession connection and slower rates of economic growth meant some very tough choices between guns and butter. The "politics of stringency"[61] and the march toward reindustrialization met upwith the revolution in income, and the latter seems to have been stalled in the Soviet Union as a consequence. Recent analyses of infant mortality in the Soviet Union, for example, indicate that more guns means not just less butter, but also class-based access to that butter.[62]

Thus, in many ways the impact of international inequalities among the Soviet bloc states set in motion a curious dynamic in which Soviet political and economic dominance generated large political and economic inequalities in the 1950s, a reduction of domestic economic inequalities and political and economic international inequalities in the 1960s, and an expansion of *both* domestic and international inequalities in the 1970s. The Soviets had created Janus-faced states in Eastern Europe, states whose external obligations increasingly forced them to choose between alienating their alliances at home and satisfying alliances abroad, or pursuing policies that placated the mass public in the short run and alienated them in the long run, by forcing austerity policies that hurt the workers, the peasants, and even the political, economic and cultural elite.[63] These states were increasingly dependent on, yet increasingly unable to please either the regional hegemon or their fickle and demanding domestic clienteles. As Jan Triska put it:

> With the growing restiveness of workers and under the pressure of dissenting intellectuals, the East European party elites' staying in office depends no longer on the Soviet leaders alone, but also on their ability to rule at home. The somewhat less demanding Soviets are easily matched by the more-demanding groups at home. The sustaining balancing of the two constituents grows heavy for Eastern European leaders.[64]

Dependency abroad had led to dependency at home and to the possibility of political and economic bankruptcy as well. The 1981 Polish crisis is a case in point, indicating one very ironic result of growing dependency relations at home. Perhaps the greatest of ironies was the Polish 1981 crisis: workers' protest against a workers' state. Leaving aside the cliché popular in Western and Polish circles that the socialist ideal seems to have the roughest going in socialist states, it can be argued that the Polish crisis does encapsulate many of the contradictions apparent in the impact of international inequalities on Eastern Europe. It is ironic, for example, that the Polish party-state, like many centrally planned one-party socialist states, seems to be far more beholden to the public in some ways and certainly more prone to short term horizons and political consumption cycles than polyarchies with market economies, systems known for their short-term economic horizons and "the electoral connection."[65] The debt trap is also ironic, not just because capitalism's inroads into socialism were unexpected and so contrary to the notion of the socialist bloc but also because of the alliances these inroads created—between workers and Western banks in the short run and between Western banks and the repressive Eastern European regimes in the longer run.

There is another ironic outcome as well. In seeking external autonomy, equality, efficiency, domestic popularity, and the maintenance of power, Eastern European elites went west, gaining in the process more economic inequality through austerity measures, possible economic collapse, more dependency, further domestic political strains, and even more pressures to give up their privileged economic and political roles within their respective societies. Instead of shoring up their points of weakness, then, they merely exposed them further by tangling with late capitalism.[66]

All this created a split for the Soviets between policies resonant with the goal of empire and policies that would enhance domestic economic growth and domestic political stability. While the Soviets achieved global power status and some security from controlling some portion of their border, they paid a very heavy price in terms of (1) subsidies in the form of loans, credits, and outright aid to prop up poorly performing economies, such as Poland, Cuba, Czechoslovakia, and Afghanistan, especially during crisis periods; (2) indirect subsidies, by offering energy—their major hard-currency asset other than gold—at below world market prices; (3) other subsidies, such as taking poor-quality consumer goods and machine tools, which are standardized, from Eastern Europe; (4) competition with their allies for scarce Western markets, capital, technology, and consumer goods, allies who have serious debt problems and parallel economic and political distortions; (5) assumption of the responsibility for safeguarding Western loans for the bloc (one reason why the overall credit rating for the bloc was so high); (6) the risk of Western contamination of Eastern Europe implied by greater contact with the West; (7) the risk of popular dissatisfaction at home, by allowing Soviet citizens to see in great numbers the relative prosperity of the satellites; (8) undermining future international influence by maintaining an empire and periodically intervening when satellites become deviant or recalcitrant; and (9) the military burden, given the free-rider effect, which is exacerbated by the unreliability of the Warsaw Pact forces and Eastern European resistance to raise contributions to the Soviet pursuit of global power status. In a time of lowered growth and rising frustrations at home, then, the Soviet Union increasingly has found Eastern Europe to be not an extension of their economic and political power but, rather, a serious liability. The Polish crisis and Soviet ambivalence about how to respond revealed the dilemmas of Soviet domination. In this case the core was distorted by its periphery—a periphery that it had to share increasingly with the West and that it even joined when pressing for greater contact with core capitalist economies.

Perhaps the biggest irony of all in the Polish case, however, was that the very process of reproducing state socialism in Poland seems to have created some of the prerequisites for a genuine proletarian revolution and a transition to real socialism. As the slogans of the Polish workers' union Solidarity indicated (as had their forerunners in Prague and Hungary), the vision of real socialism—economic and political democracy coupled with social ownership of the means of production—seems to have been taken seriously as a viable goal by large numbers of Eastern Europeans. Indeed it was the contrast between Polish socialism and real socialism, that became the target of criticism, with Socialist democracy, not bourgeois democracy, serving as the desired alternative. In this sense, the governing ideology of these regimes provided opponents with a clear standard of performance, which was not met by prevailing practices. Moreover, the form state socialism took in Poland in combination with the size of the working class, the homogeneity of the Polish nation, and the notion of a workers' state all facilitated the development of a genuine (and unprecedented) working class revolutionary movement, with characteristic recognition of a common enemy, a discredited state, and worker consciousness, cohesion, and radicalism. Third, the debt trap and dependence on the Soviet Union, precisely because of the creation of a party-state whose external interests contradicted domestic interests, led to political and economic bankruptcy—what Theda Skocpol has called the Janus-faced state in her theory of revolution.[67] Indeed, whatever theory of revolution one applies, the Polish case seems to fit unusually well, but with one missing ingredient: the state, as of this writing, still monopolizes the use of force, albeit through the military. Poland fits so well because it features to an extreme degree the contradictions noted in this chapter; that is, the complex interactions between international and domestic inequalities in the Soviet bloc and their mounting costs in generating contradictions that undermine equality, efficiency, political stability, and even empire. In this sense, the transition to socialism may be most likely not in late capitalist states, as some have argued,[68] but in late socialism, with Soviet domination having served, ironically, as a major, albeit unwitting coconspirator.

Notes

1. Quoted in Zvi Gitelman, "The World Economy and Elite Political Strategies in Czechoslovakia, Hungary, and Poland," in Morris Bornstein, Zvi Gitelman, and William Zimmerman, eds., *East–West Relations and the Future of Eastern Europe* (London: Allen and Unwin, 1981), p. 138.

    2. John Kenneth Galbraith, "Up from Monetarism and Other Wishful Thinking," *New York Review of Books* 28(August 13, 1981):29.
    3. Richard Rubinson, "The World Economy and the Distribution of Income within States," *American Sociological Review* 41(August 1976):638-659; Vince Mahler, *Dependency Approaches to International Political Economy: A Cross-National Study* (New York: Columbia University Press, 1980).
    4. For a summary of the dependencia literature, see Raymond Duvall, "Dependence and Dependencia Theory: Notes toward Precision of Concept and Argument," pp. 51-78, James Caporaso, "Dependence, Dependency, and Power in the Global System," pp. 1-12, and James Caporaso, "Dependence, Dependency, and Power in the Global System: A Structural and Behavioral Analysis," pp. 13-44, all in *International Organization* 32(Winter 1978), a special issue on "Dependence and Dependency in the Global System," edited by James Caporaso. Also see Mahler, *Dependency Approaches,* ch. 1; Johann Galtung, "A Structural Theory of Imperialism," *Journal of Peace Research* 2(1971):81-98. James Caporaso, "Methodological Issues in the Measurement of Inequality, Dependence, and Exploitation," in Steven J. Rosen and James R. Kunth, eds., *Testing Theories of Economic Imperialism* (Lexington, Mass.: D.C. Heath, 1974), pp. 87-116. On the concept of a regional hierarchical system, see William Zimmerman, "Hierarchical Regional Systems and the Politics of System Boundaries," *International Organizations* 26(Winter 1972):18-36; Zimmerman, "Dependency Theory and the Soviet-East European Hierarchical Regional System: Initial Tests," *Slavic Review* 37(December 1978):604-623. In some ways one can argue that the interaction between dependency relations and a regional hierarchical system in the Soviet bloc led to a divergence between the empire and economics.
    5. See Walter Connor, *Socialism, Work, and Equality* (New York: Columbia University Press, 1979); John Echols, "Does Socialism Mean Greater Equality?" *American Journal of Political Science* 25(February 1981):1-31; Alastair McAuley, *Economic Welfare in the Soviet Union* (Madison: University of Wisconsin Press, 1979); Murray Yanowitch, *Social and Economic Equality in the Soviet Union* (White Plains, N.Y.: M.E. Sharpe, 1977); Peter Wiles, *Distribution of Income East and West* (Amsterdam: North Holland Publishers, 1974); Frank Parkin, *Class Inequality and the Political Order* (New York: Praeger, 1971).
    6. See Zvi Gitelman, "The World Economy and Elite Political Strategies in Czechoslovakia, Hungary, and Poland," pp. 127-161; William Zimmerman, "Soviet-East European Relations in the 1980s and the Changing International System," pp. 87-104; Morris Bornstein, "Soviet-East European Economic Relations," pp. 105-126, all in Morris Bornstein, Zvi Gitelman, and William Zimmerman, eds., *East-West Relations and the Future of Eastern Europe* (London: Allen and Unwin, 1981); Paul Marer, "The Political Economy of Soviet Relations with Eastern Europe," in Steven J. Rosen and James A. Kurth, eds., *Testing Theories of Economic Imperialism* (Lexington, Mass.: D.C. Heath, 1974), pp. 231-260; Kent N. Brown, "Coalition Politics and Soviet Influence in Eastern Europe," in Jan F. Triska and Paul M. Cocks, eds., *Political Development in Eastern Europe* (New York: Praeger, 1977), pp. 241-255.

7. It must be emphasized that a careful reading of Marx or Lenin would reveal that socialism is in fact only about certain equalities, and the case for greater income equality under socialism than capitalism is *not* very easy to make in a theoretical sense. The real point has to do with some measures of equality of opportunity, the provision of economic security, and political equality. Moreover the real problem in generating greater income equality in the Soviet bloc has to do not with the contradiction between equality and growth so much as the failure to achieve socialist democracy, a world revolution, and the like—the forfeit of one value because of the failure to achieve, or at least pursue, other socialist values. See Branko Horvat, *The Political Economy of Socialism* (Armonk, N.Y.: M.E. Sharpe, 1982), pp. 285-322; David Lane, *The End of Inequality: Stratification under State Socialism* (Harmonds North, England: Penguin, 1971), pp. 11-54; Karl Marx, "Critique on the Gotha Programme," in Robert Tucker, ed., *The Marx-Engels Reader,* vol. 2 (New York: Norton, 1978), pp. 525-541; Arthur DiQuattro, "Alienation and Justice in the Market," *American Political Science Review* 7(December 1978):871-887.

8. Connor, *Socialism, Work,* p. 229.

9. The phrase is taken from Aleksander Zinoviev, *The Yawning Heights* (New York: Basic Books, 1980).

10. Rolf Dahrendorf, "On the Origins of Inequality among Men" (sic), in Dahrendorf, ed., *Essasy on the Theory of Society* (Stanford, Calif.: Stanford University Press, 1968).

11. The trade-off between equality and efficiency, Arthur Okun and others to the contrary, is a normative and not an empirical statement. Indeed, I would argue that such decisions are political and a byproduct of certain assumptions about human nature, the role of material versus normative incentives, and the like. Moreover, their relationship may not be a perfect negative correlation— large inequalities, for example, may cut into inefficiency. See Charles Lindblom, *Politics and Markets* (New York: Basic Books, 1977), pp. 222-236; Joseph Carens, *Equality, Moral Incentives and the Market* (Chicago: University of Chicago Press, 1981); Valerie Bunce and Alexander Hicks, "Capitalism, Socialisms, and Democracy: Beyond Current Political Economic Trade-offs," paper presented at the Annual Meeting of the American Political Science Association, Washington, D.C., August 28-31, 1980. For the basic theoretical argument, see Arthur Okun, *Equality and Efficiency: The Big Trade-off* (Washington, D.C.: Brookings Institution, 1975).

12. Lane, *An End to Inequality?*

13. Caporaso, "Methodological Issues," p. 87.

14. Refer to note 4 also see Ronald Herring, "International Determinents of Development Strategy Shifts: The Rise and Fall of 'Socialism' in Sri Lanka," paper presented at the Annual Meeting of the American Political Science Association convention in New York, September 3-5, 1981.

15. This has been noted, in greater detail, by William Zimmerman, "Dependency Theory."

16. Zimmerman, "Soviet-East European Relations," p. 94.

17. The term in Kenneth Jowitts. See *Revolutionary Breakthroughs and National Development* (Berkeley: University of California Press, 1971).

18. For an analysis of what Stalinism means, see Sheila Fitzpatrick, "Cultural Revolution as Class War" and Moshe Lewin, "Society, State, and Ideology during the First Five Year Plan," both in Sheila Fitzpatrick, ed., *Cultural Revolution in Russia, 1928-1931* (Bloomington: Indiana University Press, 1978), pp. 8-40, 41-77; Robert Tucker, ed., *Stalinism: Essasys in Historical Interpretation* (New York: W.W. Norton, 1977), especially T.H. Rigby, "Stalinism and the Mono-Organizational Society," pp. 53-77; Robert Tucker, "Stalinism as Revolution from Above," pp. 77-110; Moshe Lewin, "The Social Background of Stalinism," pp. 111-136; Wlodzimierz Brus, "Stalinism and the 'People's Democracies'," pp. 239-256.

19. See Alexander Erlich, "Stalinism and Marxian Growth Model," pp. 137-154 in Tucker, ed., *Stalinism*.

20. Frederick Pryor, "The Distribution of Nonagricultural Labor Incomes in Communist and Capitalist Nations," *Slavic Review* 31(1972):pp. 639-650.

21. Caporaso, "Methodological Issues," p. 91.

22. See Marer, "The Political Economy"; Borstein, "Soviet-East European Economic Relations."

23. See Marer, "The Political Economy," pp. 234-238; Jan Triska, "Workers Assertiveness and Soviet Policy Choices," in Jan Triska and Charles Gati, eds., *Blue Collar Workers in Eastern Europe* (London: Allen and Unwin, 1981):273-275.

24. See Kálmán Pésci, *The Future of Socialist Economic Integration* (Armonk, N.Y.: M.G. Sharpe, 1981), pp. 158, 166-168.

25. Rigby, "Stalinism."

26. Alec Nove, "Socialism, Centralized Planning and the One Party State," in T.H. Rigby, Archie Brown, and Peter Reddaway, eds., *Authority, Power and Policy in the USSR* (New York: St. Martin's, 1980), p. 82.

27. Ibid., p. 83.

28. The terms are Charles Lindblom's. See *Politics and Markets*.

29. Paul M. Johnson, "Changing Social Structure and the Political Role of Manual Workers," in Jan Triska and Charles Gati, eds., *Blue Collar Workers in Eastern Europe* (London: Allen and Unwin, 1981), p. 35, and, more generally, pp. 34-36.

30. Brus, "Stalinism," pp. 247-248.

31. For an analysis of de-Stalinization and the policy logic of the Khrushchev regime, see George Breslauer, "Khrushchev Reconsidered," *Problems of Communism* 25(September-October 1976):18-33; Jeremy Azrael, "Varieties

of de-Stalinization," in Chalmers Johnson, ed., *Change in Communist Systems* (Stanford, Calif.: Stanford University Press, 1970).

32. Zimmerman, "Soviet–East European Relations," p. 99; Pesci, *The Future*; Eleftherios Botsas, "Patterns of Trade," in Stephen Fischer-Galati, ed., *Eastern Europe in the 1980s* (Boulder, Colo.: Westview Press, 1981), pp. 83–120.

33. Marer, "The Political Economy," pp. 231–232.

34. Hans Herman-Hohmann, "The State and the Economy in Eastern Europe," in Jack Hayward and R.N. Berki, eds., *State and Society in Contemporary Europe* (New York: St. Martin's, 1979), p. 141.

35. Bogdan Mieczkowski, *Personal and Social Consumption in Eastern Europe* (New York: Praeger, 1977), p. 173.

36. Connor, "Workers and Power," p. 165. Also see Zvi Gitelman, "Power and Authority in Eastern Europe," in Chalmers Johnson, ed., *Change in Communist Systems* (Stanford, Calif.: Stanford University Press, 1970); Zygmunt Baumann, "Twenty Years After: The Crisis in Soviet Type Systems," *Problems of Communism* 20(November–December 1971): 45–53.

37. This correlation is based on data collected by Frederic Pryor, *Public Expenditures in Communist and Capitalist Systems* (Homewood, Ill.: Dorsey, 1968).

38. These data are summarized from Mieczkowski, *Personal and Social Consumption,* pp. 196–198, 225, 243, 241, 311; and Valerie Bunce, *Do New Leaders Make a Difference?* (Princeton, N.J.: Princeton University Press, 1981); Connor, *Socialism, Work.*

39. David Bronson and Constance Krueger, "The Revolution in Soviet Farm Household Income," in James Millar, ed., *The Soviet Rural Community: A Symposium* (Urbana: University of Illinois, 1971), pp. 214–258.

40. See Connor, *Socialism, Work*; Jaroslav Krejci, *Social Change and Stratification in Post-War Czechoslovakia* (New York: Columbia University Press, 1972).

41. Bunce, *Do New Leaders Make a Difference?* Also see Bogdan Mieczkowski, "The Relationship between Changes in Consumption and Politics in Poland," *Soviet Studies* 30(1978):263–269; Valeri Bunce, "The Succession Connection: Policy Cycles and Political Change in the Soviet Union and Eastern Europe," *American Political Science Review* 74(December 1980):966–977.

42. Theda Skocpol, *States and Social Revolutions* (London: Cambridge University Press, 1979); Herring, "International Determinants."

43. *Politics and Markets.*

44. See Connor, *Socialism, Work.* In the Czechoslovak case, it can be argued that equalization was chosen over political and economic reforms and that this is why equality correlates with lower productivity.

45. See Gitelman, "The Global Economy," for an argument emphasizing the importance of how well political leaders prepare the population for cost increases.

46. Mieczkowski, "The Relationship"; Bunce, "The Succession Connection."

47. Gitelman, "The Global Economy," p. 129.

48. Triska, "Workers' Assertiveness." For further support, see Connor, *Socialism, Work,* pp. 215–266 and Wiles, *The Distribution.*

49. See Mervyn Matthews, *Privilege in the Soviet Union* (London: Allen and Unwin, 1978), especially pp. 127–129; Jan de Weydenthal, "Poland: Workers and Politics," pp. 187–208 and Laura D'Andrea Tyson, "Aggregate Economic Difficulties and Workers' Welfare," pp. 108–135, both in Triska and Gati, eds., *Blue Collar Workers.*

50. On the Soviet case, see John Bushnell, "The New Soviet Man Turns Pessimist," in Stephen F. Cohen et al., eds., *The Soviet Union since Stalin* (Bloomington: Indiana University Press, 1980), pp. 179–199.

51. This of often overlooked in analyses of what's wrong with socialist economies. See Alex Nove, "The Soviet Economy: Problems and Prospects," *New Left Review* 38(January–February, 1980), pp. 3–19; Gregory Grossman, "An Economy at Middle Age," *Problems of Communism* 25(March–April, 1976), pp. 18–33.

52. The literature on this is immense. See, for example, M.S. Kukushkin, *Razvitoi Sotsializm: Proizvodstvo material'nykh blag* (Leningrad: Lenizdat, 1975).

53. See, in particular, Jack Bielasiak, "Workers and Mass Participation in Socialist Democracy," pp. 88–108, and Daniel Nelson, "Romania: Participatory Dynamics in 'Developed Socialism'," pp. 236–252, both in Triska and Gati, eds., *Blue Collar Workers.*

54. Triska, "Workers' Power," p. 269.

55. Gitelman, "The Global Economy"; Seweryn Bialer, *Stalin's Successors* (Cambridge, England: Cambridge University Press, 1980); Daniel Nelson, "Eastern Europe and the Non-Communist World," in Stephen Fischer-Galati, ed., *Eastern Europe,* pp. 195–224; Bunce, "The Soviet Union"; Pésci, *The Future,* p. 162.

56. Triska, "Workers' Assertiveness," p. 275. Of course, another problem was the failure of détente, which, due to space limitations, has been excluded but is, of course, *very* important. See Bunce, "The Brezhnev Era" and Cora Bell, "Soviet-American Strategic Balance, the Western Alliance, and East-West Relations," in Bornstein et al., eds., *East-West Relations,* pp. 11–30.

57. Gitelman, "The Global Economy," p. 127. For an optimistic view, see Pésci, *The Future,* pp. 162–164.

58. Cheryl Payer, *The Debt Trap* (New York: Monthly Review Press, 1974). On Eastern European and Soviet debt to the West and Eastern European debt to the Soviet Union, see Morris Bornstein, "Issues in East-West Economic Relations," in Bornstein et al., eds., *East-West Relations,* pp. 31–60; Daniel Nelson, "Eastern Europe"; Richard Portes, "East Europe's Debt to the West:

Interdependence Is a Two Way Street," *Foreign Affairs* 55(April 1977); Morris Bornstein, "East–West Economic Relations and Soviet–East European Economic Relations," in Joint Economic Committee (ed.) *Soviet Economy in a Time of Change,* vol. 1 (Washington, D.C.: U.S. Government Printing Office, 1979), pp. 291–311. For an up-to-date summary of the size of the debt, see "Down Communism's Sink," *The Economist,* February 13, 1982, pp. 11–15; Jan Vanous and Michael Marrese, "Soviet Subsidies to Eastern Economies," *The Wall Street Journal,* January 15, 1982; "Now Russia Asks for Time to Pay," *The Economist,* February 6, 1982, pp. 79–80.

59. Friedrich Levcik and Jan Stankovsky, *Industrial Cooperation between East and West* (White Plains, N.Y.: M.E. Sharpe, 1979), p. 229, pp. 158–159, and 227–229; Pésci, *The Future,* p. 159.

60. See Bornstein, "Soviet–East European Economic Relations"; Bornstein, "East–West Economic Relations"; Vanous and Marrese, "Soviet Subsidies"; Pésci, *The Future,* p. 164.

61. Seweryn Bialer, "The Politics of Stringency, in the USSR," *Problems of Communism* 29(May–June, 1980):19–33.

62. Bushnell, "The New Soviet Man"; Christopher Davis and Murray Feshbach, "Rising Infant Mortality in The USSR in the 1970's," Monograph (Washington, D.C.: U.S. Department of Commerce, 1980).

63. Skocpol, *States and Social Revolutions.*

64. Triska, "Workers' Assertiveness."

65. Lindblom, *Politics and Markets*; David Mayhew, *The Electoral Connection* (New Haven, Conn.: Yale University Press, 1974).

66. See, in particular, Alex Pravda, "East–West Interdependence and the Social Compact in Eastern Europe," in Bornstein et al., eds., *East–West Relations,* pp. 162–190. As Pravda summarizes (p. 184), greater economic contact with the West "served to stretch the system at its most sensitive points."

67. Skocpol, *States and Social Revolutions.*

68. John Stephens, *The Transition from Capitalism to Socialism* (New York: Macmillan, 1979). But see Rudolf Bahro, *The Alternative in Eastern Europe* (London: New Left Books, 1978); George Konrad and Ivan Szelenyi, *The Intellectuals on the Road to Class Power* (New York: Harcourt, Brace, and Jovanovich, 1979).

2

Leninists and Political Inequalities: The Nonrevolutionary Politics of Communist States

Daniel N. Nelson

Successful revolutionaries become rulers and bureaucrats. In the latter roles Leninists have engaged in practices similar to those followed in all political systems insofar as they preserve political inequalities. Political inequalities imply a differentiation of access to power in policymaking and thus exist in all polities. But for revolutionary movements or organizations, legitimacy turns on expectations for socioeconomic and political progress, usually seen as greater equality. More than any other modern political notion, Marxism emphasizes such equality in the presumed intimacy between party and proletariat.

Why do Leninist parties, beginning with the Communist Party of the Soviet Union, turn away from their revolutionary heritage to preserve political inequalities? What are the systemic consequences of such nonrevolutionary politics of Communist party rule? Do political inequalities impede or promote political change in communist systems?

Issues

Karl Marx would have us believe that the roots of unequal political power would dissolve in the aftermath of proletarian revolution. As economic control passed from capitalists to the industrial masses, and those who toiled came to own the means of production, the state's political machinery could be used to implement egalitarian values in the transition to communism. The rationale for political inequalities, which had in the capitalist epoch been based upon economic interests, would then cease to exist.

The tension between society's need for hierarchy[1] and Marxist expectations for an egalitarian emphasis in socioeconomic and political changes is seen no more clearly than in nation-states today ruled by Leninist parties. Any effort to develop or modernize, necessary in virtually all communist states since they are less advanced systems, will incorporate a contradiction between equality and hierarchy. Indeed the dialectic between such human needs may be critical to development.[2] Leninist organizations, however, are saddled with the necessity of seeking development while rejecting the conflictual implications of such a process. Both a need for hierarchy and expectations of equality are generated by policies to expand rapidly socioeconomic complexity and capacity. While not denying that strata exist in their societies, governing Communist parties have refused consistently to recognize conflicts of their own making and have sought to deny political outlets for the competition between requirements for hierarchy and the need for equality.

With very few exceptions Leninist party organizations have evinced little sympathy for Marxist visions. The transition of revolutionary to administrator is evident in such a gulf between the literature of Marx and the practice of Leninist rule. Gaining control of states where a proletariat was often nowhere to be found, where ethnic or linguistic schisms made a mockery of proletarian internationalism and where Communists were a tiny, insecure minority in a broad political spectrum, erstwhile revolutionaries *exploited* existing inequalities rather than sought their elimination. To protect what Roy Laird has called the "monohierarchy" of Party and state, the Communist Party of the Soviet Union (CPSU) and other Leninist parties have sought to exploit the segmentation of society through manipulation of both the involvement of citizens and resources distribution.

Leninist parties pursue socioeconomic development in the relatively less advanced areas they rule, thereby seeking an expansion of party bureaucracy and control, while denying outlets for demands that would further political equality. Elitist in their origins, Leninists find the requirement of status differentiation and structurally imposed hierarchies quite compatible with their view of themselves as a vanguard. That these same parties must encourage socioeconomic changes that engender conflict and competition regarding their political control is surely one of the more acute dilemmas to face political leaders anywhere.

My effort here is to use examples drawn primarily from communist Europe to identify types of political inequalities that exist in such systems and the ways in which former revolutionary organizations have utilized such inequalities to mitigate political change. In my explanation of the politics of such unequal access to power, I will focus on the competition and conflict over public policies that Communist parties try to control or avoid through the use of political inequalities.

Participatory Inequalities

Vernon V. Aspaturian has discussed the generic concept of involvement in three forms—participation, mobilization, and manipulation. Participation refers to citizen political activity that is autonomous. Mobilization concerns externally organized involvement in which "elements of spontaneity, volition and autonomy are largely absent." Manipulation is distinguished from mobilization via the "deception of those politically involved." Were nation-states compared in terms of political involvement[3] familiar to competitive democracies such as voting, membership in associations, or attendance at rallies and meetings, most communist systems would be among the cases highest in levels of citizen activity. As is well known, official tallies of voting often exceed 99 percent of eligible citizens. Trade unions and student and women's organizations frequently include four-fifths or more of the population from which they could potentially draw. General assemblies at enterprises, citizen assemblies or public rallies exhibit high attendance.

Within the structures of party and state, too, is a sizable proportion of the population. Party membership in communist states ranges from 6.5 percent of the total population in the USSR to 12.6 percent in Romania, and from 8 to 17 percent of adult citizens in all communist states. Membership is certainly no longer confined to the ranks of an elite vanguard or to the most powerful, but encompasses at least nominal party identity for many ordinary citizens. People's Councils or Soviets, local quasi-legislative assemblies, have hundreds of thousands of members in larger communist nations, while people's inspectors and other adjunct mechanisms vastly expand involvement in the establishment.[4]

This behemoth of involvement mobilized under the aegis of Communist parties is not broadly distributed, however. Inequalities cut two ways; both the degree of and channels for political activity are skewed by the political identification of individuals and by a variety of socioeconomic variables.

Citizens who are most frequently involved and who have the greatest commitment and sense of efficacy via such activity, are party members. (Party members are, of course, more likely to engage in participatory as opposed to mobilized or manipulated involvement.[5]) A party card does not mean its holder *will* be an activist, but membership correlates with activity; the relationship is not causal. Members of patriotic (or democratic) fronts, trade unions, or other organizations who remain outside the Communist party and citizens outside any sociopolitical organization are less frequently and less intensely involved. They attend meetings but do not speak or assist with agenda-setting or preparations; they vote but do so only when reminded and urged.[6] Since they are outside the periphery of preferred political identity, their degree of involvement is constrained and usually limited to mobilized or manipulated forms. Were individuals not belonging to the Party to attempt, singly or in groups, significant alterations in established participatory patterns, the Party would fight them and usually win. "Democracy wall" came to an end in China, even when the sentiments expressed via such a route continue. Trade union movements have been opposed vigorously in the USSR and Romania. Where the Party does not achieve an outright victory against groups seeking nonparty outlets for participation, it seeks compromise arrangements that have the potential for incremental modification in the Party's favor. In Poland the victory of Gdansk shipyard workers and the formation of Solidarity as a national independent union structure were not an outcome about which the Polish United Workers Party (PUWP) became sanguine. Under Kania and Jaruzelski, the Party tried to weaken independent unions by threats, inducements, and infiltration. When those efforts failed. Wojciech Jaruzelski pushed the Party aside, and resorted to overt coercion.

Socioeconomic status is, of course, a certain correlate of political activity.[7] But the relationship is not direct and must be analyzed with care in communist states. Segmentation of many kinds is associated with varying levels of involvement, at some times or in some cases more strongly than a measure of socioeconomic status. During years of communist rule in Eastern Europe when the presence of education or wealth were negative attributes for a political career, the typical association between socioeconomic status and involvement was reversed. Locksmiths became judges; foundry workers were named to administrative posts. As one local leader said to me in the 1970s, his country had seemingly achieved a bizarre equality—"leveling-off at the lowest level." Similarly in the Cultural Revolution catapulted many groups of low socioeconomic status into participatory activities.

Political requirements, then, can and do impose themselves to disrupt the socioeconomic association with involvement. Most dramatically, new communist regimes have not shied from a concerted attack on the link between high socioeconomic status and political activity. That such an egalitarian emphasis fades and becomes corrupted, as Djilas described in *The New Class* and Casals treated in *Syncretic Society*,[8] does not end the rhetorical commitment of communist systems to open channels for access to power by all social groups simultaneous with efforts to mitigate differences among them. While "official rhetoric and sometimes some degree of official intention"[9] call for popular initiatives, citizen involvement, socialist democracy, and other phrases, the systems ruled by Leninist parties are vertically responsive. To put it bluntly, people worry about making others beneath them do what higher authorities want. Such a non-revolutionary reward structure is not geared toward compensating public officials, bureaucrats, or economic managers for efforts to serve needs of communities in which they hold office vis-a-vis central or higher authorities. Broadening the political base of communist systems, contrary to their revolutionary heritage, does not mean strengthening of horizontal linkages, but rather the further penetration of vertically responsive organizations.

Such a vertically integrated milieu for involvement is quite different from the political life of democratic systems; federal or unitary in formal structure, communist polities are not merely centralist but antilocal and antiplural as well. The Party hierarchy cannot allow challenges at the local level since to do so would be to admit inability to subsume all subnational interests, an admission of its lack of universality. The credo of Leninist parties cannot tolerate a pluralization of political life either, and leaders use party members as one control against such tendencies. "Democratic centralism," paradox that it is to Western ears, must be applied; no one outside the Party can be in a post of responsibility. Party membership is not only associated strongly with how much one is involved but how high one may rise in posts of responsibility. A high degree of involvement without a party card is possible, as is local economic managerial status. But the combination of an important post with activism for a person outside the Party is not possible.

We penetrate communist systems to a shallow degree, however, if party membership is the only criterion observed to affect involvement. Party membership is not the only or the most pervasive political inequality where Leninist parties rule. It is not the sole determinant of access to policymaking power in communist states. Indeed participatory inequalities continued during communist regimes have been evident in many segments of society.

Women, for example, are outside top policymaking roles in all communist states. In this such systems exhibit similarity to many nation-states. Nevertheless the image of female emancipation and liberation is an important one to Leninist parties, for both ideological and economic reasons. In nations with little industry, the need for female labor in order to develop rapidly is particularly acute. But the important economic role of women has not been reflected in political power. Exceptions, as in China or Romania, seem to have been the product of familial connections. Elena Ceauşescu in Romania, for example, holds a position in the Political Executive Committee (or Politburo) as well as other high-ranking posts. Women in political life are clustered at local levels, and their economic role is predominant in only a few industries and services.[10] Even at the local level, very few provincial or regional first secretaries have been women and, among that small number, only rare examples can be cited of women who held such posts for lengthy periods. The case of Tatarkowna-Majkowska in Lodz, for instance, is unique in Poland (she was a provincial first secretary for over a decade in the mid-fifties to sixties).[11] In their attitudes working women in communist systems evince little anxiety over their political impotence, thinking of material interests as central to their lives.[12] It cannot be disputed that women are involved in the structures of state and party to a degree that compares favorably with almost every Western democracy; typically, 25 percent of party membership is female, while 33 to 40 percent of local council deputies are women. But the transformation is very incomplete, and differences between male and female in access to power remain among the most prominent political inequalities.[13]

Ethnic and linguistic minorities, likewise, are not among leading participatory elements of Leninist regimes. While Uzbeks in the USSR, Croats in Yugoslavia, or Hungarians in Romania vote, become deputies in people's councils, take high posts in local industry and are provided symbols of cultural autonomy (publications in their languages, some broadcasts, and theater performances emphasizing cultural traditions), their rate of political activity is proportionately lower. Not only are there subtle indications that minorities scorn mobilized or manipulated involvement,[14] but we also see that their route to high-level participatory roles in policymaking is constrained.[15] Prominent minority politicians in state or party roles are recruited not to speak for ethnic or linguistic interests, but to speak *to* such groups. Newspapers in native languages do not represent minority views and needs but, rather, express the positions of central leaders in local languages. People from the Armenian SSR, for example, who become participants and who appear to have some access to power are likely to be those who speak the regime's language figuratively, regardless of national identification.

Rural and urban poor are, as everywhere, denied access to power. Precisely what constitutes poverty in Communist party states is a matter for debate. Certainly, income is not alone a good indicator since status or privilege plays such an important role in perceptions of class.[16] If, however, we were to denote the lowest 20 percent of income recipients as a disadvantaged group, then even in relatively wealthy Czechoslovakia that quintile earned only 6.3 percent of individual income in 1965, whereas the top quintile earned 34.4 percent in the same year. Although some income redistribution had occurred since World War II, in other words, wealth remained concentrated.[17]

There is no debate, however, about regional inequalities within communist systems or the existence of qualitative distinctions among urban residential areas. These may be pockets of poverty and underdevelopment with long histories such as Kosovo in Yugoslavia or Bialystok in Poland. Alternatively, rapid migration to urban areas can create new zones of poverty, where first-generation industrial labor, for the most part unskilled, are clustered in massive housing projects on the periphery of older cities. Suffering from dislocation and anomie, these people are not likely to be a potent political force in any system. More easily manipulated and mobilized due to their separation from roots in the countryside, the new urban poor have no organizational basis for participation that the Party has not penetrated. Their people's councils, citizens' committees, people's courts, trade unions, and volunteer or avocational associations are all linked to the Party hierarchy. Without the infrastructure of village and extended family, the peasant-workers must rely more on party-sanctioned organizations, for health care, day care, transportation, and a whole range of employee benefits. In short, the vast number of first generation urban poor in the Balkans, the USSR, or China have been made more dependent on the Party and its adjunct organizations. The quality of their involvement in the system, then, tends to be characterized by noncommittal behavior with little knowledge about personalities or mechanisms of political life and little sense of efficacy.

The frequency of involvement, the quantity not the quality of activity, is also skewed toward the haves in communist states. In Yugoslavia this is particularly evident among workers' councils members but is also present in the political self-government bodies (local or municipal councils).[18] That the haves retain close association with political power can be seen in Yugoslav data relating political identity with socioeconomic level (see Table 2-1). Lacking comparable survey data from other communist states, one cannot replicate this cross tabulation. Nevertheless, it seems plausible that the Party will be the channel into political activity for the haves of all societies where nonrevolutionary parties rule.

Young adults have difficulty participating in anything but nominal roles in communist states. Political life in such systems has become a game of the elderly.

Table 2-1
Political Identity in Yugoslavia, by Socioeconomic Level

Socioeconomic Level	Unaffiliated (%)	Alliance Members (%)[a]	League Members (%)[b]
Lowest third	46	25	6
Middle third	34	39	23
Highest third	20	36	71
	100	100	100

Source: Sidney Verba and Goldie Shabad, "Workers' Councils and Political Stratification: The Yugoslav Experience," *American Political Science Review* 72, no. 1, (March 1978):87.

[a] Socialist Alliance but not League of Communists

[b] League of Communists; possibly also Alliance members

It was not always that way, of course, and time will alter the picture. But once in power, communist leaders, like leaders in all authoritarian regimes, do not relinquish control with grace. "Tenacious" may be an accurate description of men the age of Mao, Deng, Brezhnev, and others. One may grant that longevity is not a left-wing phenomenon (remember Franco), while still noting that access to power is not often available to people in their forties or younger in communist states—an observation associated strongly with low turnover rates of leadership posts. Systems as diverse as Yugoslavia and the Soviet Union nevertheless exhibit similarly stabilized composition of leadership levels, meaning that career advancement for younger functionaries is stalled by infrequent turnover and long tenure.[19] (See Table 2-2)

Access of industrial labor to political power has been constrained as well. Ostensibly workers' states, governments by Communist parties nevertheless incorporate inequalities perpetuating the conditions against which Marx argued. Workers have not been made owners of the means of production, nor can they negotiate with the Party leadership, which acts as the new ownership. Workers remain alienated from the product of their own labor as it is not their's to distribute. A monopoly of employment remains, albeit transferred from the capitalists to the Party. Workers are obliged to sell their labor, but no one other than the Party is allowed to buy it. Without any rival the Party need not bargain with workers; it simple demands their labor and continued sacrifice. Each worker is alone, confined to a kind of social solitude, without anything more than an imaginary means by which to defend himself.[20]

Understandably, reform efforts in communist Europe have been aimed at reducing the monopoly of employment held by the Party, and to convert the relations between party and worker to one with a negotiating basis. In the Polish case, Solidarity, the independent union structure arising from 1980 events, began as an effort to institutionalize the negotiability of worker–party relations.

Table 2-2

Age Distribution of Regional Leaders, USSR and Yugoslavia

	Percentage 45 or younger	*Percentage 46-55*	*Percentage 56 or older*
USSR, 1973 (party bureau members)	29	42	29
Yugoslavia, 1980 (party presidencies)	17.4	46.4	36.2

Sources: Lenard Cohen, "Political Management in Post-Tito Yugoslavia: The Recruitment and Composition of Regional Elites," paper presented at the Second World Congress of Soviet and East European Studies, Garmisch, Germany, September 30–October 4, 1980, p. 26; and Joel Moses, "Local Leadership Integration in the Soviet Union," in D. Nelson, ed. *Local Politics in Communist Countries* (Lexington: University of Kentucky Press, 1980), p. 33.
Note: "Regional" means eighteen oblasts in the USSR, and the six republics and two provinces of Yugoslavia. USSR data include all party bureau positions, whereas Yugoslav data include only party presidencies, i.e., a smaller sample of $N = 69$.

With equal understanding, we can observe the strenuous efforts by ruling parties to placate industrial labor with rhetoric and structures. Most often, one hears the terminology of workers' self-management channeled through general assemblies and workers' councils at the enterprise level. Enormous propaganda campaigns, involving considerable personnel and monetary resources, are mounted to create an image of access to power via participation. Until the advent of independent unions in Poland after 1980, however, no Communist party state except Yugoslavia gave any indication of workers' councils having influence on policy. Polish workers' councils established in 1956 were subverted quickly and ceased to be influential by 1958. Similar bodies established in Romania in 1971 were ignored until miners' strikes in 1977 brought about renewed propaganda emphasis in 1978-79.[21]

Workers, as a class, *do* influence politices in communist states indirectly, but have lacked institutionalized access to power. The role desired by the Party for industrial labor is clearly that of mobilized or manipulated involvement: docile and, if possible, enthusiastic obedience, coupled with high productivity on the job. Workplace behavior is essentially political in communist systems, given the Party's alleged identity with the proletariat, and the emphasis placed on socio-economic development in the realm of industry. Both the Party's ideological rationalization for dictatorship *and* the most obvious measure of its performance (economic growth) are tied to industrial labor and work place behavior.[22]

One thus finds that Communist parties are neither primarily composed of nor led by individuals with recent experiences related to the proletariat.[23] Moreover, channels established for the involvement of workers in work place governance seem designed to mitigate the participation of that stratum, restricting their access to power. For example, workers' councils do not consist of workers, per se, but frequently contain a majority of managers, directors, and party functionaries from an enterprise. When general assemblies or workers' council sessions take place, party officials or managerial personnel dominate the proceedings (setting the agenda and speaking most of the time). Workers, indeed, do not seem to know their few elected representatives to the councils very well.[24]

One kind of political inequality maintained in Communist party states, then, is differing levels of and channels for involvement. The involvement of Party members can include having access to power and hence be participatory; having a party card is clearly the most obvious variable associated with political inequality. Members not only participate more, but do so at higher levels.

But women, minorities, the poor, the young, and industrial labor are denied institutionalized access to power for policy influence; they cannot as easily *participate,* even if they are Party members, as compared with educated men of the dominant nationality who are neither poor nor young. Such an assessment is not, of course, an indictment directed solely at communist regimes. As regards political inequalities perhaps European communist states can be compared favorably with the Western democracies, not to mention authoritarian regimes of past and present. But the contrast between Marxist prescriptions and communist state realities are striking, and the failure of ruling parties to deemphasize the terminology of political equality only makes the distinction more glaring.

Resource Inequalities

Among the social axioms that appeal by simplicity is the cliché that the rich get richer while the poor get poorer. Few political systems combat such a tendency with more than rhetoric, and some polities have the effect to foster the concentration of wealth. This process both reflects and produces political inequalities. Even if the extent of and channels for political involvement were unlimited, a paucity of resources could spell impotence. Existing resources buy unequal participation. Thus one aspect of political inequality reflects an unequal distribution of resources. In any political system regions possessing great energy supplies (Canada's Alberta or Poland's Katowice) have an expanded importance based upon existing resources. In other nation-states particular constituencies receive additional attention perhaps because they are a voting bloc or a strategically important nationality.

Leninist parties, governing ostensibly Marxist systems, have often announced their intentions to mitigate income differences, regional contrasts in living standards, and inequalities arising among occupational categories. That revolutionary action has not followed revolutionary words should surprise no one. Whether communist leaders *intend* that resources be unevenly distributed notwithstanding rhetoric, or have tried but failed to redistribute resources, may be an unanswerable question. The significance of redistribution is debated but the persistence of inequalities is not.[25]

Regardless of how one looks at data from communist states, empirical evidence corroborates first-hand impressions insofar as resource inequalities are visible. Income distributions, while somewhat more egalitarian than the West, still reflect a concentration of wealth. (See Table 2-3) Even after fifteen years Communist rule, in both Czechoslovakia and Bulgaria one-fifth of the workforce were receiving one-third of the personal income. Meanwhile, regional inequalities are as stark as ever in Romania and Poland, with the net product of selected *judeţe* (countries) in the former differing greatly, and public investments and expenditures of *wojewodztwa* (provinces) highly unequal per capita. (Tables 2-4 to 2-6) Yugoslavia, despite a much more vocal commitment to equality among republics, has not achieved goals set by Tito's government years ago.[26] China's provinces exhibit vast inequalities of indigenous wealth, as suggested by agricultural production measures, which allows some locales to curtail dependency on Peking.[27] Overall, it seems that communist states (regardless of intent) exhibit regional inequalities not significantly different from what one might expect for states of their size and affluence and are about as inegalitarian as noncommunist systems.[28]

Individual and regional resource inequalities are augmented (or exacerbated) by nationalities and ethnic schisms. Although not all communist states have sizable minority populations, those that do seem to offer lower investments in minority counties or locales.[29] The relationship of other variables to resource inequality, such as an individual's social origin, reinforces the picture that the rich get richer regardless of political system. A lack of social mobility clearly prevents attaining resources that would help a person to become more

Table 2-3
Pretax Income Distribution

Major noncommunist countries	Percentage Income to Lowest 40 Percent	Percentage Income to Middle 40 Percent	Percentage Income to Top 20 Percent
United States, 1970	20	42	39
Britain, 1968	19	42	39
Japan, 1963	21	39	40
Communist Europe			
Czechoslovakia, 1965	20.3	45.3	34.4
Bulgaria, 1962	27	40	33
Yugoslavia, 1968	19	40	42

Source: Adapted by author from Hollis Chenery et al., *Redistribution with Growth* (New York: Oxford University Press, 1974), pp. 8-9, and, for Czechoslovakia, Jaroslav Krejci, *Social Change and Stratification in Post-War Czechoslovakia* (New York: Columbia University Press, 1972), p. 26.

Table 2–4
Net Industrial Production Among Romanian *Judeţe*

Total Industrial Production	Number of Judeţe		
$1 = 11.5 lei (official)	1965	1970	1975
To 5 billion *lei*	30	19	8
5.1–10 billion *lei*	6	12	4*
10.1–15 billion *lei*	3	5	7
15.1–25 billion *lei*	–	3	11
More than 25 billion *lei*	–	–	2

Source: Vasile Cucu, *Geografie şi Urbanizare* (Iaşi: Editura Junimea, 1976), p. 44; that the 1975 column does not add up to 39 *judeţe* is not explained by Cucu. His text, however, leads one to suspect that the mistake is in the 5.1–10 billion range, which probably should read *11*, not 4.

Table 2-5
Differences in per Capita Public Welfare Investments in Polish
Provinces, 1966–1972
(in zŀoty per capita)

Province[a]	Mean Investments/ Health	Mean Investments/ Education	Mean Investments/ Housing
Katowice	162	648	1249
Opole	89	380	901
Ŀodz	60	305	878
Wrocław	81	219	545
Kradów	147	370	766
Gdansk	152	670	996
Poznan	62	284	830
Szczecin	137	457	878
Warszawa	91	420	857
Bydgoszcz	93	397	959
Zielona Gora	101	387	722
Rzeszow	121	522	966
Olsztyn	99	312	719
Lublin	89	453	901
Koszalin	205	396	855
Kielce	101	388	931
Biały stok	78	371	893

Source: Adapted from data provided by Barclay Ward, University of the South.
[a]Cities classified as provinces omitted.

than nominally involved. Sons and daughters of manual workers in European communist states will most likely be manual workers. After a brief surge of political advancement given to manual occupations, workers have gained little in

Table 2-6

Differences in per Capita Public Welfare Expenditures in Polish
Provinces, 1966-1972

(in zloty per capita)

Province[a]	Mean Expenditures (Health)	Mean Expenditures (Education)	Mean Expenditures (Housing)
Katowice	793.47	523.87	201.26
Opole	718.46	707.64	174.48
Łodz	520.98	590.68	100.42
Wrocław	841.44	732.28	188.88
Kraków	548.55	565.89	106.74
Gdansk	725.70	714.12	236.15
Poznan	505.04	571.23	106.85
Szczecin	667.05	853.22	377.60
Warszawa	502.48	595.52	78.61
Bydgoszcz	575.38	641.96	128.11
Zielona Gora	819.84	776.56	212.77
Rzeszow	514.35	603.77	93.76
Olsztyn	635.07	760.74	158.68
Lublin	453.62	591.07	120.58
Koszalin	659.34	791.54	212.71
Kielce	463.37	598.70	107.60
Białystok	533.60	664.97	131.80

Source: Adapted from data provided by Barclay Ward, University of the South.

[a]Cities classified as provinces omitted.

the way of institutionalized access to power in communist systems. Any expectation held by individuals for their future influence because of rising importance or prominence would, first, have to overcome social *immobilisme*.[30] Put differently, it is extremely difficult for anyone not from background of high socioeconomic status to attain such status. A lack of social mobility means that resources of money and privilege are still concentrated in the hands of a few; the potential for access to power thus begets the same potential.

Resource availability is of course central to political activity. Individual efforts to pursue interests via an access to power and hence to participate will be unsuccessful lacking resources. Resources need not be money, per se; instead, any commodity or service wanted by someone else is a resource. Ascribed resources, often totally unproven, may be available to political actors as well.[31] The consequence of engaging in political activity sans resources is to be ignored or to be the victim of punitive countermeasures.

Authoritatian one-party states, the primary subset of which is communist systems, try to prevent the link between resource availability and political activity. In a simple metaphor, ruling Leninist parties want to keep the two components of a dangerous formula separate. Activist individuals, locales, or associations can be active until they exhaust their energies; communist regimes typically provide endless outlets for civic involvement. Meanwhile, individuals, locales, and associations with resources will not be traumatized by efforts to divest them of their concentration of wealth as long as their involvement remains within mobilized or manipulated patterns. Communist regimes, with few periods such as China's Cultural Revolution as obvious exceptions, are protectors of a new class, dependent for its success on the status quo.

Were resource availability (RA) and political activism (PA) to combine at any level, access to power (AP) could be generated for the individual, association, enterprise, or locale involved. As greater access is opened up by such activism from a position of strength, more resources and additional activism will be encouraged. These relationships might be represented simply as

$$(RA)\,(PA) = AP.$$

Such an imprecise expression is meant only to be suggestive.[32] If all three components were measured on a scale of 0 to 1.00, the multiplicative relation between resources and activity implies that access is never totally zero *or* complete. Moreover, even the most activist association (for example) would have little access were its resources very constrained.

Access does not mean a decisionmaking role, but it does imply having the ear of decisionmakers, perhaps providing crucial information or influence.[33] For a Leninist party, the specter of hearing what it does not necessarily want to hear, or listening when it does not want to listen is serious, indeed. In some communist states there may be many things leaders want to know but are afraid to ask.[34] Democratic centralism is a credo of self-preservation for party elites that they market, quite erroneously, as the basis for a Marxist system. Instead, democratic centralism is the rationale for political control, having little to do with Marx but a great deal to do with Lenin's elitism and Stalin's dictatorship. A vanguard does not want to have access forced upon it via the combination of activism with resources. Uninvited access to the party's power not only would be inconvenient but would strike at the heart of political control.

In that sense Polish workers, for the time being with intellectual allies, combined in 1980–81 political activism with the resource of strikes that threatened what remained of the economy. Insofar as the regime had to respond directly with direct negotiations and public promises, their action evidenced their access and hence threat to the Party's political control. The PUWP sought to diminish workers' access to power by severing the links between resource availability and activism. As the party failed in that effort, General Wojciech Jaruzelski responded with martial law in the face of Soviet demands for coercion.

Communist regimes, then, seek to deny access to power by constraining resource availability to activists or by limiting the activities of those with resources of personnel, money, or some other socioeconomic or political commodity such as workers' right to strike. Ideally, channels for involvement will lead nowhere; citizens, their associations, local units of government, or enterprises will exist within the system, either coopted by their very activism or satiated into inactivity by their unequal share of resources.

Inequalities and Their Political Consequences

A communist government's efforts to manipulate political activism and resource availability, such that access to power is controlled tightly, have numerous political consequences.

If successful, a ruling party will, by such a policy, retain a distinction between the elite and the masses that insulates policymaking from any but officially sanctioned voices. Noncompetitive elections, the illegality of strikes or of independent trade unions, centralized planning—these and more characteristics of communist systems are symptomatic that access to power is denied to those outside a vanguard. Although these arrangements could promote a certain efficiency in policymaking, since the range of options presented in pluralistic systems may not be present, there are nevertheless negative implications.

Excluded from policymaking processes by party-maintained political inequalities, those who are unsatisfied or reform minded have no alternative than to pursue nonsanctioned channels. A participation crisis, discussed years ago by Myron Weiner, can then occur in communist states. We have seen such a crisis develop in Poland over the span of more than two decades. Ingredients for similar, although not identical, processes can be identified in most communist states (workers' unrest in Shanghai, for example, or the Jiu Valley in Romania or Togliatti in the USSR). Less visible, but evident to anyone who has undertaken field research in communist Europe, is the presence of patron–client relationships, *blat, proteksia,* and other systemwide forms of corruption. Access to power, in other words, will always be sought because individuals, groups, enterprises, or units of government are self-interested. If routes are closed via resource limitations or constraints on activism, then political life will resort to a functional equivalent in whatever form of pull or baksheesh is culturally applicable. Competition for resources will go on, regardless of legal, structural, or ideological impediments.[35]

A second, likewise negative, consequence of efforts by Communist party regimes to manipulate political inequalities can be seen in the reduction of growth in such systems' *capacity.*[36] Capacity connotes a system's ability to meet demands and solve problems, a wider connotation than economic production alone.

The socioeconomic and political progress, offered by Marxism and promised by Lenin via Communist party rule, has not been forthcoming relative to competing systems. At best, impressive growth has been registered in the realm of heavy industry, while general standards of living have exhibited a much more modest increase. But development carries with it an impulse for both redistribution of resources and a broadening of participation.[37] Neither of these expectations has been pursued with vigor, and the continuation of both forms of inequality has short-term political utility for such regimes. It is not surprising, therefore, that popular ambivalence and passive acceptance have changed to disaffection in some societies ruled by Communist parties. Labor productivity, citizen compliance, and mass mobilization have suffered. Romanian citizens have been found to exhibit passive attitudes toward hooliganism,[38] Yugoslav citizens doubt their own efficacy,[39] and the Polish economy, even before 1980, saw declining productivity and efficiency.[40] These few examples have analogues in most communist systems, regardless of cultural or geographic differences.

To the extent that the persistence of inequalities is linked to disaffection, and the latter to lesser commitment, decreased productivity and a decline of willing obedience, systemic performance will be affected. Poland's ability to meet demands or to solve problems has, for example, been undermined by a disaffected citizenry. Indeed, by 1980, Poland's economic morass has become so severe that any offer by the regime to workers during August–September was beyond the ability of Poland to supply. Further credit had to be sought abroad, which obviously compounded the already grim level of foreign debt. In short, the PUWP no longer has a problem-solving capacity. So disaffected are citizens that they will not help themselves because it would mean aiding the Party.

Poland is an extreme case among communist states. Several unique factors contribute to and abet unrest in Poland, including a tradition of labor or student strikes, the strength of the Catholic church, and noncollectivized agriculture. Yet the curtailment of growth in a systemic *capacity* is evident elsewhere, such that the Polish example differs more in degree than kind. Even a system as tightly controlled as Ceauşescu's Romania has had labor unrest arising from, we must presume, a combination of economic complaints and the exclusion of workers from regular policymaking inputs.[41] These outbreaks and productivity concerns appear to have necessitated a costly and risky image-making campaign for self-management and self-financing of enterprises by workers' councils.

The manipulation by party leaders of involvement and resources to constrain access to power has a third consequence that has both positive and negative elements. By providing *some* resources and channels for *some* activism to citizens, ruling parties can do a great deal to augment socialization efforts. Quite simply, citizen involvement can mean their cooptation via a link to the establishment thereby avoiding disaffection. There is a wealth of evidence suggesting that, not surprisingly, most citizens of communist states will submit to nominal involvement when asked and will, thereupon, do what is demanded of them. Such nominal activities run the gamut from membership in socioeconomic organizations and voting in them, to attendance at citizens' meetings in neighborhoods, to performance of patriotic work tasks. However, commitment and enthusiasm are sometimes evinced by individuals assigned to oversee some aspect of the society's functioning, and a People's Council deputy assigned to a standing commission or a member of a socioeconomic organization acting as a volunteer public inspector may relish the task.

Asked to take a quasi-official role, there is visible evidence of the positive sentiments held by some participants; they work hard, performing their duties assiduously, often for no pay or other immediate benefits.[42] Communist systems reap considerable benefits from such enthusiastic subjects. Not only are such involved citizens obedient messengers, extending the Party's eyes and ears among a wider portion of the public, but these citizen enthusiasts are kept busy with activities helpful and innocuous. Were such citizens uninvolved, their reformist, help-oriented outlook could be problematic, whereas as part of the system they can believe their voices are being heard.

Access to power, then, can be offered in portions so insignificant to the regime that party leaders may rest unconcerned about the impact of deputies, public inspectors, and the like. The Party stands to gain goodwill and channels of communication to the populace with little risk. Officially sanctioned, but impotent, the voices of such participants in communist systems have access to power, but function to reinforce, not change, the system.

Conclusion

Sharing a principal characteristic of all political systems, today's communist regimes incorporate inequalities of access to power. Leninist parties maintain governments similar to other authoritarian systems insofar as unequal access to power is *more* evident than in systems we might label as competitive democracies. I have suggested how, in communist states, political involvement ranging from manipulated or mobilized activity to participation in policymaking is linked to resource availability.

The function of such inequalities is to control access to power and thereby to maintain political control. Two forms of inequalities are applied by Communist party regimes—those that limit political activism to levels and kinds (involvement, not participation) considered innocuous and those that constrain resources. By manipulating these two variables among social and economic segments of the population, certain groups (varying among states, or in one state over time) are kept at arms' distance from policymaking processes.

Typically, communist states follow patterns of political inequalities applied throughout history and across cultures; women, the young, national or linguistic minorities, manual laborers and other segments are excluded regularly from access to power. To a large degree, of course, these political inequalities overlap with economic stratifications.

But, aside from a functional explanation, there may be a deeper, psychological explanation for the kind and extent of political inequalities found in communist systems. Quite simply, communist leaders feel more secure when their power cannot be influenced or affected in a pluralized environment. It is altogether much more reassuring for political leaders anywhere to know that they do not face incessant demands or daily inquiries from an ever-wider spectrum of the population. Their assurance is enhanced by the degree to which those with access to power are familiar and trusted, or known quantities. Given the emphasis placed in most communist states on development and modernization, however, the thrust of socioeconomic change is not toward centralized, narrow policy processes, but toward a more pluralistic and decentralized environment inhabited by thousands of new enterprises, neighborhoods, and social organizations populated by educated citizens. In such circumstances, party leaders insecure about their links with the masses encourage the utilization of political inequalities. Without overt coercion, communist leaders can employ existing (or new) participatory and resource inequalities to insulate their political control.

That the USSR, Eastern Europe, and other communist polities share such basic features with other authoritarian systems, however, does not mean that they should not be separately considered. Unlike most junta or coup d'etat efforts, Leninist parties base their rationale for ruling on much more than opposition to a particular kind of old regime. Instead, theres is an indictment of social organization. They were, at one time, revolutionaries. Promises of Leninist parties include Marxist visions of socioeconomic equality, by which Marx meant political equality as well. But Leninists have other values holding greater weight, values stressing their vanguard status. As articulated in the phrase "democratic centralism," Leninist parties seek to insulate policymaking. Nonrevolutionary themes of elitism and centralism thus demand mechanisms to constrain the access to power of nonelites, the masses, of minorities and local units.

The perpetuation of political inequalities in communist systems is likely to be, therefore, as flagrant if not more so than in other socioeconomic systems. Certainly, clear rationales exist for Leninist parties to avoid lifting the restraints on access to power provided by political inequalities. Notwithstanding such a functional aspect to inequalities, however, I have suggested several negative consequences—the likelihood that patron-client and other noninstitutional means will expand as access to power is sought via nonsanctioned participatory channels and resources, and the possibility that systemic capacity will be harmed. Communist systems, then, maintain political inequalities in an atmosphere of calculated risk; these are stratifications from which parties can gain or lose some benefits. For the short term, at least, authoritarian rule will continue to be protected via imposed or maintained limits on participation and resources, while Communist parties wrestle with the long-term dynamic element of popular disaffection fostered by such inequalities.

Notes

1. James S. Coleman makes the point regarding a functional need for status differentiation and cites Talcott Parsons' comments relating leadership to prestige

in "The Development Syndrome: Differentiation-Equality-Capacity," in Leonard Binder et al., *Crises and Sequences in Political Development* (Princeton, N.J.: Princeton University Press, 1971), p. 82.

2. David E. Apter, *The Politics of Modernization* (Chicago: University of Chicago Press, 1965), p. 73, cited by Coleman in Binder, *Crises and Sequences in Political Development,* p. 82.

3. In this chapter I employ Aspaturian's understanding of "involvement" as a general term, used interchangeably with "activity." Involvement, therefore, can be a nominal and mobilized act. The kind of involvement denoted as "participation" not only includes elements of autonomy, as per Aspaturian's usage, but also some "access to power." Involvement, then, becomes more participatory as it increasingly means proximity to policymaking. See Vernon V. Aspaturian, "Political Participation in Eastern Europe: A Conceptual Critique," paper prepared for the Second World Congress of Soviet and East European Studies, September 30–October 4, 1980, Garmisch, Federal Republic of Germany, p. 12.

4. Jan S. Adams, "Public Inspectors in the Mid-1970s," paper delivered at the annual meeting of the American Association for the Advancement of Slavic Studies, St. Louis, Mo., October 1976, and Roy D. Laird, "The Soviet Monohierarchy and the Adjuncts," paper delivered at the Midwest Slavic Conference, Ann Arbor, Mich., May 1977. The Soviet and Chinese cases, of course, actually involve millions in one role or another, as these two papers demonstrate.

5. Aspaturian in "Political Participation in Eastern Europe" notes such a distinction.

6. Daniel N. Nelson, "Development and Political Participation in a Communist System," in Jan Adams and Donald Schulz, eds., *Political Participation in Communist States* (New York: Pergamon, 1980). Jan F. Triska and Ana Barbic distinguish among Leauge of Communist members, Socialist Alliance members, and other citizens in Yugoslavia with respect to participation, sense of efficacy, and other attitudes. See their chapter, "Evaluating Citizen Performance at the Community Level" in Daniel N. Nelson, ed., *Local Politics in Communist Countries* (Lexington: University of Kentucky Press, 1980), pp. 54–89.

7. Sidney Verba, Norman H. Nie, and Jao-On Kim, *Participation and Political Equality* (Cambridge, England: Cambridge University Press, 1978), p. 5.

8. Felipe Garcia Casals, *Syncretic Society* (White Plains, N.Y.: M.E. Sharpe, 1980); Casals is a pen name for a highly placed official in an East European State.

9. Joan M. Nelson, *Access to Power* (Princeton, N.J.: Princeton University Press, 1980), p. 396.

10. Murray Yanowitch, *Social and Economic Inequality in the Soviet Union* (White Plains, N.Y.: M.E. Sharpe, 1977), pp. 169-170; Yanowitch cites

data from Soviet sources revealing that 70 percent or more of occupations such as typists, secretaries, telephone operators, and primary and secondary teachers are filled by women. Scientific personnel and high-level industrial managers are rarely women. Wages of women range from 62 to 74 percent of men's in Soviet surveys cited by Yanowitch.

11. Radio Free Europe archives, Polish section; research by author, 1980. The only exception (before the new PUWP elections of 1981) among forty-nine provincial leaders to male domination was Grzebisz-Nowicka in Siedlce.

12. See Georgeta Dan-Spinoiu, *Factori Obiectivi şi Subiectivi în Integrarea Profesionala a Femeii* (Bucureşti: Editura Academiei, 1974), pp. 93-94.

13. Sharon Wolchik, "Women's Roles in Political Life," University of Michigan, unpublished manuscript, pp. 25-26. Susan Woodward reports that women "rarely participate even in self-management bodies" in Yugoslavia, which suggests that male dominance in workplace governance is also continuing. See Susan L. Woodward, "Yugoslavia after Tito: Evidence of Continuity and Change from Society and Economy", delivered at the 1980 Annual Meeting of the American Association for the Advancement of Slavic Studies, Philadelphia, November 5-8, 1980, p. 31.

14. Jerome Gilison, for example, found some evidence that a Soviet republic such as Estonia can be singled out as less reluctant to dissent from party candidates in elections. See his "Soviet Elections as a Measure of Dissent: The Missing One Percent," *American Political Science Review* 62(September 1968): 814-826.

15. Lenard Cohen, "Political Management in Post-Tito Yugoslavia: The Recruitment and Composition of Regional Elites," paper presented at the Second World Congress for Soviet and East European Studies, September 29-October 4, 1980, Garmisch, Federal Republic of Germany, p. 40; Cohen points out the dominant role of Serbs and Montenegrins in League of Communists presidencies. Czechoslovakia has been, during Husak's leadership, a notable exception insofar as Slovaks have had equal access to Prague ministerial posts.

16. Jaroslav Krejci details nonincome sources of status in Czechoslovakia in *Social Change and Stratification in Post-War Czechoslovakia* (New York: Columbia University Press, 1972), pp. 39-156.

17. Krejci, p. 26.

18. Sidney Verba and Goldie Shabad, "Workers' Councils and Political Stratification: The Yugoslav Experience," *American Political Science Review* 72(March 1978):85. Susan Woodward has also emphasized the association between participatory behavior and favorable material conditions and status in her paper "Yugoslavia after Tito" pp. 29-33.

19. Joel Moses has analyzed the turnover rate and tenure of regional elites (oblast level) in the USSR, finding a fairly consistent denial of promotional

opportunities to younger functionaries across time and location. See his article, "Local Leadership Integration in the Soviet Union," in Daniel Nelson, ed., *Local Politics in Communist Countries,* and see Cohen, "Political Management."

20. These ideas reflect the arguments of a prominent East European official who has published in the West under the pseudonym of Felipe Garcia Casals. One of his or her publications, "Theses on a Syncretic Society," appeared in *Theory and Society* 9(1980).

21. See Daniel N. Nelson, "Workers in a Workers' State," *Soviet Studies* 32(October 1980):542-560.

22. Yanowitch in *Inequality in the Soviet Union* details the principle of "unity of political and economic leadership," which in the USSR implies the interlocking nature of management and party (pp. 136-137). Also discussed is the broader debate in the Soviet Union of the linkage between enterprise management and workplace behavior, on the one hand, and the party's authority of the other (pp. 134-161).

23. It is, of course, true that some ruling Communist parties have up to half of their membership drawn from working class background—that is, the family of a party member was working class or the party member trained to be a worker or was, as a youth, employed in a manual occupation. These distinctions must be made when looking at party membership and can greatly reduce the image of working class presence. See Paul Shoup, "The Social Structure of the Communist Parties of Eastern Europe and the Soviet Union," paper presented at the Annual Meeting of the American Political Science Association, Chicago, September 2-5, 1976, pp. 7-10.

24. Ion Petrescu, *Psihosociologia Conducerii Colectiva a Intreprinderii Industriale* (Craiova: Scrisul Romanesc, 1977), p. 56, reports that only about one-third of employees in machine construction and chemical refining enterprises knew their few elected representatives to workers' councils.

25. There are many varying interpretations of the degree to which communist states have made headway in lessening class differences beyond what we might expect from socioeconomic changes that could have occurred in a nonsocialist environment. One might consult Yanowitch, *Inequality in the Soviet Union*; Peter Wiles, *Distribution of Income: East and West* (Amsterdam: North Holland, 1974); Peter Zwick, "Intra System Inequality and the Symmetry of Socioeconomic Development in the USSR," *Comparative Politics* 8(July 1976), pp. 501-524; David Lane, *The End of Inequality? Stratification under State Socialism* (London: Penguin Books, 1971); Walter D. Connor, *Socialism, Politics and Equality: Hierarchy and Change in Eastern Europe and the USSR* (New York: Columbia University Press, 1979), and John Echols "Politics, Budgets, and Regional Inequality in Communist and Capitalist Systems," *Comparative Political Studies* 8(October 1975).

26. See Cal Clark, "Commune Politics and Socioeconomic Parameters in Yugoslavia" in Daniel N. Nelson, ed., *Local Politics in Communist Countries.*

27. Frederick C. Teiwes, "Provincial Politics in China," in John M.H. Lindbeck, ed., *China: Management of a Revolutionary Society* (Seattle: University of Washington Press, 1971), pp. 174–178.

28. Cal Clark, "Regional Inequality in Yugoslavia", paper delivered at the Annual Meeting of the American Association for the Advancement of Slavic Studies, Philadelphia, November 5–8, 1980, p. 15 and pp. 27–38; Clark regressed a measure of inequality (coefficient of variability) on affluence and size. The USSR is the anamolous case, apparently reducing regional inequalities to a greater degree.

29. Mary Ellen Fischer, "Nation and Nationality in Romania," in George W. Simmonds, ed., *Nationalism in the USSR and East Europe* (Detroit: University of Detroit Press, 1977), p. 518. In the Soviet case, the Russian Soviet Federated Socialist Republic (RSFSR) had a 1975 per capital investment of 409 rubles vis-a-vis 265 rubles for the rest of the USSR, and some republics in the Ukraine and Georgia have declined in investment shares during the Khrushchev and Brezhnev years. See Martin C. Spechler, "Regional Developments in the USSR, 1958–1978," in *Joint Economic Committee, Soviet Economy in a Time of Change* (Washington, D.C.: U.S. Government Printing Office, 1979), p. 159. The distinctions among nationalities however, *exceed* regional inequalities (controlling for the dispersion of Russians in other republics). See Brian Silver, "Levels of Sociocultural Development among Soviet Nationalities: A Partial Test of the Equalization Hypothesis," *American Political Science Review* 68(December 1974):1618–1637.

30. Yanowitch reports on aspects of social mobility in the USSR. Data from Soviet sources are cited that suggest that parents' occupational position is strongly related to elite occupational groups (faculty, engineers, medicine, arts), that offspring of manual laborers tend to become manual laborers, and that intergenerational mobility is less than Soviet ideology might lead outsiders to believe. "Unrealistic occupational aspirations" of Soviet youth, indeed, may be a serious problem. See pp. 113, 118, 124, and 131 of Yanowitch.

31. Lenard Cohen brought out the point about ascribed resources in conversation. Of course Robert Dahl listed kinds of resources many years ago and suggested how they could be employed to influence policy. See Dahl's "The Concept of Power," *Behavioral Science* 2(July 1957):201–215 and "A Critique of the Ruling Elite Model," *American Political Science Review* 52(July 1958): 463–469. Later work by James C. Coleman pointed out the different forms of resources applicable in different arenas of action (from family to legislatures and courts). See James C. Coleman, *Resources for Social Change* (New York: Wiley, 1971), p. 85.

32. Other analysts have expressed this relationship in analogous ways. Terry N. Clark, in his monograph *Community Power and Policy Outputs* (Beverly Hills, Calif.: Sage, 1973), pp. 42–43, for instance, offers the equation $I = P_a R$, where I = influence, P_a an activation probability, and R = resources.

33. Clark's formulation makes I, or influence, the product of the link between resources and the probability of their activation. The only component of such an equation similar to that being used in this chapter is R, or resources. These terms are not identical, however, since I refer to resource availability, not all resources present. In a sense, the terms differ in ways similar to net and gross income. Clark's probability of activation is exemplified by comparing the electoral influence of a political party to a steel factory (p. 43), with the smaller resources of the party being more likely to be activated because of its political purpose and greater concern about the election. This term differs from my political activism variable insofar as Clark is, apparently, referring more to the purpose or character of an organization, and conveys little about the degree or intensity of involvement by individuals, groups or other actors. Finally, I am less certain that influence, per se, results from the relationship between activism and resources, and prefer to discuss access to power, which *may* mean influence in policy processes. Some people, groups, or locales with access are not heeded, however, even when they are assured a hearing.

34. Empirical social scientists *have* dared to ask questions about the values held by citizens, for example, or their sense of efficacy in society and government. Except for Yugoslavia, however, these studies have been periodic, without national samples. In some cases, such as Romania, social scientists with such interests have suffered official sanctions varying from denial of passports to loss of jobs.

35. Jacek Tarkowski, "Wpyw Lokalny w Scentralyzowanym Systemie: Zascby Lokalne i Lokalny Aktyw Kiercwnicizy (Local Influence in a Centralized System. . .)", Institute of Sociology, University of Warsaw, mimeo, December 1976, pp. 3–13; See also, by the same author, "A Study of the Decisional Process in Rolnowo Powiat," *The Polish Sociological Bulletin* 2(1967):94.

36. Coleman, *Crises and Sequences*, p. 81.

37. Joseph LaPalombara, "Distribution: A Crisis of Resource Management," in Binder et al., eds., *Crises and Sequences in Political Development*, p. 279.

38. Ioan Vida and Mircea Preda, "Interferenţe ale Eticului, Politicului şi Juridicului la Nivelul Conştiinţei Individuale," *Viitorul Social* (1975).

39. Triska and Barbic in Nelson, *Local Politics in Communist Countries*, p. 64: (Table 2.6).

40. See, for example, *RFE Research Reports* by Henry Trend during the 1970s; frequent newspaper articles refer to Poland's economy such as dispatches written by John Darnton for the *New York Times* in 1980.

41. Daniel N. Nelson, "Worker-Party Conflict and the Dialectics of Developed Socialism", in Maurice Simon and James Seroka, eds., *Developed Socialism,* (Boulder, Colo.: Westview Press, 1982).

42. Two good accounts, in the Soviet case, of such activists are included in Jan Adams's "Political Participation in the USSR," in Daniel Nelson, ed., *Local Politics in Communist Countries,* pp. 121-144, and Theodore Friedgut's, *Political Participation in the USSR* (Princeton, N.J.: Princeton University Press, 1979).

3 Welfare Ideologies and Policy Styles: Soviet, American, and British Roads to Equality

John D. Robertson

No advanced industrial society of the world today has an explicit policy goal of achieving a totally equitable distribution of rewards, benefits, and services. Social democracies and Communist party states hold out the promise of achieving a gradual eradication of the stratification structures that reinforce the distributive inequalities in their respective societies, yet none has gone so far as to claim the present circumstances can accommodate the costs associated with this change.

Societies that have reached advanced stages of industrial development have, however, also displayed noticeable concern for the needs of the less fortunate in their societies. How much concern and whether this promises to relieve the distribution gaps existing in modern society are still unclear. It is certain, however, that the welfare state has become a fixture on the contemporary scene. The modern welfare state is distinguished from previous versions of politically expedient benevolence by an institutionalized policy process for redistributing portions of society's wealth to those who are denied some minimum standard of living.[1]

Essential to the welfare effort has been the extension of public authority in advanced industrial society.[2] Comparative studies that have explored differences in levels of equality across nations have focused primarily upon the targets of policy—wage differentials across strata in society, relative freedoms and opportunities for political participation, and mobility opportunities to various segments of society—and have shown these targets to vary extensively.[3] The purpose of this chapter is not to measure the levels of inequality across communist and noncommunist systems. Rather, it is to address the following question: Assuming persistent inequality is a common feature of capitalist and Communist party states, how may we arrive at a general explanation of their condition from which futher comparative analysis may be built?

One way is to examine both the welfare ideology of a society and the dominant policy style that directs the public welfare effort. The central thesis of this chapter is therefore that inequalities in advanced capitalist and Communist party systems are largely a function of the prevalent welfare ideologies that determine the methods and parameters of public activity directed at forging the road to equality.

In the course of developing this argument I shall first consider as examples the British, American, and Soviet welfare ideologies and policy styles. I shall then employ a continuous aggregate time series design to test the validity of the predicted logical relationship between the specific welfare ideologies and the policy styles. The findings confirm that for each country, the predicted welfare ideology–policy style structure is present, which provides evidence to support the chapter's central thesis. The implications of these findings and conclusions follow the data analysis.

Welfare Ideologies: Three Examples

The policy tools of the modern welfare state that serve to pave the roads to equality are social security and public assistance programs. The former is a combination of state expenditures and earned benefits at the disposal of an individual for purposes of assistance during periods of unexpected hardships and economic dislocation. Public assistance grants are income maintenance allotments to individuals, irrespective of some previous contribution, which are designed to redistribute the wealth more actively of society to those who are seriously deprived and in danger of remaining permanently below some minimum standards of living.[4] Taken together, these represent an important component of the welfare effort in modern societies. The justification for the welfare effort in society is found within the context of the welfare ideology.[5] Three common ideologies are (1) the social right ideology, (2) the self-help ideology, and (3) the collective dependency ideology.

The Social Right Welfare Ideology

An obligation of society to provide for the minimum security provisions and well-being of a population is stressed by the social right ideology. It reflects the liberal view that the various elements in a society can be integrated through a network of reinforcing contributions and benefits progressively structured to eradicate sharp distributional differences within a population. Individual citizens within advanced society are assumed to bear a large responsibility for the welfare of society as a whole by contributing to a general social fund from which those who fall below some level of defined subsistence will be eligible to draw upon in portions equal to their degree of suffering. The only criterion of eligibility is citizenship.

The British social security and public assistance programs reflect the social right welfare ideology. The modern version of the present British system may be found in the Beveridge Report of 1942, and institutionalized into public policy by the National Treasury Act of 1946, the National Assistance Act of 1948, the

Social Security Act of 1966, the Family Income Supplement Program of 1970, and a series of further elaborations and expansions of previous social welfare laws enacted since the end of the Second World War.[6]

Although the early enthusiasm espoused in the language of the Beveridge Report has been eroded in the face of a steady economic decline in Great Britain, the British welfare effort still stands as vigorous public commitment to eradicating extreme differences in wealth and economic hardships through a universal system of redistribution and public assistance. At the end of the 1970s, for instance, 85 percent of all major medical costs of British citizens were subsidized by public expenditures. The employer's contribution to social insurance is nearly twice that of the employees (13.5 percent to 6.5, respectively), and unemployed workers can expect the state to subsidize up to 85 percent of the individual's previous earnings.[7]

The Self-Help Welfare Ideology

Whereas the social right welfare ideology stresses the obligation of society to provide for the minimal personal security of its less fortunate citizens, the self-help system sanctifies the right of individuals to choose their own form of protection against economic dislocation. While this may be supplemented in part by some role of public authority acting in the name of society, the self-help ideology instructs society that beyond providing for a minimum base upon which individuals may build, government's role is to be limited and the citizens in that society are expected to guarantee their own fate through the market mechanism. Social integration is not the goal of the state, although it may be a byproduct of a properly balanced market process. By leaving individuals to their own resources in the welfare effort, economic productivity and growth are thought to be more likely.

The American social security and public assistance programs are shaped largely by the values of the self-help ideology. The role of public authority in such an effort is primarily one of encouragement, relative to the more institutionalized commitments found in the British, Swedish, and Dutch welfare systems.[8] What effort exists in terms of the total commitment is a product of a halting, gradual, and marginal expansion upon existing programs—each designed to stimulate a response on the part of the market without significantly influencing the market in a manner that would stifle the individual management component. Such public commitments are therefore intended to enhance the skills of the less fortunate as well as to provide investment potentials for employers, rather than administer direct public assistance and income-maintenance benefits to its public. The emphasis, in short, is on social assistance through public example, not public authority.

American federal assistance in the form of a national relief program began in 1935 with the Social Security Act. Until then the American citizen had very little form of relief to economic hardship other than outright private donations and fewer than half of the forty-eight states had any form of social insurance.[9] Interstate labor and the growth of business competition kept further public assistance and social security to a bare minimum. There is little doubt that the American version of the welfare state in practice has grown in terms of a fiscal commitment that might be interpreted as contrary to the tenets of the self-help welfare ideology. Yet the restraint imposed by the lingering shadow of the self-help ideology can be seen when one compares the ratio of total public consumption expenditures to expenditures on social welfare services in the United States and United Kingdom. In 1977 the British ratio was $9.04:$1.00, while the American ratio was $30.22:$1.00.[10]

The Collective Dependency Welfare Ideology

Communist systems espouse a third welfare ideology in which social security and public assistance serve important roles, both as vehicles for minimum personal security and provision and as a medium for expanding and guaranteeing the authority of the political elite. Social welfare is not seen strictly as a right guaranteed members of society nor as an obligation of the state. Rather, it is an instrument of the state designed to assist the political elite in mobilizing the efforts of the public in a manner consistent with the interests of the political elite.[11] To the extent that material growth is an important and tangible value for which the elite can claim to have ultimate responsibility, it is the primary purpose of the welfare effort to serve as a tool for bringing aggregate supply and demand levels in society into line with the general targets of growth.

This is not to suggest that concern for the public and its welfare is not important to this society or to its political elite, who primarily control the welfare resources. Concern that does exist on the part of public authority, however, is probably less a product of public pressure and persuasion than political calculation. This is particularly true when elites embed the justification for the welfare effort within a larger, more encompassing messianic goal. In such cases each policy instrument such as social security or public assistance is valuable in direct proportion to its contribution to the continued progress of development toward the end goal.[12] Expanding or restricting a particular policy output such as welfare is therefore largely a function of the elite's own discretion. The welfare effort in a collective dependency system thus both provides for public security, as in the self-help and social right systems, and fosters public dependency upon the political elite as the sole legitimate source of welfare. A collection dependency welfare ideology, then, has the dual purpose of mobilizing and directing public energies while pacifying and subordinating that public.

The Soviet welfare effort approximates the values of the collective dependency welfare ideology. During the past three decades the USSR has gradually expanded its social security and public assistance effort to the point where total benefits offered to its citizenry are often loosely construed as an exemplary model of public welfare. The Soviet welfare picture remains somewhat marred, however. Only recently has need been a legitimate criterion for determining eligibility of social security and income-maintenance distributions to families and individuals. Throughout most of the post-Stalin era, need has taken a second place to both earned benefits and employment as the main consideration of an individual's welfare benefits. The primary concern for the Soviets seems to have been the fear of undermining the incentive system.[13] As a result, progress toward subsistence support by the state, without accompanying concerns for merit and employment contribution to the socialist endeavor, has been halting and erratic.[14]

Yet concern that incentives for the workforce be maintained is only one of the motives driving the Soviet welfare effort. In a system where elites' legitimacy is based largely on economic growth and specified standards of living for their population, social security and welfare disbursements play an important role in enticing political compliance from segments of the nation whose skills are required for the management of the economy. In addition to well-known privileges extended to those in such positions of prestige, the data of Okun and Vinokur show that the Soviet social wage fund (*obshchestvenny fondy potreblenyia*) may also be an instrument for structuring a dependency relationship within the Soviet society. Their data reveal that in 1973, for example, approximately 65 percent of the wage fund was distributed to families earning a per capita monthly income of 75 rubles, while only 13 percent was going to those families earning 50 rubles of less.[15]

This apparent concern for both incentive maintenance and compliance is evident also when one examines the available data on Soviet wage distributions. Though lower than the days of Stalin, income differentials remain rather high for a country claiming to be progressing rapidly and steadily toward communism and the elimination of class antagonisms. Recent estimates by Yanowitich indicate that socialized sectors of Soviet society earn an annual real income three times as great as their nonsocialized counterparts—the *kholkozniki*.[16] And whereas the *kholkozniki* are today granted many of the cash transfer benefits afforted their socialist bretheren, they remain a group discriminated against on the basis of their contribution to the development of socialism. As McAuley observes:

What Soviet writers derive from Marx and Lenin is justification for relating reward to achievement or merit, for maintaining disparity in income, power, and status in the USSR. Further, socialism as it has been interpreted in the Soviet Union has raised objections to, if it has not precluded, the provision of assistance to those in need; after all, did not Lenin write "He who shall not work, neither shall he eat"? And although Lenin was threatening those who had previously lived off income from property, his strictures have been applied to those thought to be the idle poor as well as the idle rich . . . All this implies that Soviet socialist ideology has more in common with the meritocratic views of a social democrat like Crosland than the egaltarianism of a thinker like Tawney.[17]

Thus the Soviet welfare effort may be seen as a reflection of many of the elements comprising the self-help and social-right welfare ideologies. Although a citizen has a right to expect minimal assistance from the state, this assistance is structured carefully to prevent it from serving as a disincentive to contribute to the building of a strong collective, socialist state, while controlled disbursements concurrently build a degree of public dependency upon the political elite in the Soviet Union.

Styles of Welfare Policy

Public policy is action taken by government to address issues in society. The style of public welfare policy can therefore be understood as the manner and method by which the welfare effort (social security and public assistance disbursements) is administered by public authority. A welfare ideology defines the acceptable parameters of a welfare effort, while policy styles are the manner by which the respective welfare ideologies are institutionally translated into welfare efforts. Thus the three welfare ideologies should find their expression in three styles of welfare policy. The three welfare policy styles are the state-initiative style, the need-responsive style, and the discretionary-caution style.

State-Initiative Style of Welfare Policy

A welfare effort emerging from the growth of state authority in the affairs of economic and social management in society may be denoted as a state-initiative policy style. That such a style may characterize welfare policy is linked to the expanding fiscal responsibilities transferred to central government. In most industrial democracies, the decision to enlarge or contract welfare disbursements may depend on cost/benefit analyses by public officials who must weigh the value of the welfare effort against that of other public programs for which they are responsible. Policy direction emerges from the central authority of government, although this initiative may be effected variously by public opinion, depending on the degree to which the society is polyarchical.[18]

Therefore the state-initiative style of welfare policy depicts a commitment of public resources to achieve a welfare effort consistent with societal goals predominantly interpreted and administered by a burgeoning state authority. The welfare effort is shaped by a policy style reflecting an expansion of the state's fiscal authority.

The Need-Responsive Style of Welfare Policy

A second style is one that shapes welfare effort in society as a response to economic changes in the environment. Welfare is not an instrument for state expansion but a tool of temporary relief for a population suffering from economic dislocation. As such, it is much less the institutional program found in those countries where the style is one of state initiative. Thus the welfare effort is not a cumulative process but a halting, stop and go activity that often is erratic in nature. A large-scale public commitment to any comprehensive provision of social insurance and public assistance for minimum subsistence is unlikely to be evident in this style of welfare policy.

The Discretionary-Caution Style of Welfare Policy

Finally, the welfare effort in society may be shaped by a gradual, marginal expansion (or contraction) of the welfare effort. This style reflects the severe constraint imposed on decisionmakers by a public still unsettled about the value of the welfare effort, or by a political elite unwilling to initiate a more cumulative and comprehensive program of social security and public assistance. Thus since political costs are uncertain and popular support unclear, policymakers who shape the welfare effort are likely to follow a far more incremental, low-risk course, careful not to alter extensively the existing program design in a way that may mobilize potential opposition to their efforts.

Linking Welfare Ideologies and Policy Styles: Propositions and Hypotheses

Welfare ideology and policy style are the determinants of the manner in which a system pursues equality. To assess the validity of the thesis that inroads on inequality can advance no further in any country than the bounds established by the welfare ideology and policy style, it must first be demonstrated that each welfare ideology shapes a unique style. If verified, we are in a stronger position comparatively to evaluate the prospects for further eradication of persistent inequalities in communist and noncommunist systems.

The following pages, then, utilize American and British data vis-a-vis the Soviet case. Four general propositions are formulated that establish the logical relationship between the three welfare ideologies and the three policy styles. These four propositions will be operationalized and tested, using cross-national aggregate time series data for each country.

Proposition 1:   Countries espousing a collective dependency welfare ideology will demonstrate a state-initiative welfare policy style.

In a collective dependency welfare society, the political elite cannot afford to shape their welfare effort simply on the basis of temporary economic dislocations affecting their society. As a policy tool consuming a portion of the scarce resources that play an important part in achieving the economic growth for which the political elite is responsible, the welfare effort must be largely monopolized by the state. Therefore, social security and welfare disbursements in a collective-dependency society will be controlled by the initiative of a state already assuming substantial responsibility for the economic welfare of a population.

Proposition 2:   Countries espousing a self-help welfare ideology will demonstrate a discretionary-caution welfare policy style.

The political costs associated with a more encompassing public welfare policy are likely to be prohibitive to public authority in a self-help welfare society. Thus the most that can be expected from public authority in these societies is marginal alteration of existing programs, devoid of major programmatic modifications that may be more noticeable to the public and to potential opposition groups. Consequently welfare effort in self-help societies is likely to reflect the incremental style of discretionary caution.

Proposition 3:   Countries espousing a social right welfare ideology are likely to demonstrate a mix between the state-initiative and the discretionary-caution style of welfare ideology.

State initiative to provide minimal subsistence support to individuals from public funds is certainly implied in the social right welfare ideology. Yet, when this ideology is combined with political pluralism, the result is likely to be an awkward attempt by public authority to harmonize the various public interests into a policy of consensus that renders the innovation and reform of existing policies difficult to achieve.[19] While the expanding fiscal authority of the state may transfer to government the burdens and responsibilities of public welfare, there is no reason to suspect that state action will be guided by anything other than political and bureaucratic rationality derived from inherent oppositional constraints of a polyarchy. The consequence is a welfare effort directed and administered by agents of public authority in an incremental and cautious administrative manner.

Proposition 4:   A need-responsive policy style is no longer a distinctive feature of advanced industrial states. Thus this style of welfare policy is largely absent from all countries having progressed to the point of industrial modernization.

In none of the three welfare ideologies should a need-responsive policy style characterize the welfare effort in advanced society. The social right welfare system cannot politically or practically afford to ignore a mandate to assist the public in escaping the harsh effects of economic decline or loss of employment.

The self-help welfare system seems to be the likeliest candiate for such a policy style. It is likely that for most self-help systems, a need crisis (such as the American depression of the 1930s) provided the initial impetus for an expanded public welfare effort. However, once such disbursements became an active part of the policy agenda, their political value began to surpass their need value until they could no longer be extracted from the responsibilities of public authority. Thus they became an institutionalized feature of modern society; need is second to political expendiency.

Most of all, public authority in a collective-dependency welfare society has both practical and political needs for a carefully controlled, yet consistent welfare effort. Therefore, simply responding to events after the fact either violates a moral obligation (social right), sound principles of economic and political management (self-help) or prudent concerns for the securing of political power (collective dependency).

Data and Operationalizations

In terms of specific countries, these four propositions predict that a discretionary-caution style of welfare policy will be observed in the United States; state initiative in the Soviet welfare effort; and a combination of the state-initiative and discretionary-caution styles in the British welfare effort. To provide sufficient scope for testing these four propositions, a continuous time series design will be employed. All data for these three countries are annual observations for the years 1960-1979, consecutively.[20]

The phenomenon we seek to explain is the welfare effort—the product of the welfare policy style. This welfare effort will be defined as the per capita welfare disbursement by a government in a given year. For the United States and Great Britain, this concept is operationalized as the total social security and social welfare expenditure by central government during a specific year, and will be represented by the expression: $(SSPA/c_t)$, where $SSPA$ denotes the social security and public assistance disbursement, and c population, both at time t. In the case of the Soviet Union, an equivalent measure is more difficult to obtain because of accounting differences between it and the West. However, the Soviet social wage fund (*obshchestvenny fondy potrebleniya*) is functionally comparable to the measures used in Britain and the United States for a measure of the welfare effort.[21] Thus for the USSR, the welfare effort will be operationalized as the total per capita outlay of the social wage fund during a given year $(SSPA/c_t)$. Though the Soviet measure is not identical to the American and British measure, each serves a principal role in redistributing wealth to the population and therefore is at the heart of the central government's welfare effort.

The discretionary-caution style of welfare policy suggests that $SSPA/c_t$ will change incrementally. As Wildavsky and others have shown, this is understood as a given year's expenditures being shaped by the previous year's base.[22] Thus the discretionary-caution variable is operationalized as the total social security and welfare expenditure by government, lagged one year $(SSPA_{t-1})$.

The state-initiative style of welfare policy suggests that $SSPA/c_t$ is primarily a function of the expanding fiscal authority of the central government. This fiscal authority is operationalized as the total expenditures of central government expressed as a proportion of a national economy during a given year. The national economy is measured in terms consistent with the accounting principles common in each of the three countries. For the United States and Great Britain this means that the national economy is simply the gross domestic product, while for the USSR it is the national income for a particular year. Therefore the state-initiative policy style variable symbolically is represented as (E/V_t), where E is the total central governmental expenditure and V is the respective measure of national economy for the particular country at a specific time point (t).

Finally, the need-responsive style of welfare policy suggests that $SSPA/c_t$ will vary as a function of some alteration in the economic environment of a society. This economic variance is measured as the rate of growth of the national economy for a given year (ΔV_t) and is calculated as

$$\Delta V_t = \frac{V_t - V_{t-1}}{V_t} \times 100.$$

The measure of the national economy V is consistent with the fiscal authority component found in E/V_t. Thus for the United States and Great Britain, it is a measure of the gross domestic product, while for the USSR it is the national economy. Table 3-1 summarizes each of the three independent variables and their respective measurements. The formal relation of the four variables as suggested by Propositions 1-4, is summarized in the equation below, which will be referred to as the *welfare effort model*.

$$(SSPA/c_t) = a + b_1 (SSPA_{t-1}) + B_2 (\Delta V_t) + b_3 (E/V_b) + e$$

Based on the logic and structure of the model, the four propositions may be restated in formal terms.

Table 3-1
Summary of Independent Variables and Operationalizations

Style of Policy	Suggests $SSPA/c_t$ to be function of[a]	Measured as
Discretionary caution	Last year's total social security and welfare disbursement of government	Social security and welfare expenditure of government, lagged one year ($SSPA_{t-1}$)
State initiative	Expansion of central government's fiscal authority	Total expenditure of central government as proportion of total national economy (E/V_t)
Need responsive	Changes in economic environment of society	Rate of growth of national economy (ΔV_t)

[a]$SSPA/c_t$ = total per capita social security and social welfare expenditure of central government in a given year.

Hypothesis 1: Controlling for the independent effects of ΔV_t and E/V_t, $SSPA/c_t$ is positively and significantly related to $SSPA_{t-1}$, in the United States only.

Hypothesis 2: Controlling for the independent affects of ΔV_t and $SSPA_{t-1}$, $SSPA/c_t$ is positively, and significantly related to E/V_t in the Soviet Union only.

Hypothesis 3: Controlling for the independent affected of v_t, $SSPA_{t-1}$ and E/V_t are each independently related positively and significantly to $SSPA/c_t$ in Great Britain only.

Hypothesis 4: Controlling for the independent affects of $SSPA_{t-1}$ and E/V_t, $SSPA/c_t$ is unrelated significantly to V_t in all of the three countries.

Data Analysis

To evaluate the validity of these four hypotheses, the welfare effort model was tested for each country. To reduce the biasing and inflating effects of autocorrelation present in the original samples, aggregate data for each sample were transformed by first different design to facilitate a generalized least squares application of the regression model.[23] The results of this analysis are presented in Table 3-2.

The results confirm each of the four hypotheses.[24] First, the U.S. sample supports the idea that the American welfare effort has been shaped less by need and strong state authority, and more by ad hoc incremental decisions consistent with the self-help welfare ideology ($SSPA/c_t$, $\beta = 0.773$). Second, the Soviet sample

Table 3-2
Regression Results of Tests on Welfare Effort Model

Dependent Variable (SSPA/c_t)	United States (Self-help Ideology) (N=19)		Great Britain (Social-right Ideology) (N=19)		Soviet Union (Collective-dependency Ideology) (N=19)	
	b (Standard Err)[a]	β	b (Standard Err)[a]	β	b (Standard Err)[a]	β
Independent variables:						
Discretionary-caution ($SSPA_{t-1}$)	.004[d] (.000)	.773[d]	.017[d] (.001)	.965[d]	.001 (.000)	.335
Need responsive (ΔV_t)	−.082 (.306)	−.051	.027 (.030)	.067	.043 (.041)	.272
State initiative (E/V_t)	1.229 (1.201)	.197	.586[d] (.114)	.391[d]	.249[c] (.097)	.677[c]
R^2	.595		.929		.411	
Intercept (a)	1.007		.038		.992	
Durbin-Watson d[b]	2.134		1.721		2.61	

[a]Pertains to first-differenced data. Correlation of ordinary least squares residuals $(\rho) \geqslant 0.993$.
[b]d statistic conclusively significant at the 0.01 range, indicating insignificant autocorrelation.
[c]Significant at the .02 range.
[d]Significant at the .001 range.

depicts a welfare effort where the disbursement patterns are best understood as an extension of substantial state authority and perogative (E/V_t, $\beta = 0.677$). As predicted, this policy style is not incremental, nor a result of need considerations solely. A third policy style is shown to exist in the British case. Welfare disbursements are fashioned incrementally ($SSPA_{t-1}$, $\beta = 0.965$), yet, as one would expect given the consensual nature of British politics, these decisions appear to be confined almost exclusively to the relevant ministerial personnel within government (E/V_t, $\beta = 0.391$).

These findings lend strong support to the central thesis of this chapter that specific welfare ideologies will find their overt expression in particular welfare policy styles, which, it is argued, will ultimately determine the opportunities for further reductions of persistent inequalities within advanced capitalist and Community party systems. What remains is to consider how these particular welfare ideology–policy style linkages provide a comparative framework from which to assess the likely success these countries are to have in eradicating persistent inequalities.

Three Roads to Equality: Prospects for and Limits to Progress

Political and economic equality is unlikely in modern society without the active intervention of public authority. Social security and welfare expenditures have been two instruments with which public officials in advanced industrial society variously have experimented to achieve relief from inequality prevalent in their societies. The limits to progress are ultimately shaped by the country's welfare ideology. An empirical comparison of different welfare ideologies, given the sorts of data required for such an endeavor, is beyond the bounds of the present study. Nonetheless, one can compare the welfare policy styles that follow logically from the specific welfare ideology in a country. Consistent with the logic of the three welfare ideologies, the expected welfare policy styles have appeared for each country as predicted. These findings reveal that the Soviet Union does differ from principal capitalist states in the road it has taken toward equality. Each road presents its own distinctive set of obstacles to the further progress toward greater equality, and each therefore provides a slightly different set of implications for the future encroachments on economic and social forms of inequality.

The first road to equality, that of the Soviet Union and other Communist party states, is pursued by a centralized, entrenched political elite bound to principles of a messianic ideology. Welfare expenditures are designed primarily to provide some form of economic relief and are generally free from pluralistic scrutiny. It is here that one finds a glimmer of hope for real inroads to be made on inequality. Yet a more careful examination of the collective-dependency welfare ideology reminds us that welfare disbursements are not obligatory activities of a sanctioned public authority. Rather, welfare efforts in these systems are more likely to stimulate labor productivity and to encourage conformity to proper norms of political behavior. The Soviet record over the past twenty-five years demonstrates some movement toward a more benevolent welfare effort. Gains made, however, particularly in regards to the *kolkhozniki,* probably have been initiated out of political expediency as much as concern for the welfare of a segment of Soviet society suffering from official discrimination.[25] As long as the welfare effort is shaped and administered by the political elite, equality by means of a welfare effort is indirect at best, albeit potentially easier to achieve in the collective-dependency welfare society than in more pluralistic countries.

The second road to equality, that of the United States, is via pluralistic politics characterized by federalism and a complex array of multiple subgovernments. Whatever gains to be made on the socioeconomic equality front will be slow and tenuous. Yet some advances have been realized through the circuitous route of social welfare. The American example demonstrates the importance of expertise within bureaucracy for such purposes. When the political system is complicated by numerous checkpoints to policy innovation, welfare redistribution is likely to be opposed at each stage of the policy process. As Heidenheimer et al. note, examples such as the Family Assistance Program and Supplementary Security Income demonstrate the difficulty of making significant strides toward equality.[26] The bottom line is that the prospects for progress toward equality via this road ultimately will be constrained by frustration and imposing political obstacles often absent in the Soviet Union.

An alternative road to equality, which preserves the values of political opportunity found in the United States while offering hope for the leadership required to move society away from the traditional practices of distributive policies, such as the USSR, may lie in Britain's social right welfare ideology. Data reported, however, suggest that, although the state-initiative style is important to the welfare effort, public disbursements are much more constrained by discretionary caution. Ashford and McQuail and Smith provide an important understanding of the inherent limits to the achievement of equality in the United Kingdom clues consistent with data cited earlier.[27] First, as Ashford notes, the insulation of the British mandarins provides some escape from the pluralism confronting their American counterparts. Yet this insulation has led to a degree of caution and conservation due in part to the lack of any real pressure or incentive to seek innovation through political risk. In addition, laws that define the welfare effort are complex and intricate, making the technical obstacles to innovation and expansion a foreboding prospect. Taken together, the price to be free from effects of pluralistic politics and separate branches of government is bureaucratic inertia, yet without any less technical complexity to the existing welfare effort. The third road to equality therefore seems to provide more commitment than the American route, though far less potential than the Soviet state-initiative style.

Conclusion

Given the difficulties associated with redistributive policies in communist and developed capitalist systems, it seems clear that greater equality will have to come at the political expense of those either unable, unwilling, or unlikely to assume these costs. Each system promises different prospects for achieving strides toward equality; yet each is characterized by a public authority that must structure welfare policies within an environment greatly affected by particular welfare ideologies. Equality in each of these countries is limited primarily by welfare ideologies that have complemented and perhaps shaped welfare policy styles that inherently lack the capacity to implement policy reforms. The irony for advanced capitalist and noncapitalist states over the next decade may be that the net result of their expanded public commitments to the welfare effort only serves as a vivid reminder about how far they have yet to go before major gains are made on persistent inequalities.

Notes

1. See Robert J. Lampman, "Transfer and Redistribution as Social Process," in Shirley Jenkins, ed., *Social Security in International Perspective* (New York: Columbia University School of Social Work, 1969), pp. 29-54, and Organization for Economic Cooperation and Development, *Public Expenditure on Income Maintenance Programmes* (Paris: OECD, 1976).

2. David Cameron, "The Expansion of the Public Economy," *American Political Science Review* 72(December 1978):1243-1261. Also see Daniel Tarchys, "The Growth of Public Expenditures: Nine Modes of Explanation," *Scandanavian Political Studies* 10(Fall 1975):9-31, and Harold L. Wilensky, *The Welfare State and Equality* (Berkeley: University of California Press, 1975).

3. Peter Wiles, *Distribution of Income: East and West* (Amsterdam: North-Holland, 1974); Frank Parkin, *Class Inequality and Political Order* (London: MacGibbon and Kee, 1971); David Lane, *The End of Inequality* (New York: Penguin, 1971).

4. Arnold J. Heidenheimer, Hugh Heclo, and Carolyn Adams, *Comparative Public Policy* (New York: St. Martin's, 1975), pp. 188-89.

5. Gaston V. Rimlinger, *Welfare Policy and Industrialization in Europe, America and Russia* (New York: John Wiley and Sons, 1971).

6. See Heidenheimer, Heclo, and Adams, *Comparative Public Policy,* pp. 198-200, and Douglas E. Ashford, *Policy and Politics in Britain* (Philadelphia: Temple University Press, 1981), pp. 199-220 passim. Also consult Derek Fraser, *The Evolution of the British Welfare State* (New York: Macmillan, 1973) for more detailed treatment.

7. U.S. Department of Health and Human Services, *Social Security Programs throughout the World 1979* (Washington, D.C.: U.S. Government Printing Office, 1980), pp. 250-51.

8. See Organization for Economic and Cooperative Development, *Public Expenditure on Income Maintenance Programmes,* 1976.

9. Heidenheimer, Heclo, and Adams, *Comparative Public Policy,* pp. 196-97.

10. Organization for Economic and Cooperative Development, *National Accounts of OECD Countries,* 1960-1977, 2 vols. (Paris: OECD, 1979), vol. 2, pp. 2-27.

11. Rimlinger, *Welfare Policy and Industrialization in Europe,* pp. 321-322.

12. Ibid., pp. 321-326.

13. For a thorough analysis of this point, see Alastair McAuley, *Economic Welfare in the Soviet Union* (Madison, Wis.: University of Wisconsin Press, 1979), pp. 265-269 passim.

14. Ibid., p. 285. Also see Richard B. Dobson, "Socialism and Social Stratification," in Jerry G. Pankhurst and Michael Paul Sacks, eds., *Contemporary Soviet Society* (New York: Praeger), p. 99.

15. Gur Offer and Aaron Vinokur, "The Distribution of Income of the Urban Population in the Soviet Union," mimeo, cited by Gur Offer, "Review of

Alastair McAuley, *Economic Welfare in the Soviet Union:* Poverty, Living Standards, and Inequality," *Soviet Studies* 33(October 1981):624.

16. Murray Yanowitch, *Social and Economic Inequality in the Soviet Union* (White Plains, N.Y.: M.E. Sharpe, 1977), p. 53.

17. McAuley, *Economic Welfare in the Soviet Union,* pp. 316-317.

18. See Robert A. Dahl. *Polyarchy* (New Haven, Conn: Yale University Press, 1971). For more specific discussions of this theme, consult either Douglas A. Hibbs, Jr., "Political Parties and Macroeconomic Policy," *American Political Science Review* 70(December 1977):1033-1058 or John D. Robertson, "Economic Policy and Election Cycles: Constraints in Nine OECD Countries," *Comparative Social Research* 5((1982):129-145.

19. See Ashford, *Policy and Politics in Britain* pp. 215-220.

20. All data for the United States and the United Kingdom (Great Britain) were drawn from the OECD, *National Accounts of OECD Countries,* vol. 2, 1979. British data are in pounds sterling, and American data are in dollars. All data for the Soviet Union were drawn from Tsental'noye Statisticheskoye Upravlennye, *Narodnoye Khozyaistvo SSSR Statisticheskie Yezhegodnik* (various years, 1960-1979) (Moscow: TSU). Data are in rubles.

21. The Soviet social wage fund is broader in coverage than the American and British measures. The latter do not include functions such as bonuses for employees, annual leaves from employment, and housing maintenance costs, as does the Soviet wage fund. For further detail, see McAuley, pp. 262-265, and Robert J. Osborn, *Soviet Social Policies* (Homewood, Ill.: Dorsey Press, 1970), pp. 38-39.

22. Aaron Wildavsky, *The Politics of the Budgetary Process,* 2nd ed. (Boston: Little, Brown, 1974).

23. Charles W. Ostrom, Jr., *Time Series Analysis: Regression Techniques* (Beverly Hills, Calif.: Sage Publications, 1978).

24. Utilizing the r^2-delete procedure and a subsequent examination of each F statistic, in conjunction with the model's probability of the individual regression coefficients, it has been determined that there is no reason to suspect the presence of extremely harmful multicollinearity among any of the model's independent variables. See Jan Kmenta, *Elements of Econometrics* (New York: Macmillan, 1971), p. 390, for further elaboration of this procedure.

25. McAuley, *Economic Welfare in the Soviet Union* pp. 302-310.

26. Heidenheimer, Heclo, and Adams, *Comparative Public Policy,* pp. 204-205.

27. See Ashford, *Policy and Politics in Britain,* pp. 13-24, and D. McQuail and J.H. Smith, "Britain—A Post-Welfare Society?", in M. Donald Hancock and Gideon Sjoberg, eds., *Politics in the Post-Welfare State* (New York: Columbia University Press, 1972), pp. 117-146. Also see James. B. Christoph, "High Civil Servants and the Politics of Consenualism in Great Britain," in Mattei Dogen, ed., *The Mandarins of Western Europe* (New York: John Wiley and Sons, 1975), pp. 25-62, for an extended discussion of the insulation of British civil servants and the consequences for public policy.

4

Regional Inequality in Communist Nations: A Comparative Appraisal

Cal Clark

Communist regimes come to power with a strong ideological impetus to promote equality in the political, economic, social, and cultural realms. Communist commitment to and success in ending exploitation and achieving equality among their citizenries have varied greatly over these dimensions. Most analysts agree that the communist regimes in the Soviet Union and Eastern Europe have made substantial progress in ameliorating the massive class differences that existed in most of these societies on their advent to power.[1] On the other hand, a general consensus exists, at least in the West, that these governments tore down the old structures of political privilege and inequality only to replace them with similar, if not more inegalitarian, institutions that concentrate effective power in the hands of the vanguard rather than the proletariat.[2]

While most scholarly concern with inequality in communist countries has focused upon the socioeconomic and political dimensions, increasing attention has been devoted to inequality among regions, especially where regional differences are intertwined with nationality ones. Differences among regions might appear inevitable and of only secondary concern to regimes that are attempting to eradicate class inequalities. Still, pronounced differences among regions in popular living standards would seemingly create a new class differentiation; and, where regions form the homelands for national groups, continuing regional inequality would contradict the communist promise to ensure national equality and end the oppression of national minorities. This chapter hence examines data on regional inequality in communist countries to assess the communist record in this realm.

Regional Inequality: Overview, Hypotheses, and Measurement

Substantial regional inequality, typical of less-developed economies, existed in most of the European countries that were taken over by communist regimes. In several (Russia, Yugoslavia, and Czechoslovakia), moreover, regional inequality was tightly intertwined with national rivalries that had weakened the previous

An earlier draft of this chapter was presented at the Twelfth National Convention of the American Association for the Advancement of Slavic Studies, the Sheridan Hotel, Philadelphia, November 5-8, 1980.

governments. Especially in the Soviet Union and Yugoslavia, the new communist governments appealed to previously alienated minorities and based their legitimacy on claims that they were reversing past policies of discrimination against minority nationalities and the regions they inhabited. Communist ideology, especially in multinational states, thus committed these governments to reducing regional disparities in living conditions in these societies. Furthermore, the monopolies exercised by these governments over economic investment, the setting of wages and salaries, and welfare transfer payments gave them a unique capability to alter radically the existing state of affairs.

Regional equality was obviously not the only economic goal and these countries sought to pursue, however. The prime objectives of the USSR under Stalin and of the East European countries once they came under Stalin's sway were rapid economic growth and the industrial transformation of society.[3] Such an overriding emphasis on growth might well be expected to have retarded a movement toward regional equality since growth is usually maximized by concentrating resources in the most advanced part of the country—which would accentuate, not ameliorate, regional inequality. Substantial development, however, creates additional economic resources that can subsequently be used for the redistributive purposes of attacking regional inequality. Williamson found that the relationship of regional inequality to development level among a sample of noncommunist nations followed an "envelope curve" in which inequality is greatest in countries at medium development levels.[4] Thus one might hypothesize that their industrialization programs initially lead to greater regional inequality in communist nations, but that the fruits of industrialization would be used to promote more egalitarian societies.

Regional inequality has several distinct facets, and the degree of inequality on these dimensions may vary substantially. Regional inequality is most commonly conceptualized and measured in terms of the aggregate development level of various parts of a nation as indicated by their gross national product per capita (or net material product per capita, for communist states). A major determinant of development level, but one that is conceptually distinct from it, is a region's economic base as indicated by, for example, the extent of industrialization proportion of national product or employment accounted for by individual enterprises). In addition, governmental policies may have a separate impact on the inequality in living conditions among regions, which adds several further dimensions to regional inequality. Bahry and Nechemias, for instance, distinguish three separate phases or stages of governmental policies.[5] First are aggregate spending policies reflected in budgetary allocations; second are the outputs of services and investments purchased by these outlays (new factories, medical facilities, school building or student/teacher ratios, and so on); and third are the outcomes that measure how the outputs affect the target population (infant mortality, literacy rate, consumption per capita, and so on). One would expect these three stages to be significantly correlated, but large discontinuities may still occur between them.[6] Increased budget allocations may not always bring increased services; and public services can be rather limited in their impact on social conditions.

Figure 4-1 sketches these five subdimensions of regional inequality and a presumed set of causal linkages among them. The social outcomes or living conditions probably represent the key element since they measure the ultimate inequality in life-style and opportunity. Obviously, these social outcomes should be very strongly affected by regional affluence. In addition the sociopolitical outputs financed by government spending should have some impact on outcomes as well. Moving one step back in the causal order, the level of regional affluence should largely be conditioned by a region's economic base; and government spending should have a substantial impact on service levels. Government policies can also affect regional economic bases either directly through investment (spending) in plants and enterprises (outputs) or indirectly through tax and regulatory policies.

The relations described so far are all positive in the longitudinal sense that increases in each of the independent variables should bring subsequent increases in each of the items that they are presumed to influence. Cross-sectionally, regional affluence should be positively correlated with economic base and with social outcomes (unless the government is pursuing an improbably high redistributive policy); and the relation between government spending and services should also be positive. The direction of service outputs' impact on social outcomes and economic base is more problematic, however, depending upon the correlation (or absence of one) between regional affluence and the amount of government spending directed toward a region. If a nation's fiscal system is highly decentralized, the relation between affluence and spending is very probably positive since richer regions will have far greater resources with which to

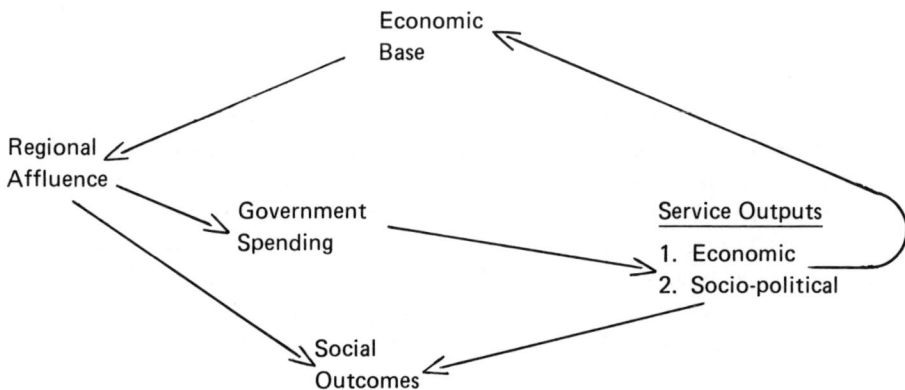

Figure 4-1. Causal Links among Dimensions of Regional Inequality

finance governmental services. Higher spending in turn should produce more services, so that governmental policy should exacerbate the impact of developmental differences upon inequality in living conditions. The same situation could occur in a more centralized system if the government wanted to concentrate resources in the more developed parts of a country, because, for instance, it believed that such strategy would maximize economic growth. A centralized regime could, though, pursue a policy of reducing regional inequality by redistributing resources from richer to poorer regions through progressive spending and service delivery. In this case correlations would be negative between regional affluence and spending and between service levels or the economic base. Thus actual living conditions would be more equal than the regional development environment. As a third alternative the government may be neutral or indifferent toward regional inequality, resulting in no correlation at all between governmental policy and regional affluence.

The model sketched in figure 4-1 should indicate the special advantage that communist countries have in combating regional inequality. Government control of the economy and new economic investment means that radical manipulations of the economic base, unthinkable in societies with large private sectors, are theoretically possible; and, if government so desires, almost unlimited resources can be directed to redistributive social services. When this greater capability to combat regional inequality is combined with an ideology that generally views inequality as illegitimate, the following might well be inferred:

Hypothesis 1:   Regional inequality will decline faster and be at lower levels in socialist countries than in comparable capitalist ones.

On the other hand, communist commitment to rapid industrialization might force these regimes to ignore opportunities for redistributive policies:

Hypothesis 2:   Regional inequality in communist countries will be no different than, and perhaps even higher than in capitalist ones.

Although the second hypothesis may be true for certain periods of time or dimensions of inequality, communist regimes might be expected to make special efforts to use the fruits of industrialization either in the long run by gradually spreading industrial growth to backward areas or, in the short run, by using wage scales and transfer payments to equalize living conditions (social outcomes) among regions at different levels of development. Thus, if hypothesis 2 is found to hold under certain circumstances, communist commitment to regional equality might still be shown if one or both of two other hypotheses are supported:

Hypothesis 3:   Communist countries will demonstrate an envelope curve record in attacking regional inequality in that economic development will initially result in greater inequality, but will ultimately bring a reduction in regional differences.

Hypothesis 4:   Communist nations, to a significantly greater extent than comparable capitalist ones, will use governmental power over wage scales and transfer payments to make living conditions significantly more equal than regional development environments.

One communist country, Yugoslavia, deviates substantially in its structural features from other communist states in a manner that should affect its policies concerning regional inequality. The Yugoslavs have instituted a system of market socialism and extreme political and fiscal decentralization. (Political reasons for such decentralization are examined by Susan Woodward later in this volume.) For example, as early as the mid-1950s, Yugoslavia had the greatest degree of fiscal decentralization to subnational units among the sample of command and market economies in Pryor's comparative budgetary analysis.[7] This decentralization in turn should inhibit the ability of the Yugoslav government to pursue redistributive policies equalizing the living conditions among regions. Thus the following hypothesis is implied:

Hypothesis 5:   The difference between the degree of inequality on regional affluence and social outcomes will be substantially less in Yugoslavia than in other communist countries.

There are many ways in which regional inequality might be measured. Most of the studies of communist inequality, however, have applied the same index—the coefficient of variability, or CV. This is a standardized measure of the dispersion in the distribution of some variable, such as regional GNP per capita, literacy rate, or the percentage of industrial employment. It is calculated by dividing the standard deviation of the distribution by the mean or average value.

One difference among the studies discussed here is whether the regional scores used in the calculation of CV are or are not weighted according to the region's population. Some analysts use weighted CV's (CV_w) arguing that they are based on the actual proportions of a population who are advantaged or disadvantaged on the item in question. Others, primarily interested in the differences among regions per se, use unweighted CV's (CV_u), which count each region equally. If the regions are approximately equal in size, CV_w and CV_u will be approximately equal. However, if one is disproportionately large or small or several regions are (for example, one of the fifteen Soviet Republics, the RSFSR, contains about half the national population), there will probably be a substantial difference between these two statistics.

In the following pages I attempt to test these competing hypotheses with three different analyses, although data limitations make this test far from as complete or systematic as would be desirable. First, the gross level of regional inequality in the European communist states is compared to that in other non-communist countries, testing hypotheses 1 and 2. Second, the possibility that communist regimes are combating regional inequality through the more subtle means suggested by hypotheses 3 and 4 is examined. Finally, hypothesis 5, concerning the difference between Yugoslavia and other communist states will be tested.

The Socialist Record on Aggregate Regional Inequality

In this section the socialist record on regional inequality is assessed through comparison between levels of and changes in regional inequality within communist and noncommunist states of Europe. Williamson conducted the seminal study of regional inequality in global perspective by calculating weighted and unweighted CV's for regional inequality on per capital income in twenty-four nations during the 1950s.[8] Without presenting specific statistical tests, Williamson concluded that regional inequality is affected strongly by affluence (poorer nations are more inegalitarian) with geographic size having a secondary impact (larger countries are more inegalitarian). Williamson's conclusions are supported by a regression of these nations' degree of inequality as measured by CV_w, on their income per capita and area.[9]

Table 4-1 summarizes the regression results. Wealth and area in combination have a fairly strong impact on regional inequality (multiple $R = 0.68$); and both influences are in the predicted direction. The beta (standardized regression) coefficients, which show the relative effect of the explanatory variables, indicate

Table 4-1
Impact of Wealth and Area on Regional Inequality

Summary Statistics		Impact of Wealth and Area		
			Income per Capita	Area
Multiple R_2	.68	r	−.59	−.03
Multiple R	.46	b	−.000210	.000019
F	8.93	Beta	−.80	.39
Significance level	1.01	F	17.81	4.30
Standard error	.12	Significance level	.001	.05

Sources: These coefficients were calculated from data in John G. Williamson, "Regional Inequality and the Process of National Development: A Description of the Patterns," *Economic Development and Cultural Change* 8, no. 4 (July 1965, Part II) p. 12 for CV_w's. Bruce M. Russett, Hayward R. Aiker, Jr., Karl W. Deutsch, and Harold D. Lasswell, *World Handbook of Political and Social Indicators* (New Haven, Conn.: Yale University Press, 1964), pp. 139-141 and 155-157, for income per capita and area.

that income per capita has a much stronger influence on regional inequality than does area, although both these effects are highly significant statistically.

The b's (unstandardized regression coefficients) in Table 4-1 can be used along with the constant of the regression equation (which equals 43.00) to give predicted values for all the nations in the analysis. These values can then be compared to a nation's actual degree of regional inequality to see whether it has more or less inequality than would be predicted on the basis of its physical size and development level. Since the standard error of the regression equation (the standard deviation of the distribution of residuals between the actual and predicted CV_w's for the 24 states in the regression analysis) is 0.122, an actual score must be 1.96 standard errors, or approximately 0.24 greater, more or less than the predicted value to be significantly different at the .05 level.

Unfortunately Williamson included only one socialist country, Yugoslavia, in his study. To expand the comparison between communist and noncommunist nations in the present analysis, therefore, the preceding equation was applied to the other European communist nations to derive predictions of their expected degree of inequality for the late 1950s. These results are reported in Table 4-2. For instance, Yugoslavia's actual value for CV_w on income per capita is 0.34 which is slightly, but far from significantly, less than a predicted score of 0.38.[10] These predicted values can then be compared with the data in table 4-3 on Koropeckyj's calculations of CV_w for the socialist states for net material product (NMP) per capita, industrial production and industrial employment over the 1950s and 1960s, supplemented for the USSR by McAuley's estimates of inequality in personal income per capita (which includes monetary earnings, in kind receipts, and personal transfer payments from the government).[11] The comparability of these variables to the income per capita figures on which the estimates in table 4-3 are based is admittedly somewhat crude.[12]

Table 4-2
Predicted Value for CV_w of Communist States

Czechoslovakia	.29
East Germany	.31
Hungary	.33
Poland	.34
Bulgaria	.36
Romania	.36
Yugoslavia	.38
Soviet Union	.73

Sources: These coefficients were calculated from data in John G. Williamson, "Regional Inequality and the Process of National Development: A Description of the Patterns," *Economic Development and Cultural Change* 8, no. 4 (July 1965, Part II) p. 12 for CV_w's. Bruce M. Russett, Hayward R. Aiker, Jr., Karl W. Deutsch, and Harold D. Lasswell, *World Handbook of Political and Social Indicators* (New Haven, Conn.: Yale University Press, 1964), pp. 139–141 and 155–157 for income per capita and area.

Table 4-3
Regional Inequality in Communist States[a]

		Industrial Employment	Industrial Output	NMP	Personal Income
Soviet Union	1950	.31	.28		
	1958	.28	.22	.15	.11[b]
	1968	.27	.26	.20	.12[b]
	1974				.15
Czechoslovakia	1961	.32			
	1968	.28			
East Germany	1955	.36	.31		
	1968	.31	.22		
Bulgaria	1957	.52			
	1968	.31			
Yugoslavia	1953	.42	.62	.30	
	1967	.36	.46	.38	
Romania	1959	.48			
	1968	.39			
Poland	1950	.81	.93		
	1960	.51	.50	.19[c]	
	1968	.40	.38	.18[c]	
Hungary	1963	.71			
	1968	.50			

Sources: I.S. Korpeckyj. "Equalization of Regional Development in Socialist Countries: An Empirical Study," *Economic Development and Cultural Change* 21, no. 1 (October 1972): 73 for industrial employment, industrial output, and NMP. Alastair McAuley, "Personal Income in the USSR: Trends and Prospects," in NATO Directorate of Economic Affairs. *Regional Development in the USSR: Trends and Prospects* (Newtonville, Mass.: Oriental Research Partners, 1979), p. 46 for personal income.

[a] All coefficients are CV_w's

[b] 1960 and 1970 instead of 1958 and 1968.

[c] 1961 and 1967 instead of 1960 and 1968.

Still, the data in Table 4-3 strongly suggest that the European communist states have levels of regional inequality approximately equal to what would be expected from their environmental characteristics. Three of these eight nations— Czechoslovakia, East Germany, and Yugoslavia—had approximately the level of inequality predicted for them at the end of the 1950s and recorded modest decreases over the subsequent decade. There are a couple of noteworthy facets of the Yugoslav data, though. First, despite a significant reduction in regional inequality in industrial base between 1953 and 1967, the CV_w for Yugoslav NMP per capita rose from 0.30 to 0.38 between these two time points, suggesting that the correlation between economic base and regional affluence is far from perfect. Second, unlike the other three socialist states for which data on both industrial employment and output are available (East Germany, Poland, and the Soviet Union), Yugoslav regional inequality on output was substantially greater than on employment, although this difference narrowed somewhat over time. This reflects the much higher productivity in Yugoslavia's industrially advanced northwest Republics of Slovenia and Croatia, as opposed to the rest of the country, which may well account for the different temporal trends in regional inequality on national product and industrial structure.

The Polish data are slightly contradictory. In 1960 regional inequality was greater than predicted on industrial structure and less than predicted on NMP per capita, although both these differences missed the .05 significance level. Industrial production and employment, however, were in the middle of a fairly rapid drop between 1950 and 1968. Thus regional inequality in Poland appears roughly comparable to the expected level. For Bulgaria and Romania, regional inequality in the late 1950s was somewhat greater than predicted, although not to a statistically significant extent. During the subsequent decade it fell to approximately predicted levels. It should be noted, however, that the rapid economic growth of these and the other East European nations throughout the 1960s means that the predicted levels of inequality for them would have fallen somewhat as well. Hungary, the remaining East European state, was the only communist country to have significantly greater regional inequality than predicted at the beginning of the 1960s. Hungary's CV_w fell substantially from 0.71 to 0.50 over just five years between 1963 and 1968, but was still somewhat higher than would have been expected in a country of Hungary's affluence and geographic size. Thus with the exception of Hungary, which was slightly more inegalitarian then comparable countries, the East European communist states appear to match the degree of regional inequality in comparable noncommunist nations. Echols reached the same conclusion that communist states have no better records than capitalist ones on regional and ethnic inequality.[13]

The Soviet Union deviates from East European cases in two respects, which have contradictory implications for Soviet success in reducing regional inequality. On the one hand the degree of regional inequality in the USSR appears substantially lower than predicted. The predicted CV_w of 0.73 for the Soviet Union was twice as great as that for any of the East European states; yet the Soviet Union had the lowest degree of regional inequality in the bloc. It might also be noted, parenthetically, that these figures are based on republic data with the huge RSFSR being treated as a single unit. Including subregions in the RSFR and Ukraine in the analysis, for a total of twenty-six regions, results in somewhat higher CV_w's, but they are still significantly less than predicted.[14] That the USSR was the one state in the European communist community to have significantly less inequality than predicted thus suggests that Soviet policy should be regarded as quite successful in promoting regional equalization.

On the other hand the Soviet Union also deviated from the East European pattern of decreasing inequality over the 1950s and 1960s. After 1958, regional inequality increased somewhat in industrial structure, net material product, and personal income.[15] This trend and findings about substantial regional differences in industrial base and social outcomes and about similar levels of inequality in the USSR when compared with advanced Western nations have led some analysts to question the efficacy or the intent of Soviet policies aimed at reducing regional inequality.[16]

Several other considerations, however, still argue for giving the Soviets credit for significant success in their attempts at fighting regional inequality. First, the increases in inequality cited are relatively small and come from a base that is much lower than would have been expected on the basis of the USSR's affluence and size. As Bahry and Nechemias argue, limited data have forced Western studies to concentrate on the USSR after 1950:

> As a result, redistribution of resources in the 1920's and 1930's—when the drive to integrate the outlying regions was at its height—is largely ignored. Only Nove and Newth (1966) consider this early Soviet effort, which may help explain why they conclude that Moscow has moved toward equal development, while authors who focus on later periods ... find less evidence of equalization.[17]

Bahry's analysis of social spending policies also showed marked redistributive efforts during this earlier period which were considerably reduced after 1950.[18] Thus in historical perspective the earlier major gains in regional equality should more than counterbalance the recent slight rise in inequality. Second, in comparison to the advanced industrial nations of the West, the West, the Soviet Union's lower development level and huge size mean that it would be expected to have a greater degree of regional inequality.

Third, taking regional diversity in the huge RSFSR into consideration modifies the conclusion about growing regional inequality in the Soviet Union during the 1960s and 1970s. In the 1960s, Schroeder points out, income per capita was more evenly distributed in the RSFSR than among the fifteen republics, although Koropeckyj's findings indicate that industrial base was more inegalitarian in the RSFSR.[19] In terms of the temporal trend, statistical analysis of twenty-six Soviet regions composed of ten subregions in the RSFSR, three subregions in the Ukraine, and the other thirteen republics indicates that regional inequality in affluence actually declined somewhat over the 1960s and then remained constant for the first half of the 1970s.[20] Nechemias, using smaller *oblast* and *krai* (provincial) units, also found a greater reduction of regional inequality within the RSFSR than among the republics over the 1959-1975 period.[21] A diminution of regional inequality may still be occurring, but its focus seems to have changed from among the republics to within the RSFSR.

Fourth, there are several indications that the trend of increasing inequality among the republics may well be reversed in the near future. Bahry has found that investment has become more equally distributed since 1960, which might well presage a renewed narrowing of inequality in economic base and regional affluence.[22] In fact Abouchar, looking at planned industrial production for the late 1970s, concluded that significant regional redistribution was occurring to the benefit of the less developed republics.[23] However, this policy seems to be motivated more by the location of raw materials than by concern over regional inequality per se.[24]

Finally there are several indications that Soviet policies aimed at regional redistribution have been blunted by subtle social and economic factors that Soviet planners did not and possibly could not anticipate. First, industrial productivity in the less developed republics has proved to be significantly lower than elsewhere in the USSR.[25] Investments in the poorer regions therefore might not have yielded the expected returns. Second, because of the reliance of the less developed areas upon more industrialized regions for intermediate and manufactured products, new investment in poorer regions may stimulate almost as much output and income in existing industrial heartlands, thereby undermining its redistributive effects.[26] Gillula applied a sophisticated input-output model to Soviet data that indicated that this theory was valid for the Soviet Union.[27] Third, demographic differences among the republics (the less developed areas have by far the highest birth rates) mean that equal investment, production, and wage scales have higher per capita effects in the more developed regions. McAuley, for instance, found that a major determinant of poverty was the number of dependents in a household.[28] Thus some regional inequality may result from shortfalls in the Soviet welfare system that have nothing to do with regional policy.

Fourth, the reluctance of parts of a region's population to take advantage of opportunities provided by Soviet attempts to develop the poorer republics might also have significantly hindered equalization. Economic development, higher standards of living, and progress in general are normally associated with the process of urbanization; Nechemias, Schroeder, and Zwick all conclude that relative levels of urbanization provide the primary explanation for differences in regional affluence and social outcomes in the USSR.[29] Yet many members of the indigenous nationalities in Central Asia do not seem willing to move to urban areas and take higher paying industrial jobs.[30] Similar findings have also been reported by Clayton concerning the role of women.[31] This is not to say that cultural aversions to progress are always unwarranted but only to point out that the reactions of supposed beneficiaries of development policies can contribute to the continuation inequality.

Finally, McAuley has demonstrated that

While the Soviet government was successful in reducing the variance of elements under its direct control, changes in other factors and the way in which policies were implemented led to a general failure in reducing disparity.[32]

In particular, regional variations among state employees in earning per employee and social welfare payments dropped significantly between the 1960s and the 1970s, but this was offset by changes in the relations between the participation rate of job-holding in the economy and earning per employee and between social welfare payments and other sources of income (both of which moved in the direction of reinforcing regional inequality). Over the 1960s, in addition, the income gap between state employees and collective farmers and the regional differences in proportion of *kolkhozniki* both narrowed appreciably, which should have produced more equal income across regions. Again, however, these positive changes were offset by a shift in the relation between the proportion of *kolkhozniki* and income differences between state and collective farmers.

In short, the Soviet government in the 1960s was able to reduce most of the individual components of regional inequality. This progress was undermined, though, by changing relationships among the individual elements of inequality as they became much more coherent. Unlike 1960, then, when there was some counterbalance between republics ranking high on some but low on other dimensions of inequality, by the beginning of the 1970s republics that were advantaged in terms of one component were generally advantaged in terms of the others.[33] Zwick found a similar pattern of growing cohesion in regional inequality on various social outcome indicators.[34]

Although such considerations of frustrated policy intensions do not make the Soviet record any better, they do vitiate the conclusion that regional inequality resulted from Russian colonialism or from the political power of the richer republics.[35] Overall therefore the Soviet Union seems to qualify, albeit with a few caveats, for the specification in hypothesis 1 that regional inequality has been reduced more than would be expected based on the experience of comparable capitalist states. Inequality is much less than predicted; and recent increases seem marginal for the various reasons cited. Eastern Europe, in contrast, clearly follows the second hypothesis's expectations of no significant difference from nonsocialist states.

Indirect Policies for Reducing Regional Inequality

If hypothesis 2—the null hypothesis of no difference—holds for most of the European socialist community, is there any evidence to support the extenuating circumstances suggested in hypothesis 3 about an envelope curve movement in regional inequality or in hypothesis 4 about communist governments' making special efforts to equalize social outcomes among regions at different development levels? Two analyses explicitly argue that regional inequality in communist countries conforms to Williamson's envelope curve theory Koropeckyj shows that, except for the low inequality in the USSR, a cross-sectional ranking of the socialist countries on regional inequality follows an envelope curve.[36] The countries in the middle in terms of NMP per capita (Hungary and Poland) display the greatest inequality; and the most developed East European states (Czechoslovakia and East Germany) are slightly more egalitarian than the least developed (Bulgaria, Romania, and Yugoslavia). In addition, Brian Silver found some longitudinal support for the envelope curve theory in educational inequality among major Soviet nationality groups (not regions).[37]

Most striking about changes in regional inequality among European communist states, however, is their failure to replicate what Williamson called the classic pattern of first increasing and then decreasing inequality. In the Soviet bloc, by contrast, regional inequality began to narrow almost as soon as the communist industrialization drives began. Koropeckyj argues that this indicates a substantial concern by these communist regimes for promoting regional equalization:

> This decrease, although at various rates, took place despite significant differences among the countries in terms of the level of economic development. There is probably no doubt that this has something to do with the Socialist system of economics. Such factors as the centralization or degree of decentralization in decision making, the full employment of all resources, the general emphasis on rapid economic growth and all the structural changes can be influential on the reduction of interregional inequality.[38]

This decrease by itself does not seem very significant, however, since regional inequality fell for most of the countries for which Williamson had longitudinal data after 1940.[39] That their industrialization drives very quickly led to reduced regional inequality rather than following the envelope curve pattern does suggest special success for European communist nations.

Hypothesis 4 receives some support in that several communist states clearly do use governmental powers in a redistributive manner to make living conditions much more equal than regional affluence. Table 4-3 suggests that this is the case for the Soviet Union because personal income is more equally distributed than regional affluence, which in turn is more equally distributed than economic base. Thus while industry seems to be concentrated in the most productive areas, overall regional affluence is less skewed than industrial base, and, in particular, government manipulation of wage scales and transfer payments has led to a distribution of personal income that is much more egalitarian than differences in NMP per capita. Koropeckyj's analysis of Poland, summarized in table 4-4, produces similar results: Consumption is more evenly distributed than regional affluence, while industrial structure shows the greatest degree of regional concentration.

Other data on social services, consumption, and budgetary allocations also support the hypothesis that the USSR has utilized government spending and services to equalize social outcomes among regions at different developmental

Table 4–4
Regional Inequality in Poland[a]

	1950	1955	1960	1965	1970	1974
National economy						
GNP per capita			.19[b]	.19	.18	
Gross fixed capital per capita			.48	.44	.37	.33
Industry						
Gross output per capita	.91	.67	.50	.40	.36	.28
Gross fixed capital per capita			.70	.63	.52	.42
Consumption						
Consumed material product						
per capita			.12	.12	.11	
Retail sales per capita		.24	.21	.18	.15	.12

Source: I.S. Koropeckyj. "Regional Development in Postwar Poland," *Soviet Studies* 29, no. 1 (January 1977):1,14.
[a] All coefficients are CV_W's.
[b] 1961.

levels.[40] Clayton, found, for example, that regional inequality in Soviet consumption was fairly low, especially by international standards.[41] Schroeder's analysis of several dimensions of regional inequality in the USSR provides more comprehensive support for hypothesis 4.[42] Table 4-5 reports CV_u's that were calculated from Schroeder's data on regional variations in national income, budgetary outlays, medical facilities, retail trade, housing, and educational achievement (CV_u's were used since this is the measure that has been applied in most of the studies of regional inequality in the spending, service, and outcome realms.) In comparing the CV_u's in table 4-5 with the previously discussed CV_W's for the USSR, CV_u tends to be significantly higher than CV_W for the same variable since the RSFSR is usually close to the national mean.[43] Regional inequality in national income per capita, which indicates regional affluence, rose from 0.30 to 0.39 between 1960 and 1970. As hypothesis 4 predicts, most of the other indicators of spending, service levels, and social outcomes have significantly lower or decreasing levels of inequality. Of the three spending categories, health and educational expenditures were much closer to equality than national income among the republics. Social consumption expenditures (which include both individual transfer payments and spending on some public services) had approximately the same CV_u as national income in 1960 but became more equally distributed over the next decade. Furthermore, the two most direct indicators of service levels—housing space and hospital beds—also manifested low levels of inequality. Doctors per capita represent a service level slightly less subject to government control given the understandable tendency of physicians to try to find desirable locations. Such efforts seem to have borne some fruit because doctors were distributed substantially more unequally than hospital beds with CV_u's of 0.29 in

Table 4-5
Regional Variation in the Soviet Union[a]

	1960	1965	1970
Regional affluence			
National income per capita	.30	.34	.39
Government spending			
Educational expenditures per student	.13	.13	
Health expenditures per capita	.15	.15	
Social consumption expenditures per capita	.34	.23	.21
Service levels			
Urban housing space per capita	.16	.16	.16
Hospital beds per capita	.14	.10	.09
Doctors per capita	.29	.24	.23
Social outcomes			
Retail trade per capita	.28	.29	.31
Persons with secondary education per capita	.17[b]		.10

Source: These coefficients were calculated from the data presented by Gertrude E. Schroeder, "Regional Differences in Incomes and Levels of Living in the USSR," in V.N. Bandera and Z.L. Melnyk, eds., *The Soviet Economy in Regional Perspective* (New York: Praeger, 1973), pp. 169, 171, 182, and 184–186.

[a] All coefficients are CV_u's.

[b] 1959.

1960 and 0.23 in 1970. Moving to the two indicators of social outcomes, educational achievement had a low and declining level of regional inequality, while retail trade and sales per capita was the variable in table 4-5 whose CV_u's were most similar to per capita income's. This contrasts with Clayton's finding of low inequality in consumption,[44] an incongruity perhaps explained by regional variations in sales on the collective farm market and in the size of agricultural in kind income.

Changes in regional inequality in education also imply that the Soviet regime has been pursuing policies aimed at moderating regional differences. Education appears the key to upward mobility in the USSR. Education is a central prerequisite for attaining higher status jobs, and educational opportunities are limited. Thus access to education is a major determinant of various (say, class or nationality) groups' social status.[45] Table 4-6 demonstrates that the USSR has made major strides in reducing educational differences among both the fifteen republics and fifteen nationality groups represented by them. Inequality has been reduced for basic educational achievements as indicated by literacy rate and attendance up through secondary school (the high CV_u for kindergarten enrollment is probably caused by variations in the number of children of less than kindergarten age among the republics because of differing birthrates.) Again these CV_u's would usually be higher than the previously discussed CV_w's for a given degree of Soviet inequality. Thus by 1970 basic

Table 4-6
Educational Inequality in the USSR[a]

	1929	1939	1959	1970
Regions				
Kindergarten enrollment per capita under 10		.56[b]		.42
Vocational school enrollment per capita over 10		.40[b]		.19
Higher education enrollment per capita over 10		.65[b]		.17
People with secondary education per capita over 10		.45[b]		.10
Nationalities				
Literacy rate	.87	.77	.26	
Incomplete secondary education per capita over 10			.22	.14
Specialists with higher education per capita			.49[c]	.38
Specialists with secondary education per capita			.42[c]	.44
Scientific workers per capita		.88	.64[c]	.58

Sources: Brian Silver, "Levels of Socioeconomic Development among Nationalities: A Partial Test of the Equalization Hypothesis," *American Political Science Review* 68, no. 4 (December 1974):1624–1628 for nationalities. Peter Zwick, "Intrasystem Inequality and the Symmetry of Socioeconomic Development in the USSR," *Comparative Politics* 8, no. 4 (July 1976):507 for regions.

[a] All coefficients are CV_u's CV's before World War II are for eleven groups. Postwar comparison of eleven and fifteen groups shows this to have little impact on CV_u.

[b] 1940.

[c] 1960.

education was much more evenly distributed among both republics and nationalities than their relative degrees of affluence were, suggesting changes in human capital that might promote the narrowing of the gap between the more and less developed regions. However, the substantial educational differences that remain in terms of higher education, as indicated by the data on specialists and scientific workers, show that major efforts still need to be made.

The redistributive policies hypothesized by hypothesis 4 should be reflected in budgetary allocations; and several studies have assessed the regional inequality of budgetary expenditures by subnational governments. However, as Bahry has pointed out, such data are far from exhaustive of the total spending in a region.[46] Other governmental and nongovernmental units contribute to the financing of public services, so that regional spending data among countries and in one country over time may be far from strictly comparable. Although budgetary figures must be treated with a good deal of caution, Echols's comparative analysis of regional spending is still suggestive.[47] Table 4-7 presents summary figures from this study for Echols's sample of socialist and nonsocialist nations. CV's are given for income per capita, as a measure of regional affluence, and three indicators of budgetary commitment—total revenues, educational expenditures, and health spending per capita. For three budgetary items, the letter *P* following them denotes a progressive relation (negative correlation) with regional

Table 4-7
Inequality in Regional Spending[a]

	Income per Capita	Revenues per Capita	Educational Spending per Capita	Health Spending per Capita
Australia				
1956	.08	.15 (P)[b]	.14 (P)	.10 (P)
1970	.09	.14 (P)	.10 (P)	.18 (P)
Canada				
1956	.27	.45		
1963	.24	.18	.21	.14
1972	.20	.08	.14	.14
China				
1956	1.22[c]	.47	.41	.36
India				
1958	.24	.31	.36	.32
1965	.23	.21	.33	.24
1972	.24	.25	.32	.28
Japan				
1958	.27	.11	.10 (P)	.25
1968	.25	.15 (P)	.15 (P)	.26 (P)
Poland				
1958	.20	.21	.17	.27
1965	.22	.27 (P)	.13 (P)	.30
1971	.20	.24 (P)	.14 (P)	.17
Soviet Union				
1940	.31	.33	.32	.30
1950	.30	.29	.17	.22
1958	.26	.24	.12	.17
1965	.32[d]	.23	.11 (P)	.13
United States				
1940	.35	.29[e]	.36	.47[e]
1950	.23		.25	
1957	.23	.22	.22	.35
1970	.17	.18	.19	.33

Source: John M. Echols, "Politics, Budgets, and Regional Equality in Communist and Capitalist Systems," *Comparative Political Studies* 8, no. 3 (October 1975):264–265, 269, 272, and 277–278.

[a] All coefficients are CV_u's.

[b] P indicates a progressive situation in which the poorer regions spend more.

[c] Industrial output per capita, 1957.

[d] 1969.

[e] 1942.

affluence. Such progressive relation indicate major regional redistributional policies. A lesser, but still significant, abatement of regional inequality occurs when there is less inequality in budgetary resources than in regional affluence.

Three of the eight countries in table 4-7—Australia, Poland, and Japan—meet the strictest criterion of having greater budgetary resources in poorer regions, although overall inequality in the former is so small that progressive redistribution might not be particularly significant. In terms of the second criterion, budgetary inequality is much less than developmental inequality in China, somewhat less in the Soviet Union, and slightly less in Canada. India and the United States, in contrast, evince no regional redistribution.

Several other analyses of the Soviet Union are also consistent with hypothesis 4. Bahry's more detailed budgetary analysis reached the same conclusion that social welfare spending is significantly more egalitarian than overall regional affluence among the Soviet republics.[48] Dellenbrant found that social outcomes in the republics were more equal than differences in economic structure.[49] Bielasiak's analysis of republic budgets provides further support for the thesis that governmental policy has been aimed at making social outcomes more equal than economic structures, although he introduces a significant caveat. Table 4-8 presents the CV_u's that Bielasiak calculated for the republics' economic and sociocultural outlays. Sociocultural expenditures were substantially closer to equality than economic spending except for social maintenance and state assistance payments, which were targeted at urban and rural populations respectively and which, thus, offset each other.[50]

However, because of the continuing very high correlation (approximately .85) between per capita sociocultural expenditures and urbanization as an indicator of development level, Bielasiak concluded that Soviet policymakers focus their attempts to reduce inequality on trying to equalize urbanization rather than social transfers per se. This impact of urbanization upon inequality in social outputs and outcomes is taken a step further by Kordan and Hubert in their study of intrarepublic variations among Ukrainian *oblasti* on urbanization and

Table 4-8
Inequality in Soviet Republic Budgets[a]

	1960	1965	1970
All economic expenditures per capita	.40	.35	.39
Industry and construction	.48	.43	.37
All sociocultural expenditures per capita	.18	.16	.15
Education	.16	.14	.15
Health	.15	.13	.11
Social maintenance	.48	.47	.44
State assistance	.48	.71	.88

Source: Jack Bielasiak, "Policy Choices and Regional Equality among Soviet Republics," *American Political Science Review* 74, no. 2 (June 1980):398.
[a]All coefficients are CV_u's.

on various indicators of outputs and outcomes.[51] Although the CV's for the latter were lower than for urbanization, and although their positive correlations with urbanization decreased over time, Kordan and Hubert argue that growing equality in urbanization over time should have produced greater equalization in the output and outcome indicators than actually occurred for most of them. This suggests that a similar objection might be raised to Echols's and Bielasiak's conclusions supporting hypothesis 4.

The communist nations in Echols's sample, hence, all have spending patterns aimed at ameliorating regional differences, but so do about half of the noncommunist ones (Australia and Japan clearly do; India and the United States clearly do not, and Canada is in the middle.) Echols himself concluded that the communist-capitalist dichotomy does not have a significant effect on budgetary responses to regional inequality but that the major determinants are development level and governmental centralization. Thus socialist states appear to be making the redistributive effort posited by hypothesis 4, but it is much less certain whether they are significantly different from nonsocialist countries in this regard, especially in view of the tentative nature of the data.

The Yugoslav Road for Combating Regional Inequality

Yugoslavia is a multinational state with a federal system basically structured on national groups.[52] The Tito government, which came to power at the end of World War II, inherited a cauldron of national hostilities and conflicts, especially between the two largest national groups—the Serbs and the Croats. Although Susan Woodward's chapter later gives detailed consideration to these and other cleavages within Yugoslavia, my goal here is to place that case in comparative perspective regarding regional inequality.

One of the major appeals of Tito's partisans during and immediately after World War II was that they constituted the only major political force with support among all nationalities; and the new communist government put a high priority upon defusing national rivalries and tensions. At least after the period of "administrative centralism," a continuing series of reforms implementing economic and political decentralization were used to assuage national or republic fears of domination and exploitation.[53] Pronounced regional economic differences between the northwest and southeast parts of the country, furthermore, are widely perceived as a salient political issue. On the one hand the more developed areas in the northwest advocate a more rational distribution of economic investment and resources that would benefit their more productive economies. Poorer regions meanwhile argue that substantial redistributive policies are necessary to promote the socialist goal of an egalitarian society.[54] In Yugoslavia, hence, regional inequality is quite pronounced and is at the center of the nationality conflicts that periodically have erupted.

Table 4-9 gives an overview of Yugoslav inequality for regional affluence, as measured by total production per capita, industrial base, investment patterns, productivity, and regional spending. Four years between 1952 and 1978 are included in the analysis with two indicators of regional inequality presented for each year. The first is CV_u, which shows the amount of variation among eight regions (the six Republics of Bosnia–Hercegovina, Croatia, Macedonia, Montenegro, Serbia, and Slovenia, and the two autonomous provinces within Serbia of Kosovo and Vojvodina); and the second is the correlation between an item and total production per capita, which shows how closely these variations are tied to regional affluence.

Inequality in regional affluence increased significantly over the 1952-1978 period. Almost no change took place in the relative ranking of the regions during 1952, 1958, 1968, and 1978 as the correlations among total production per

Table 4-9
Regional Inequality in Yugoslavia

	1952		1958		1968		1978	
	CV_u	r with wealth	CV_u	r with wealth	CV_u	r with wealth	CV_u	r with wealth
Regional affluence								
Total production per capita	.40	–	.47	–	.48	–	.55	–
Industrial base								
Industrial production per capita	.77	.93	.72	.95	.62	.96	.64	.98
Performance industrial production	.32	.63	.23	.62	.13	.53	.12	.26
Basic capital per capita[a]	.69	.96					.47	.95
Investment								
Total investment per capita	.54	.67	.33	.77	.27	.94	.40	.95
Industrial investment	.59	.69	.40	.35	.29	.53	.42	.89
Productivity[a]								
Industrial output per worker	.85	.93					.64	.98
Basic capita per worker	.21	.46					.16	.15
Personal Income								
Personal income per worker					.11	.93	.13	.95
Government spending per capita[b]								
Rep budget			.56	.13			.50	.49
District budget			.30	.78			–	–
Commune budget			.29	.73			.38	.78
All local budget			.28	.68			.37	.70

Sources: These coefficients were calculated from the date in *Statisticki Godisnjak Jugoslavije, 1960* (Beograd: Savezni Zavod za Statistiku, 1960), sec. 3-130 for the 1959 budgetary figures, and *Statisticki Godisnjak Jugoslavije, 1979* (Beograd: Savezni Zavod za Statistiku, 1979), pp. 403-404, 411, 431, 434-435, and 456-457 for all other data.

[a] 1953 and 1977 instead of 1952 and 1978.

[b] 1959 and 1977 instead of 1958 and 1978.

capita in those four years ranged from 0.94 to 0.99. The regions' industrial levels as indicated by industrial production per capita and basic capital per capita were almost perfectly correlated with regional affluence for all four years; and correlations of .93 in 1953 and .98 in 1977 show that the richer regions clearly led the nation in industrial productivity as operationalized by output per worker. In 1952 these three industrial structure variables had much higher CV_u's than regional affluence, indicating that Yugoslavia's industrial resources were being concentrated in the most advanced and productive regions, similar to the situations in Poland and the Soviet Union. Over the next twenty-five years, in contrast, regional inequality on those items dropped appreciably, while basic capital per capita had even moved to a less inegalitarian distribution.

The reason for this change can be seen in Yugoslav investment strategy. The CV_u's for both total and industrial investment per capita fell from over 0.5 in 1952 to just under 0.3 in 1968. Furthermore, regional variations in investment, especially industrial investment, were less tied to the level of regional affluence than were industrial production and productivity. The correlation between industrial investment and total output per capita fell from .69 to .35 between 1952 and 1958 and then grew to .53 in 1968. Throughout the 1950s and 1960s therefore investment, while not being progressively higher in the poorer regions, at least ameliorated developmental differences. As a result, the proportion of a region's national income generated by industry and its basic capital per worker became fairly equal throughout the country (in 1978 CV_u was 0.12 for the former and 0.15 for the latter) with these variables being generally uncorrelated with development level. The muted redistribution of these investment policies was evidently reversed during the 1970s, however, as the CV's for both total and industrial investment rose to over 0.4 in 1978, and as both became very strongly correlated (at about the .90 level) with regional affluence.

Another indication of redistributive intent is that personal income per worker was very evenly distributed among regions (CV_u = 0.11 in 1968 and 0.13 in 1978)—more than might have been expected in view of the decentralized economy and large regional variation in economic prosperity. Thus, there does seem to be a significant commitment to equalizing wages, although regional variations in economic "participation rates" and in the proportion of population working in private agriculture are both disadvantageous to the less developed republics and, as will be seen, result in much greater regional inequality on personal income per capita.

The spending of governments below the federal level also suggests a limited redistributive impact. Again, Bahry's caution about the incomplete nature of the data should be repeated. The decentralized nature of the Yugoslav fiscal system means that the federal government spends very little on public services affecting living conditions compared to most other regimes, particularly communist ones. However, the spending data in table 4-9 exclude communities of interest, quasi-governmental bodies that provide many Yugoslav public services like health.[55]

By the late 1970s, these organs spent more than the republic and commune governments combined.[56] Since the spending levels of the communities of interest are positively correlated with the wealth of their commune,[57] the statistics in table 4-9 almost certainly overstate the egalitarianism of regional governmental outlays.

In addition to the spending of the republics and autonomous provinces, the total spending of communes and in 1959 districts in the eight regions are reported separately. Republic, district, and commune spending is then summed to calculate total subfederal government expenditures. The republic budgets were much less correlated with wealth than were the communal and district ones. In 1959 there was almost no correlation between per capita republic spending and development, although the r jumped to about 0.5 in 1977. Commune and district budgets had correlations of about .75 with total production per capita, implying that local government resources are constrained by the availability of local resources. On the other hand there was substantially less variation among commune and district spending levels than among republic ones. Overall, the CV_u in total subfederal spending rose between 1959 and 1977 from 0.28 to 0.37 (both well below the variation in regional affluence), while its correlation with regional affluence remained at 0.7. Thus regional government spending, like investment funds, was in a slightly redistributive direction, but also like investment this effect seems to have decreased over time.

Table 4-10 describes regional inequality on a variety of social outcomes for 1968. These data are for the six republics only; Kosovo and Vojvodina are combined with Serbia. The CV_u's for total production and industrial production per capita are almost exactly the same as the figures in table 4-9 for the eight regions in 1968. Thus merging by far the poorest region (Kosovo) and a slightly above average region (Vojvodina) with a region near the national average (Serbia) seems to cancel out the effects on the overall degree of variation. Table 4-10 is also consistent with the preceding analysis about the relation between regional affluence and industrial base. Industrial production per capita is almost perfectly correlated with and somewhat more unequally distributed than regional affluence. Effects of Yugoslav investment policy, moreover, can be seen in the lower CV_u's and lower correlations with development level of basic capital and working capital per capita.

The data in table 4-10 clearly support the supposition that social outcomes have not been greatly equalized among Yugoslav regions. Personal consumption with a CV_u of 0.36 is slightly more equal than regional affluence which has a CV_u of 0.48, but this difference is proportionately much less than in the Soviet Union or Poland. Almost all the other social outcome indicators, in addition, had levels of regional inequality approximately equal to that of regional affluence. This is true of personal income in the social sector, retail trade, consumer credit, household electricity, and the possession of radios, televisions, and telephones. Savings were slightly more unequally distributed than regional affluence

Table 4-10
Republic Variations in Yugoslavia, 1968[a]

	CV_u	r with wealth
Regional affluence		
Total social product per capita	.48	–
Industrial base		
Industrial production per capita	.63	.99
Basic capital per capita	.37	.76
Working capital per capita	.49	.69
Industrial electricity	.77	.86
Social outcomes per capita		
Personal income in the social sector	.45	.99
Personal consumption	.36	.99
Retail trade	.42	.99
Consumer credit	.52	.84
Savings	.59	.84
Household electricity	.46	.99
Housing area	.22	.87
Radio subscriptions	.47	.98
Television subscriptions	.44	.93
Telephones	.49	.99
Personal cars	.74	.99
Service levels per capita		
Doctors	.27	.89
Hospital beds	.33	.89
Spending policy per capita		
Central credits	.43	−.18

Source: These statistics were calculated from the data in Vladimir Farkas, Branko Kubovic, Jakov Sirotkovic, and Vladimira Stipetica, "Politka Regionalnog Razvoja," in Vladimir Farkas, Branko Kubovic, Jakov Sirotkovic, and Vladimira Stipetica, *Ekonomika Jugoslavije* (Zagreb: Novinsko-Izdavacki, Stamparski, i Birotehnicki Zavod, 1970), p. 431.

[a]These coefficients are computed for the six republics only with Vojvodina and Kosovo being combined in Serbia.

while passenger cars, ownership of which was concentrated in the northwest republics of Slovenia and Croatia, had by far the most unequal distribution of the variables in the table. Only housing area with a CV_u of 0.22 displayed a fairly low level of regional variation. All these social outcome indicators, moreover, were very strongly associated with development level as their r's with total social product per capita ranged from 0.84 to 0.99.

The three other variables in this analysis do suggest some attempts at redistribution, though. The distribution of doctors and hospital beds per capita were much more even than development levels (CV_u = 0.27 and 0.33, respectively.) However, this difference was again not as great as the one in the USSR: and both the variables had correlations of .89 with regional affluence. Credits from central sources do appear to be used in a redistributive manner as they had a low negative correlation of –.18 with total social product per capita (along with a CV_u of 0.43.) Still, given the high degree of inequality on most of the social outcome items, these redistributive efforts obviously have been muted at best.

Yugoslavia's unique system of economic and political decentralization in a socialist polity, therefore, seems to have had a decided impact on the government's quite substantial efforts at reducing regional inequality. Yugoslavia has followed a different path from what might be called the classic communist pattern. In most communist countries the major route for attacking regional inequality is to manipulate wage rates and to provide social services so as to make social outcomes much more equal than regional affluence. Changes in economic base are much more incremental as the communist regimes try to spur economic efficiency in their overall developmental drives. The large degree of fiscal and governmental decentralization in Yugoslavia, in contrast, means that the mechanisms for such a policy simply are not present, and indeed Yugoslavia fails to exhibit the differences between inequality in wealth and in service levels and social outcomes found in other communist states.

Yugoslav investment policies on the other hand do show significant evidence of being directed toward an equalization of regional economic base. Very substantial progress has been made toward equalizing the republics and autonomous provinces in terms of the proportionate industrial composition of their economies, but this had only a slight dent in the large inequality among them in total production levels and regional affluence. Yugoslavia, then, is beset by a north-south split in which industrialization in the underdeveloped south does not bring with it the well-rounded development of the economy and society that had previously accompanied economic growth in the more advanced north.[58]

Furthermore, economic and governmental decentralization has finally caught up with this redistributive policy. By curtailing central authority to transfer resources to the poorer regions, the previous pattern of investment redistribution was reversed druing the 1970s. Until the 1965 economic reforms, central control of economic investment made this attempt to equalize economic bases a viable strategy. The decentralization of investment decisions to the enterprise level and banking system in that year obviously created problems for this approach to equalizing regions. The Yugoslavs responded by setting up a special Fund for the Development of Underdeveloped Regions, the size of which was set at a specific proportion of national income. Through the late 1960s it proved sufficient to continue the redistributive investment strategy.[59] However, data from the 1970s indicate that Yugoslav decentralization seems to have caught up with the policy of redistributive investment. In addition to the republic data just presented, this is confirmed by Seroka's study of six categories of communal investment in 1976—total, industrial, agricultural, housing, cultural, and social. He found that income per capita was the most important determinant of most of these types of investment, followed by 1973 investment level (regional location and several political factors had little impact).[60] Thus, commune investment was evidently moving in a more regressive direction over the 1970s.

Implications

A review of the communist record on regional inequality provides mixed results in evaluating whether communism's postulated greater interest in combatting differences among regions has produced discernible effects. In comparative terms, with the exception of the Soviet Union, which does appear to have achieved substantial success in reducing regional inequality, Communist nations seem to be about as inegalitarian on regional affluence and economic structure as comparable noncommunist ones, indicating that they were not meeting with any extraordinary success in eradicating developmental differences. On the other hand the communist countries did begin reducing inequality earlier in their developmental drives than many other states that followed Williamson's classic pattern of an envelope curve relation between development and inequality. Finally the two European communist states for which data were available (Poland and the Soviet Union), as well as China, evidently used government spending and services to make living conditions (social outcomes) much more equal than regional affluence. Unfortunately, not enough comparative data can be found to tell whether this is a sole characteristic of communist states.

Yugoslavia, however, forms a significant exception to this general communist pattern of immediately reducing regional inequality and of placing greater emphasis on reducing inequalities in social outcomes than in economic structures. Rather, Yugoslavia has followed a gradual envelope curve relation between development and inequality on regional affluence, which is only now peaking well after considerable progress was made in equalizing regional economic structures. Extreme governmental decentralization is probably the principal reason why Yugoslavia has not emulated other communist states in making service levels and social outcomes much more equal than regional affluence and economic structures (see Woodward's chapter for further discussion of the genesis of such inequalities and their consequences for system stability). Yugoslavia may not be the only communist state to follow the deviant pattern of manipulating economic structures as the major strategy for reducing regional inequality in social outcomes. For example, the work of Lampton and Lardy suggests that this may be true of China, especially during the 1950s, despite China's adherence to hypothesis 4 in Echols's study.[61]

Overall therefore communist regimes evidently have paid significant attention to reducing regional inequality when more indirect policy effects are taken into account. The industrialization drives that they initiated normally would be expected to exacerbate regional inequality. Yet inequality in regional affluence and especially in living standards began to decrease immediately after the initiation of the forced-draft industrialization programs instead of following the normal envelope curve pattern. Attempts at promoting regional equality were particularly pronounced in countries like the Soviet Union where socioeconomic inequalities fueled the resentment of previously oppressed national minorities.[62]

The greater emphasis of most communist states on reducing inequality in living standards, as opposed to regional affluence or economic structure hence appears a fairly rational strategy for combining efficiency in promoting economic growth with equity in reducing disparities in living conditions. In this light the Yugoslav deviation from this pattern is ironic. Yugoslavia's decentralized political and fiscal systems certainly appear liberal in the communist context, but their very existence prevents Yugoslavia from using redistributive fiscal means to pursue the liberal objective of equalizing social outcomes despite continuing differences in regional affluence and economic structures.

Notes

1. For various perspectives on this question see Walter D. Connor, *Socialism, Politics, and Equality: Hierarchy and Change in Eastern Europe and the USSR* (New York: Columbia University Press, 1979); Leonard J. Kirsch, *Soviet Wages: Change in Structure and Administration since 1956* (Cambridge, Mass.: MIT Press, 1972); David Lane, *The End of Inequality? Stratification under State Socialism* (London: Penguin Books, 1971), and *The Socialist Industrial State: Toward a Political Sociology of State Socialism* (London: Allen and Unwin, 1976); Alexander Matejko, *Social Change and Stratification in Eastern Europe: An Interpretation of Poland and Her Neighbors* (New York: Praeger, 1974); Mervyn Matthews, *Class and Society in Soviet Russia* (New York: Walker, 1972), and *Privilege in the Soviet Union: A Study of Elite Life Styles under Communism* (London: Allen and Unwin, 1978); Alastair McAuley, *Economic Welfare in the Soviet Union: Poverty, Living Standards, and Inequality* (Madison: University of Wisconsin Press, 1979); Frank Parkin, *Class Inequality and Political Order* (New York: Praeger, 1971); Peter Wiles, *Distribution of Income East and West* (Amsterdam: North Holland, 1974); Murray Yanowitch, *Social and Economic Inequality in the Soviet Union: Six Studies* (White Plains, N.Y.: M.E. Sharp, 1977); and Murray Yanowitch and Wesley A. Fisher, eds., *Social Stratification and Mobility in the USSR* (White Plains, N.Y.: International Arts and Sciences Press, 1973).

2. Zbigniew Brzezinski and Samuel P. Huntington, *Political Power: USA/ USSR* (New York: Viking Press, 1963); Connor, *Socialism, Politics, and Equality*; and Daniel N. Nelson, "The Politics of Political Inequalities in Leninist Regimes," chapter 1 in this book.

3. The program of forced-draft industrialization was probably implemented for several reasons: ideological commitment, a pragmatic attempt to destroy old elite classes and provide opportunities for massive upward social mobility, and a desire to increase military power and potential.

4. John G. Williamson, "Regional Inequality and the Process of National Development: A Description of the Patterns," *Economic Development and Cultural Change* 8, no. 4 (July 1965, Part II):3–84.

5. Donna Bahry and Carol Nechemias, "Half Full or Half Empty? The debate over Soviet Regional Inequality, *Slavic Review* 40, no. 3 (September 1981):368-369.

6. Ira Sharkansky, "Governmental Expenditures and Public Services in the American States," *American Political Science Review* 61, no. 4 (December 1967):1066-1077, presents data from the American states supporting this hypothesis.

7. Frederic L. Pryor, *Public Expenditures in Communist and Capitalist Nations* (Homewood, Ill.: Richard D. Irwin, 1968). Also see Tosa Tisma, "Financing of Public Services in Yugoslavia," paper presented at the North American Seminar on Federation, University of Indiana, June 1967.

8. Williamson, "Regional Inequality and National Development," pp.3-84.

9. The data on inequality in Williamson, "Regional Inequality and National Development," p. 12 were regressed on those countries' GNP per capita and area.

10. Williamson, "Regional Inequality and National Development," p. 12.

11. Alastair McAuley, "Personal Income in the USSR: Republic Variations in 1974," in NATO Directorate for Economic Affairs, *Regional Development in the USSR: Trends and Prospects* (Newtonville, Mass.: Oriental Research Partners, 1979):41-57.

12. Net material product per capita will usually understate regional inequality as compared to gross national product per capita because it excludes the tertiary sector of the economy, which is normally much better in the more developed parts of a nation, according to I.S. Koropeckyj, "Equalization of Regional Development in Socialist Countries: An Empirical Study," *Economic Development and Cultural Change* 21, no. 1 (October 1972):69-70.

13. John M. Echols, III, "Racial and Ethnic Inequality: The Comparative Impact of Socialism," *Comparative Political Studies* 13, no. 4 (January 1981): 403-444.

14. Koropeckyj, "Equalization of Regional Development in Socialist Countries," p. 73.

15. This conclusion is also supported by data from such other analyses as McAuley, *Economic Welfare in the Soviet Union*, ch. 5; Gertrude E. Schroeder, "Regional Differences in Incomes and Levels of Living in the USSR," in V.N. Bandera and Z.L. Melnyk, eds, *The Soviet Economy in Regional Perspective* (New York: Praeger, 1973):167-195, Gertrude Schroeder, "Regional Income Differences: Urban and Rural," in Nato Directorate for Economic Affairs, *Regional Development in the USSR,* pp. 25-39; Gertrude Schroeder, "Soviet Regional Development Policies in Perspective," in NATO Directorate for Economic Affairs, *The USSR in the 1980's* (Brussels: NATO Directorate for Economic Affairs, 1978):125-141; Martin C. Spechler, "Regional Developments in the U.S.S.R., 1958-78," in Joint Economic Committee, *Soviet Economy in a*

Time of Change (Washington, D.C.: U.S. Government Printing Office, 1979): 141-163; and V. Zlatin and V. Rutgaizer, "Comparison of the Level of Economic Development of Union Republics and Large Regions," *Problems of Economics* 12, no. 2 (June 1969):3-24.

16. Echols, "Racial and Ethnic Inequality," pp. 403-444; and "Does Socialism Mean Greater Equality? A Comparison of East and West along Several Major Dimensions," *American Journal of Political Science* 25, no. 1 (February 1981): pp. 1-31; Vsevold Holubnychy, "Some Economic Aspects of Relations among Soviet Republics," in Erich Goldhagen, ed., *Ethnic Minorities in the Soviet Union* (New York: Frederick A. Praeger, 1968):50-120; and Peter Zwick, "Intrasystem Inequality and the Symmetry of Socioeconomic Development in the USSR," *Comparative Politics* 8, no. 4 (July 1976):501-524.

17. Donna Bahry and Carol Nechemias, "Regional Development in the Soviet Union: The Debate over Inequality," paper presented at the Annual Meeting of the Southwestern Social Science Association, Fort Worth, Texas, March 1979.

18. Donna Bahry, "Regional Influence and Soviet Public Policy," paper presented at the Annual Meeting of the Southwestern Social Science Association, Houston, March 1978.

19. Koropeckyj, "Equalization of Regional Development in Socialist Countries," p. 73; and Schroeder, "Regional Differences in Incomes," pp. 170-171.

20. Koropeckyj, "Equalization of Regional Development in Socialist Countries," p. 73; and James W. Gillula, "The Economic Interpendence of Soviet Republics," in Joint Economic Committee, *Soviet Economy in a Time of Change*, p. 621.

21. Carol Nechemias, "Regional Differentiation in Living Standards in the RSFSR: The Issue of Inequality," *Soviet Studies* 32, no. 3 (July 1980):366-378.

22. Donna Bahry, "Measuring Communist Policy: Budgets, Investments, and Priorities in the USSR and Eastern Europe," *Comparative Political Studies* 13, no. 3 (October 1980):267-292.

23. Alan Abouchar, "Investment at Regional Level: Industrial and Consumer," in NATO Directorate for Economic Affairs, *Regional Development in the USSR*, pp. 93-103.

24. Zbigniew Fallenbuchl, "Comment," in NATO Directorate for Economic Affairs, *Regional Development in the USSR*, pp. 113-117; Gillula, "Economic Interdependence of Soviet Republics," pp. 618-655; and Nechemias, "Regional Differentiation in Living Standards in the RSFSA," pp. 366-378.

25. Schroeder, "Soviet Regional Development Policies," pp. 129-130, and Spechler, "Regional Developments in the U.S.S.R., 1958-78, p. 149.

26. Hollis B. Chenery, "Regional Analysis," in Chenery and P. Clark, eds., *The Structure and Growth of the Italian Economy* (Rome: U.S. Mutual Security Agency, 1953).

27. Gillula, "Economic Interdependence of Soviet Republics," pp. 618-655.

28. McAuley, *Economic Welfare in the Soviet Union,* ch. 4.

29. Nechemias, "Regional Differentiation in Living Standards in the RSESR," pp. 372-373; Schroeder, "Regional Differences in Incomes," pp. 181-183 and 188-190; and Zwick, "Intrasystem Inequality in the USSR," pp. 519-520.

30. Murray Feshback, "Prospects for Outmigration from Central Asia and Kazakhstan in the Next Decade," in Joint Economic Committee, *Soviet Economy in a Time of Change,* pp. 656-709.

31. Elizabeth Clayton, "Regional Distribution of Medical Services in the Soviet Union," paper presented at the Annual Meeting of the American Association for the Advancement of Slavic Studies," Atlanta, October 1975; and Brian Silver, "Levels of Sociocultural Development among Soviet Nationalities: A Partial Test of the Equalization Hypothesis," *American Political Science Review* 68, no. 4 (December 1974):1618-1637.

32. McAuley, *Economic Welfare in the Soviet Union,* p. 149.

33. This growing cohesion of the dimensions of inequality that accompanied the reduction of regional variation in most of these items probably accounts for the finding of Ellen Mickiewicz, *Handbook of Soviet Social Science Data* (New York: Free Press, 1973), pp. 35-40, of fairly constant clusters of Soviet republics over time with similar rankings on indicators of education, housing, organization memberships, agricultural structure, health facilities, and electric power.

34. Peter Zwick, "Ethnoregional Socio-Economic Fragmentation and Soviet Budgetary Policy," *Soviet Studies* 31, no. 3 (July 1979):380-400.

35. Holubnychy, "Economic Aspects of Relations among Soviet Republics," pp. 50-120; and Schroeder, "Regional Differences in Incomes," p. 193.

36. Koropeckyj, "Equalization of Regional Development in Socialist Countries," pp. 74-77.

37. Silver, "Levels of Sociocultural Development among Soviet Nationalities," pp. 1618-1637.

38. Koropeckyj, "Equalization of Regional Development in Socialist Countries," p. 84.

39. Williamson, "Regional Inequality and National Development," pp. 25-26.

40. Jeffrey W. Hahn, "Stability and Change in the Soviet Union: A Developmental Perspective," *Polity* 10, no. 4 (Summer 1978):542-567; and Schroeder, "Soviet Regional Development Policies," pp. 130-135.

41. Elizabeth Clayton, "Regional Consumption Expenditures in the Soviet Union," *ACES Bulletin* 17, nos. 2, 3 (Winter 1975):27-46.

42. Schroeder, "Regional Differences in Incomes," pp. 167-195.

43. When the largest unit's score is near the mean, the variance and standard deviation will be lower in the weighted than the unweighted analysis because the contribution of the extreme scores to the variance will be proportionately greater in the latter. A lower standard deviation will obviously reduce the value of CV.

44. Clayton, "Regional Consumption Expenditures," pp. 27–46.

45. Yanowitch, *Inequality in the Soviet Union*, ch. 3.

46. Bahry, "Measuring Communist Policy," pp. 267–292.

47. John M. Echols, "Politics, Budgets, and Regional Inequality in Communist and Capitalist Systems," *Comparative Political Studies* 8, no. 3 (October 1975):259–292.

48. Bahry, "Regional Influence and Soviet Public Policy."

49. Jan Ake Dellenbrant, *Soviet Regional Policy: A Quantitative Inquiry into the Soviet Republics* (Atlanta Highlands, N.J.: Humanities Press, 1980), ch. 6.

50. Jack Bielasiak, "Policy Choices and Regional Equality among the Soviet Republics," *American Political Science Review* 74, no. 2 (June 1980):394–405.

51. Bohdan R. Kordan and Richard L. Hubert, "Social Welfare and the Issue of Equality in the Ukrainian SSR, 1970–1978," paper presented at the Convention of the Western Social Science Association, San Diego, April 1981.

52. Dennison Rusinow, *The Yugoslav Experiment, 1948–1974* (Berkeley: University of California Press, 1977); and M. George Zaninovich, *The Development of Socialist Yugoslavia* (Baltimore: Johns Hopkins University Press, 1968) provide good overviews of Yugoslav politics and regional differences.

53. Gary K. Bertsch, "The Revival of Nationalisms," *Problems of Communism* 22, no. 6 (November 1973):1–15; Rusinow, *The Yugoslav Experiment*; Paul Shoup, *Communism and the Yugoslav National Question* (New York: Columbia University Press, 1968); and Wayne S. Vucinich, "Nationalism and Communism," in Wayne S. Vucinich, ed., *Twenty Years of Socialist Experiment* (Berkeley: University of California Press, 1969):236–284.

54. Deborah D. Milenkovitch, *Plan and Market in Yugoslav Economic Thought* (New Haven, Conn.: Yale University Press, 1971), pp. 175–186. For more detailed discussions of Yugoslav development see F.E. Ian Hamilton, *Yugoslavia: Patterns of Economic Activity* (New York: Frederick A. Praeger, 1968); and George W. Hoffman, *Regional Development Strategy in Southeast Europe: A Comparative Analysis of Albania, Bulgaria, Greece, Romania, and Yugoslavia* (New York: Praeger Publishers, 1972).

55. James H. Seroka, "Local Sociopolitical Organizations and Public Policy Decision-Making in Yugoslavia," *Balkanistica* 2, no. 1 (1975):117–145; and Tisma, "Financing of Public Service."

56. *Statistaicki Godisnjak Jugoslavije, 1978* (Boegrad: Savezni Zavod za Statistiku, 1978), p. 176.

57. Cal Clark, "Commune Policies and Socio-Economic Parameters in Yugoslavia," in Daniel N. Nelson, ed., *Local Politics in Communist Countries* (Lexington: University of Kentucky Press, 1980):148–175.

58. Karl F. Johnson and Cal Clark, "Priorities in the Policies of Yugoslav Communes: Developmental Imperatives *v* Regional Style," paper presented at the Annual Meeting of the Southwestern Social Science Association, Houston, March 1978.

59. Mary B. Gregory, "Regional Economic Development in Yugoslavia," *Soviet Studies* 25, no. 2 (October 1973):213–228.

60. James H. Seroka, "The Impact of Local Public Policy Planning in Yugoslavia," paper presented at the Annual Meeting of the American Association for the Advancement of Slavic Studies, Columbus, October 1978.

61. David M. Lampton, "The Roots of Interprovincial Inequality in Education and Health Services in China since 1949," *American Political Science Review* 73, no. 2 (June 1979):459–477; and Nicholas R. Lardy, "Centralization and Decentralization in China's Fiscal Management," *China Quarterly* 61(March 1975):25–60.

62. Bahry, "Regional Influence;" Alex Nove and J.A.N. Newth, *The Soviet Middle East: A Communist Model of Development* (New York: Frederick A. Praeger, 1966); and Ann Sheehy, "Some Aspects of Regional Development in Soviet Central Asia," *Slavic Review* 31, no. 3 (September 1972):555–563 for the Soviet Union. For Yugoslavia see Hamilton, *Yugoslavia,* and Hoffman, *Regional Development Strategy in Southeast Europe.*

Part II
Case Studies

Through the comparative analyses of Part I, we have considered similarities and differences among communist states regarding inequality patterns and their political correlates. The links between inequalities and a political economy within communist Europe of dependency relationships, between party political control and inequalities, among welfare ideologies, policy styles, and inequalities, and between inequalities of wealth and inequalities of state investment across communist states have all been analyzed in Part I. These comparative generalizations gleaned from aggregate data set the stage for and guide the analysis of studies at nation-state and subnational levels. To see the politics of inequalities we must consider the nation-state and local context; in Yugoslavia, for example, we need to move beyond the observation that interregional inequalities remain relatively large to assess the political antecedents and consequences of this and other forms of inequality in that state.

Donna Bahry's chapter about the Soviet Union challenges past emphases that attributed to Moscow all blame for failure or commendation for success in combating inequalities. Bahry hypothesizes instead that political inequalities among union republics and their leaders affect the allocation of resources by central authorities. In the Soviet context she seeks political explanations for socioeconomic differences among regions; she is particularly concerned to learn why some regional leaders "are more successful or which political inequalities count the most." Bahry states and tests three hypotheses about the connection between political inequalities and policy—that Politburo representation, rule by native elites in a non-Russian republic, and change in the top regional party leadership post mean higher per capita appropriations for a republic. Her findings do not confirm these hypotheses; most strikingly, Politburo representation does not aid regions in gaining higher levels of per capita investments. Neither native rule nor succession have significant influence on appropriations either. Bahry thus turns to other explanations for investment differences—incrementalism, the cross-cutting pressures on policymakers when allocating resources, and pressures not to grant more to politically priviledged regions. In such an environment politicians can bargain in pursuit of regional interests, seeking outcomes beneficial to their locale.

China's interprovincial socioeconomic gaps were enormous in 1949. During the Maoist era, the two and half decades in which Mao Zedong held nominal or actual power, strong emphasis was placed on bridging such gulfs. After Mao's death, however, Deng Xiaoping has devoted less attention to combating inequalities. The degree to which such a policy change is important depends on how effective China's performance regarding inequalities had been under Mao. To answer questions about past Chinese efforts to mitigate inequalities, as well as to consider how inequalities may affect post-Mao political life, David Lampton examines two policy arenas, education and health services. Using budgetary data from five provinces for 1949-1976, Lampton isolates economic variables decisive for the performance of Maoist equalization programs in education and health services and finds that central leadership choices regarding investment priorities, funding strategies, and program priorities influence interprovincial differences. He concludes that the post-Mao era will likely incorporate more and greater interprovincial inequalities than before 1976. The values promoted by Deng do not stress the redistribution of resources but, rather, their concentration to produce growth. Were that growth to occur, Lampton raises the possibility that some "measure progress for everyone" might be permitted thereby reducing the immediate danger of instability from a sense of inequality. But the political dangers if some elites try to "mobilize . . . dissatisfactions" are real and considerable.

The link between inequalities and political stability is likewise the focal point of Susan Woodward's contribution concerning Yugoslavia. As Tito aged, Yugoslav political stability was of worldwide concern. When he died, the fears of many did not materialize. Nevertheless the association between inequality and uncertainty in political life is important to Yugoslavia's future; without Tito system performance has become even more important to the legitimacy of rule of the Communist party (the League of Yugoslav Communists). Woodward sees evidence that, even prior to Tito's death, economic difficulties and persistent inequalities combined to foment social turmoil between 1967 and 1971. That Yugoslav economic performance in combating inequality has suffered setbacks in the late 1970s and early 1980s, with the regional maldistribution of resources increasing and social mobility stiffled, raises the potential for renewed schisms. In her evaluation of how discontent over such inequalities might be translated into discontent with the political order itself, Woodward finds that discontent is present. The structure of the system disaggregates this discontent such that it has not posed a challenge to party hegemony. The population segments that suffer most from inequalities are not those which are most politically active. Indeed Woodward concludes that the discontent of the advantaged presents "a greater threat to Yugoslav political stability." Persistent and growing distributional inequalities among the republics, however, may disrupt the delicate system of federalism, leading to intraelite competition and open discontent from below. In a sense, then, Woodward views inequalities of distribution as a potential trigger (my word) for the decay of Yugoslav political stability.

National schisms have been at the root of many inequalities that are found in communist systems. Ruling Communist parties have had to deal with complex, longstanding and tense situations among nationalities within states they govern. Notwithstanding the precepts of Marxist internationalism, ethnic or linguistic minorities have had difficulty rising much beyond the statutory equality guaranteed to them by party/state constitutions. Mary Ellen Fisher's chapter provides a detailed look at the "Politics of National Inequality in Romania," a case that reflects many of the issues between communist systems and national identity. Fischer points out tension between Ceauşescu's nationalistic foreign policy and minorities, especially Hungarians whose previous elite status leads them to regard even the rhẹtoric of equality as a sign of national persecution. She suggests many other sources for discontent among Hungarians in Romania, including their sense of deprivation relative to citizens of Hungary. Although Fischer indicates that Romania's ethnic map is becoming simplified because of emigration and assimilation, she also notes that the discontent of minorities, especially Hungarians, poses a danger to "Ceauşescu's foreign policy as well as his domestic control." Fisher assesees Ceauşescu's strategies for political control as much less successful among minorities, a failure that can harm economic growth. That educational opportunities, cultural outlets, economic growth rates, and central investments for Hungarians and other nationalities are matters of debate suggests that anxieties run high about the link between inequalities and minority antagonism toward the Romanian Communist Party. Fischer concludes that, while outbreaks of nationality unrest have been thus far avoided, increased tension in the next decade because of unequal treatment is quite possible.

Inequalities played a central role in the politicization of Polish workers both before and during 1980. In Jack Bielasiak's chapter, the reader is introduced to strong evidence that egalitarianism formed the nucleus of Solidarity's appeal, which enabled it to become a national movement linking an "end of economic and social inequality to the elimination of discrimination in political participation." As the Polish working class saw its position erode during the 1970s, while "increasing stratification and conspicuous power and privilege" became more evident among the Party elite, its alienation from party and government grew. The injustice, Bielasiak writes, of "bearing the burden of economic failure while the elite continued to enjoy its privileges" spawned in Poland a "movement for the restoration of economic equality and social justice." These connections are explored by Bielasiak citing survey research conducted in Poland during the 1970s and the 1980–81 period, as well as economic indicators for the same decade. The statistical portrait drawn by Bielasiak demonstrates clearly that the pessimism with which workers (and lower income groups generally) viewed their circumstances was warranted. Declining material prospects and lessened prospects for mobility and advancement faced workers as elites expanded their wealth and privilege. Attribution of such discontent to the system and the adoption by workers of militant collective action completed the process of politicization. Such militancy was, finds Bielasiak, "forced upon the laboring class by the lack of political channels to express their discontent." This denial of political representation is further examined by Bielasiak, citing disproportionate Polish United Workers Party recruitment from white-collar groups, higher rates of party resignations by workers, and generally lower rates of political activism within the enterprise by manual labor. Cognizant of both their economic malaise and political impotence within official channels, Polish workers sought equality through collective action.

Sharon Wolchik begins her chapter on Czechoslovakia by noting that there, as in Poland, class inequalities have led to political conflict. But Wolchik argues that Czechoslavak political life is most affected by social cleavages based on ethnicity. Her foci are the many aspects of Czech versus Slovak inequality and trends in that gap over time since the Communist party gained control in Prague. Wolchik evaluates the extent to which Slovakia has improved compared to the Czech Lands since the late 1940s. She also discusses the effect of federalism (since October 1968) on the pace of equalization and the potential political consequences of continued difference in the Czech Lands and Slovakia. The picture of intrastate inequalities found by Wolchik is one that continues to evince limitations on Slovak opportunities and welfare, but much less on many indicators than at the end of World War II. Notwithstanding such absolute and relative progress, it may be that Slovaks are less impressed with their progress since 1948 "than they are with . . . continued differences which exist today." Wolchik implies, therefore, the continued volatility of inequalities related to ethnicity in Czechoslovakia despite the diminished size of such inequalities.

Such case studies emphasize different dimensions of inequalities in communist systems because, quite simply, the importance of certain inequalities varies from case to case. From Bielasiak's chapter, it becomes clear that class-based inequalities are highly salient to Polish politics, whereas nationality and ethnicity (of limited importance in Poland) continued to play a major political role in Romania and Czechoslovakia, with potential conflictual implications in both. That certain kinds of inequalities receive greater emphasis in one Communist party state vis-à-vis another does not mean that most categories of inequity are not present; for example, like Poland, Czechoslovakia and China have experienced workers' discontent and strike activity, but the salience of these to Party control may be less than the problems of ethnicity in Czechoslovakia and interprovincial inequalities in China. The inequality that poses the greatest threat to party hegemony therefore will vary among political cultures, but the politicization potential of inequalities will be evident in all cases.

5 Political Inequality and Public Policy among the Soviet Republics

Donna Bahry

After almost twenty years of research on the socioeconomic gap among Soviet regions, Western scholars are divided in their appraisals of the Soviet record. Some show that the USSR has fostered greater equality, while others argue just the opposite.[1] In either case the results are treated as "made in Moscow." If the data suggest that underdeveloped regions are catching up to the others, then the Soviet regime's efforts to promote equality are deemed a success. If on the other hand the figures reveal a persistent or growing gap, then the Party is presumed to lack the will to promote equality.

Although this emphasis on the long arm of the center is clearly well founded, it all but ignores the effect of grassroots politics on the making of regional policy. In a system where officials in every republic capital constantly assert local interests, and where party and government decisions presumably grow out of bargaining among such interests, policy choices ought to be intimately connected with regional politics. And since regional leaders have unequal bargaining resources at their disposal, policy choices ought to reflect such political inequality. That is my point of departure in this chapter; I will be measuring the effect of political inequalities on socioeconomic policy among the Soviet national republics.

This approach is somewhat unorthodox. Studies of Soviet regions typically treat politics and policy as separate issues. Granted, decisions about regional investment, services, and other distributive policies are highly politicized. But when Western attention turns to policy outputs, politics is usually offered as a residual explanation. If funds are distributed unequally or irrationally (in comparison with the availability of resources or the rate of return), then political factors are presumed to intervene.[2] This is hard to dispute, but it reduces the decision-making process to a "black box."

When Western studies *do* focus on republic politics, the emphasis shifts to party and government leaders' careers and to their constant demands for additional funds from Moscow. As Jerry Hough points out, much of politics below the national level centers on the quest for funds from above.[3] Regional leaders take virtually every opportunity—including Congresses of the Communist Party of the Soviet Union (CPSU) and meetings of the Central Committee and

I would like to thank the National Academy of Sciences and the Department of Politics and Faculty of Arts and Sciences at New York University for supporting the research reported here.

and Supreme Soviet—to highlight local needs as they recite the achievements of socialism. Given their continual demands, Seweryn Bialer concludes, "There is no doubt that bargaining with central authorities is at the heart of local politics in the Soviet Union.[4]

The critical question, however, is how this bargaining affects public policy. Presumably the better the lobbying effort and the more political pressure a regional leader can bring to bear on Moscow, the greater his success in acquiring funds. But what kinds of political pressure work? Western analysts have yet to explain *why* some leaders are more successful or which political inequalities count the most when regional politicians attempt to influence contral policies. There is certainly no lack of hypotheses about the most important political resources. My aim here is to determine whether unequal political resources do in fact make a difference.

The following section reviews evidence on each of these political variables and outlines their likely effects on republic policy. A second section of this chapter describes the methods and data I used to measure their impact and the final part presents results of the statistical analysis and a reappraisal of links between regional political inequality and public policy.

The Political Inequality of Soviet Republics

Few pieces of conventional wisdom are more firmly established than the notion that the Soviet republics are politically unequal. Virtually every study of Soviet regional politics points to certain advantages that set some republics apart: Some have superior connections to central leaders in Moscow; some non-Russian regions are "self-administered" and deemed more politically trustworthy than others; and some seem to gain at least a temporary advantage in the aftermath of a republic succession.

The importance of connections, of course, cannot be overemphasized. Philip Stewart suggests, for example, that

> a Republic's or a region's ability to resolve issues affecting its welfare, whether it be a question of locating major new industry or assuring delivery of critical goods in short supply, is improved by having supporters at the top. The more influential the supporters, the better.[5]

Teresa Rakowska-Harmstone makes the same point: A republic's success in having its demands met often depends on the quality of its leadership's contacts at the center.[6] And other authors—economists and political scientists alike—agree.[7]

Of all the possible contacts available in Moscow, none is more valuable than direct access to the Politburo. Access means an edge in bargaining over key policies. As Donald Kelley observes,

> Policy-making takes place within a complex and interlocking network of party and government agencies. In practice, this has usually meant that decisions emerge through the informal bargaining of high-level Politburo figures and the party and bureaucratic interests with which they are linked.[8]

Representation in the Politburo is thus an important political resource, since it allows a regional leader the opportunity to defend local interests where his comments will have the greatest impact.[9] As a result, republics with a spokesman in this top decisionmaking arena (currently, seven republics in all—the RSFSR, Ukraine, Belorussia, Uzbekistan, Kazakhstan, Georgia, and Azerbaidzhan) must therefore enjoy considerable direct and indirect political leverage.

Inclusion in the Politburo offers direct benefits by providing republic leaders with a national forum for airing local needs and grievances. And, according to Stewart, republic spokesmen take full advantage of this opportunity in their public appearances; their speeches consistently focus on the development and welfare of their own regions.[10] This is hardly surprising, since they spend the great majority of their days dealing with republic affairs. A count of their daily appearances reveals that republic leaders elevated to the Politburo spend all but a fraction of their time in their own regions, addressing party plenums, dedicating new factories, greeting visiting dignitaries, and otherwise managing their republics' political and economic life.[11] Thus although they have become nationally prominent by virtue of their inclusion in the Politburo, local concerns still dominate their time and attention. In this sense they are no different from their counterparts in other republics. But inclusion in the Politburo makes them insiders in a system where commuications between center and periphery often travel all too slowly. They can focus attention on their own republics' needs and provide immediate feedback on new central initiatives or proposals affecting their own republics' welfare.

Representation in the Politburo must also improve a republic's political leverage indirectly as well. A republic leader with Politburo rank can, for example, facilitate contacts for officials in his home region who need information or assistance from central ministries, state committees, and other agencies in Moscow. Given the frequent complaint in the republics that information and assistance are difficult to extract from the center, having a highly placed connection in the capital is especially important.[12] Representation in the top echelons of the CPSU offers yet another advantage to a republic. Central planners and other government and party officials, like agency heads in the United States, surely must avoid proposals that would seriously disadvantage Politburo members and their constituencies.[13] This kind of anticipated reaction probably gives Politburo members and candidate members a tacit veto, preventing the most undesirable proposals from ever reaching the political agenda and perhaps providing compensation when a new policy does threaten their interests.[14] In effect, then, the direct access of a republic leader to the commanding heights of the party apparatus must be of enormous help to his home region, even if he himself *never* lobbies openly.

Aside from the unequal distribution of representation in the Politburo, divergent patterns of native versus Russian rule in the non-Russian republics suggest a second type of political inequality: Moscow seems to play favorites among the non-Russian regions. To use Bialer's phrase, some are "self-administered," with native leaders in top party and government posts, while other republics are subject to what Grey Hodnett terms "on-the-spot surveillance" by outsiders serving as second secretaries of republic party organizations or deputy chairmen of republic councils of ministers.[15] The distinction, as Western scholars argue, is a measure of political favor in Moscow. John Miller contends, for example, that it is a "matter of policy to have one Russian among the two top party officials in non-Russian areas," and the exceptions—regions with native leaders in these key posts—are "areas that Moscow has best reason to trust."[16]

Thus in the view of Western researchers, the preeminence of natives over outsiders in a non-Russian republic indicates the region's political standing with central leaders. And, according to Hough, it is a form of political privilege that ought to be reflected in regional policy. In his view, a republic's influence over public policies may depend on the degree to which it is self-administered.[17]

A third major source of at least temporary regional advantage in the quest for funding is reportedly the appointment of a new republic first secretary. Valerie Bunce concludes that new party leaders take advantage of a "honeymoon effect" to push new priorities. She notes that "[s]uccession seems to breed great opportunities and capabilities for policy change," and therefore "[t]he rotation of republic leaders in the Soviet Union produces a corresponding change in budgetary expenditures."[18] Hough suggests that a similar pattern may exist at the local level; his study of *oblasti* in the Russian republic indicates that some expenditures rose more rapidly than average after the appointment of a new first secretary.[19] We should therefore expect that a new party boss will enjoy increased political leverage, and this will make his requests for funding far more successful.

The three propostions linking political inequalities and public policy in the republics can be stated more formally as testable hypotheses:

Hypothesis 1: Representation in the Politburo will, other things being equal, enable a republic to gain higher than average per capita appropriations from Moscow.

Hypothesis 2: Self-administration, or rule by native elites, in a non-Russian republic will, other things being equal, enable it to win higher than average per capita appropriations from Moscow.

Hypothesis 3: The succession of a new party boss will, other things being equal, mean higher than average per capita appropriations for a republic in the immediate postsuccession period.

Before describing my test of these propositions, two important points need clarification. One is the use of the phrase "other things being equal," the infamous ceteris paribus clause. It is all too clear that the political inequalities described here are only a few of the variables likely to influence appropriations decisions among the republics. Incrementalism, the availability of natural resources and skilled labor, and the level of economic development in each republic must also figure prominently when Moscow decides where to allocate funds. Accordingly I have been careful to include each of these variables in my analysis, in order to weigh their influence against the effects of political privilege in explaining "who gets what" among the republics.

A second point that should be noted is the control Moscow exerts over the appropriations process. As Soviet accounts make clear, republic officials may offer proposals for expenditures, but it is the Politburo, the Council of Ministers, Gosplan, and the Ministry of Finance that ultimately decide where funds are to be allocated.[20] Even when central and republic agencies are supposed to share budgetary responsibilities, as in union-republic ministries, central officials control the corresponding portion of the republic budget.[21] Small wonder then that regional leaders direct constant requests for extra funds to central authorities. During the 1981 budget debate, for example, M.G. Gapurov, first secretary of the Turkmenian Communist party, requested assistance from union-level ministries to boost local industry and agriculture; another delegate from Turkmenia asked for a new institute to train Russian-language teachers; and a delegate from Georgia asked for added capital investments for local education and public health care—and these were just a few of the requests put forward by regional spokesmen.[22] In every case, from industry and agriculture to social programs such as education and health care, all-union officials were the ones deciding how funds would be spent. Thus, no matter what a republic leader's agenda or priorities, his success in promoting local interests depends on his ability to persuade his superiors of local needs. In this sense regional policies are definitely made in Moscow; the important question is whether and how regional politics affects the outcome.

Measuring the Effects of Political Inequality

To discover whether the political inequalities among Soviet republics do lead to unequal funding, I ran several types of empirical tests, using government spending from 1956 to 1975 to measure policy choices. I analyzed expenditures because, as Aaron Wildavsky is fond of observing, money talks.[23] Expenditures speak volumes about the reigning political favorites among programs and regions.

This assumes, of course, that we *can* measure expenditures among the republics. The USSR does publish some data on regional spending, but the statistics can be misleading. Official *budget* data for the Soviet republics conceal just how much Moscow commits to each region. They give *republic-level* budgetary expenditures by major categories such as industry, agriculture, education, and health care, but they count only the programs under direct republic subordination.[24] And since the Soviet republics have few programs under their own direct subordination, their budgets significantly underestimate total government spending in each region. In other words Moscow appropriates funds to the republics by several different means, and republic budgets are a relatively minor one. This is most obvious in the critical area of expenditures on the "economy" (industry, agriculture, and services): less than 25 percent of Moscow's allocations to the republics are actually included in republic budgets.[25]

Any study of Soviet regional expenditures thus faces the question of how to compensate for gaps in republic budgetary data—particularly since the gaps affect each republic budget differently and thereby exaggerate the apparent inequality of spending across regions.[26] Moreover, the Soviet practice of frequent budgetary reorganization has also led to exaggerated fluctuations in the size of republic budgets from one year to the next. There have been both dramatic increases and steep dips in regional revenue and expenditure data simply because Moscow reassigned budget items.[27] The best strategy to minimize these problems is to find the most complete expenditure data available. With this strategy in mind, I chose to analyze three types of expenditures: on capital investment, education, and health care. Capital investment was a natural choice, since Soviet publications offer complete data on total funds invested in each republic (they include all expenditures and thus eliminate problems caused by incomplete data and by fluctuations in budgetary organization). More important, investment policy is the issue that figures most prominently in regional requests to the center. It gives rise to what Leslie Dienes calls a "perennial struggle" over the territorial allocation of funds, so regional investment decisions ought to be especially sensitive to regional political influence.[28]

On the other hand the republics play a greater direct role in administering social programs such as education and health, and regional political pressure could well be more pronounced and more effective in these two policy areas than in the area of investment decisions. In this case I chose to analyze republic budgets, since the budgetary statistics for these two items are relatively complete and consistent.[29]

To assure that the findings were as valid and reliable as possible, I cross checked the results using several different statistical methods. The most important (and most powerful) method was a multivariate regression analysis that included both an assessment of policy changes over time and a comparison of policy variability among the republics. In other words I wanted to determine just how uniform policy choices have been since the early years of the Khrushchev era *and* how uniform they have been across regions.

I also wanted to determine whether it makes sense to compare policy outputs across all the republics—the RSFSR as well as the non-Russian regions—or whether the size, economic importance, and traditional political dominance of the Russian republic set it apart when the time comes to allocate funds among regions. Testing this proposition was straightforward: I ran the statistical analysis two ways, once counting the RSFSR in with the other fourteen republics and a second time excluding it. If the results turned out to be the same, there would obviously be no reason to treat Russia any differently in the rest of the analysis.

Finally, I wanted to compare the impact of several variables on regional spending and therefore relied on standardized regression analysis. This indicates what percentage of the total variance in expenditures is explained by each independent variable. Standardization allows us to weigh one explanation against another.

The Impact of Political Inequality

Of the three political variables I analyzed, I expected republic representation in the Politburo to be the best predictor of relatively high appropriations. No political advantage could be more valuable than direct, institutionalized access to the top decisionmaking elite. Yet the results of every test I devised offer striking evidence that republics with a leader in the Politburo have no measurable advantage over the others in the appropriations process. In fact, regions with a local spokesman in the top echelon of the CPSU typically receive *less* than others do. As table 5-1 illustrates, for example, average investment per capita has been higher in regions without direct institutionalized access to the Politburo. Indeed, two of the republics with the longest access—Georgia and the Ukraine—saw their furtunes decline relative to the other republics, while other regions—such as Estonia and Lithuania, which have never been represented in the Politburo—were experiencing higher than average increases in investment (see table 5-5).

The investment gap between regions with representation and those without it did shift from 1965 onward (see table 5-1). By 1975 regions *with*

Table 5-1
Politburo Representation and Public Expenditures in the Soviet Republics[a]

Expenditures	1956	1960	1965	1970	1975
Per capita investment[b] Republics represented					
in Politburo[c]	69.38	123.85	169.33	257.34	347.91
Other republics	88.21	137.34	203.25	259.26	306.39
Per capita expenditures on education[d] Republics represented					
in Politburo	24.45	35.46	51.72	66.50	86.36
Other republics	26.26	38.08	58.61	76.08	98.75
Per capita expenditures on health care[e] Republics represented					
in Politburo	13.45	18.24	25.68	34.11	40.06
Other Republics	14.26	18.60	26.49	33.40	39.20

Sources: See Appendix 5A.

[a]In rubles, with a post-1960 decimal.

[b]Gross capital investment expenditures, excluding private housing investment, divided by population. Since Soviet sources provide no consistent figures on annual investment among the republics, I chainlinked data from successive statistical handbooks.

[c]Republics whose First Secretary of the Communist Party or Chairman of the Council of Ministers is included among the full or candidate members of the Politburo.

[d]Budgetary expenditures on enlightenment (education and culture) minus outlays on science, divided by population.

[e]Budgetary expenditures on health and physical education, divided by population.

representation had a decided edge. The reason lies in the shifting composition of the Party's highest decision-making elite: Kazakhstan, a high-investment region, gained a seat in the Politburo in 1966, and this automatically raised the average level of investment for regions with representation. Then Georgia, a low-investment region, lost its spokesman in the Politburo when V.P. Mzhavanadze retired in 1972, and this necessarily raised the average level of investment even more for the republics with representation. Thus the changing investment gap revealed in table 5-1 is the result of personnel changes; there is little evidence that access to the Politburo itself caused any shift in investment among republics.

The fact that access does not explain per capita investment levels was so surprising that it warranted further tests to see if the effects of political privilege might be more subtle. Access to the Politburo could easily have a significant effect that is not evident in table 5-1. Regions with a spokesman in the Politburo, for instance, could have even lower levels of investment were it not for their privileged position. The combined influence of incrementalism, natural resources, skilled labor, and level of development alone might justify a far lower level of investment, but privileged areas receive more because of their access to top decisionmakers. In other words a true test of the effect of Politburo representation must hold other factors constant, by relying on multivariate analysis.

Yet even this stringent test yields the same result; once we factor out differences in resources, levels of economic development, skilled labor, and past funding among the republics, there is still no significant advantage for regions that are represented on the Politburo. (See table 5-2.) If anything, the multivariate

Table 5-2
Determinants of Public Expenditures among the Soviet Republics, 1956-1972[a]

Explanatory Variable	Per Capita Investment	Per Capita Educational Expenditures	Per Capita Health Care Expenditures
"Incrementalism" (level of expenditure in previous year)	.94*	.99*	.97*
Level of economic development (per capita retail trade in previous year)	.05*	-.003*	.03*
Representation in Politburo (in previous year)	-.01*	-.003*	.007*
Degree of native rule (in previous year)[b]	.008*	-.008*	.002
Republic succession (replacement of republic first secretary in previous year)	.001	-.002*	.002
Availability of skilled labor (in previous year)[c]	.006	-	-
Availability of natural resources[d]	.01*	-	-
R^2	.99	.95	.95

Sources: See Appendix 5A.

[a]The numbers are standardized regression coefficients or beta weights, which indicate the percentage of the variance in each expenditure category that is explained by the variables in the left-hand column. The regression analysis relies on a combined cross-section and time-series or "panel" model, which is described in Jan Kmenta, *Elements of Econometrics* (New York: Macmillan, 1971), pp. 508-517.

[b]This is a binary variable, where a 1 indicates that all four top posts in the republic hierarchy—first and second secretary of the Communist Party and chairman and deputy chairman of the Council of Ministers—are held by native elites; a 0 indicates that one or more of these slots is held by an outsiders.

[c]Availability of skilled labor is defined as the number of workers with secondary specialized or higher education. There were some gaps in the published data on this variable, and therefore some observations were interpolated.

[d]Availability of natural resources is a binary variable based on Soviet calculations of the resource potential of each republic. A 1 indicates abundant resources, and a 0 indicates relatively low resouce potential.

analysis bears out the conclusion that politically privileged republics have a slightly lower average level of investment than do other regions.

Finally, one could argue, along with Jerry Hough, that the process of bargaining over republic appropriations is really a "micropolitical affair," in which regional lobbying results in only small adjustments in appropriations or specific victories over individual projects.[30] In this case the advantage of Politburo representation would not be evident in republic appropriations until a number of years passed and all the small victories could be added up. The marginal adjustments won by a republic leader in the Politburo would show up only cumulatively. Yet even when the cumulative effects are considered, the results are the same: Politburo representation still does not lead to higher levels of investment. If the bargaining process does give rise to specific victories over individual projects, then the victors include both politically privileged and non-privileged regions alike.

The same basic patterns characterize republic appropriations for education and health care. For education, as for investment, average expenditures have been higher in regions *without* institutionalized access to the Politburo. The level of health care spending is almost identical between republics with representation and those without it. Of course the argument could again be made that having a spokesman in the Politburo simply means higher appropriations than we would expect on the basis of other features in a republic's economic profile, but the findings in table 5-2 reemphasize that political privilege does *not* boost republic fortunes in the budgetary process. Once other background variables are considered, privileged republics still have lower educational expenditures than do other regions. Privileged areas fare better than others with appropriations for health care (when other variables are counted in the analysis), but their advantage is slight: representation in the Politburo explains only 0.7 percent of the variance in health care spending across the republics. Moreover, the cumulative impact of representation is essentially the same. Bargaining by regional spokesmen in the Politburo may lead to an occasional victory over an individual project, but all told, regions with institutionalized access to top party circles win no more than any other republics.

At first glance, native rule or self-administration does seem to mean higher average investment and educational expenditures in non-Russian republics (table 5-3). Yet the effect all but disappears in the multivariate analysis (table 5-4): native-run regions have slightly lower expenditures on education than other regions, and they spend roughly the same amounts on investment and on health.

The third political variable—succession—has even less influence on republic appropriations. Once again other things, from incrementalism to the level of economic development in a region, prove to be far more important in explaining policy choices among the republics. The selection of a new party boss (or, in the RSFSR, of a new Chairman of the Council of Ministers) has no effect

Table 5-3

Native Rule and Public Expenditures in Non-Russian Soviet Republics[a]

Expenditures	1956	1960	1965	1970	1972
Per capita investment					
Native-ruled republics	82.31	123.60	193.81	275.16	275.188
Other republics	81.47	136.07	188.05	246.08	275.09
Per capita expenditures on education					
Native-ruled republics	28.66	39.51	60.32	77.09	83.67
Other republics	24.78	35.74	54.81	71.22	80.81
Per capita expenditures on health care					
Native-ruled republics	14.71	18.45	27.43	34.93	35.01
Other republics	13.64	18.33	25.45	32.74	35.47

[a]In rubles, with a post-1961 decimal. For definitions, see notes to Tables 5-1 and 5-2.
Sources: See Appendix 5A.

at all on investment or health care spending in the republics and has a minor, *negative* impact on education. "Old" republic leaders have virtually the same leverage over regional policies that new ones exhibit.

This is not to say that successions do not coincide with shifts in expenditure; they frequently do. But in most cases the policy change originates in Moscow. Consider for example two cases of succession—in Belorussia and in Kazakhstan. In 1957, the year after K.T. Mazurov became head of the Belorussian party, welfare expenditures in his republic nearly doubled. What had been a 26.5 million ruble budget item the year before jumped to 52.4 million rubles.[31] This might be interpreted as a product of Mazurov's succession, except for the fact that welfare spending nearly doubled in *all of the republics* that same year, because of a nationwide pension reform.[32] The appointment of Mazurov was simply coincidental to the shift in republic welfare outlays. In Kazakhstan, expenditures on health and education increased significantly in 1965, the year after D.A. Kunaev was reappointed as first secretary of the Kazakh Communist Party.[33] Here too, however, the shift in Kazakh expenditures matched increases across the republics during the same year, all because Nikita Khrushchev had raised wages for workers in education and health care.[34] Once again a central, rather than republic, initiative produced the change in republic policies. When the effects of central decisions are identified and accounted for, as they are here, it becomes clear that succession has virtually no effect on republic spending policies.

The same conclusions about the impact of political inequalities apply whether the Russian republic is counted with the other fourteen regions or not.

Table 5–4

Determinants of Public Expenditures among the Non-Russian Republics, 1956-1972[a]

Explanatory Variable	Per Capita Investment	Per Capita Educational Expenditures	Per Capita Health Care Expenditures
"Incrementalism" (level of expenditure in previous year)	.95*	.99*	.97*
Level of economic development (per capita retail trade in previous year)	.05*	-.002*	.03*
Representation in Politburo (in previous year)	-.01*	-.004*	.007*
Degree of native rule (in previous year)	.01	-.006*	.002
Republic succession (replacement of republic first secretary in previous year)	.003	-.008*	.003
Availability of skilled labor (in previous year)	-.005	—	—
Availability of natural resources	.002	—	—
R^2	.99	.99	.97

Sources: See Appendix 5A.

[a]The numbers are standardized regression coefficients or beta weights, which indicate the percentage of the variance in each expenditure category that is explained by the variables in the left-hand column. For a description of the regression analysis and definitions of variables, see the notes to Table 5-2.

Results which include the RSFSR (table 5-2) are virtually identical to the ones obtained when Russia is excluded from the analysis (table 5-4). In both cases expenditures prove to be highly incremental and to be just as immune to political inequalities among regions.

Likewise, there appear to be few major differences in regional spending policies between the Khrushchev and Brezhnev eras. My preliminary analysis indicates that both regimes followed an incremental policy, but neither distributed a significantly larger share of the budget to regions represented in the Politburo, administered by native leaders, or ruled by newly appointed party bosses.

Political Inequalities and Distributive Policy: A Reassessment

Given the empirical evidence, political inequalities among the Soviet republics are far less significant in the policy process than our preoccupations with them imply. Having a powerful friend at court, a representative at the apex of the party hierarchy, confers virtually no tangible benefits on a republic when it comes to distributive policymaking. In fact republics with a spokesman in the Politburo have typically fared worse on appropriations for investment and for education. One need only think of the below average level of investment in politically privileged regions like the Ukraine and Georgia to recognize that high political connections do not translate into higher expenditures.

Self-administration or native rule, another sign of political privilege, also provides no tangible benefits for republics in the budgetary arena. Regions with native elites in top political posts and those with outsiders in the same positions spend almost equal amounts on capital investment, education, and health. Thus native rule, and by implication the political trustworthiness of a republic administration, offer no leverage to a regional leader in pursuit of extra funds.

Nor does political succession in a republic lead to substantially higher expenditures. A new republic party leader may well go through a honeymoon period when his minor mistakes are overlooked and his political standing in Moscow is relatively high, but he enjoys no special influence over the budgetary process. He is typically no more or less successful than any other republic leader in gaining additional funds.

Obviously our assumptions about the importance of all three political variables need to be reexamined. The explanation for this rather surprising conclusion is not hard to understand. In the first place distributive policies are highly incremental, and it is difficult for regional leaders (or central ones, for that matter) to disrupt the routine of planning new appropriations on the basis of last year's budget. This is evident in that the level of spending in the previous year explains 94 percent or more of the variance in every expenditure category (tables 5-2 and 5-4). Soviet leaders face the same problems as policymakers everywhere else: too little time, too many choices to make, too little information about alternative decisions, and too little hard data on the likely consequences of each policy choice. Soviet complaints about all these problems are legion, especially among the republics.[35] As a result planners typically rely on past decisions in determining new appropriations.[36]

In addition Moscow is caught between conflicting pressures in making regional policy. Allocations among the republics are supposed to meet diverse and sometimes contradictory criteria. Regional policy is to equalize conditions among the republics, promote national defense by dispersing industry, even out urban-rural differences, and at the same time make the best use of land, labor, and capital for the country as a whole. There is considerable disagreement within the USSR on the operational definitions of each of these criteria and on the best strategies to meet each one. This too makes incrementalism all the more likely.

More important from a political standpoint are the substantial costs in granting significantly higher appropriations to politically privileged regions. For example, while central officials may actually favor republics with high political connections, they *need* high performance from every republic. After all, Soviet regions are economically interdependent and lagging performance in one is bound to be exported to others. This implies equal political leverage for regions *without* key connections. A similar dilemma arises with respect to policy choices in self-administered regions. Native-run (and politically trustworthy) republics could be rewarded with higher than average appropriations, but extra funds could just as profitably be spent to strengthen the loyalties of *less* trustworthy areas. Finally, consider the dilemma that arises when a republic first secretary has just been replaced. The newly appointed leader could easily have higher political status in Moscow than his counterparts in other republics; but if his predecessor was removed for poor performance, any grant of extra funds would actually be a reward for the previous incumbent's failures. In other words higher appropriations after the removal of a "failed" party leader would penalize regions where incumbent leaders continued to perform well in managing their republic's development.

The point is that there are pressures on Moscow to fund *both* regions with and those without spokesmen in the Politburo, to fund regions with native leaders in key posts and those with outsiders in the same positions, and to fund regions with "old" party bosses as well as new ones. The net result, as Seweryn Bialer predicts, is a draw: expenditures are remarkably equal among the republics.[37] Several authors have shown, for example, that interrepublic inequality in social expenditures—on education, welfare, and health—is relatively modest and has diminished with time.[38] This is borne out in my analysis here. There is more uniformity in per capita expenditures *among* regions than within the republics from year to year.[39] If spending policies have been highly incremental, with extremely small fluctuations over time, variations in spending across republics have been even smaller.

Capital outlays have also been relatively equal among the republics, and have tended to grow more equal with time. As the coefficients of variation in table 5-5 make clear, the regional investment gap closed from 1950 onward, with a slight upturn in inequality by 1975. In effect, by allocating funds relatively even among the republics, Moscow has redistributed resources from more developed to less developed areas. Poorer republics, primarily in Central Asia and the Caucasus, have received more than we would predict on the basis of local economic conditions alone.[40]

This emphasis on roughly equal appropriations stems partly from an ideological commitment to close the regional gap, partly from a strategic imperative to disperse industry, and partly from the countervailing demands of the republics themselves. Taken together, regional demands tend to offset each other, and the result is a politics of compromise. As Robert Taaffe explains about the debate over investment in eastern versus western regions of the USSR,

> the national plan directives usually provide compromise solutions
> that encompass some of the objectives sought by both of the regional

Table 5-5
Per Capita Investment in the Soviet Republics, 1950-1975[a]

Republic	1950	1960	1965	1970	1975
RSFSR	67.54	175.93	223.45	315.89	446.08
Ukraine	53.32	131.26	172.28	231.51	302.16
Belorussia	31.74	88.42	143.33	243.01	325.32
Uzbekistan	41.19	103.12	169.96	217.50	263.96
Kazakhstan	67.92	230.01	288.87	342.96	402.03
Georgia	64.97	99.78	137.63	193.18	220.29
Azerbaidzhan	104.23	132.30	152.06	195.08	238.97
Lithuania	22.93	102.50	188.88	297.0	372.77
Moldavia	28.38	94.98	147.14	219.31	300.53
Latvia	41.15	140.56	228.02	315.57	430.51
Kirgizia	43.12	109.50	154.54	199.73	217.50
Tadzhikistan	44.40	114.61	175.99	179.35	204.99
Armenia	63.85	122.87	201.97	273.23	288.44
Turkmenia	85.21	178.28	237.38	301.20	382.60
Estonia	65.63	181.97	257.66	352.88	407.28
Mean	55.04	133.74	191.94	258.49	320.23
Coefficient of Variation	.402	.304	.240	.227	.256

[a]Gross capital investment expenditures, excluding private housing investment, divided by population. For an explanation of how the data were derived, see the notes to Table 5-1.
Source: See Appendix 5A.

interest groups (East vs. West); advocates of differential directions of regional development normally can find support for their positions in the national economic plans.[41]

Samuel Beer found much the same result in his study of general revenue sharing legislation in the United States. States that stood to gain most from the distribution of funds according to revenue effort pressed for a distribution formula based on effort, while states that stood to gain more from distribution by need lobbied for a formula based on need. This led to a classic case of log-rolling: in the effort to get the bill passed, the proponents compromised and adopted *both* formulas, which tended to "cancel each other out and to result in an equal per capita distribution."[42]

The same equal but opposite pressures arise in Soviet decisions on regional policy. Since the decisions are supposed to further several diverse (and even contradictory) goals at the same time, regional spokesmen can legitimately choose to emphasize the goals that will benefit local interests the most. The outcome, as Taaffe points out, is a set of compromises the net effect of which is to even out expenditures among the regions. The impact of regional bargaining is thus to blunt, rather than sharpen, policy differences across republics. Political resources that supposedly increase a region's bargaining power turn out on closer examination to have no substantial effect on distributive policies. Even representation in the Politburo does not improve a republic's furtunes in the appropriations process. This is clear evidence that Western analysts need to reevaluate both the importance of the political inequalities among Soviet republics and the nature of center-republic bargaining over regional policy.

Notes

1. Compare Martin Spechler, "Regional Developments in the USSR, 1958-78," in U.S. Congress, Joint Economic Committee, *Soviet Economy in a Time of Change,* vol. 1 (Washington, D.C.: U.S. Superintendent of Documents, 1979), pp.141–163; James W. Gillula, "The Economic Interdependence of Soviet Republics," ibid, pp. 618-655; Jack Bielasiak, "Policy Choices and Regional Equality among the Soviet Republics," *American Political Science Review* 74, no. 2 (June 1980): 394-405; and John M. Echols, "Politics, Budgets and Regional Equality in Communist and Capitalist Systems," *Comparative Political Studies* 8, no. 3 (October 1975): 259-292. Carol Nechemias and I reassess the debate over equality in "Half Full or Half Empty: The Debate over Soviet Regional Equality," *Slavic Review* 40, no. 3 (Fall 1981): 366-383.

2. Bielasiak, "Policy Choices and Regional Equality among the Soviet Republics," pp. 399-401; and Vsevolod Holubnychy, "Some Economic Aspects of Relations among the Soviet Republics," in Erich Goldhagen, ed., *Ethnic Minorities in the Soviet Union,* (New York: Praeger, 1968), pp. 86-93.

3. Jerry F. Hough and Merle Fainsod, *How the Soviet Union Is Governed* (Cambridge, Mass.: Harvard University Press, 1979), p. 510.

4. Seweryn Bialer, *Stalin's Successors: Leadership, Stability and Change in the Soviet Union* (New York: Cambridge University Press, 1980) p. 218.

5. Philip D. Stewart, "Politburo Perceptions of Soviet Regions and Economic Development," paper presented at the national conference of the American Association for the Advancement of Slavic Studies (September 1981), p. 4.

6. Teresa Rakowska-Harmstone, "Ethnicity and Change in the Soviet Union," in Teresa Rakoswka-Harmstone, ed., *Perspectives for Change in Communist Societies* (Boulder, Colo.: Westview Press, 1979), pp. 182-183.

7. F.E. Ian Hamilton, "Spatial Dimensions of Soviet Economic Decision-Making," in V.N. Bandera and Z.L. Melnyk, eds., *The Soviet Economy in Regional Perspective* (New York: Praeger, 1973) pp. 88-89; Seweryn Bialer, "How Russians Rule Russia," *Problems of Communism* 5 (September–October 1964): 51-52.

8. Donald Kelley, "Environmental Policy-Making in the USSR: The Role of Industrial and Environmental Interest Groups," *Soviet Studies* 28, no. 4 (October 1976): 571.

9. Archie Brown, "Political Developments, 1975-1977," in Archie Brown and Michael Kaser, eds., *The Soviet Union since the Fall of Khrushchev* (London: Macmillan, 1978), p. 241.

10. Stewart, "Politburo Perceptions," p. 24, table 2.

11. According to the CIA's *Appearances of Soviet Leaders, January-December 1977,* (Washington, D.C.: National Foreign Assessment Center, CIA, 1978). for example, all but a fraction of Azerbaidzhan First Secretary G.A. Aliev's 107 public appearances in 1977 were in his own region; the public record shows that he visited Moscow only four times, once for the anniversary of the Revolution and the other three times for meetings of the Supreme Soviet and Central Committee. Other republic leaders in the Politburo did much the same, appearing in Moscow at the same times, and spending the rest of their days attending to republic affairs.

12. See, for example, F.I. Kotov, *Organizatsiia planirovanie narodnogo khoziaistva SSSR* (Moscow: Ekonomika, 1974), pp. 214-215; I.A. Avetisian, *Voprosy territorial 'nogo finansovogo planirovaniia* (Erevan: Izdatel'stva Erevanskogo Universiteta, 1979), pp. 41-42.

13. This argument was suggested by R. Douglas Arnold's study of Congressional committees and the allocation of federal funds among members' districts: federal bureaucrats attempt to "sell" their own budgets by including benefits for committee members' districts. See Arnold, *Congress and the Bureaucracy: a Theory of Influence* (New Haven, Conn: Yale University Press, 1979).

14. In this sense, as Peter Bachrach and Morton Baratz emphasized in their classic "Decisions and Nondecisions: An Analytical Framework," *American Political Science Review* 57 (September 1963): 632-642, the critical advantage of insiders is the power of nondecisions—the power to see that unwelcome policies never receive serious consideration.

15. Bialer, *Stalin's Successors,* p. 222; Grey Hodnett, *Leadership in the Soviet Natonal Republics: A Quantitative Study of Recruitment Policy,* (Oakville, Ontario: Mosaic Press, 1978), p. 114.

16. John H. Miller, "Cadres Policies in Nationality Areas: Recruitment of CPSU First and Second Secretaries in Non-Russian Republics of the USSR," *Soviet Studies* 29, no. 1 (January 1977): 18-19.

17. Hough and Fainsod, *How the Soviet Union Is Governed,* p. 517.

18. Valerie Bunce, "Leadership Succession and Policy Innovation in the Soviet Republics," *Comparative Politics* (18 July 1979): 395.

19. Hough and Fainsod, *How the Soviet Union Is Governed,* p. 512.

20. I.D. Zlobin et al., *Soviet Finance* (Moscow: Progress, 1975), p. 37.

21. S. N. Dosymbekov, *Problemy gosudarstvennogo upravleniia promyshlennost'iu v soiuznoi respublike* (Moscow: Nauka, 1974), pp. 118-119; N.I. Khimicheva, *Pravovye osnovy biudzhetnogo protsessa v SSSR* (Saratovsk: Izdatel'stvo Saratovskogo Universiteta, 1966), p. 96.

22. *Izvestiia,* November 19-21, 1981.

23. Aaron Wildavsky, *Budgeting: A Comparative Theory of Budgetary Processes,* (Boston: Little, Brown, 1975), pp. 3-5.

24. For a description of the way expenditures are divided between central and republic budgets, see V.V. Bescherevnykh, *Kompetentsiia Soiuza SSR v oblasti biudzheta* (Moscow: Iuridicheskaia literatura, 1976).

25. Less than half of Soviet budget expenditures on the economy are counted in republic budgets; and the budget as a whole makes up less than half of all government expenditures on the economy. For more on this point, see my "Measuring Communist Priorities: Budgets, Investment and the Problem of Equivalence," *Comparative Political Studies* 13, no. 3 (October 1980): 267-292.

26. See my "Measuring Communist Priorities" and Carol Nechemias's and my "Half Full or Half Empty."

27. Ibid.

28. Leslie Dienes, "Issues in Soviet Energy Policy and Conflicts over Fuel Costs in Regional Development," *Soviet Studies* 23, no. 1 (July 1971): 26-58.

29. Over the years I examine here, republic budgets have accounted for an average of over 70 percent of all budget expenditures on education, and over 90 percent of all budget expenditures on health care. See *Gosudarstvennyi biudzhet SSSR i biudzhety soiuznykh respublik. Statisticheskii sbornik* (Moscow: Statistika, 1962, 1966, and 1972), passim. (Hereafter, these budget handbooks are referred to as *Gosbiudzhet.*

30. Hough and Fainsod, *How the Soviet Union Is Governed,* pp. 510-511.

31. *Gosbiudzhet* 1962), p. 63.

32. Ibid.

33. *Gosbiudzhet* (1966), pp. 31,57.

34. Ibid.

35. See, for example, O.D. Vasilik, "Planirovanie raskhodov na soderzhanie vuzov v usloviiakh OASU," *Finansy SSSR,* no. 7 (July 1980): 45; N.S. Zenchenko, ed., *Sochetanie territorial'nogo i otraslevogo planirovaniia* (Moscow: Ekonomika, 1979), p. 23.

36. Vasilik, "Planirovanie raskhodov," p. 45; Kotov, *Organizatsiia planirovaniia,* pp. 145-146.

37. Bialer, *Stalin's Successors,* p. 218.

38. Bielasiak, "Policy Choices and Regional Equality," pp. 397-400; Echols, "Politics, Budgets, and Regional Equality," p. 271; Bahry and Nechemias, "Half Full or Half Empty," pp. 374-375. [From a comparative standpoint, Cal Clark's chapter in this book places the Soviet Union's performance in perspective—Ed.]

39. Part of my analysis included a variance components regression model, which breaks down the unexplained or residual variance left over in republic expenditures after the effects of all the explanatory variables have been calculated. In other words it measured the goodness of fit of the regression model

across regions and over time; and it showed a better fit (less unexplained variance) across regions.

40. James Gillula provides a more detailed analysis of redistribution among regions in his "The Economic Interdependence of Soviet Regions," pp. 630-636.

41. Robert N. Taaffe, "Soviet Regional Development," in Stephen F. Cohen, Alexander Rabinowitz, and Robert Sharlet, eds., *The Soviet Union since Stalin* (Bloomington: Indiana University Press, 1980), pp. 164-165.

42. Samuel Beer, "The Adoption of General Revenue Sharing: A case Study in Public Sector Politics," *Public Policy* 24, no. 2 (Spring 1976): 142.

Appendix 5A:
Sources for Data
Presented in
Tables 5-1 to 5-5

Investment

Narodnoe khoziaistvo SSSR. Statisticheskii sbornik (Moscow, Statistika, (annual)–hereafter, *Narkhoz*.

Population

Narkhoz (annual); A.A. Rakov, *Naselenie BSSR* (Minsk, Nauka i tekhnika, 1969), passim.

Education and Health Expenditures

Gosudarstvennyi biudzhet SSSR i biudzhety soiuznykh respublik. Statisticheskii sbornik (Moscow, Statistika, 1962, 1966, 1972).

Retail Trade

Narkhoz (annual).

Politburo membership

Boris Lewytzky, *The Soviet Political Elite* (Stanford, Calif.: The Hoover Institution, 1970); *Current Soviet Leaders* 1, nos. 1-2 (1975); Grey Hodnett, "Succession Contingencies in the Soviet Union," *Problems of Communism* 24, no. 2 (March-April, 1975): 1-21.

Native rule

Grey Hodnett and Val Ogareff, *Leaders of the Soviet Republics, 1955-1972: A guide to Posts and Occupants* (Canberra: Department of Political Science, Research School of Social Sciences, The Australian National University, 1973).

Republic succession

Hodnett and Ogareff, *Leaders of the Soviet Republics; Current Soviet Leaders.*

Skilled labor

Narkhoz (annual); *Narodnoe obrazovanie, nauka, i kul'tura v SSSR. Statisticheskii sbornik* (Moscow, Statistika, 1971); *Vysshee obrazovanie v SSSR. Statisticheskii sbornik* (Moscow, Statistika, 1961); *Trud v SSSR. Statisticheskii sbornik.* (Moscow, Statistika, 1968); *Narodnoe obrazovanie, nauka, i kul'tura v SSSR. Statisticheskii sbornik* (Moscow, Statistika, 1977).

Natural resources

A.A. Mints and T.G. Kakhanovskaia, "An Attempt at a Quantitative Evaluation of the Natural Resource Potential of Regions in the U.S.S.R.," *Soviet Geography: Review and Translation* 15, no. 9 (November 1974): 554-565.

6 Interprovincial Inequalities in Education and Health Services in China

David M. Lampton

Under Mao Zedong's stewardship, the People's Republic of China made important and comparatively rapid progress in reducing inequalities in real income, consumption, and in making primary education and basic medical services more universally available.[1] Between 1949 and 1976 generally the regime pursued policies of keeping urban wages relatively constant while boosting real rural incomes. In 1949 cities like Beijing (Peking) had between 10 and 20 percent of their populations in primary school while outlying provinces had less than 1 percent; by the mid-1970s, Chinese authorities claimed to have practically universalized primary education. Between 1968 and 1976 equally vigorous attempts were made to equalize access to basic health services by building a system based on paramedical workers.

Despite these serious attempts at achieving equality of access to specific categories of educational and health services, however, inequalities among the provinces remained. These inequalities are both practically and theoretically important. This study will ask: How did five major Chinese provinces perform comparatively in providing access to primary and secondary education, hospital beds, and rural medical services during the 1949-1976 period? What factors best account for the observed variations, after we have considered many possible variables? Were economic factors decisive in determining program performance, as most of the literature pertaining to industrial societies suggests, or must leadership choice be considered as well? If both played a role, what was the relationship between choice and economic determinism? Also when economic variables are considered, were different educational and health programs sensitive to different parts of the economy? When one looks at leadership choice, which leaders, at what levels, were most important with respect to which policy areas? Finally, what do these findings suggest may be the fate of equality in the post-Mao era?

The major findings of this study are threefold: (1) Economic variables

I would like to thank Professors Lawrence Baum, Joyce Kallgren, John Kessel, Daniel N. Nelson, Dorothy Solinger, and Edwin Winckler, and Dr. Christopher Clarke, Keun-sang Lee, and Suzette Oi-chun Lu for their trenchant comments and help. As well, I would like to thank Patti Anne Kirst for her assistance in data manipulation and Samuel Tyus for his excellent typing. Of course, any shortcomings that may remain are my responsibility. This chapter is an updated and slightly revised version of a piece by the same title appearing in *The American Political Science Review* 73, no. 2 (1979): 459-477. The author gratefully acknowledges *The American Political Science Review* for permitting republication.

were the principal determinants of the pattern of interprovincial performance for *any given* program during the 1949-1976 period, but leadership choices relating to program financing, investment strategies, and program priorities demonstrably affected the way in which the economy interacted with the program. As Huntington and Nelson have persuasively argued, the kind of economic determinism that asserts "that the causal flow would be from economics to politics rather than in the reverse direction" is overly simplistic.[2] While the studies of Dye and of Wilensky are important in relating economic factors to program performance, the study of interprovincial variation in China gives substance to Huntington's assertion that leadership choice decisively influences economic variables.[3] Also leadership choices affect which economic variables are most salient to which program.

(2) This study clearly suggests that the critical political choices are those concerning investment priorities, funding strategies, and program priorities. These decisions are invariably made in Beijing leaving provincial leaders with responsibility for implementing and refining policy. Confirming Falkenheim's findings for Fujian Province, this study suggests that interprovincial variations in performance *do not* represent the accumulated result of independent decisions made at the provincial level.[4] As Dye found in his analysis of the United States, we have found that the political characteristics of subnational units in China have not been the principal determinants of provincial performance.

(3) In the post-Mao era, investment priorities, funding strategies, and program priorities all have changed; greater interprovincial inequalities in the provision of primary and middle school education and basic medical services will be the likely result. Although economic growth will determine the absolute level of services provided, relative inequalities between provinces and between urban and rural areas almost inevitably will increase, in the absence of strong compensatory measures.

Methodology and Rationale

The costs and difficulties of collecting data for all possibly important variables for all twenty-nine province-level units in China would be staggering. Consequently I have adopted an alternative strategy. Five important and variably performing provinces (accounting for about 28 percent of China's population) have been intensively examined: Anhui, Hunan, Guangdong, Shanxi, and Shandong. This analysis identifies variables that best account for the observed interprovincial variations in performance. Having formulated clear hypotheses from the case provinces for the 1949-1976 period, the next step would be to collect appropriate data for the remaining two dozen provincial-level units in order to test the degree to which the observed relations hold nationally.

Moreover, the hypotheses to emerge from the 1949-1976 data provide us a basis to access the likely impact of post-Mao policies on equality in China.

Two criteria were employed in selecting the case provinces: (1) Relatively complete and reliable performance data had to be available. The indicators of performance to be used were: the percentage of provincial population separately enrolled in regular primary and general middle schools, the number of hospital beds per 1000 population, and the percentage of a province's production brigades with "cooperative health programs."[5] From those provinces for which suitable performance data were available, I selected provinces that provided a wide variety of educational and health service levels. (2) The provinces had to be dispersed geographically in order to assess the possible importance of various preliberation experiences, North-South differences, economic disparities, and region.[6] Defense areas and sparsely populated minority regions were excluded from consideration because their military and political sensitivity has given them a salience to the national leadership that has altered their performance patterns.[7] Also, immigration to these areas has made demographic data for these areas particularly unreliable.

Data reliability and the implicit biases of the measures employed are issues that must be addressed. The reliability and availability of Chinese statistical data have varied over time. During the late 1950s the statistical system broke down as a consequence of the Great Leap Forward. In the early 1960s, provincial budgets, so freely available during the 1950s, were no longer disseminated in ways that made them accessible to outside analysts. Finally during the Cultural Revolution of 1966-1969, the statistical system once again was in disarray. Consequently, the most reliable statistical data are available for the 1950s and the 1970s. I obtained provincial-level data on hospital beds, school enrollments, insurance coverage, budgetary expenditures, and gross value of industrial output for the 1950s from provincial newspapers, which printed government work reports and budgets.

For the 1970s I culled statistics from the national press and provincial radio broadcasts. Recent figures are comparable with the pre-1958 series. For instance, Emerson, Lardy, and Field have found that figures on Chinese gross value of industrial output (used below) are of sufficient reliability and consistency to be very useful in economic analyses. Tom Wiens has found provincial agricultural performance data equally useful.[8] While the reliability of Chinese data is accepted with the noted qualifications, one should nevertheless refrain from profound conclusions based on small isolated variations.

As to the problem of implicit biases, several observations are required: First, all of the measures employed in this study have been used by the Chinese themselves. It is true, however, that outside analysts have not employed all the performance measures that the Chinese have used at any given time. This is the case because some of the indicators appear to be more reliable, meaningful, and comparable across provinces than others. However, the fact that we have used some measures to the exclusion of others is potentially important. For instance, the use of hospital beds as an indicator of health service availability distorts the assessment in favor of urban (curative) health care when Chinese priorities *may* stress rural (preventive) services. Alternative measures such as health personnel might have alleviated this particular problem, but these data were not regularly released on a provincial basis. Health personnel variably includes as well, nurses, doctors, herbalists, acupuncturists, sanitary workers, and paramedics; one cannot be confident that the term has much uniformity of meaning across either time or space. Finally the fact that the Chinese kept regular statistics on hospital beds during the 1950s tells us something about their priorities at that time. When the Chinese government became more interested in rural medical care in the late 1960s and 1970s, they began to release appropriate performance measures that we have used for that period.

Primary Education in the 1950s and Mid-1970s

Making primary education almost universally available in the five provinces during the mid-1970s was a tremendous achievement (see table 6-1). Table 6-2 shows that inequality in provincial rates of primary school enrollment was evident during the 1949-1957 period.[9] During that time Shanxi Province performed best in providing primary enrollments, Anhui did least well in this respect, and the other three provinces were arrayed between these two. What

Table 6-1
Percentage of School-Age Children in Regular Primary Schools
1965 and 1972-1976, by Province

	1965	1972	1973	1974	1975	1976
Anhui			88.9[a]	92.2		96.0
Guangdong	83.5		92.0			
Hunan			98.9		95.0	
Shandong				94.3		
Shanxi						

[a]This figure was for *rural* areas, so the provincewide rate is undoubtedly somewhat higher.

Note: It would be desirable to make tables 6-1 and 6-2 statistically comparable, but this cannot be done without data on the age structures of each province. Such information presently is unavailable.

Source: All enrollment data from which these statistics were generated are from Chinese provincial radio broadcasts as monitored by the *Foreign Broadcast Information Service: Daily Report, People's Republic of China* (1973-1976) and *Summary of World Broadcasts* (1973-1974). Individual citations not included for space reasons will be provided upon request.

Table 6-2
Primary Enrollments in Five Case Provinces, 1949-1958
(Percentage of Provincial Enrolled in Regular Primary School)

	1949	1950	1951	1952	1953	1954	1955	1956	1957	1958
National average	4.5	5.2	7.6	8.8	8.7	8.5	8.7	10.1	10.0	13.1
Anhui							6.5	8.6	8.4	
Guangdong	5.7		6.9	8.6	9.4	9.1	8.7	10.9	10.7	13.7
Hunan				8.2			9.1	10.9	10.2	13.2
Shandong	4.3						8.2	9.3		
Shanxi	7.0			11.2			10.4	12.0	12.1	

Source: All enrollment data from which these statistics were generated are from the following Chinese provincial newspapers: *Anhui Ribao, Xin Hunan Bao, Nanfang Ribao, Shanxi Ribao, Dazhong Ribao, Qingdao Ribao,* and *Wen Hui Bao.* Precise documentation will be provided upon request. These figures were collected by the statistical departments in each province and they were internally consistent.

factors appear to account for these divergences in the 1949-1957 period and what has produced the more uniform enrollment rates of the mid-1970s?

Per capita gross value of industrial output (hereafter per capita GVIO) and percentage of provincial population in urban areas (with which per capita GVIO is intimately associated) are most closely linked to the observed interprovincial differences in primary enrollment levels during the 1949-1957 period. These relationships appear to have existed because primary education required both a local revenue base adequate to finance educational programs and sufficient community stability to assure continuity in primary school attendance. Both of these conditions were more prevalent in urban and industrial settings than in rural areas.

Beijing's conscious commitment to equalizing industrial and urban growth during the 1950s[10] appears to have provided the basis for more equal distribution of primary enrollments across provinces that was evident by the mid 1970s. Central policymakers sought, as well, to change the way primary education was funded so as to reduce some of the financial advantages that accrued to urban areas in the 1950s. In short, while we have found quite predictably that economic and structural variables are decisive in determining program performance, the analysis of these five Chinese provinces strongly suggests that conscious central policy choices can affect these master variables in such a way as to promote or retard the realization of equality among provinces.

Provincial political and social attributes such as leadership stability (see table 6-3, column g), percentage of provincial population in the Chinese Communist Party (table 6-3, column i), and the availability of surface transportation (table 6-3, columns e and f) do not appear to be powerful predictors of provincial performance for any of the programs examined in the case provinces.

Before considering the correlations among urbanization, average per capita GVIO, and level of primary school enrollment, and before we explain why such relationships exist, a brief qualitative description of Shanxi (the most successful province in providing primary school enrollments in the 1949-1957 period) and Anhui (the province least successful in this respect) will provide an important qualitative context for the rest of the analysis.

In the early and mid-1950s Anhui was a province with severe social, political, and economic difficulties; it ranked poorly along most comparative dimensions. Anhui was a middling producer of food grain per capita,[11] had the lowest urbanization rate among the five provinces, and had the lowest average per capita GVIO. These problems reflected and contributed to a particularly knotty set of environmental and administrative problems in Anhui. Anhui's leaders desperately sought to control the Huai, Ying, Yangtze, and the many other rivers in the province. In 1955-1956, 50 percent of the province was affected by natural disasters. The year before (1954), Anhui's leadership acknowledged that it was only thanks to timely central aid that "the people of Anhwei [Anhui] basically tided over the famine and achieved the target

Table 6-3
Selected Characteristics of Five Chinese Provinces and Ranking of Each by Attribute

	Grain Output per Capita (Catties) (a)	Rank	GVIO per Capita, 1949 and 1957 Average (yuan) (b)	Rank	Percentage of Population Urban, 1953 (c)	Rank	Capital Investment per Capita (yuan) (d)	Rank	Roads-km/ 1000 km² Circa 1950 (e)	Rank	RR's-km/ 1000 km² Circa 1950 (f)	Rank	Teiwes's Stability Category (g)	HEW Expenditures per Capita, 1956 (yuan) (h)	Percentage of Population in CCP, Mid-1956 (i)	Rank
Anhui	521	3	28	5	6.7	5	3.6	2	54.3	3	4.6	3	III	4.9	.83	4
Guangdong	551	2	64	2	12.2	2	3.6	2	58.1	2	2.9	5	II	5.1	.93	3
Hunan	570	1	31	4	7.0	3	N.A.		26.8	5	4.3	4	III	3.5	.80	5
Shandong	423	5	47	3	6.9	4	2.0	4	94.7	1	7.3	2	IV	3.6	2.14	2
Shanxi	486	4	66	1	12.9	1	6.9	1	53.9	4	7.9	1	I	6.7	2.92	1

Source:

(a) Column A gives the average of the yearly per capita food grain production of each province for the entire 1949-1957 period. Grain figures from Kang Chao, *Agricultural Production in Communist China, 1949-1965* (Madison: University of Wisconsin Press, 1970), pp. 302-303. These are official Chinese figures and exclude soybeans. The population figures are from John Aird, "Population Estimates for the Provinces of the People's Republic of China: 1953 to 1974," *International Population Reports*, Series P-95, No. 73 (Washington, D.C.: U.S. Department of Commerce, 1974), p. 23. All numbers have been rounded to the nearest catty.

(b) The indicator in column b is the average of the per capita gross value of industrial output (GVIO) for the years 1949 and 1957. Yearly provincial per capita GVIO figures are displayed in table 6-4. Absolute GVIO figures are from Robert M. Field, Nicholas Lardy, and John Emerson, "A Reconstruction of the Gross Value of Industrial Output by Province in the People's Republic of China: 1949-73," *Foreign Economic Report*, no. 7 (Washington, D.C.: U.S. Department of Commerce, 1975), p. 9. The same population data were used for this computation as cited for column a.

(c) These percentages represent the proportion of persons living in urban places of 2000 or more in 1953. These estimates may be found in Morris B. Ullman, "Cities of Mainland China: 1953 and 1958," *International Population Reports*, Series P-95, No. 59 (Washington, D.C.: U.S. Department of Commerce, 1961), pp. 11-12.

(d) This figure is the average of annual provincial per capita budgetary allocations for "state economic construction" from 1955 to 1957. The population data are from Aird (1974), p. 23.

Table 6-3 – *Continued*

(e) Both road and railroad miles were ascertained by using an official Army Map Service 1:250,000 map series with data current through approximately 1950. All road and railroad miles were counted, even though some of the mileage may not have been serviceable at this time. Roads included were "fair, dry weather, loose surface or dirt" and "all weather." With respect to railroads, both single and double track lines have been included.

(f) See note for e.

(g) These rankings were assigned by Frederick Teiwes in his article, "Provincial Politics in China: Themes and Variations," in John M.H. Lindbeck, ed., *China: Management of a Revolutionary Society* (Seattle: University of Washington Press, 1971). pp. 152-53. These stability categories refer only to *leadership* continuity as measured by the number of first party secretaries and changes in the composition of various leadership core groups in the 1956-1966 period. A low number indicates high stability and a high number low stability.

(h) These per capita "health, education, and welfare" expenditure figures are from Nicholas R. Lardy, "Centralization and Decentralization in China's Fiscal Management," *China Quarterly* 61 (1975):37.

(i) From Frederick C. Teiwes, "Provincial Politics in China: Themes and Variations," in John M.H. Lindbeck, ed., *China: Management of a Revolutionary Society* (Seattle: University of Washington Press, 1971), p. 165.

of saving people from starvation."[12] These calamities, the subsequent social dislocation, and the government's ill-advised grain procurement policies in 1955 produced substantial violence.[13]

In contrast to Anhui's plight, Shanxi did exceptionally well in providing primary education (table 6-2). In 1953 Shanxi was the most urbanized of the five provinces (but was by no means the most urbanized provincial-level unit in China) and it has the largest and most rapidly growing per capita GVIO (see table 6-4). The designation of Shanxi as an industrial keypoint for the first five-year plan (1953-1957) meant that it would receive greater than average funds for state construction, funds that helped increase the local tax base, created demand for education, and created a stable social base that would permit children to attend school without frequent interruptions. In the 1955-1957 period almost twice as much state construction investment per capita was pumped into Shanxi as any of the other case provinces (table 6-3, column d). Finally, while this contribution is impossible to quantify, Shanxi's preliberation leader, Yen Hsi-shan, had provided vigorous leadership in the development of primary education.[14] What evidence is available to support this assertion that average per capita GVIO (table 6-3, column b) and the percentage of provincial population living in urban places (table 6-3, column c) were the most potent determinants of a province's performance in providing primary school enrollments in the 1949-1957 period? What would account for such relationships? And finally, was the greater equality in provincial primary school enrollment rates characteristic of the mid-1970s accompanied by corresponding changes in these variables?

Table 6-4
Per Capita Gross Value of Industrial Output for Five Chinese Provinces, 1949-1957
(yuan)

	1949	1952	1953	1954	1955	1956	1957
Anhui	11.0	20.9			28.5	35.5	45.1
Guangdong	25.5	50.5	64.5	75.5	78.7	91.7	101.6
Hunan	11.5	23.5				45.2	49.8
Shandong	20.5	42.6					74.2
Shanxi	16.7	46.0					116.1

Source: The absolute GVIO figures are from Robert Field, Nicholas Lardy, and John Emerson, "A Reconstruction of the Gross Value of Industrial Output by Province in the People's Republic of China: 1949-73," *Foreign Economic Report*, no. 7 (Washington, D.C.: U.S. Department of Commerce, 1975), pp. 20-22. Population data are from John Aird, "Population Estimates for the Provinces of the People's Republic of China: 1953 to 1974," *International Population Reports*, Series P-95, No. 73 (Washington, D.C.: U.S. Department of Commerce, 1974), pp. 5. 23.

Looking at the pattern of enrollments in primary education among the provinces during the 1949-1957 period (see table 6-2), and comparing that to the provincial attributes displayed in table 6-3, we can see that Shanxi, the most urbanized province with the highest average per capita GVIO in the 1949-1957 period, consistently had the largest primary school enrollments. The least urbanized province, with the smallest average per capita GVIO, Anhui, was persistently lowest. Similarly, the second most urbanized province, with the second highest average per capita GVIO in the 1949-1957 period (Guangdong), was the second best at providing primary school enrollments. Conversely, Shandong, the second to the last province in degree of urbanization (but not average per capita GVIO) was second to last in primary enrollments.

Relationships among average per capita GVIO, percentage of provincial population residing in urban places, and a province's level of primary enrollment also are apparent from statistical tests.[15] While statistics generated with so much missing performance data and a small number of provinces is of quite limited significance, such analysis supports the conclusions drawn.

What concrete factors account for the apparently close linkage between urbanization, average per capita GVIO, and the level of primary school enrollment? Clearly, variables affecting both the system's capacity to *supply* education and the public's *demand* for primary education are important.

Looking at the supply side of the equation first, we note that the method by which primary education was funded during the 1949-1957 period was critical. Throughout the 1950s, primary education was importantly supported by locally controlled extrabudgetary funds generated from the local industrial surtax, the local agricultural surtax, the commercial enterprise levy, house taxes, utilities surcharges, wharfage fees, and other minor levies.[16] Although the specifics of the tax system changed somewhat throughout the 1949-1957 period, these locally controlled extrabudgetary resources remained of genuine importance to primary education.[17] While we have no systematic and comprehensive data with which to demonstrate what percentage of these local extrabudgetary funds came from the industrial surtax and what percentage from other levies, we do know that industrial and commercial taxes were generally two to four times as large a component of *provincial* revenue as were agricultural taxes.[18] One presumes that local revenues generated from surtaxes on these levies reflected the same predominance of industrial and commercial areas.

Provincial officials in Shanxi and Shandong provinces explicitly noted the importance of these locally derived and locally controlled revenues to primary education.[19] For instance, Shanxi's Wu Guangtang explained,

Expenditures for the social, cultural, and educational program come to 105,708,000 *yuan*. . . . With the addition of 5,234,000 *yuan* in local supplementary funds to meet the needs of the primary schools, the total figure represents an increase of 44.82 percent over the final budget figures for 1955.[20]

As a consequence of these financing arrangements, the provision of primary education in the 1950s (prior to 1958) was importantly influenced by the locality's revenue-generating ability; there had to be a revenue base sufficient to support primary education. This aspect of the tax system appears to have favored localities with extensive industrial and commercial development; they would have had the most plentiful local extrabudgetary resources with which to support primary education. In short the way in which primary education was funded rewarded relatively urbanized provinces like Shanxi and Guangdong and made it more difficult for provinces like Anhui and Shandong to achieve parity in enrollment levels.

In evaluating the case of Guangdong, in addition to its comparatively substantial industrial and agricultural base, we must recognize an idiosyncratic factor. The province had 6.4 million overseas Chinese; many received financial support from relatives abroad. Chinese abroad were exhorted to use these remittances to support schools and other construction activities. The amounts involved were far from trivial and they had a disproportionate impact on education.

> The CCP [Chinese Communist party] gave its blessing to existing Overseas Chinese schools and revived some which had become defunct, it created new ones and in some cases simply conferred the title "Overseas Chinese" on existing schools, and it persuaded groups of dependents to "request" the establishment of such schools in their own districts. The Party then appealed for donations from Chinese abroad and suggested to their dependents in China that they might donate some of their savings or "surplus" remittances.[21]

If we conclude from the Shanxi and Guangdong cases that a solid local revenue-generating ability was essential for the development of primary education, and industrial and commercial development were crucial to providing such resources, our analyses of Shandong and Anhui reinforce that finding. Anhui, which had comparatively few children enrolled in primary schools, had the least developed urban sector and had the lowest average per capita GVIO (see table 6-3). Shandong had only a slightly more developed urban and industrial sector. This, combined with the fact that neither province was a major recipient of per capita capital construction investment (see table 6-3, column d), meant that both provinces lacked the financial foundations to encourage primary enrollments. Finally, much of what investment there was had to be used for water management projects. Anhui, for instance, "put in more than half of the 93.3 percent that constitutes the productive investment for the five years under the program of capital construction for the erection of water conservancy works."[22]

In explaining interprovincial variations in the provision of primary education, economic variables affect not only the government's ability to *supply* such services, they also affect popular *demand* for primary education. In both Shandong and Anhui the frequency and scope of natural calamities has meant that villages are frequently uprooted. Dike repair and construction require workers. Both factors made it difficult to assure continuity in school attendance and made it likely that families were more frequently unable to afford the inevitable sundry expenses associated with school.[23] While neither officials in Shandong nor Anhui publicly articulated the close relation between the stability of rural life and primary school enrollments, Shanxi officials did: Total enrollment in elementary schools . . . fulfilled only 92.4 percent of the planned goal because of the high mobility of the students as the result of natural calamities in agricultural production.[24]

It cannot be demonstrated that *provincial-level* political characteristics were important variables in explaining interprovincial variations in the provision of primary education in the 1950s, but this should *not* lead one to conclude that political leadership and conscious policy choice is unimportant at the *national level*. Conscious central political choices concerning taxation strategies, investment allocation, and policy priorities all determine how the economy will interact with the program, as well as determining the long-run configuration of the economy itself. For instance, the economy will variously affect the distribution of primary education depending upon whether it is funded locally or through the national treasury and whether or not the central govenment subsidizes backward provinces. Likewise, the decision to invest heavily in one province (such as Shanxi) to the exclusion of others has demonstrable consequences for the distribution of primary enrollments among provinces.

How well do these generalizations predict the patterns of primary education in the 1970s? Table 6-1 shows that the four provinces for which we have early and mid-1970s data were performing approximately equally. The hypotheses derived from the examination of the 1950s would suggest that this convergence should have been accompanied by one or more of the following: (1) relatively more rapid increases in GVIO on the part of Anhui, Shandong, and Hunan than Guangdong and Shanxi provinces, (2) changes in the financing system so as to make schools less dependent upon variable and unequal local revenues, (3) changes in investment policy. Much of this appears to have occurred.

Table 6-5's GVIO index numbers (column c) clearly demonstrate that the provinces with the lowest per capita GVIO in the 1950s grew more rapidly than Shanxi and Guangdong, though the absolute gaps probably were still significant. Unfortunately, we have no data on provincial-level investment or urbanization for the 1970s. We must assume that those alterations that may have occurred along these two dimensions were consistent with the direction of change in GVIO. The apparent trend toward convergence in the industrial sector, alone, would lead one to predict a narrowing of the differences in primary school enrollment rates between the case provinces.

Table 6-5

Selected Attributes for Five Chinese Provinces in the 1970s

	Grain Output per Capita, 1974-75 (Catties) (a)	GVIO per Capita 1973 (yuan) (b)	Index of GVIO, 1972 (1965=100) (c)	Roads, 1972 (km/1000km²) (d)	Railroads, 1972 (km/1000km²) (e)
Anhui	683 rank 3	N.A.	225 rank 3	100.5 rank 4	9.2 rank 3
Guangdong	684 rank 2	340.55	182 rank 4	84.8 rank 5	2.0 rank 5
Hunan	747 rank 1	N.A.	240 rank 2	133.4 rank 2	4.3 rank 4
Shandong	451 rank 5	253.66	254 rank 1	135.3 rank 1	12.6 rank 1
Shanxi	565 rank 4	N.A.	174 rank 5	126.7 rank 3	12.5 rank 2

Source: As follows:
(a) All figures have been rounded to the nearest catty. The grain figures for the 1970s, unlike those for the 1950s, *include soybeans*. The food grain output data are from "China: Agricultural Performance in 1975," Research Aid, ER-10149 (Washington, D.C.: Central Intelligence Agency, 1976), p. 18. The figures displayed are the average of the per capita figures for two years (1974 and 1975) for each province.
(b) Reported and estimated absolute GVIO figures (in 1952 constant prices) are reported in Robert Michael Field, Nicholas R. Lardy, and John Emerson, "A Reconstruction of the Gross Value of Industrial Output by Province in the People's Republic of China: 1949-73," *Foreign Economic Report* no. 7 (Washington, D.C.: U.S. Department of Commerce, 1975), p. 9.
(c) Field et al. "Gross Value of Industrial Output by Province in China," pp. 34-35.
(d) All road and railroad miles include all lengths of route as of 1972.
(e) See note for d.

As predicted, another factor was apparently particularly important in producing the observed convergence in primary enrollment rates among provinces. In 1957 it was announced that "in accordance with the decision of the State Council, the salaries of elementary school teachers, *which have been appropriated from locally raised funds*, will be appropriated from the *National Treasury*" (emphasis added).[25] One important obstacle to establishing schools in relatively impoverished localities was thereby removed, and we presume this policy was still operative in the 1970s. The effect of this alteration was to make primary school programs less dependent upon variable and unequal local revenues; this promoted the equalization of enrollment rates between provinces.

We must consider one other factor that would not have been forecast from the 1950s cases. The length of primary education in the early and mid-1970s was, generally, five years, whereas prior to the Cultural Revolution it was six.

As ex-Minister of Education Zhou Rongxin told a delegation of American educators, "Some of the factors which have made possible the progress in universalizing elementary and secondary education are the simplification of schooling materials and shortening the number of years of schooling."[26] Shortening the number of years in school has made it possible to divert resources from the old practice of keeping fewer students in school longer to the newer system of keeping more students in school for a shorter time. At the same time when the number of years was reduced, it became increasingly difficult for the provinces that led in the 1950s to boost their rates further. As Orleans explains, "There is a normal slowing up as the proportion in school approaches the school-age population."[27] One reason for this convergence has been that the indicators are measuring the enrollment levels of a somewhat altered system of primary education. This favored the "poor performers" of the 1950s.[28]

To conclude, the factors that affected the levels of primary enrollment in the five provinces during the 1950s appeared to account for interprovincial convergence in the early and mid-1970s. Relatively rapid increases in the GVIO index in the previously low-ranking provinces contributed to a trend toward convergence; presumably trends in urbanization paralleled changes in industrial output, but that is not certain. Also the movement toward interprovincial equality reflects changes in financing patterns that attenuated the link between local financial resources and the provision of primary education. Finally the length of primary schooling was generally shortened, making it easier for poorly performing provinces to boost enrollment levels. Concisely stated, while economic variables appear to be important determinants of program performance with respect to any given program, and urban areas will always enjoy benefits (especially on the demand side), the shape of the program and the financial relationships governing it are not given. Political choices concerning which sectors of the economy to emphasize, which provinces to target for investment, levels and kinds of subsidization, length of curriculum, and how to fund a given service, all ultimately determine the pattern of interprovincial performance. The Chinese case, then, suggests that models of strict economic determinism in which political leaders are mere putty in the hands of economic forces beyond their control may need to be modified, as Chenery and Huntington and Nelson have suggested.[29]

General Middle School Education in the 1950s and the Mid-1970s

General middle school education has not been nearly as available as primary education (compare table 6-1, 6-2, and 6-6). In 1975, 3.8 percent of the national population was enrolled in middle schools while about 14.5 percent was enrolled in primary schools. Despite this relatively low enrollment rate, there were variations in the performance of the five provinces. The following analysis suggests

Table 6-6
Enrollments in General Middle School in Five Chinese Provinces, 1949-1975
(Percentage of Provincial Population Enrolled)

	1949	1952	1953	1954	1955	1956	1957	1960	1965	1975
National average	.19	.43	.49	.59	.63	.82	.98	N.A.	N.A.	3.8
Anhui					.32	.39	.63			
Guangdong	.39	.67	.71	.80	.82	1.12	1.35			
Hunan		.36			.45	.57	.56	.73	.98	3.36
Shandong	.08				.33	.42	.50			
Shanxi	.076	.40			.58	.86	.99			

Source: All enrollment data from which these statistics were generated are from the following Chinese provincial newspapers: *Anhui Ribao, Xin Hunan Bao, Nafang Ribao, Shanxi Ribao, Dazhong Ribao, Da Gong Bao, Qingdao Ribao,* and *Wen Hui Bao.* The figures for 1965 and 1975 were obtained from *Foreign Broadcast Information Service: Daily Report, People's Republic of China,* no. 99 (1975), p. H2. The specific citation for each figure will be provided upon request.

that interprovincial variations in middle school enrollments during the 1950s were very closely tied to rates of urbanization and industrial growth.[30] For instance Shanxi and Guangdong provinces (the most urbanized case provinces with the highest average per capita GVIO) had the highest levels of middle school enrollment by 1955 (see table 6-6). The apparent association is also demonstrable if statistical tests are run for years for which we have complete middle school enrollment data (1955-1957).[31]

But what accounts for this strong relationship between a province's middle school enrollment level and its degree of urban and industrial development in the 1950s? How did early and mid-1970s policies deal with those relationships?

Four reasons suggest themselves: On the demand side, urbanization and industrial expansion created needs for technical and managerial skills. In the more agrarian provinces, such requirements were fewer. Also in agricultural settings, a peasant family could not forgo a child's labor power for the length of time necessary for the child to receive a middle school education. As well, middle schools generally were located in central places of some size. An urbanized province simply afforded easier access to more people than was the case in rural units.

On the supply side the relatively urbanized provinces had greater resources with which to provide middle school facilities. An important asset was the state enterprise that could establish attached secondary technical and general middle schools. A provincial leadership that had a concentration of state enterprises had an advantage in achieving higher rates of enrollment. Finally, in Guangdong, the availability of resources provided by the overseas Chinese came into play with respect to *both* industrialization and middle school education.

> In 1956, for example, Overseas Chinese investment was reported to have accounted for 10 percent of the total local industrial investment in the two provinces [Guangdong and Fujian]; and in the same report it was stated that 23 percent of all middle school students in Fukien [Fujian] were enrolled in schools established with Overseas Chinese capital.[32]

While the latter half of this report referred only to Fujian, the situation almost certainly was similar in neighboring Guangdong. How were these variables manifested in the provinces under examination?

In 1949 Shanxi had a smaller per capita GVIO than both Guangdong and Shandong (see table 6-4). Shanxi did less well than either in middle school enrollments (see table 6-6). However, once Shanxi was designated an industrial keypoint, its GVIO per capita rose rapidly in the 1952-1957 period (see table 6-4), as did its middle school enrollment rate. Guangdong, which had the second highest rate of growth of per capita GVIO during this period, had the second most rapid rate of middle school expansion.

Levels of middle school enrollment apparently did not depend on agriculture during the 1949-1957 period. The Shanxi and Hunan cases offer striking indication of this. While Shanxi was forging ahead industrially and its rate of urbanization was comparatively high, it did poorly in per capita food-grain production (table 6-3, column a), ranking ahead only of Shandong. Conversely, while Hunan led the five provinces per capita food-grain output, it did only marginally better than Shandong and Anhui in middle school enrollment. A tentative conclusion, then, is that urban development and industrial growth are the most powerful factors affecting the provision of middle school education. This suggests that if policymakers in China wish to achieve interprovincial equality in access to middle school education, they will be most successful by promoting a program of equalization of urban and industrial growth among provinces. Lardy argues that the pre-1976 fiscal system was designed to accomplish just this.[33]

Unfortunately, because of the absence of middle school enrollment data for the 1960s and 1970s for all of the case provinces except Hunan (see table 6-6), we are unable to determine whether or not a trend toward equalization of middle school enrollment rates developed during that period. However, given the apparently close links between urbanization, average per capita GVIO, and middle school enrollment levels in the 1950s, it is probable that the relatively more rapid growth in GVIO in Hunan, Anhui, and Shandong during the 1965-1972 period (see table 6-5, column c) would have produced some reduction in disparities among the provinces. One would predict, however, that it would take much longer to overcome inequalities in middle school enrollments than was the case with primary education.

One further piece of evidence links rates of middle school enrollment to the degree of urbanization for the 1970s. In April 1975 visiting American educators were told by a Suzhou official that, "we have the principle of enrolling the students who live nearby the schools. . . . Nearly 100 percent of the primary school pupils go on learning in the middle school."[34] If only a small percentage of primary school graduates (nationally about 1 in 3.5) could go to regular middle schools in 1972,[35] and one finds that the percentage of urban children going to such schools is much higher, it means, *ipso facto*, that there is a marked urban bias in the availability of such education.

This suggests that the conscious choices of political leaders in Beijing, where allocations to the various provinces are made, are important. If they promote policies of equalizing urban and industrial growth among provinces, they will then probably enhance equalization of middle school enrollments. Conversely, decisions to focus industrial investment and urban growth in selected areas would have the reverse effect. It appears that Mao Zedong's successors are pursuing the latter course, as we shall see.

The Origins of Interprovincial Inequalities in Hospital Beds in the 1950s and 1970s

As with secondary education, relatively urbanized provinces were able to provide more hospital beds per thousand population than other provinces for which we have data (table 6-7). Comparing the performance of the four provinces for which we have information with their aggregate attributes, the province that was almost twice as urbanized as the others did approximately twice as well as the other provinces in providing hospital beds. Food-grain output per capita was apparently not a major factor. If agriculture had been a more salient factor, one would have expected Hunan (the leading per capita food-grain producer) to have done significantly better than Shandong, the province which ranked last (see table 6-3, column a).

While data on the number of hospital beds are exceedingly fragmentary, the appearance of a positive association between percentage of provincial population residing in urban places and level of hospital beds holds if statistical tests are performed.[36]

Several factors account for the apparently close relation between urbanization, industrial output, and hospital bed availability. First, effective demand for hospital facilities is greater in urban areas.

> In a developing country distance is a critical determinant of medical care, and it is widely realized that only those close to a medical unit can derive the full benefit from its services. . . . The average number of outpatient attendances per person per year will be seen to halve itself about every two miles. . . . The number of persons per square mile determines the possibility of providing them with medical care nearly as profoundly as does the distance of a patient's home from a medical unit.[37]

Also, the financial terms of access to curative facilities favored areas with high concentrations of workers covered by the 1951 labor insurance regulations.[38] Starting in 1951, many employees of large or critical industries were covered by labor or medical insurance.[39] For those with medical coverage, most financial barriers to receiving medical care had been removed. Also by at least 1957 medical facilities were receiving periodic allotments proportional to the number of workers for which the hospital was responsible.[40] These benefits and the method by which hospitals were paid linked demand for hospital services to urban areas.

Additionally, workers were concentrated in cities where they could constitute a limited political force. There were continued tensions among the All China Federation of Trade Unions, its membership, and the regime over the level of material and fringe benefits. The stress was particularly acute in 1956 and 1957 in provinces such as Shanxi and Guangdong, which had high

Table 6-7
Hospital Beds per Thousand Population in Four Case Provinces, 1949-1957 (Includes Hospital and Sanatorium Beds)

	1949	1950	1951	1952	1953	1954	1955	1956	1957
National average	.15			.31		.41	.45	.52	.56
Anhui	.0061					.28	.23	.31	.33
Guangdong						.37	.44	.68	
Hunan				.33					.39
Shandong	.06							.32	.32

Source: All hospital bed data from which these statistics were generated are from the following provincial newspapers: *Anhui Ribao, Xin Hunan Bao, Nanfang Ribao, Dazhong Ribao,* and *Qingdao Ribao.* Aggregate national-level data are from *Ten Great Years* (Beijing: Foreign Languages Press, 1960), p. 220. Precise documentation will be provided for each figure upon request.

concentrations of workers. At the Second Congress of the Taiyuan Municipal Party, Party leaders observed that, "many people, and even some Party members and cadres, were not fully aware of the important significance of the production-increase and economy campaign. These people . . . insisted on the improvement of living standards for individuals."[41]

If the relationships suggested are correct, there should be an association between the provision of hospital facilities and the percentage of provincial population with labor insurance.[42] The available data are consistent with the presumed set of relations (table 6-8). In 1956 Canton City had more insured workers than the entire province of Anhui had that year and Shandong had the following year. Guangdong ranked ahead of all the provinces for which data are available.[43]

Identifying the probable sources of interprovincial inequalities in the availability of hospital beds during the 1950s suggests that the twin (and highly correlated) factors of urbanization and the level of per capita GVIO are most important and that both of these variables are reflected in the number of insured workers (see table 6-8). This finding implies that hospital bed inequalities among provinces could be reduced by a policy of equalization of industrial and urban growth. Lardy's work suggests that, prior to 1976, the central authorities in China adopted this approach, and the relatively rapid growth of GVIO in Anhui, Hunan, and Shandong (see table 6-5, column c) seems to reflect the policy.[44]

Table 6-8
Number of Insured Workers, by Province, 1951-1957

	1951	1952	1953	1954	1955	1956	1957
Anhui					62,500 (.20)	63,300 (.19)	
Canton[a]				37,398 (2.33)	46,000 (2.87)	64,000 (3.43)	
Guangdong			78,333 (.23)	94,000 (.27)	150,400 (.42)		
Hunan		50,000 (.15)			141,000 (.41)	283,000 (.80)	280,000 (.78)
Shandong							51,000 (.09)

Source: The absolute numbers of workers with insurance were obtained from the following provincial newspapers: *Anhui Ribao, Xin Hunan Bao, Nanfang Ribao, Dazhong Ribao,* and *Wen Hui Bao.* Precise documentation will be provided upon request.

Note: The numbers in parentheses are the percentage of provincial population with labor insurance.

[a]Nonprovincial-level unit included for information purposes.

Once again, while factors such as degree of urbanization and per capita GVIO are linked to performance, leadership choice at the central level can play a critical role in shaping the long-term structure of the economy and thereby ultimately affect the distribution of hospital beds among provinces.

Did these generalizations hold into the 1960s and 1970s? Because the Chinese have released almost no provincial-level data on hospital beds since 1960, we cannot be certain. A few inferences may be drawn, however. Because Cultural Revolution criticisms of the medical system were aimed at the concentration of medical resources in urban areas, it is almost certain that before 1966, rural provinces continued to do substantially more poorly than relatively urban ones. Even today the largely urbanized provincial-level units of Shanghai and Beijing have hospital resources far in excess of those to which they would be entitled if all resources were distributed equally.

The persistence of interprovincial (and urban-rural) gaps explains the post-Cultural Revolution alterations in the health system. Indeed it is the apparently strong relation between urbanization, industrial output, and hospital beds that led central policymakers in Beijing to try to find an alternative to a hospital-based system. In 1968 a new health care delivery system began to take shape: the cooperative health care system.

Two features of this system are particularly significant. First, production brigade health clinics and commune medical clinics have been established. These clinics employ paramedics, the barefoot doctors, who provide diagnostic, preventive, and limited curative services. Cases requiring additional treatment are supposed to be referred to more comprehensive facilities. The second significant feature is that these services were meant to be financed locally using the resources of cooperative welfare funds and individual contributions; both the welfare funds and individual incomes are very dependent upon the well-being of local agriculture. In contrast to a health system based on hospital care, then, the presence or absence of these medical programs is much more a function of the local agricultural situation than trends in the urban-industrial sector. Indeed, cooperative health programs have had to deal with highly variable local revenues because of their close ties to the local agricultural economy.

The Determinants of Cooperative Health Care Availability in the Late 1960s and the Mid-1970s

The capacity of production brigades to establish and maintain cooperative health programs is tied intimately to local agricultural production; the financial provisions described make it inevitable. The size of commune and brigade welfare funds is directly tied to local agricultural output. These funds receive a fixed percentage of cooperative receipts. Also, peasant incomes are linked directly to agricultural production; as their incomes drop, their ability to pay for medical care declines.

Ideally, in order to demonstrate rigorously the links between local (commune and brigade) agricultural production and the availability of cooperative health programs at these same levels, one would like local production and performance data. Unfortunately such systematic statistics are unavailable. Consequently we have had to assume that program and production increases and decreases occurring at the *provincial level* reflect trends and relationships that we are unable to observe directly at the local level. Using such reasoning the analyst would predict the following sets of relationships between provincial (aggregate) food-grain output and the availability of cooperative health programs at the provincial level: Increases in the percentage of a province's production brigades with cooperative health programs should be associated with increases in aggregate grain production for that same province the preceding year. Conversely, declines in a province's aggregate food-grain output one year should be followed the next year by a decline in the percentage of that province's production brigades with cooperative health programs. The reason for the one-year lag between grain production and program performance is that one year's agricultural increases or decreases are not fully felt until the following year. Quantitative and qualitative data for our case provinces, and national-level aggregate data, all support these presumed relationships.

To test these linkages during the 1971-1975 period, Chinese provinces were divided into those which achieved aggregate increases in food-grain output and those that experienced declines (see Table 6-9). Table 6-10 provides data on each province's performance in providing cooperative health programs during the 1969-1976 period. There were variations in program level within and between provinces.

In table 6-9 and 6-10 there are seventeen provinces for which we have both the food-grain production and program performance data necessary to test the hypothesized relationships. (These provinces are designated by asterisks in table 6-9.) In twelve of the seventeen cases provincial food-grain increases for one year were followed in the next by increases in the availability of cooperative health programs within these same provinces, as predicted. In two of the seventeen cases, documented provincial food-grain declines were followed the next year by decreases in the availability of cooperative health programs within those provinces, as predicted. Only three cases deviated from the hypothesized outcome. One of these cases (Anhui) actually supports the hypothesis when understood. In 1972 provincial grain output in Anhui rose slightly, but the increase was less than the expansion in population; there had been a per capita food-grain decline. This suggests that per capita food-grain production would be a better indicator. Unfortunately we lack sufficient quantitative data to systematically use that variable. Conservatively speaking, fourteen of seventeen cases fit the hypothesis. The odds that this occurred by chance are less than 2 percent.[45]

Examining the case provinces, we find that these aggregate relationships

Table 6-9
Provincial Increases and Decreases in Food-Grain Production, 1971-1975

1971	1972	1973	1974	1975

Provinces with a decline in food-grain production over the previous year:

1971	1972	1973	1974	1975
Guangdong	Guangdong[a]		Anhui	Guangdong[a]
	Guizhou		Sichuan	Guizhou
	Hebei		Xinjiang	Hebei
	Henan			Henan
	Xinjiang			Inner Mongolia
				Jiangsu
				Jiangxi
				Ningxia
				Zhejiang

Provinces with an increase in food-grain production over the previous year:

1971	1972	1973	1974	1975
Anhui[a]	Anhui[a]	Anhui	Guangdong	Anhui
Hebei[a]	Fujian[a]	Fujian	Guangxi	Fujian
Henan	Gansu	Guangdong	Hebei	Gansu[a]
Shanxi	Guangxi[a]	Guangxi[a]	Hubei	Guangxi
Yunnan[a]	Qinghai[a]	Guizhou	Hunan	Heilongjiang
	Shandong	Hebei	Jiangsu	Hubei[a]
		Heilongjiang	Liaoning	Hunan[a]
		Henan		Jilin[a]
		Hubei		Liaoning
		Hunan		Qinghai
		Inner Mongolia[a]		Shaanxi
		Jiangsu		Shandong[a]
		Jilin[a]		Shanxi
		Liaoning		Tibet
		Shaanxi		Xinjiang
		Shandong		
		Sichuan		
		Xinjiang		
		Yunnan		
		Zhejiang		

Source: Provincial performance in food-grain output was determined from "China: Agricultural Performance in 1975," *Research Aid* (Washington, D.C.: Central Intelligence Agency, 1976), p. 18; *Foreign Broadcast Information Service: Daily Report, People's Republic of China* (1972-1973); *China News Summary*, nos. 411, 447, 452, 454, 475, 476, and 497; (American Consulate General, Hong Kong) *Survey of China Mainland Press,* No. 5041 (December 27, 1971), p. 15. Precise documentation for each province will be provided upon request.

[a]A province for which both grain data and the two appropriate consecutive years of cooperatiive health care performance data are available.

hold, except for Anhui in 1971-1972. For instance, Guangdong suffered grain production declines in 1972 and 1975. The years immediately following witnessed reductions in the percentage of production brigades providing cooperative health care. Conversely, both Shandong and Hunan experienced increases

Table 6-10
Percentage of Production Brigades with Cooperative Health Programs,
by Province, 1969-1976

	1969	1970	1971	1972	1973	1974	1975	1976
Anhui			70	68.7	50			
Beijing					75			
Fujian				80	74		80	87
Gansu			80	85			85	90
Guangdong	50	87		100	80		97.3	93
Guangxi				66.7	70	90		95
Guizhou				67.5				
Hebei			80	80.6				
Heilongjiang							94	
Henan							75	
Hubei					83		80	93
Hunan		97.4		February 90 June 50			79	83
Inner Mongolia					33[a]	50	71	
Jiangsu		June 80 September 95						95
Jiangxi				93				
Jilin					68[a]	90[a]	90	
Liaoning								90
Ningxia							80	
Qinghai				42	70	50	70	
Shaanxi		84						86.4
Shandong			50			53	85	90
Shanxi			85					
Sichuan				80				
Tianjin							95	
Xinjiang		70			90			
Yunnan		90		100		80		
Zhejiang			71					

Source: These figures were obtained from provincial radio broadcasts monitored by *Foreign Broadcast Information Service: Daily Report, People's Republic of China* (1973-1976), *Summary of World Broadcasts* (1969-1974), and *The Chinese Medical Journal* 1, no. 1(1975):3-12. One must be critical of figures that allege participation rates of 100 percent. However, the rates of each province taken as a set are in all probability accurate indicators of trends in that province. Precise documentation for each statistic will be provided upon request.

[a]This statistic is for a model area only; the provincewide rate was probably lower, if anything.

in food-grain production in 1975; the following year both provinces achieved increases in program availability.

The close link that appears to exist between agricultural production and cooperative health care in the aggregate provincial-level data also is apparent in the qualitative information coming from lower level units within the case provinces. For example, some basic-level cadres in Xin County, Shandong, were denounced for having let a cooperative health program collapse for allegedly economic reasons. They reportedly, "spread the word that since economic conditions here were so poor, and commune members had no money, the medical cooperative system could not exist any longer."[46]

While it is clear that agricultural prosperity is essential to the survival and growth of cooperative health programs, can it be argued that provincial-level leadership stability is a significant factor affecting a province's capability to implement these programs? Although provincial leadership data are defective in several respects, the data acquired in the course of this study would lead one to conclude that there is little discernible relationship between program performance and the stability of provincial leadership. For instance Guangdong had more shifts in first party secretaries during the 1972-1976 period than any of the other case provinces.[47] While one might hypothesize that such instability would disrupt administration and thereby impair performance, Guangdong did well in providing cooperative health programs. Conversely Hunan had greater continuity of first party secretaries in the 1970-1976 period, with Hua Guofeng providing continual leadership. Yet Hunan did less well in establishing continuity in its cooperative health program than Guangdong. This suggests that while the central leadership in Beijing makes critical choices concerning funding and investment strategies, subsidies, and program shape, the choices made by provincial leaders are not demonstrably important factors in determining provincial performance.

The Fate of Equality after Mao

With the death of Mao Zedong in September 1976, one sees what political analysts since Machiavelli have argued: it makes a difference who, with what skills and values, is leader. During most of Mao's reign, the central policy tendency, as we have seen, was toward equality in the delivery of basic educational and medical services, equality along both the urban-rural and interprovincial dimensions. Educational equality at the primary level was promoted by investment and subsidization policies that facilitated relatively rapid urban and industrial growth in relatively poorer and less urban provinces. Similarly, comparatively rapid industrial and urban growth in previously lagging provinces should (eventually) have produced more equality in middle school education, though the data on this were weaker and the time lags longer. Finally, the cooperative medical service and the deemphasis on hospital facilities in the late-1960s and the first half of the 1970s was an attempt to reduce urban-rural and interprovincial inequalities in the provision of curative health services.

Although the jury is still out, many of the policies identified as having contributed to interprovincial equality have been modified, or abandoned, by Mao's successors. Why? Because his heirs believe that these egalitarian efforts retarded economic growth and were inefficient ways of allocating exceedingly scarce resources. This leads one inexorably to the conclusion that inequalities in the provision of primary and secondary education and medical services will increase, *if* these policies are implemented persistently and effectively. Rising inequalities, of course, do not exclude the possibility that, simultaneously, absolute levels for everyone may climb.

Because the Chinese have not released provincial-level hospital bed and school enrollment figures for the case provinces for the late-1970s and early 1980s, it is not possible to present data comparable to that for the 1950s in order to assess the effects of post-Mao policies. The very nature of these policy changes, however, in the light of the hypotheses presented here, leads one to expect widened interprovincial and urban-rural gaps, unless strong counter-vailing measures are taken. For instance, present investment and budgetary policies should aggravate interprovincial inequalities. Under Mao the central collection of revenues and the central distribution of investment capital, on balance, worked to the advantage of less industrial and less urban provinces because they generally receive relatively more from the central authorities. This policy was reflected in the relatively high GVIO growth figures (table 6-5, column c) for Anhui and Hunan Provinces in the 1960s and early 1970s. However, China's present leaders would agree with Lardy's assessment that "The cost of rapid development of backward areas, in terms of national growth foregone, appears to have been quite high."[48] Now, Beijing is advocating the allocation of investment through banks and charging interest on loans. Provinces and areas with the brightest prospects for repaying the loans presumably would be the first recipients of credit. In the absence of compensatory mechanisms, this would channel investment toward already developed areas. Recent calls to use capital to renovate and expand existent enterprises would further concentrate investment in already advanced locales. Because school enrollments and hospital services are so tied to urban and industrial expansion, these policies should increase relative interprovincial disparities.

Turning specifically to education, school enrollments grew so rapidly during the Cultural Revolution, especially at the middle school level, that the state budget now is unable to provide anything but the most rudimentary service to students. To illustrate, in 1980, a deputy from Sichuan Province to the National People's Congress said that "the average annual fund for a middle school student had gone down by a half since 1965."[49] In order to train a corps of highly competent students, key schools have been reestablished and superior teachers, students, and facilities are provided these institutions on a priority basis.[50] Unsurprisingly, these schools are concentrated in urban areas. In 1978, only four of twenty-five key provincially run primary and secondary schools in Beijing were located in suburban counties where around one-half of the municipality's population lives. Moreover, Beijing, with its twenty-five provincially run key schools had many more such facilities than all of Sichuan Province, which only had nine.[51] As a result, the capital had one such facility for every 332,000 persons while Sichuan had one for every 11.1 million residents. Concurrently, the regime has begun to talk about the need for rural areas to shoulder more educational expenses themselves.

> In view of the fact that the state is still unable to finance the operation of all the schools, it remains necessary to encourage the communes and production brigades to run their schools largely at their own expense, namely, to practice the traditional method of "having people run schools with government subsidy."[52]

The implication is that rural provinces will do less well (qualitatively *and* quantitatively) in providing education than comparatively urbanized areas. Gaps will probably widen.

Another area of policy should increase inequalities in the provision of educational opportunities. Provinces and various enterprises are being given incentives to increase production by being permitted to retain a share of the revenues created by above-quota production and profits. Although much remains unclear, provinces with a large industrial base should have relatively more extrabudgetary funds. In the past, education has been a major recipient of such monies. It was no accident that the first secretary of relatively industralized and urbanized Jiangsu Province said in 1980, "the province planned to increase its appropriations for education by retrenching other expenditures, [and] *drawing on local financial resources*" (emphasis added).[53]

Finally, in the earlier discussion of the determinants of educational enrollments in Guangdong (and Fujian), we noted the importance of an idiosyncratic factor—the role of Overseas Chinese remittances used to support education. In 1980 the authorities in Guangdong noted,

> Guangdong Province is encouraging Overseas Chinese and compatriots in Hong Kong and Macao to contribute to education in their home towns. The work of running schools with funds from Overseas Chinese has been resumed now after a ten-year halt. A number of new school buildings funded by Overseas Chinese compatriots in Hong Kong and Macao are now under construction.[54]

This inflow of resources will be an additional factor allowing relatively industralized coastal areas to make comparatively large gains, thereby widening interprovincial gaps. Too, coastal areas are aggressively soliciting foreign investment; this should further accelerate industrial and urban expansion along the eastern seaboard, presuming the policy endures.

Turning to the delivery of health services, it was precisely because of the close linkage between urban and industrial growth and the availability of hospital services that Mao argued for the creation of a rural paramedic-based system. Although this rural system probably will not be entirely abandoned, several post-Mao policy decisions have reemphasized hospitals at the county levels and above, accorded less emphasis to the rural delivery system, and have, to some extent, weakened the financial underpinnings of the cooperative health system.[55] Emphasis on hospitals inevitably exacerbates urban-rural gaps and, given varying rates of provincial urbanization, interprovincial disparities in the delivery of curative medical services.

To be precise, in 1979 Minister of Public Health Qian Xinzhong announced his ministry's intention to modernize one-third of China's county hospitals. Both the 1979 and 1980 state plans called for the construction of 80,000 hospital beds each year, an annual rate of construction well above the annual rates for the previous thirty years.[56] Second, there have been documented declines in both the numbers of production brigades with cooperative health programs and the numbers of barefoot doctors.[57] Besides the vagaries of agricultural production, which explain some yearly variations, two new policies have contributed to this decline. First, cooperative health programs, funded substantially from collective welfare funds are to some extent redistributive. Beijing is trying to diminish the redistributive functions of communes in order to enhance individual production incentives. Second, with the assignment of production quotas to households (with the household able to freely market above quota production), many barefoot doctors simply feel it now is more lucrative to work for the household than the collective.[58]

To summarize, it still is too early to document the effects (either generally or vis-à-vis the five case provinces) of post-Mao policies on the distribution of educational enrollments and curative health services among provinces. However, given the very close ties between urban and industrial growth and the provision of educational enrollments and hospital services, one would expect greater interprovincial disparities to result.

One cautionary note by way of conclusion is essential. To say that interprovincial and urban-rural gaps probably will widen is not to assert that large numbers of people necessarily will become worse off in absolute terms. Economic growth could permit some measure of progress for everyone, with only relative gaps increasing. Whether or not this occurs is a central question for the future. Moreover, inequality is not the only possible danger to stability. Growth itself is a destabilizing process and, of course, prolonged economic stagnation would present explosive problems. There is no assuredly safe course. The growth-versus-equality dilemma has been, as discussed in chapter 1, a feature of European communist systems as well.

This raises one final question. What are the probable political consequences of increased inequalities? One could hypothesize that inequalities in the context of absolute declines for some (or all) people would be more explosive than increasing inequalities in the context of progress for all. In the final analysis, much will depend on whether or not some members of the elite seek to mobilize possible dissatisfactions. The denunciation of cadres in Anhui who called for *more* educatonal equality ought to give one pause.

> They also smeared enrolling those who are outstanding as widening the differences between town and countryside, between worker and peasant. . . . They even threateningly said: If such things go unchecked, we would like to see if the poor and lower middle peasants will oppose you.[59]

Conclusions

Three theoretically and practically important conclusions emerge from this study, findings relevant to developmental theorists, policy analysts, and sinologists. First, no single economic variable accounts for the observed interprovincial variations in performance across all of the policy areas examined. Agricultural growth is a precondition to success in cooperative health care (as it is presently funded) and not particularly helpful in obtaining high levels of primary or middle school enrollments, or hospital facilities. While the specific linkages between these particular programs and the economy are peculiar to China, it suggests that policy analysts in the Third World setting (where there is a great bifurcation of the economy into rural and urban sectors) must be sensitive to varying linkages between specific programs and specific sectors of the economy. More particularly, Mao's successors are emphasizing policies that are particularly linked to urban/industrial growth and they are concentrating the resources necessary to produce such growth. This will widen interprovincial and urban-rural inequalities, in the absence of compensatory efforts.

Second, the foregoing finding leads one to refine and revise the conventional wisdom of many developmental and policy studies. Policy studies emerging from rather wealthy industrial societies, such as those of Dye and Wilensky, have generally concluded that program performance is most closely tied to economic variables (usually per capita gross national product). This finding in turn has fit nicely with the prevailing developmental notion that if one emphasizes economic growth, other fundamental values such as equality and participation will automatically be realized in its wake. As Huntington and Nelson and Chenery have begun to argue, both trends have tended to negate the importance attached to leadership choice, making it appear that the only job of the political leader is to maximize aggregate economic growth. Such a conclusion is not warranted by this study.

Central policymakers in China (as elsewhere) face an enormous array of difficult choices. As this study has shown, equality of education and medical services among Chinese provinces is affected by the leadership's choice of financing arrangements, by choices concerning which areas to designate as key points for investment, by decisions about whether to emphasize investment in agriculture or industry, by decisions about whether or not to subsidize various programs and provinces, and by the particular provisions and configurations of programs themselves.

The critical point is that while leaders can never eliminate economic constraints, their political choices do shape the long-term structure of those constraints and, in the short run, determine how those economic variables will manifest themselves through concrete programs. Most important, leadership policy choice reflects value choice. With Mao's death, policy choices have changed and we anticipate this will have distributional effects, as well as incentive and productivity effects.

Third, one need not assume that interprovincial variation in program performance reflects significant discretionary authority available to provincial leaders. The layering of authority is such that the decisions that most affect levels of provincial performance are generally made in Beijing. This suggests that provincial leaders have a stake in influencing national policymakers in at least two respects: first, provincial leaders who wish to maximize the performance of "their" provinces would be well advised to attempt to encourage central authorities to adopt programs they believe to be consistent with the constraints imposed by each province. Second, provincial leaders should push for more state investment and they should marginally prefer those forms of investment that will most strengthen the provincial economy in the areas most important to achieving priority objectives. A major question for further research is how these presumed interests have been concretely articulated and whether Chinese leaders define their interests in this way. Certainly what little information we do have on the budgetary process in China suggests that provincial leaders do seek consciously and openly to minimize the outflow of provincial resources and maximize the allocations made to their respective provinces.

To conclude, the provision of education and health services in China, as elsewhere, is shaped by economic variables. However, policymakers need not only to know this, but also to understand which program is affected by which sector of the economy and how. These complex relationships provide national policymakers with important areas of choice. These choices in turn are guided by fundamental values and the interaction of local and national political leaders. The task of future research is to identify more precisely how much latitude for choice in fact exists, why certain values come to dominate any given decision process, how various political actors seek to influence these critical choices, and what are the long-term consequences of present decisions.

Notes

1. David M. Lampton "Performance and the Chinese Political System: A Preliminary Assessment of Education and Health Policies," *China Quarterly* 75

*(*1978): 509-539; William L. Parish, "Egalitarianism in Chinese Society," *Problems of Communism* (January-February 1981): 37-53; Nicholas R. Lardy, "Regional Growth and Income Distribution: The Chinese Experience," Yale University Economic Growth Center Discussion Paper 240.

2. Samuel P. Huntington and Joan M. Nelson, *No Easy Choice: Political Participation in Developing Countries* (Cambridge, Mass.: Harvard University Press, 1976), p. 20.

3. Thomas R. Dye, *Politics, Economics, and the Public: Policy Outcomes in the American States* (Chicago: Rand McNally, 1966); Harold L. Wilensky, *The Welfare State and Equality: Structural and Ideological Roots of Public Expenditures* (Berkeley: University of California Press, 1975).

4. Victor C. Falkenheim, "Provincial Leadership in Fukien: 1949-66," in Robert A. Scalapino, ed., *Elites in the People's Republic of China* (Seattle: University of Washington Press, 1972), pp. 199-244.

5. For a more thorough discussion concerning the choice and reliability of these indicators, see Lampton, "Performance and the Chinese Political System," pp. 511-514.

6. G. William Skinner, "Regional Urbanization in Nineteenth-Century China," in G. William Skinner, ed., *The City in Late Imperial China* (Stanford, Calif.: Stanford University Press, 1977), pp. 211-249.

7. Frederick C. Teiwes, "Provincial Politics in China: Themes and Variations," in John M.H. Lindbeck, ed., *China: Management of a Revolutionary Society* (Seattle: University of Washington Press, 1971), pp. 116-189.

8. Tom Wiens, "Transcript: Advanced Training Seminar on Subnational Politics and Development in the PRC," (New York: East Asian Institute, Columbia University, 1976), pp. 89-94.

9. For such provincial-level units as Tibet, Guizhou, or Qinghai, the inequalities would have been much greater.

10. Nicholas R. Lardy, "Centralization and Decentralization in China's Fiscal Management," *China Quarterly* 61 (1975): 25-60; also, Lardy, "Regional Growth and Income Distribution."

11. Wiens, "Transcript," p. 90.

12. Yu Yao-nung, "Speech by Yu Yao-nung," in *Current Background* 356 (Hong Kong: U.S. Consulate General): 41.

13. Ibid., pp. 41-42.

14. Donald G. Gillin, *Warload: Yen Hsi-shan in Shansi Province, 1911-1949* (Princeton, N.J.: Princeton University Press, 1967), p. 302.

15. We analyzed the relationship between average per capita GVIO (Table 6-3, column b) and the level of primary enrollment for those years for which we have the *relatively* most complete primary education performance data (1949, 1952, 1955, 1956, and 1957). When the data were analyzed as interval-level data, the strength of positive association, as measured by Pearson's R, varied from 0.91 (significant to the .12 level) to 0.64 (significant to the .27

level). When the data were expressed as rank orders for each year, the Tau *B*'s varied from 1.0 to .6. The percent of provincial population in urban areas (table 6-3, column c) is positively correlated with the level of primary school enrollment. The strength of association as measured by Tau *B* varied from 1.0 to 0.8 and when measured by Pearson's *R*, varied from 0.92 (significant to the .12 level) to 0.67 (significant to the .10 level). Complete statistical data will be supplied upon request.

16. *Nanfang Ribao* [Southern Daily], August 27, 1951. In *Current Background* 128 (Hong Kong: U.S. Consulate General): 3-6.

17. Audrey Donnithorne, *China's Economic System* (New York: *Praeger*, 1967), pp. 389 and 393.

18. Nai-ruenn Chen, *Chinese Economic Statistics* (Chicago: Aldine, 1967), pp. 451-467.

19. *Dazhong Ribao* [The Masses Daily], August 17, 1957, in Joint Publications Research Service, DC-196, CSO: DC-1529.

20. *Shanxi Ribao* [Shanxi Daily], December 9, 1956.

21. Stephen Fitzgerald, *China and the Overseas Chinese* (London: Cambridge University Press, 1972), p. 132.

22. *Anhui Ribao* [Anhui Daily], October 1, 1957, in *Survey of China Mainland Press* 1639 (Hong Kong: U.S. Consulate General):29.

23. *Dazhong Ribao* [The Masses Daily], August 17, 1957.

24. *Shanxi Ribao* [Shanxi Daily], May 12, 1958, in Joint Publications Research Service, DC-438, CSO:DC-2226, p. 8.

25. *Dazhong Ribao* [The Masses Daily], August 17, 1957.

26. Delegation of the American Association of State Colleges and Universities to the People's Republic of China, *Impressions of Modern China* (Washington, D.C.: American Association of State Colleges and Universities, 1975), p. 21.

27. Leo A. Orleans, *Professional Manpower and Education in Communist China* (Washington, D.C.: National Science Foundation, 1961), p. 32.

28. Hunan Provincial Service, February 2, 1972, in *Summary of World Broadcasts* (London: British Broadcasting Corporation), FE/3923/BII/7.

29. Hollis B. Chenery et al., eds., *Redistribution with Growth* (London: Oxford University Press, 1974).

30. Peter Zwick, "Intrasystem Inequality and the Symmetry of Socioeconomic Development in the USSR," *Comparative Politics* 8 (1976): 501-523. Zwick finds that this is true in the Soviet Union.

31. When the data were analyzed as interval-level data, the strength of positive association between the percentage of population living in urban places (table 6-3, column c) and middle school enrollment levels, as measured by Pearson's *R*, varied from 0.9 (significant to the .01 level) to 0.85 (significant to the .03 level). When the data were expressed as rank orders for each year, the Tau *B*'s varied from 0.8 to 0.4. Average per capita GVIO (table 6-3, column b) is positively correlated with the level of middle school enrollment. The

strength of association as measured by Tau *B* varied from 0.6 to 0.2 and when measured by Pearson's *R* varied from 0.81 (significant to the .04 level) to 0.75 (significant to the .06 level).

32. Fitzgerald, *China and the Overseas Chinese,* p. 125.

33. Lardy, "Centralization and Decentralization."

34. Delegation of the American Association of State Colleges and Universities to the People's Republic of China, p. 29.

35. Lampton, "Performance and the Chinese Political System," p. 525.

36. The strength of positive correlation between percent of population in urban areas (table 6-3, column c) and a province's provision of hospital beds per thousand population (for the years 1956 and 1957), when measured by Pearson's *R*, varied from 0.99 (significant to the .002 level) to 0.66 (significant to the .26 level). When the data were expressed as rank orders for each year, the Tau *B*'s varied from 1.0 to 0.33. As well, I suspect and statistical tests confirm in all but one case, that average GVIO per capita (table 6-3, column b) is positively associated with hospital beds per thousand population.

37. Maurice King, ed., *Medical Care in Developing Countries* (London: Oxford University Press, 1966), pp. 2:6-2:8.

38. Joyce Kallgren, "Social Welfare and China's Industrial Workers," in A. Doak Barnett, ed., *Chinese Communist Politics in Action* (Seattle: University of Washington Press, 1969), pp. 540-573.

39. Donnithorne, *China's Economic System,* p. 213.

40. *Weekly Information Report on Communist China* 205, Summary no. 1777 (May 26, 1958): 37.

41. New China News Agency, February 2, 1957, in *Survey of China Mainland Press* 1471 (Hong Kong: U.S. Consulate General):16.

42. We chose the number covered by labor insurance instead of medical insurance because the data are better for the former than the latter.

43. See Table 6-8. There is an ambiguity in the coverage of the 1953, 1954, and 1955 figures for Guangdong, but this does not affect the analysis.

44. See notes 1 and 10.

45. The chi-square test was applied. For an explanation, see Hubert M. Blalock, Jr., *Social Statistics* (New York: McGraw-Hill, 1972), pp. 275-285.

46. Shandong Provincial Service, March 20, 1974, in *Foreign Broadcast Information Service: Daily Report, People's Republic of China* (hereafter cited simply as *FBIS*) 61 (1974):C2.

47. Zhao Ziyang, Ding Sheng, and Wei Guoqing.

48. Lardy, "Regional Growth and Income Distribution," p. 45.

49. *FBIS* 174 (1980):L4.

50. *FBIS* 2 (1981):04.

51. David M. Lampton, "New 'Revolution' in China's Social Policy," *Problems of Communism* (September-December 1979):31.

52. *FBIS* 171 (1979):L16; also *FBIS* 242 (1979):L5.

53. *FBIS* 174 (1980):L4.

54. *FBIS* 161 (1980):P1.

55. *FBIS* 55 (1980):L4.

56. *FBIS* 123 (1979):L9; also *FBIS* 69 (1981):K19.

57. *FBIS* 204 (1980):P1; also Lampton, "New 'Revolution' in China's Social Policy," p. 27.

58. *FBIS* 57 (1981): L18.

59. *FBIS* 113 (1978):G1.

7 Inequalities and Yugoslav Political Stability

Susan L. Woodward

The cause of sedition is always to be found in inequality. . . . There are some who stir up sedition because their minds are filled by a passion for equality, which arises from their thinking that they have the worst of the bargain in spite of being the equals of those who have got the advantage. There are others who do it because their minds are filled with a passion for inequality, which arises from their conceiving that they get no advantage over others although they are really more than equal to others. Thus inferiors become revolutionaries in order to be equals, and equals in order to be superiors. —Aristotle[1]

Thus begins Aristotle's lecture on the cause of revolution. Its origin is inequality, but the measure of inequality depends on one's principles of justice. With some historical perspective, one can see that perceptions of injustice also "depend substantially," as Amartya Sen puts it, "on possibilities of actual rebellion." He continues, "The Athenian intellectuals discussing equality did not find it particularly obnoxious to leave out the slaves from the orbit of discourse, and one reason why they could do it was because they could get away with it."[2]

With the death of President Tito in May 1980, the Yugoslav political system entered a period of political uncertainty. No longer able to rely on Tito's personal authority to soothe popular discontent, the socialist regime must find its security in the social and economic changes taking place under its governance. The potential for stability of the Yugoslav state in the the 1980s depends on its vulnerability to disorder. That is, is there inequality? Is it perceived as unjust by some? And, are they likely to rebel? Three kinds of evidence are necessary to answer those questions: (1) what principles guide perceptions of justice in Yugoslavia, (2) whether governmental action conforms to those principles, and (3) what means are available to express discontent should some feel unfairly treated—keeping in mind, of course, Sen's injunction.

Principles of Justice

Socialism aims at equality. It emphasizes the common humanity and thus equal worth of human beings and identifies the origin of inequality in the social arrangements created by men and women, not in their nature. The fundamental social relations are those defined by the system of property; the division of people into classes of owners and producers prevents the free development

165

of the producers and treats them as unequals. With the abolition of private property, humans can be treated as equals, differentiating among them according to needs rather than property. This ethical principle has a practical correlate. Social welfare is maximized once the equal freedom of individuals fosters their self-development and the goods of society are fully available for social use.

The leadership's response to the Cominform Resolution of 1948, excommunicating Yugoslavia from the socialist commonwealth of Eastern Europe, had a profound effect on the definition of socialist equality in Yugoslavia. Declaring Stalinism a bureaucratic deformation of the principle of social ownership, the League of Communists began a total reorganization of economy and society on the principle of self-management. Treatment as equals was redefined as the equal right to participate in all social decisions—among workers at their workplace, citizens in their neighborhoods and communes, and nations within the federation. To make this formal, political equality effective, constitutional guarantees of the preconditions for human development and treatment as equals were reaffirmed: the right to work, to education, and to cultural expression.

As for distribution, they returned to Marx's argument in *Critique of the Gotha Program* that equal right during the first stage of communist society must still be "in principle—bourgeois right," by which he meant:

> The right of the producers is *proportional* to the labour they supply; the equality consists in the fact that measurement is made with an *equal standard*, labour. But one man is superior to another physically or mentally and so supplies more labour in the same time, or can labour for a longer time; and labour, to serve as a measure, must be defined by its duration or intensity, otherwise it ceases to be a standard of measurement. This *equal* right is an unequal right for unequal labour. It recognises no class differences, because everyone is only a worker like everyone else; but it tacitly recognises unequal individual endowment and thus productive capacity as natural privilege. *It is, therefore, a right of inequality, in its content, like every right.*[3]

Distribution, in other words, would be according to work, not need. Decisions over distribution were handed over to associations of workers as the fundamental right of self-management, of workers to distribute the products of their labor. Any interference with the outcome of those decisions was rejected as bureaucratic, hence illegitimate. Workers within the association who were also members of sociopolitical associations such as the League of Communists and the trade unions would represent society's interest in moving toward communist equality, nurturing a new consciousness in the process, by warning against excess or illegitimate inequalities in wages and benefits and by urging *solidarity* —economic assistance—with workers in enterprises doing less well economically.

A different contract altogether was made with peasants and some craftsmen.

They could choose to exempt themselves from the social sector of associated workers and own their land and tools instead. They would, however, continue to be subject to the sphere of exchange; the market would distribute their income and from it, they would pay taxes to society for public goods. In addition, between 1948 and 1965, the country moved slowly but inexorably away from planning and toward market principles for the entire economy, so that distribution of income within work associations came increasingly to depend on the productivity of labor as measured by world market prices.

It is not clear that the redefinition of equality by the introduction of self-management has been adopted by all Yugoslavs. Evidence from work stoppages and strikes, student demonstrations, conflicts within workers' councils, and sociological research of public opinion all points to a fundamental and in some cases intensely felt disagreement over what is fair and equal in Yugoslav society. On one side, there are those who define equality in terms of self-management and social ownership. They find inequality in wages and benefits acceptable and, for some, even desirable as an incentive to greater productivity and economic growth. On the other side are those who also value economic development but who focus on the substantive concept of equal distribution instead of self-management.

This division follows the Aristotelian distinction between those less advantaged by social distribution and those who have benefited. The poorer and less secure are the material circumstances of Yugoslavs and the lower their social status, the more strictly egalitarian are their principles of distribution; the wealthier, more secure, and higher status the Yugoslav, the more inequality is acceptable and self-management valued.[4] This is especially apparent among youth, but it is also the case in work associations. Strikes and work stoppages overwhelmingly originate among unskilled and semiskilled workers protesting the inegalitarian distribution of income in their enterprise.[5] Response from enterprise directors or even local officials comes, however, if the protest turns to claims that rights to self-management have been usurped. In Ellen Comisso's study of a large machine tool factor in Zagreb, this divide found expression in the definition of self-management itself. Executives regarded self-management as a procedure, but blue-collar workers thought of self-management in terms of substantive outcomes.[6] In a general attitude survey of the Serbian population, researchers identified a "modernist" ideology among respondents who were politically supportive and materially better off; they valued social ownership and self-management but tended to ignore material possessions and egalitarian ideas. Their opposites, labeled traditionalist in the research, were individualistic, localist, materialist, supporters of private property, and radical egalitarians.[7] Finally, there is disagreement as well on the criterion that should guide distribution according to work. In surveys peasants, artisans, and shopfloor workers say that income should be distributed in terms of the amount, quality, difficulty, and danger of the work performed. Middle strata within both factories and offices, however, think educational qualifications should determine income, whereas managers and political leaders would add to those educational qualifications the complexity of the work.[8]

Policies and Inequality

Governmental policy in Yugoslavia sets the conditions under which self-management and distribution according to work as determined by the autonomous decisions of workers operate. It assumes that distribution according to work can produce unacceptable inequalities if the conditions under which enterprises earn incomes and individuals obtain jobs give prior advantage to some, that is, if individual income is not directly a result of labor. The government tries to prevent privileged access to work and income, in particular, through its policies on employment, education, regional development, and general economic conditions.

Income, social security and status, and the effective right to participate in social and governmental decisions are defined by employment in Yugoslavia. By the economic reform of 1965, however, political leaders allowed that socialism and unemployment might coexist on the grounds that a more efficient allocation of labor resources would result and thus an increase in the productivity from which all would benefit. Fighting serious inflation and balance-of-payments deficits since at least 1961, policymakers were also under international pressure to impose classical adjustment and stabilization policies on the Yugoslav economy. These policies led to a deep recession by 1966 and 1967 when employment levels in the social sector declined absolutely. At the same time the demand for jobs was at its highest since 1945 as a result of the postwar baby boom.

It does not seem too far-fetched to suggest that the social turmoil of 1967-1971, and in particular the Croatian events, was a response to these conditions.[9] In all regions of Yugoslavia between 1966 and 1972, except for a momentary surge in 1968 in response to the invasion of Czechoslovakia, party membership declined. The drop was greatest in Croatia.[10] Temporary migration to northern Europe in search of employment, a more frequent choice of Yugoslavs after 1964, came earliest and most massively from Croatia. Particularly in those areas experiencing the worst outflow, this revived historically conditioned nationalist anxiety about declining population, loss of identity, and discrimination at the hands of the federal government or of Serbs. That this nationalism culminated in a student strike against federally defined economic conditions (especially those relating to foreign trade) is hardly surprising if one looks at the unemployment figures: of registered unemployment at the time of the strike (1971), 65.5 percent were under age of 29 and 48.5 percent were younger than 25.[11] Nor is the political restraint of the Slovenes during this time of troubles surprising if one looks at the miniscule unemployment rate for that republic. The riots in Kosovo in 1968, and again in 1981, were also the complaints of university students against miserable employment conditions in Kosovo, a region severely hit by the recession, and against the discriminatory conditions for gaining employment that had resulted from the pro-Serb policies in schools and jobs of the republican government before the purge of Ranković in 1966. Not even the maligned Serbs escaped the unemployment anxiety as the student explosion in Belgrade in June 1968 made abundantly clear.

Unemployment not only threatens political stability because it denies to some the right to treatment as equals. The resulting dependence of the unemployed on others leads to longer term social problems as well. Communal budgets must increase the funds for unemployment compensation. The economic status of the unemployed declines drastically, with consequences for economic growth as well as inequality. The unemployed become "disappointed, indignant, and suspicious of people and society,"[12] both out of their frustration and their growing loss of self-respect. Researchers document greater family disputes and divorce, problems of psychological and social stability, and a growing belief in the greater efficiency of the private sector.[13]

The official unemployment rate has hovered around 8 percent of the labor force since 1965-66, while revisions to include those not registered or temporarily employed abroad usually bring this rate to 10 percent or higher. According to the Organization for Economic Cooperation and Development (OECD), labor market conditions were weakening by the end of 1979 with a faster than average rise in the number of job seekers among the more highly educated and skilled, among women, and among youth.[14]

Governmental policies to reduce unemployment in Yugoslavia are indirect; monetary, and to some extent fiscal, policies are aimed at reducing inflation and stimulating production so that enterprise can employ more workers. There is no effort to create works programs or increase government spending. The difficulty is that these policies have increasingly become dictated by the need to restore some equilibrium to the balance of payments, both by expanding exports and reducing imports, and by deflationary policies—devaluation and restrictive credit and incomes policies. The consequences of such policies, however, are lower growth and greater unemployment. Federal economic resolutions of the last few years have begun to recognize this and so project reduced growth in employment, a trend that will continue as a result of the restrictive monetary and incomes policies of the 1980 and 1981 stabilization efforts (3 percent growth in employment was predicted for 1980 in contrast to 4.25 percent in 1979, and at a time when, as in 1966 and 1967, the number of first job seekers was rising rapidly).[15] The legally binding obligation on republican and communal governments to balance their budgets quarterly also restricts employment growth, and official limits are now being placed on investment in social services, where employment has been greatest in recent years. These austerity measures had extended to unemployment compensation by the middle of 1981. At the enterprise level, increasing resort to methods of improving productivity without adding workers, such as honoraria to pensioners for part-time work and overtime,[16] also limits new employment opportunities.

This situation has been exacerbated by the recession in Europe since 1974 because it has slowed the employment of workers abroad and even sent many home, on the average of 80,000 a year to Yugoslavia (although only 15,000 a year in 1977 and 1978). The government's response to the problem of employing returned workers was to encourage expansion of the private, nonagricultural sector and to create means by which a worker can invest his earnings in an enterprise in exchange for the guarantee of employment. Although this policy might gain the short-term flexibility needed (it has not been successful thus far), it also creates troublespots in rural areas. Local conflicts between returned workers and the rest of a village have arisen, and there is discontent at the visible inequalities in consumption that foreign exchange deposits make possible. If workers remain in northern Europe, on the other hand, their children encounter disadvantages in both schooling and employment that only prolong inequalities into another generation.

Despite a high unemployment rate, the rate of job vacancies was also on the rise in 1978 and 1979, and unemployment varied significantly across regions (in 1979, Slovenia's unemployment rate was 1.5 percent of its social sector labor force whereas in Macedonia, the rate was 20 percent and in Serbia, 25 percent.)[17] In other words a significant aspect of the unemployment problem is its regional imbalance. The solution proposed by most Western observers and Yugoslav officials is to increase labor mobility among regions. Implementing a program to encourage such mobility where forced labor is constitutionally forbidden and centrally directed manpower policy would violate both self-management and federalism is difficult, however. The current educational reform is designed, among other goals, to improve the coordination of manpower plans between schools and firms.

Yet the methods remain indirect, and some of the problems that result have been studied. For example, the cultural and ethnic barriers to labor mobility in Yugoslavia are high; where people do move across republic or provincial lines in search of work, they tend to join relatives and friends, usually in the next republic, rather than move to the republic with the greatest number of job vacancies.[18] This pattern, of movement from Kosovo or Macedonia to Serbia, for example, only exacerbates current unemployment problems. According to Slovenian surveys, secondly, workers from less developed republics travel to jobs in Slovenia because of the higher rates of social benefits—social insurance, housing subsidies, health care, pensions—not because of employment opportunities alone. Since the central government has now established limits on the amounts enterprises may spend on collective consumption goods as a part of its deflationary economic policies, the effective incentive to labor mobility will be removed. (The OECD presents this as the first step in a long-term policy to transfer much of the burden of such services to individuals; the amounts spent by enterprises in Slovenia on collective consumption began to decline as early as 1978.[19]) Third, whether or not this flow slows down, the conflicts often produced by labor migration—prejudice, ghettoization, reinforced patterns of disadvantage—have been documented in Slovenia since the early 1970s.[20] In homogeneous Slovenia, at least, the policy to reduce one inequality appears to be creating others.

The regional maldistribution of employment opportunities reflects a larger inequality that government policy is pledged to erase. No government in Yugoslavia is secure, as the destructive conflicts of the 1918-1945 period show, that does not attempt to reassure each nationality that it is being fairly treated. The current policy declares its standard in the opening lines of the 1974 Constitution:

> The nations of Yugoslavia, proceeding from the right of every nation to self-determination, including the right to secession, on the basis of their will freely expressed in the common struggle of all nations and nationalities in the National Liberation War and Socialist Revolution, and in conformity with their historic aspirations, aware that further consolidation of their brotherhood and unity is in the common interest, have, together with the nationalities with which they live, united in a federal republic of free and equal nations and nationalities and founded a socialist federal community of working people—the Socialist Federal Republic of Yugoslavia.[21]

Just as self-management was designed to guarantee political equality to citizens, so the federal structure, defining republican and provincial boundaries along ethnic lines where possible, was to guarantee self-determination to nations. Conflicts between the republics and the federal government over the distribution of economic and political power, particularly the claims by wealthier republics that federal policy does not serve their interests, have usually been met with further decentralization of the federation (extending powers to the republics and the scope of the market). When federal coordination of policy is required, the representatives of nations meet on the basis of parity and take decisions on consensus where each has a veto.[22]

Because of the significant differences in economic development among Yugoslav regions, these formal guarantees of equality, as well as the extensive decentralization of power, put the less developed regions at a disadvantage. To remove this disadvantage, the federal government has reserved the power to define and implement regional development policy. This policy has changed several times since 1945. Since the early 1960s policy has aimed at fiscal redistribution. Revenues, based until 1971 on a capital tax on enterprises, are transferred through a federal fund for development from the more developed

regions (MDRs) as subsidies of governmental budgets and supplements to investment funds in the less developed regions (LDRs). More recently, hopes have
been pinned on reducing federal mediation; the current proposal is to encourage
direct transfers of labor (northward) and of capital (southward) between regions.
Regional development policy has been subject to intense debate over the distribution of relative burdens, whether it harms development in LDRs or hinders
growth in MDRs for example, as well as over the appropriateness of the strategy
itself. As with individuals, the measurement of regional differences depends on
normative definitions of development, and perceptions of fairness depend on
one's perspective, in this case exacerbated by historical antagonisms and past
discrimination. These conflicts make it difficult, therefore, to find generally
acceptable analyses of the consequences for inequality of development policy.

One attempt by a Slovenian development economist to create a dynamic
measure of regional disparities provides interesting evidence, however.[23] If one
looks simply at annual disparities among regions between 1954 and 1974, the
growth rates of gross material product (GMP), employment, and productivity
in the social sector have been the same or higher in LDRs than in MDRs. Differences in per capita income have not decreased and in some cases even
increased somewhat, but this inequality has been produced mainly by the larger
proportion of the agricultural sector in LDR economies, that is, in the aggregate,
by a lower productivity of labor in the south. Regional disparities in per capita
income even decrease in years of good harvest. Regional disparities in living
standards may not be as great, furthermore, if one believes that larger households in the LDRs, where population growth rates are much higher, can benefit
from economies of scale. Since differences in consumption between northern
and southern households can be seen mainly in the purchase of luxury goods,
one might also argue that income inequalities do not reflect as great a difference
in welfare levels. Life expectancy differences between north and south had
closed by1970; mortality rates were nearly identical, although their composition
differed (for example, higher rates before the age of five in Kosovo and higher
rates at all age categories above five years in Slovenia); and the differences in
caloric intake were far greater between agricultural and nonagricultural households within a region than were the differences among regions. Federal income
transfers had reduced the differences in budgetary expenditures on public and
social services from those that would have resulted from the local income
base.

Development is a measure of change, however, and the mixed picture
from annual comparisons tells even less about whether the disparities in regional
economies are being reduced over time. Sicherl tries to measure whether the
time it will take a poorer region to reach the level of the developed regions
has been declining. He finds that this "time-distance" among regions has been
growing. Further, the most important factor in the regional disparity in per
capita income is the difference in employment opportunities. (Of the 11.5

years time-distance for GMP per capita between LDRs and MDRs in 1971, 5.1 were due to employment structure, only 2 to demographic trends, and 4.4 to productivity, itself largely due to employment structure also.[24] Employment opportunities have been growing at a faster rate in the LDRs from 1954 to 1974, except for 1966 and 1967. Thus in addition to more impoverished initial conditions, the LDRs suffered disproportionately from the slowdown in investment and production after the 1965 reform of investment and development planning and the accompanying restrictive monetary policies. It was not until 1968 that employment in the country reached its 1965 level, while employment in the social sector reached the 1965 level only in 1970. This two-year stagnation in employment had far deeper consequences for the less developed regions, however, as is revealed in Sicherl's time-distance measure for employment. In 1961 after extensive expansion of employment in the south, the time distance between MDRs and LDRs was 7 years. By 1965 it has *grown* to 9 years, and by 1970 the projected 14 years was instead 16.[25]

Other measures of regional inequality can be devised, and the results of the 1981 census will reveal a far clearer picture. It does seem clear that federal policy of economic stabilization harms the less developed regions more than the north because of the cumulative impact of slower growth and less investment on less industrialized, less self-sufficient economic structures. According to this analysis differences among regions might appear to be declining if some static measures, such as growth rates or in some years per capita income, are examined, but if one looks at dynamic measures of development, the regional differences have in fact worsened. As a result of this increase in dynamic disparities among regional development, furthermore, inequalities within republics and provinces are on the rise. By 1975, to take one measure, the intraregional spread of incomes (measured among communes) was greater than the interregional spread, and the widest gap was that between the social and private sectors within each region.[26] Within the last few years, by another measure, the variation in net personal earnings for the same kind of work has been increasing.[27] And within the social sector, escalator clauses recently added to pensions and wages in the service sector increase the remuneration of those jobs over industrial occupations.

Finally these data mean that continued high growth rates and assistance from the MDRs are essential to closing the gap between the richer and poorer regions. Yet growth rates have been declining and the regional development policy is again under attack by the wealthier regions (Slovenia in particular) as they feel the pinch of international economic conditions and of the austerity measures prescribed by the International Monetary Fund (IMF) for loans. This potential tax revolt will be strengthened by the effect of these conditions and policies on distribution within republics, for example, the influence of inflation and tight credit on luxury consumption, the restrictions on those collective consumption expenditures by enterprises that made the difference between northern and southern living standards, or the overall decline in real household earnings which the OECD predicts will be marked in 1980 and 1981.[28] Strikes are already on the rise in the north, mainly in Croatia but also Slovenia, particularly in those enterprises where wages have been insecure because of world market fluctuations.[29]

Regional development, opportunities for employment, and government economic policy all create inequalities within Yugoslavia. Which individuals benefit and which suffer, however, is largely a matter of the level and kind of their education. More than any other criterion, income and status in Yugoslavia tends to reflect education. Distribution according to work within associations of workers has tended to become distribution according to formal qualifications. The higher people's education the more they participate in self-management organizations and decisionmaking as well. Unhindered, equal access to education is thus crucial to a sense of fair distribution.

Until recently governmental policy toward education had two aims: to eliminate illiteracy through universal, free, obligatory, elementary schooling, and to include as many students as possible in secondary and higher level training through an expanded network of schools, government stipends, dormitories, two-year colleges, and, in the early days, adult education in literacy programs and trade union seminars. The most recent reform, begun in the mid-1970s, addresses inequalities that the eduational system itself perpetuates: through differences in the kinds of secondary education, access to universities, and links between educational preparation and the workplace. Its goals are to make the choice of occupation fairer by weakening the tie between education and an individuals' social origin that persists, and to reduce unemployment by improved manpower planning and counseling.

The first aim has led to a reform of secondary education. It establishes a common program for the first two years of secondary education, eliminates the *gimnazija* and thus the traditional two-track schooling system of college preparatory education for the more privileged and vocational education for everyone else, and introduces work experience into every curriculum. It also reorganizes educational institutions and programs to bring educators and workers together to coordinate educational and manpower policy (in school centers at the secondary level, in the self-managing communities of interest in education that finance education and establish policy, and in forums yet to be created for planning at the secondary and postsecondary level between enterprises and schools).

The second aim has led to greater direction of the process by which individuals are trained for and distributed among occupations. Legislatures revised the list of occupational categories (from several to several hundred) and unified the previously dual scale of skill levels (one for manual occupations, one for white-collar positions). The number of places available at each secondary school and university faculty are being redefined, planned, and in most cases limited in accordance with the needs of the economy. Priority in secondary school enrollment will be given to youth who have contracted with an organization of associated labor for employment after schooling and a stipend. The purpose of this contractual arrangement is to train individuals for a specific job and thus eliminate the allocational irrationalities causing unemployment, to guarantee jobs to youth, and to make organizations of associated labor more responsible for the educational and manpower planning that is ultimately in their interest to do.

A third aspect of the current reform is more directly addressed to the apprehension over political stability during the last years of Tito's life. Personnel commissions to assess the moral-political fitness of candidates for teaching positions, particularly at the university level, have been reintroduced. Marxist teachings have returned to a prominent place in the curriculum of secondary and university level education. The elimination of the *gimnazija* may even be viewed as part of an ideological campaign against the status and influence of professionals and managers.

In principle this educational reform threatens the entire process of cultural inheritance and social mobility in Yugoslavia, that is, the ability of parents to pass on social privileges to their children through a place in the educational system.[30] Its potential consequences have not been lost on those parents and teachers who stand to lose, and their resistance has slowed its implementation, diverted much of its activity into procedural questions, and led to distortions in the contracting process.[31] In particular the pervasive use of personal connections to circumvent rules in Yugoslavia has thus far allowed some parents to undermine the equalizing intent of the reform. Enterprise contracts have become the object of intense competition among parents. In the first years of the reform the demand for places in nonmanual occupations has been intense, filled more often by parents' connections than their childrens' qualifications. Many contracts have even been falsified. Places for manual occupations, on the other hand, have gone partly or completely unfilled. Education ministry officials are trying to develop regulations for the contracts, against their own intentions to hand such decisions over to organizations of associated labor, to ensure that contracts become "neither a privilege for individuals nor a way to prevent the best students from getting places."[32] Many parents of former *gimnazija*-bound students have also hired private tutors for their children to assure their previous advantage in access to preferred university faculties. Thus far the social origin of students who gain places in schools that train for higher prestige occupations has changed little.

In the long run this new system should break up the sharp social distinction that resulted from *gimnazija* and vocational school tracking.[33] Yet the reform ignores the elementary school where the problem begins: children of peasant and unskilled workers' families tend not to continue their education at the secondary level at all.[34] The reform makes it easier for authorities to limit the demand for white-collar positions through restricted school enrollments, if they are willing to assert that power, but it does not reduce the importance of formal skill qualifications to individual welfare and status; in fact, the multiplication of skill and occupational categories may intensify that bond. Like earlier manpower plans, it assumes no substitutability in skills, factor mixes, production technologies, or even qualities of education,[35] and so makes no real reform of the current relation between education and work. Finally, in terms of the structure of unemployment in Yugoslavia, the reform makes no provision for manpower needs arising out of the proposed expansion of the private sector or for interregional imbalances between labor supply and demand.

In conclusion, if the reform begins to work as intended, there are significant groups who stand to lose status and privilege and who can be expected to increase their resistance to the reform, including attempts to reassert the value of meritocratic over political or egalitarian criteria. If the reform continues to operate as it has begun, the frustrations associated with the scarcity of social sector jobs will not abate and feelings of injustice in the access to contracts for nonmanual occupations could grow. But these developments will not take place independently of the economy itself. If the current contraction from the austerity measures of stabilization policy and the world recession continues, and Hammel's conclusions about social mobility from the 1915-1965 period hold after 1980,[36] the reform may have little effect *and* the more privileged groups will be relatively secure. If the intent of the reform is justice—opening up positions to those unfairly excluded on the basis of social origin—as well as a more efficient labor market, and the measures of the reform continue as begun, the Yugoslav economy will have to continue to grow, and certainly at higher rates than were projected for employment in 1980 and 1981.

This discussion has focused on three sources of inequality in access to the means of individual welfare, that is, to work. Any attempt to analyze the outcome of economic distribution in Yugoslavia is beyond its scope and would be plagued not only by the inadequacy of data but also by the need to confront more precisely what social welfare function would form the basis of the measurement of inequality. Evidence presented here suggests that inequalities do exist, that they may have grown over time, and that they give rise to feelings of unfairness and even occasionally to protest. The question therefore becomes what the chances are that these feelings will become translated into discontent with the political order itself and what the possibilities are for expressing that discontent.

The Possibilities of Actual Rebellion

In surveys of public opinion taken over the last fifteen years, 60-65 percent of the Yugoslav population report that they are generally satisfied with current conditions, the political system, and self-management. Of the other 35-40 percent, many plead no opinion or abstain. As in their attitudes toward equality, however, this satisfaction tends to be very highly correlated with the respondent's material and status circumstances: the more urban, more highly educated, and the wealthier the Yugoslav, the more supportive he or she is of the current system. Upwardly mobile workers, particularly peasant-workers and routine white-collar workers, are particularly positive. Differences between men and women do not show up in their responses to attitude surveys, and those between urban and rural residents decline rapidly over the period from 1965 to 1978. Critical and oppositional attitudes, on the other hand, are found in two groups: those of very poor material circumstances, and especially the unemployed; and those identified earlier as traditional, above all among those employed full time in agriculture and in the private sector.[37]

Avenues for Discontent

While no rumble of rebellion can be heard in these surveys, discontent is there. What avenues for its expression exist? Of the three main methods the most common is a personal one: to find a private, individual solution. The scramble for contracts in education, the increased recourse to overtime, part-time work, and moonlighting, the strength of kinship ties in urban settings and between urban and rural relatives, and the persistence of VIP (resort to connections and acquaintances), now grown into NAVIP (particularly influential connections), all attest to this. The particular methods and likelihood of success depend, of course, on personal resources. The greater an individual's resources—wealth, education, political influence, urban residence, influential friends and relatives—the more possibilities he has for advantageous private solutions. Although legislation to further individual equality can be undermined this way, this outlet also protects the political system from the discontent of the privileged over their loss of advantage, the form of sedition that is most likely and dangerous in Aristotle's scheme. The fewer a Yugoslav's resources, the more he tries to improve his personal position by entering the sector of advantage (finding a social sector job or joining the League of Communists perhaps) or removes himself entirely, through migration, privatization (women and peasants mainly), or crime (increasing among youth). In all cases, the action is apolitical.

A second avenue for discontent is the workplace and the right to self-management. Here complaints over working conditions can be lodged, and decisions are made on the distribution of both income and material benefits and on contributions to local social programs. Since 1975 the selection of delegates to governmental assemblies also begins here. Protests at the workplace are a common affair—strikes, work stoppages, or at least disagreements within workers' councils—and, according to Jovanov, they overwhelmingly concern wage inequalities.[38] The striking characteristic of this form of collective action is the extent of its disaggregation. Unless workers take their grievances to the trade union or League of Communists, there is no way to organize on a broader front than the level of the enterprise, or even its internal unit, the basic organization of associated labor.[39] This decentralization probably has the effect described by Michael Burawoy for American workers of "manufacturing consent" because it offers some "limited but nonetheless critical freedom" and choice at the same time that the participation "generates consent to the rules."[40] This pluralism, together with the frequent changes in organizational forms and lines of authority in Yugoslavia, diffuses the potential threat, if any, to political stability. As Burawoy describes it for the United States, "the internal state has the effect not only of organizing struggles but also of dispersing them among enterprises. It prevents struggles from reaching beyond the enterprise and coalescing in struggles aimed at the global state."[41]

Although the organization of work contributes to political stability through dispersion, it does not resolve conflicts over inequality. Workers' councils, delegations, and party and trade union actives are as a rule dominated by those who benefit from distribution: urban, highly skilled and professional, secondary and university educated, males of forty years or older. The discontented, at least those who participate in strikes, are also urban resident males, but they have usually had only an elementary school education, are unskilled or semi-skilled, are downwardly mobile, and often belong to a minority at their workplace.[42] As researchers in a seven-nation study of the socioeconomic stratification of political participation find in Yugoslavia, "Those mobilized to activity through the League are disprotionately from the haves; those locked out because of absence of League membership are disproportionately from the have-nots.[43] Most people are inactive, however. Women rarely, if ever, take part in self-management or sociopolitical bodies, and 95 percent of men and women in a 1974 survey in Serbia offered reasons why they would prefer *not* to be elected to delegations.[44] Furthermore, since the cause of most internal disagreements over inequality is to be found in the economic conditions under which an enterprise works and workplace decisions do not influence the terms of productive activity in the country, such disagreements can only be resolved temporarily. Delegates to governmental bodies that do make economic policy are selected indirectly at each level above the enterprise, or even its basic organizations; this effectively eliminates the chance for individual workers to influence policy early on. Finally, workplace decisions are no solution for the unemployed or for those employed in the private sector of agriculture and crafts.

The third channel for expressing discontent is to influence the decisions of party and government. Although the opportunities for participation are again quite numerous at the neighborhood and communal level, this suffers from the same problems as workplace influence—such action is too dispersed to have much effect on fundamental policy. Influence over policymaking must reach the provincial and republican leaders, the main participants in federal decisionmaking. Attitude surveys, however, find that Yugoslavs are more critical of policymaking arenas the closer they are and less likely to criticize distant decisions. Perhaps more important, since republics and provinces exist to give expression to ethnic identity and the principle of national equality, however justified a protest against inequitable policies that occurs at the republic or federal level, it will almost inevitably be interpreted as a nationalist protest, endangering the unity of the country.

Short of a crisis, the ability of a republic's leaders to influence political decisions to its advantage will depend on its power vis-à-vis other republics. To the extent that this power depends on vital resources, the continuing inequalities in regional development give the advantage to the wealthier republics. Organizational resources also matter, and here the trend toward increasing inequality and differentiation within republics, particularly in those inequalities that do not arise within a particular enterprise, take on a crucial importance. The strength of a republic in negotiations with other republics depends on its ability to control and speak for its own population.[45] Unity behind republican leadership permits greater flexibility in bargaining to its own advantage because it need not worry about placating internal conflicts and because it can guarantee support for the policies it agrees to make. Increasing heterogeneity within republics endangers this unity, as the most obvious example, the threat to Serbia from the shifting fortunes and numerical strength of its two provinces, the Vojvodina and Kosovo, illustrates. In addition, political groups that are based on ethnic identity, as the Yugoslav republics and provinces are, require more intransigent or extreme leadership in the face of disunity than natural groups (for example, those based on sex or race) or groups based on less inclusive characteristics (for example, religion in a secular society or class).

To cultivate unity within an ethnic or communcal group, leaders seem to have three choices. The first is to take extreme, polarizing positions on issues. This would undermine the consensual, bargaining give-and-take of the Yugoslav decision-making structure. The second is to reinforce the identity of the group by tactics that emphasize differences among the groups (republics) rather than within them, a favorite being to define all disagreements as issues of membership and communal identity whatever their substantive origin. Not only is the issue lost, but the threat of nationalism also brings quick repression. The third is to override republican autonomy with an externally imposed concensus or to negotiate a consensus among leaders that their concord is more important than substantive disagreements they may have had. Again this loses sight of the issue, and it strengthens the force that imposed or negotiated consensus.

For example, crises in federal decisionmaking have occurred when a republican leadership was unable to control its constituency (the Slovenian road crisis of 1969, the Croatian nationalism of 1967-1971) or when it took extreme positions and pushed ethnic loyalty to increase its bargaining strength (the Croatian leadership in 1970-71). Crises have been resolved by redefining an issue as procedural rather than substantive, as the stalemate over the federal budget in 1972 was resolved by enlarging the membership of the Federal Executive Council. Much of the time, however, these conflicting pressures have brought neither crisis nor resolution but only inefficiency, often by combining substantive and procedural issues in the same decision (for example, Steven Burg's description of the drafting of the 1974 Constitution, where the distinction between whom to tax and what decisionmaking procedures were appropriate within the government became blurred[46]). Crises are ultimately concluded, but not necessarily resolved, by a unity imposed from above—by the intervention of President Tito, reauthoritarianization of the party, repression, or reinvigoration of an external danger. With the death of President Tito, this third option is less easily secured, and the political stability of Yugoslavia depends more on the willingness of republican and provincial leaders to find another third option to avoid the past dangers of the first two. This will matter not only to reduce the current inefficiencies, stalemates, and even crises in federal decisionmaking, but also to avoid encouraging extraparliamentary expression of popular discontent.

Discontent and the Orbit of Political Discourse

Social inequalities exist in Yugoslavia in access to employment, to housing in cities (not discussed here), to income and work-related benefits, and to the quality of schooling. The disadvantaged tend to be youth and women who are disproportionately burdened with unemployment; residents of poorer regions and towns that have fewer resources for schools, health care, pensions, industrial investment, and so forth; agricultural households outside the export crop, cooperative sector; and increasingly those with the fewest resources (low wages, few savings, or few skills to earn extra income) to withstand the stabilization policies that have cut real incomes and begun to transfer the cost of public goods to individual incomes. These disadvantaged, moreover, tend to judge these inequalities by standards of justice emphasizing the equal distribution of goods and services, and the right to employment and to unhindered educational opportunities, regardless of social or ethnic origin.

The politically active, however, do not share these standards, and valuing self-management and the current policy of economic development, including its necessary inequalities, they are unlikely to perceive injustice. As Sen notes for the Athenians, this reduces the possibilities for actual rebellion. We can see in Yugoslavia, indeed, that protests have occurred at moments when political actions gave the impression that an inequality was illegitimate and therefore that protest was permissible. The Croatian nationalists, for example, were surely encouraged by the freedom with which the Croatian Writers' Club protested the Novi Sad Accord (on a united Serbo-Croat language) in 1967 or *Hrvatski Tjednik* was allowed to become increasingly open on Croatian griev-ances or the students' election of blatantly nationalist and non-communist Čičak and Budiša was allowed to stand; students in Kosovo were surely respond-ing to the ouster of Ranković two years earlier and the recognition of past discrimination against Albanians; and the Belgrade students took courage from the television and newspaper reports of youth power in other countries during spring 1968.

Since this encouragement was the inadvertent consequence of the struc-turing of conflicts among political leaders, it was predictable that there would be increased party vigilance in the 1970s and greater restrictions on intellectual freedom. The base from which political leaders is drawn, the League of Com-munists, appears stronger—if membership figures, unity, and positive self-image are satisfactory measures—than it has been for some time. The "leadership stratum," to use a Yugoslav expression, also continues to be the more advan-taged. One study suggests that it is becoming socially more exclusive as well, sharing this life-style and exclusion with members of the managerial and professional strata. The study also asserts that this exclusion does not arouse envy and resentment from the majority of the working class because they are too occupied with their struggle for existence and material and social security (although this does not prevent them from expressing sharp criticism of those middle and upper strate for "living off others").[47] This political and social exclusiveness could also be reinforced by a change in the basis of political struggles, since the ruling group is becoming more internally differentiated along functional lines.

The League is undergoing a change of generations as well. The changing of the guard in Yugoslavia has not been precipitous as was once thought it would be; a major replacement took place in 1972-73 and another is going on now, but it nevertheless entails a profound change in outlook. The following observations are an amalgam of unlikely evidence,[48] but it converges on qualities necessary for the consensual decisionmaking now in place and on perceptions of injustice. The older political generation held positions primarily on the basis of ideological and political soundness and on experience; they tended to be morally puritanical (with some exceptions), highly egalitarian, and paternal in their notion of authority, that is, strong on discipline but responsive to popular opinion. Above all, they valued social harmony, humane personal relationships, and the avoidance of conflict. Locally at least, these leaders tended to see the League as a representative of various social forces and interests rather than a single party line, and so they included persons of many values and sought the support of many groups. Their revolutionary activity before and during the war taught them to be secretive, and they in-spired profound personal devotion in people around them, unless they were clearly opportunists. The newer political generation is less easily characterized by one set of personal traits or skills, but it does tend to gain positions because of its skills—its specific expertise, its formal education, or its talent for management, and preferably all three. They are less egalitarian, value efficiency and performance of tasks more than social harmony, and are willing to tolerate more conflict than the older generation. As a result of these last traits, however, they see less need to gather support from many groups or to incorporate many different views; they are impatient with time spent to smooth relationships, and they have a tendency to prefer procedural rather than substantive solutions to problems. They did not grow up in an atmosphere of secrecy and conspiracy, although they do share in the socially exclusive life-style mentioned previously.

The difference between these two generations is not the Red-versus-expert of politics-versus-skill distinction so often made about leaders in socialist political systems. The new generation is as likely to be persuaded by the dictates of political considerations as those of their functional expertise. But their recruitment primarily on grounds of skill rather than political grounds does seem to make a difference in the nature of interpersonal relationships that they value, in their views on equality, and on the foundations of their authority. If the literature on consensual decisionmaking among elites from other countries is relevant to Yugoslavia, the changes described could be inauspicious since secrecy, fundamental consensus on basic principles, cohesion against the outside, and harmony among members of the political elite are all essential to stability.[49] Instead it appears that these traits are secure but that their basis is different, namely, public support for the methods of decisionmaking and affinity that comes from social ties and consensus on the new values, rather than from the social relations of revolutionary activity.

On the first, if my study of sixty teachers and directors in Croatian secondary schools in 1970 is reliable, the majority of Yugoslavs consider the procedural norms of the political elite legitimate. Given eleven criteria for legitimate decisions, the respondents showed a marked preference for rules made by consensus among political elites. The best decisions were those, 40 to 65 percent said, that began with a careful, "rational" study of a problem by experts, then gained the agreement of all those in authority and people with proven experience in the field, and only then were subjected to popular discussion. Although a majority of the teachers and directors expressed personal sadness at the loss of older generation directors and their qualities, their principles correspond to those of the newer generation.[50] On the second, the vacillation of a Tito on the conflict between equality and economic development is no longer apparent, and the value consensus reinforces the divide between the advantaged and disadvantaged discussed earlier. In brief, this consensus is that inequalities in wages, employment conditions, and regional (urban-rural and north-south) development will disappear with economic development; those that remain will be inevitable and harmless. Inequalities within the workforce are the jurisdiction of self-management, where the equal relation of all to social property and the equal right to participate will result in an equal standard—labor—for reward but not necessarily an equal reward. Those who protest social and economic inequalities must in most cases therefore be opponents of self-management.

The unemployed, the average agriculturalist, and the worker who spends much of the day making ends meet would scarcely find their dissatisfaction with circumstances unaffected by the conspicuous consumption and competition for prestige among the middle and upper strata. Students often express this sentiment with the slogan, "Down with the Red Bourgeoisie" (a favorite in Belgrade in 1968, it reappeared on the tenth anniversary in 1978). But the consensus among the advantaged and the few "possibilities for actual rebellion" (as Sen pointed out) limit the likelihood that the disadvantaged will perceive their condition as unjust and translate their discontent into protest. The most critical and angry, the unemployed, are the least participant. Youth are internally divided between students and workers, they disagree on the extent of desirable equality in society and on the best method to achieve change, and they tend to be very favorable toward self-management. Their criticism, moreover, is directed most often at the older generation who are not living up to the principles of the revolution rather than at the system or its principles. Rural residents are highly critical, but in a traditional sense, preferring autonomy, while their children want more than any other youth to be accepted into party membership. Women find the dual shift of work and household so demanding as to reduce their participation drastically. A feminist movement has begun, but it is predominantly an organization of younger, highly educated, and materially well-off women. Workers returning from temporary employment abroad tend to be geographically dispersed and unemployed; although recent studies may reveal changes after their experiences in northern Europe, they above all chose individualistic, apolitical solutions to their discontent. Regardless of an individual's social identity, finally, surveys of Yugoslavs suggest a high level of personal ignorance about political issues, methods of participating, and even ways to solve specific, small-scale, local problems. The number of highly active and well-informed Yugoslavs appears to be small.

Add to this the difficulty of mounting a united challenge to the party's authority even if (and this appears to be a major if) there were people intensely committed to trying. The near impossibility of organizing action on a broader front than the workplace and the dominance in decisionmaking bodies of the more advantaged members of society have been discussed here. The diligence with which the party has tried to neutralize intellectual dissent from Djilas on, the employment of workers against students when actual confrontation occurs (as a "political reserve army" in Alfred Meyer's useful metaphor), and the complex organization of power and lines of authority all act against the possibility without undue repression. In the meantime the middle strata of administrators and professionals in service, financial, and government positions are growing most rapidly, a buffer of like-minded individuals between political leaders and discontent from below. Nor is there any reason to suggest that many of the disadvantaged have lost the hope of upward social mobility.

Conclusion

The stability of the socialist regime in Yugoslavia, particularly without the authority in both party and country of President Tito, will depend on many factors, including several crucial economic and international developments over which current leaders have only partial control. This chapter has explored some of the social sources of disorder, yet it is only a first approximation. To study this further, one could look more directly at the outcome of economic distribution (as long as a social welfare function is specified) or at other policies, such as housing. The extent to which informal coalitions of interests perpetuate inequalities has not been examined, although the move to negotiation and bargaining to coordinate economic activities since 1974 should strengthen the influence of such groups. Economic conditions and policies appear very important in shaping actual inequalities. Above all, the perceptions of individuals and their inclination to act depend on the changes that take place in their own conditions over time, which remains to be studied carefully.[51]

The evidence thus far shows the relation between inequality and discontent in Yugoslavia to be very much as Aristotle predicted: the lesser pressing for equality, the equal for inequality. The potential for destructive conflict has been circumvented, however, by an Aristotelian prescription for stability, that is, by combining two principles of equality, that of self-management and federalism, on the one hand, and of distribution according to work, on the other. As Aristotle writes:

> a constitutional system based absolutely, and at all points, on either the oligarchical or the democratic conception of equality is a poor sort of thing. The facts are evidence enough: constitutions of this sort never endure. . . . The right course is not to pursue either conception exclusively, but to use in some cases the principle of numerical equality, and in others that of equality proportionate to desert.[52]

The difficulty is that these two principles interact. The proportionate inequalities of distribution affect the operation of the numerical equality of self-management and federalism. Thus those who benefit from distribution participate more fully in self-management and political organizations while the disadvantaged tend to withdraw. Since there is disagreement on what is "deserving," that is, how to measure the equal standard of labor, the most participant are thus in a position to impose the measure to their advantage, namely, educational qualifications, managerial responsibilities, and increasingly, seniority (for men more than for women) and market-based determination of productivity, rather than "duration or intensity." A major source of societal inequality is the very decentralization–self-management, the market, and federalism–designed to guarantee political equality. In other words, the operation of self-management tends to reproduce the patterns of inequality and reinforce the priority of self-management among those who benefit.

The "possibilities of actual rebellion" are thus reduced as Sen predicted, and the threat to stability from below diminished. The discontented among the disadvantaged seek private solutions, and egalitarians are labeled traditional. Sociologists who study inequalities focus primarily on the stratification of participation and influence at the workplace. Collective protest is most likely among the downwardly mobile, who attack inequalities in the distribution of reward not as inherently unjust but as evidence that self-management failed to operate. Protests from above, on the other hand, cannot be ignored. The discontent of the advantaged presents a greater threat to Yugoslav political stability. This threat is increased, however, if the delicate balance of coalition building and consensual decision making at the federal level that the principle of national equality requires is upset by growing inequalities of distribution; if this stable balance is upset, in turn, the tactics of competition among political leaders can inadvertently encourage the expression of discontent from below.

Notes

1. Aristotle, *The Politics*, tr. Ernest Barker (Oxford: Oxford University Press, 1946), pp. 205, 207.

2. Amartya Sen, *On Economic Inequality* (Oxford: Oxford University Press, 1973), p. 1.

3. Karl Marx, *Critique of the Gotha Program*, in Robert C. Tucker, ed., *The Marx-Engels Reader* (New York: W.W. Norton, 1972), p. 387, italics in original.

4. One survey of these attitudes can be found in Susan L. Woodward, "An Overview of Survey Research in the Socialist Federal Republic of Yugoslavia," in William A. Welsh, ed., *Survey Research and Public Attitudes in Eastern Europe and the Soviet Union* (Elmsford, N.Y.: Pergamon Press, 1981).

5. Neca Jovanov, *Radnički Štrajkovi u Socijalističkoj Federativnoj Republici Jugoslaviji od 1958. do 1969. godine* (Beograd: Zapis, 1979); see also Goldie Shabad, "Strikes in Yugoslavia: Implications for Industrial Democracy," *British Journal of Political Science* 10, no. 3 (July 1980):292-315.

6. Ellen Comisso, *Workers' Control under Plan and Market: Implications*

of Yugoslav Self-Management (New Haven, Conn.: Yale University Press, 1979), ch. 8; see also Sharon Zukin, "Beyond Titoism," *Telos* (Summer 1980):11.

7. Mihailo V. Popović et al., *Društveni Slojevi i Društvena Svest* (Beograd: Centar za Sociološka Istraživanja, Instituta društvenih nauka, 1977).

8. Popović et al. *Društveni: Slojevi i Društvena Svest.*

9. See Dennison Rusinow, *Crisis in Croatia,* American Universities Field-staff Reports, Southeast Europe Series, 19, nos. 4-7 (1972).

10. Boris Vuškovic, "Promjene temeljnih obilježja strukture članstva S.K.J. u razdoblju 1968-1976," *Naše Teme* 22, no. 5 (May 1978):1034-1057.

11. Dušan Tomašević, "L'insertion des jeunes dans la vie professionelle en Yougoslavie," *Entry of Young People into Working Life: Technical Reports* (Paris: Organization for Economic Cooperation and Development, 1977), p. 278.

12. Mladen Žuvela, "Grupe stanovnika pojačeno izložene nezaposlenosti i neke njene socijalne i psihološke posljedice," *Sociologija* 10, no. 4 (1968): 91.

13. Žuvela, "Grupe Stanovnika," Velimir Filipović and Sulejman Hrnjica, "Psihološki aspekti nezapošljavanja omladine," *Gledišta* 8 (1967):1693-1699.

14. Organization for Economic Cooperation and Development, *Economic Survey of Yugoslavia* (Paris: OECD, 1980).

15. Ibid.

16. Zukin, "Beyond Titoism" p. 20.

17. OECD, *Economic Survey of Yugoslavia,* 1980.

18. Oli Hawrylyshyn, "Ethnic Affinity and Migration Flows in Postwar Yugoslavia," *Economic Development and Cultural Change* 26, no. 1 (October 1977): 93-116.

19. OECD, *Economic Survey of Yugoslavia,* 1980.

20. Interviews with sociologists of migration studies in Ljubljana, 1978.

21. *The Constitution of the Socialist Federal Republic of Yugoslavia* (Belgrade: Secretariat of the Federal Assembly Information Service, and Ljubljana: Dopisna Delavska Univerza, 1974), p. 53.

22. The best analysis of this to date has been by Steven Burg, "Decision-making in Yugoslavia," *Problems of Communism* (March-April 1980):1-20.

23. Pavle Sicherl, "A Dynamic Analysis of Regional Disparities in Yugo-slavia," Unpublished manuscript. For different methods, see Martin Schrenk et al., *Yugoslavia: Self-Management Socialism; Challenges of Development* (Baltimore: Johns Hopkins University Press, 1979), and Mary B. Gregory, "Regional Economic Development in Yugoslavia," *Soviet Studies* 25 (October 1973):213-228.

24. Sicherl, "Regional Disparities in Yugoslavia," p. 81.

25. Sicherl, "Regional Disparities in Yugoslavia," pp. 61-62.

26. Schrenk et al., Yugoslavia; see also D. John Grove, "Research Note: Ethnic Socio-economic Redistribution, a Cross-Cultural Study," *Comparative*

Politics 12, no. 1 (October 1979):87-98, who finds significant statistically the trend toward ethnic parity (measured by republic) in Yugoslavia, 1961-1974, and increasing within group variation.

27. OECD, *Economic Survey of Yugoslavia,* 1980.

28. Ibid.

29. Zukin, "Beyond Titoism."

30. For a discussion of this in Romania, see Mitchell S. Ratner, "Schools, Jobs, and Young People in Romania: An Anthropological Account," *Studia Univ. Babes-Bolyai, Philosophia* 26, no. 2 (1981):10-17.

31. Lazo Antić, "Ugovori samo radi vpisa Kandidata ili radi programiranog osiguravanja Kadrova?" *Naše Teme* 22, no. 12 (234) (December 1978):2776-2779; also "Platforma i Forma Reforme," *Ekonomska Politika* 1410 (April 9, 1979):20-21.

32. Antić, "Ugovori. . . ."

33. Susan L. Woodward, "Training for Self-Management: Patterns of Authority and Participation in Yugoslav Secondary Schools," Unpublished doctoral dissertation, Princeton University, 1974, and Velimir Tomanović, *Radnička i Intelektualna Omladina: Promene Socijalnih Razlika* (Beograd: Institut Društvenih Nauka, 1971).

34. Blagoje Mujović, "Obrazovanje u sklopu strukturalnih promjena savremenog jugoslavenskog drustva," *Naše Teme* 20, no. 6 (June 1976).

35. Amartya Sen, "Models of Educational Planning and their Applications," *Journal of Development Planning* 2 (1970):11-18.

36. In periods of economic contraction or stability, "levels of occupational hierarchy have tended to recruit from within themselves, each one replenishing its own labor force"; in periods of expansion, each level tends to recruit from below itself, eventually reaching into the peasantry; the date of an individual's first job is the key to the economic conditions that will affect him. Eugene A. Hammel, *The Pink Yo-Yo: Occupational Mobility in Belgrade, ca. 1915-1965* (Berkeley: Institute of International Studies, University of California, 1969).

37. See Woodward "Survey Research in Yugoslavia," and Popović et al., *Društveni Slojevi i Društvena Svest.*

38. Jovanov, *Radničk: Štrajkovi u Socijalističkoj Federativnoj Republici Jugoslaviji od 1958 do 1969.*

39. On the limits of trade union activity, see Ellen Comisso, "Workers' Councils and Labor Unions: Some Objective Tradeoffs," *Politics and Society* 10, no. 3 (1981):251-279; and Sharon Zukin, "The Representation of Working-Class Interests in Socialist Society: Yugoslav Labor Unions," *Politics and Society* 10, no. 3 (1981):281-316.

40. Michael Burawoy, *Manufacturing Consent* (Chicago: University of Chicago Press, 1979), p. 199.

41. Ibid., p. 198.

42. Popović et al., *Društveni Slojevi i Društvena Svest; Izvještaji-Projekt: Funkcioniranje i Ostvarivanje Delegatskog Sistema* (Zagreb: Institut za Političke Nauke Fakulteta Političkih Nauka, 1977), 5 vols.; Vladimir Arzenšek, "Otudjenje i Štrajk," *Revija za Sociologiju* 6, no. 2 (August-September 1976): 2-3; and Miro A. Mihovilović et al., *Žena Izmedju Rada i Porodice* (Zagreb: Institut za Društvena Istraživanja Sveučilišta u Zagrebu, 1975).

43. Sidney Verba, Norman Nie, and Jae-On Kim, *Participation and Political Equality: a Seven-Nation Comparison* (Cambridge, England: Cambridge University Press, 1978), p. 233.

44. Popović et al., *Društveni Slojevi i Društvena Svest; Izvještaji-Projekt;* Mihovilović et al., *Žena Izmetju Rada i Porodice.*

45. This discussion depends on Brian Barry's interpretation of consensualism found in "Review Article: Political Accommodation and Consociational Democracy," *British Journal of Political Science* 4:477-505 and "The Consociational Model and Its Dangers," *European Journal of Political Research* 3 (1975):393-412; for the model in Yugoslavia, see Burg.

46. Steven Burg, "Decision-making in Yugoslavia," paper presented to the annual meetings of the American Association for the Advancement of Slavic Studies, Columbus, Ohio, 1978.

47. Popović, et al., *Društveni Slojevi i Društvena Svest.*

48. Philip Jacob et al., *Values and the Active Community* (New York: Free Press, 1970); Woodward, *Training for Self-management;* and Woodward "Survey Research in Yugoslavia."

49. Barry; also Ezra Suleiman, *Elites in French Society* (Princeton, N.J.: Princeton University Press, 1978), and Arendt Lijphart, *The Politics of Accommodation* (Berkeley: University of California Press, 1968).

50. Woodward, *Training for Self-Management.*

51. A good example is Tord Høivik, "The Development of Romania: A Cohort Study," *Journal of Peace Research* 11, no. 4 (1974):281-340; another approach to inequality in Yugoslavia can be found in Boris Vusković, "Social Inequality in Yugoslavia," *New Left Review* 95 (January-February 1976): 26-44.

52. Aristotle, V:i, &14-15, p. 206.

8 The Politics of National Inequality in Romania

Mary Ellen Fischer

Relations among the nationalities in comtemporary Romania are complex, and the lack of systematic and objective data makes any assessment of their status somewhat tentative.[1] The goal of this study is not to supply more ammunition to either Hungarians or Romanians in the verbal battle over Transylvania. Rather, I hope to place current developments into a broader context of ethnic politics and inequality. Hence this study is suggestive, not definitive, and several themes run throughout.

First, the complexity in Romania is becoming simplified as the smaller ethnic groups emigrate or come to identify themselves at least officially in census interviews as Romanian. Second, this simpler solution is no less difficult for the Romanian polity since the largest nationality, the Hungarians, seem to be more unified and actively hostile to the Bucharest government than before 1975. Finally, there is a striking contrast between the Hungarians and the other minorities in attitudes toward the Romanian Socialist Republic (RSR), and here the concept of inequality is crucial. Indeed, perceptions of inequality form the basis of ethnic politics in the Romanian system.

The very existence of ethnic minorities in Romania stems from past inequalities in the international system when southeastern Europe was the focus of imperial rivalries. These international differences were perpetuated in internal politics, producing inequalities among the ethnic groups in political, economic, and social status. For example, Transylvania was part of the Austro-Hungarian Empire until 1918, and the Hungarians and Germans in this area were granted special political and economic privileges. The largest national group in Transylvania, the Romanians, for centuries were not legally equal to these other groups and, even as late as the 1966 census, the Hungarian and German minorities in the RSR retained higher group levels of urbanization and education than the Romanians and were concentrated in the more industrialized counties.[2] Any attempt by Bucharest to reduce inequalities among regions has been perceived by the previously advantaged Hungarians as persecution or even genocide.[3] In contrast, other ethnic groups such as Yugoslavs, Ukrainians, and Gypsies, have not been historically privileged and can more easily accept egalitarian goals. The politics of nationality in Romania therefore involve both historically powerful minorities that deeply resent political domination from Bucharest and perceive past and present inequalities as advantageous to themselves, and smaller ethnic groups with more limited desires for upward mobility within the Romanian system leading them toward accommodation and assimilation.

The current foreign policy of the Romanian government tends to complicate relations among the nationalities. The present territory of the RSR before 1918 formed a frontier area in which the Austro-Hungarian, Russian, and Ottoman Empires vied for political influence. Today the Romanian government strongly resents any attempt to challenge its sovereignty or its historical right to areas in which Romanians form a majority of the population, and it rejects interference in its internal affairs by any foreign state. This rejection of outside interference, while based on a genuine sense of nationalism within the Romanian elite, has also proven a very useful strategy for achieving broader internal support for the regime. But the strategy does not attract the support of the minority ethnic groups whose members are not susceptible to appeals based on Romanian nationalism. In fact the extremely nationalistic statements of President Nicolae Ceauşescu have often alienated the smaller groups as they interpret his remarks to be evidence of prejudice against them and disregard for their rights.[4]

The status of national minorities in Romania, and more specifically that of the Hungarians in Transylvania, has long been a matter of controversy. However, that controversy became especially vitriolic in the late 1970s as a result of several quite separate developments. First, the Helsinki Final Act of 1975 and the subsequent linkage of economic credits and trade to observance of its human rights provisions raised hopes inside Eastern Europe and in the West that the socialist governments would ease restrictions on emigration, communication, and visits, raise living standards, and allow more intellectual freedom. These hopes were quickly dashed in the case of Romania, although the government did ease emigration for Germans and Jews. Meanwhile, the Hungarian economy had produced considerably higher living standards for its population due to its New Economic Mechanism and Soviet subsidies and, like West Germany and Israel, could attract the envy of conationals inside Romania. Hungarians in Romania began to feel a sense of relative deprivation compared to their relatives across the border in Hungary; they compared themselves not to other citizens of Romania but to other Hungarians, and the comparison apparently left them dissatisfied. Also in the mid-1970s, ethnic Romanians in the RSR were becoming disillusioned with Ceauşescu and his policies, especially the continued low standard of living and the absence of cultural freedom. The popular hopes of the 1965-1974 period for political relaxation and economic improvement had not been realized by the RCP, and after mid-1974 ethnic Romanians gradually became more and more disappointed.[5] Only their nationalism encouraged them to support Ceauşescu; Romanian nationalism, aside from its anti-Soviet component, did not appeal to the Hungarians.

This combination of factors—Helsinki, Hungarian economic successes, and Romanian disappointment with Ceauşescu's policies—intensified the discontent of Hungarians inside and outside the RSR, and led to bitter attacks on Ceauşescu and his regime. Romania was granted most favored nation (MFN) trade privileges by the United States in 1975, and Hungarian groups in Western Europe and North America have accused the Bucharest government of systematic persecution of ethnic Hungarians and violations of their human rights and have testified against Romania's MFN status on this basis. Romanians in Europe and America have risen to the defense of Ceauşescu's nationality policy, regardless of their attitude toward his other strategies. The publications of both sides present excellent examples of the biased use of statistics,[6] and the international environment once more is affecting ethnic relations in Romania.

This case study in the politics of nationality therefore presents a number of problems. Implicit in any attempt to analyze inequality are the ambiguous relation between policy intent and outcome in a political system and the dilemma of defining equality among groups rather than individuals. The latter difficulty produces exceptionally bitter disputes when nationality (reinforced by language and religion) appears to be threatened. I shall begin by suggesting some implications of these general issues for the Romanian case. Among problems specific to Romania that demand more extensive treatment are the internal relations among the ethnic groups and the effect of international events on internal policy. The groups differ sharply in their backgrounds and current attitudes toward the Romanian government. What was their past role in society? What changes have taken place in the circumstances of these groups in the last three decades under Communist rule? What implications does this background have for the future of Romanian politics?[7] Particularly crucial is the attitude of the Hungarians. Is their intense resentment of the late 1970s merely a stage in the process of industrialization and urbanization of the RSR,[8] or will it prove a serious and permanent obstacle to the Romanian Communist Party (RCP) as the party and Ceauşescu try to build their version of socialism in Romania?

Policy Outcomes and Definitions of Equality

That "outcomes are an imperfect guide to policy commitments" has been demonstrated convincingly with respect to the equality of nationalities and regions in the USSR.[9] Even the positive or negative nature of the outcome can be difficult to assess. Too often, "strategies used to evaluate . . . equality . . . determine the results"; measuring regional compensation, for example, is less likely to produce findings of equalization than comparing funding.[10] Another difficulty in measuring outcomes is the lack of data available on ethnic groups. In the Soviet case this is solved (imperfectly, as those who work on the subject are the first to admit) by equating regions with ethnic groups.[11] In Romania the coincidence of ethnicity and political divisions is much less perfect; in fact only two counties are predominantly Hungarian, all others having a Romanian majority. Variation over time in county economic statistics, which-ever measures are selected, is therefore an even less accurate measure of policy outcome in Romania than in the USSR, although some findings have been suggestive.[12]

The basic question in the USSR, of course, is whether Moscow has been able to reduce the gap between rich and poor regions. Since the Russian republic tends to be wealthier than other areas, an egalitarian commitment by Moscow usually is regarded as favorable to non-Russian nationalities. The exceptions are the Baltic republics, whose populations consider equalization to be persecu-tion, as do the Hungarians in Transylvania. In Romania, therefore, even the original policy commitment to equality on the part of Bucharest is rejected by the Hungarian minority, regardless of policy outcome.

No less difficult than evaluating policy commitments and measuring out-comes is defining the equality that policy is meant to effect. Is the goal equal opportunity, or is it equal distribution of resources? That question, now being debated in the West, is controversial in communist systems, where the tension grows between Marxist egalitarians and pragmatic reformers advocating the "performance principle."[13] In China, for example, the Cultural Revolution was in part a revolt of the egalitarians against the unequal reward system used to stimulate economic development. Romania also had its mini-cultural revolu-tion in 1971, when Ceaușescu the egalitarian attacked some privileges of the New Class in Romania. Ceaușescu, in fact, like most long-surviving communist rulers, has shifted his emphasis back and forth from egalitarian principles to pragmatic reform with unequal rewards. While he attracts and alienates some Romanians with each shift, Hungarians in the RSR view both emphases with suspicion. Egalitarianism is detrimental because they fear for their past advantages, and pragmatic reform because they regard the economic incentives as structured to entice the younger generation out of their ethnic communities, thus hastening assimilation.[14]

Still another consideration in defining equality involves the distinction between individual equality and group equality. An irony of the present situa-tion is that the rights now claimed by the Hungarian minority from the Roman-ian government are those Budapest refused to grant to Romanians in Transyl-vania a century ago. In each case the existing government offered full legal equality to all *individuals* as citizens of the larger political entity, Hungary before 1918 or the RSR today. In both cases it was the group right of national-ity that the nonruling group perceived to be threatened. In 1869 a group of Romanian intellectuals voted to boycott the upcoming elections to the Hungarian parliament; they were permitted to vote as individuals but were guaranteed no rights as a nation. One Romanian argued that the Hungarians "offered civil liberties as the price of nationality."[15]

This distinction between individual and group rights is crucial when nationality is at issue, for language, culture, and often religion are involved, and all require unrestricted activity within a group or community. Individual members of that group regard autonomy—insulation from the outside world to preserve the special interaction of the group—as a prerequisite to individual rights. Today an individual Hungarian, like any citizen of the RSR, enjoys legal rights under the RSR constitution, but the rights of the Hungarian minority as a group are limited by political centralization. The Romanian Communist Party, dominated by Ceauşescu, sets all economic and cultural priorities. This threatens the individual rights of all Romanian citizens, regardless of ethnic background, but it presents a special threat to the group rights of the nationalities. "Nationality rights . . . are essentially collective rights, and do not exist in any other way, because the nationality is a form of communal existence. The restriction of these rights meant practically the deprivation of the nationalities of any rights."[16] As it happens, this is the lament of a Hungarian in Transylvania describing the 1950s. It could also be a Romanian complaint from the preceding century. In both cases the stress on individual rights seems eminently fair to the rulers and totally unacceptable to the ruled. National autonomy, the latter would argue, is a prerequisite for national equality.

The Romanian Environment: Complexity to Simplicity

According to the 1977 census, national minorities make up less than 11 percent of the RSR population (see table 8-1).[17] But the various groups are geographically dispersed and diverse in socioeconomic background, reflecting the complex history of the region. The principalities of Moldavia and Wallachia formed the original core of Romania, which gained independence in 1877. After World War I the Versailles Treaty allowed the Romanians extensive territorial gains: in the northwest, Transylvania from Austria-Hungary, with its Hungarian and German (Saxon) minorities; in the northeast, Bessarabia from Russia and Bucovina from Austria-Hungary, with Russian, Ukrainian, and Jewish minorities; in the southwest, the Banat, again from Austria-Hungary, with more Germans (Swabians) and Yugoslav groups; and in the southeast, the southern Dobrogea from Bulgaria. Almost all of the lands gained, however, did have a Romanian majority and in 1930 Romanians composed over three-fourths of the population of Greater Romania.[18] Many of the new territories were then lost in 1940, but all except the southern Dobrogea, Bessarabia, and northern Bucovina were reacquired after 1945. Since Romanians today generally recognize Bulgaria's ethnic claim to the southern Dobrogea, only the area of Bessarabia and nothern Bucovina in the USSR remains an irredenta.

Table 8-1
Total Population of Romania by Nationality, 1930, 1956, 1966, 1977

Nationality	1930	(%)	1956	(%)	+/-	1966	(%)	+/-	1977	(%)	+/-
Total	14,280,729	(100)	17,489,450	(100)	+22.5	19,103,163	(100)	+ 9.2	21,559,910	(100)	+12.9
Romanians	11,118,170	(77.9)	14,996,114	(85.7)	+34.9	16,746,510	(87.7)	+11.7	19,207,491	(89.1)	+14.7
Hungarians	1,423,459	(10.0)	1,587,675	(9.1)	+11.5	1,619,592	(8.5)	+ 2.0	1,670,568	(7.7)	+ 3.1
Germans	633,488	(4.4)	384,708	(2.2)	−39.3	382,595	(2.0)	− 0.5	332,205	(1.5)	−13.2
Gypsies	242,656	(1.7)	104,216	(0.6)	−57.1	64,197	(0.3)	−38.4	75,696	(0.4)	+17.9
Ukrainians, Ruthenians	45,875	(0.3)	60,479	(0.3)	+31.8	54,705	(0.3)	− 9.5	51,503	(0.2)	− 5.9
Serbs, Croats, Slovenes	50,310	(0.4)	46,517	(0.3)	− 7.5	44,236	(0.2)	− 4.9	38,252	(0.2)	−13.5
Russians	50,725	(0.4)	38,731	(0.2)	−23.6	39,483	(0.2)	+ 1.9	17,480	(0.1)	−55.7
Jews	451,892	(3.2)	146,264	(0.8)	−67.6	42,888	(0.2)	−70.7	24,667	(0.1)	−42.5
Tatars	15,580	(0.1)	20,469	(0.1)	+31.4	22,151	(0.1)	+ 8.2	20,508	(0.1)	− 7.4
Slovaks	50,772[a]	(0.4)[a]	23,331	(0.1)	−	22,221	(0.1)	− 4.8	19,513	(0.1)	−12.2
Turks	26,080	(0.2)	14,329	(0.1)	−45.1	18,040	(0.1)	+25.9	20,750	(0.1)	+15.0
Bulgarians	66,348	(0.5)	12,040	(0.1)	−81.9	11,193	(0.1)	− 7.0	9,267		−17.2
Czechs			11,821	(0.1)	−	9,978	(0.1)	−15.6	5,507		−44.8
Greeks						9,088			5,092	0.1	−44.0
Poles						5,860	1.3		3,481		−40.6
Armenians						3,436			1,410		−59.0
Others	105,374[b]	(0.7)[b]	42,756[b]	(0.2)[b]		4,681			56,520[b]	0.3	
Undeclared						2,309					

Sources: 1930, 1956, and 1966, see Anuarul Demografic al Republicii Socialiste România, 1974 (Bucharest: Direcția centrală de statistică, 1974), pp. 106–107. 1977: Recensămîntul populației și al locuințelor din 5 ianuarie 1977, vol. 1, Populație–Structura demografică (Bucharest: Direcția centrală de statistică, 1980), pp. 614–615.

[a]Includes Czechs.

[b]Includes undeclared.

Rival Claims to Transylvania

The one major foreign claim to territory in the RSR is the Hungarian irredenta in Transylvania. The Hungarians base their claim on historical precedence: the Magyars appeared in the Danubian Basin in the ninth century and established control over Transylvania in 896. Hungarian historians cite Byzantine sources to document Magyar presence (and that of the Székelys) during the tenth century and thereafter. They recognize the Saxon migrations in the twelfth century but assert that the nomad Vlachs, as they term the Romanians, did not appear until the thirteenth century, seeking asylum from the south.[19] Transylvania is therefore perceived as a "natural, political, and economic unit . . . [of] the Hungarian Kingdom" from 896 to 1918.[20] The Romanians are regarded as latecomers who crept through the Carpathian passes to seek shelter from the Turks and then proliferated rapidly until they formed the majority of the population. The exclusion of the Vlachs from the three recognized nations of medieval Transylvania is interpreted by Hungarians as an indication "that they were not yet a decisive factor in Transylvania" in the thirteenth century,[21] and they were subsequently excluded from the Union of Three Nations (Saxons, Magyars, and Székelys) in the fifteenth century and from the Constitution of 1542.

These medieval nations, of course, did not yet have the ethnic significance of modern nations but were based on the medieval *natio*, a concept that "excluded the mass of the population from membership" since it applied to "a relatively small group set apart from the mass of men by legally sanctioned privileges."[22] In other words, only the privileged strata among the Hungarians and Germans were included in those nations, not the peasants; and since there were no privileged Romanians, they had no *natio*. Hungarian sources demean the Romanians throughout, both directly and by implication. For example: "In view of the fact . . . that the victims of the anti-Habsburg and anti-Turkish struggles were predominantly Magyars and Székelys, by the close of the eighteenth century the Wallachians formed the real majority in Transylvania proper."[23] The Wallachians (Romanians), it is implied, became a majority in Transylvania by allowing the Hungarians to do the fighting! The Romanians, of course, claim that they were always the majority in Transylvania and regard their exclusion as a *natio* to be irrefutable evidence of their suppression and persecution under Hungarian rule.

The Romanian claim to Transylvania is based on historical continuity: their ancestors were the descendants of the indigenous Dacians and Trajan's Roman legions. They speak a Latin language and have inhabited Transylvania without interruption since the Romans left in the third century.[24] The Hungarians and the Saxons are the late arrivals who invaded and suppressed the peaceful native Romanians. There is no conclusive documentary evidence to prove the Romanian theory of continuity, but Romanian historians have amassed an impressive amount of material evidence (coins and other artifacts) to support their contention. Unfortunately, in their enthusiasm and determination to build an unassailable case, they have made such extreme assertions as to weaken their cause. For example, the two thousand fiftieth anniversary of the Dacian state under Burebista was celebrated in 1980, and the pageantry of the occasion implied a direct line of Romanian heroes from the Dacian leader down to Ceauşescu.[25] Statements by Romanian historians that might be accepted as probable are made so dogmatically that they must be rejected. History has been so politicized in Romania as to render it no longer history.[26] These extremes of Romanian historiography have been generated as much by perceived internal needs as by the quarrel with the Hungarians—for example, the need to associate the RCP and its leaders with Romanian antecedents, to create a glorious national tradition for the current leaders to continue. Such elaborate excesses are simply not necessary in the dispute over Transylvania for, while the Romanians cannot prove their case, the Hungarians cannot disprove it. And Romania's claim rests on more practical bases than history: possession and ethnicity.

Ethnic Minorities in the RSR

Transylvania has long had a majority of ethnic Romanians in its population. The rough proportions in the eighteenth and nineteenth centuries were 50-55 percent Romanian, 30-35 percent Hungarian, and 10 percent German.[27] Although the minorities are for the most part dispersed, living in small groups among the Romanians, they tend to concentrate in southeastern Transylvania along the former frontier of the Austro-Hungarian Empire, but now in the very center of the RSR. The Saxon cities—Sibiu, Sighişoara, Braşov, for example—form a rough east-west line in southern Transylvania, while the most compact Hungarian group, the Székelys, are just to the east, in the bend of the Carpathian mountains. The Székely counties are among the least industrialized in Romania, providing the main exception to the historically advantaged position of the Hungarians.

The bitterness of Hungarian-Romanian relations does not characterize German attitudes toward the Romanians. This is partly due to the escape valve of emigration: the most dissatisfied members of the German community have been able to leave for West Germany in recent years. But there are also important differences in the historical roles of these two nationalities who for centuries composed the ruling nations of Transylvania.[28] The Germans, although granted privileges, never expected to rule the entire province. Their leaders were urban, middle class, and engaged in trade; they were not landowners like the Hungarian aristocracy. The Germans had no political aspirations except to reach an accommodation with the political structure, Hungarian or later

Romanian, and protect their autonomy within the commercial sphere. Their use of the German language is suggestive in this respect: the Saxons tended to use Hungarian or Romanian in their communications with the other nationality and reserved German as an exclusive vehicle of communication among themselves. Thus they maintained their separate small communities over the centuries and accepted the need to acquire the language of the external environment.[29] Germans after 1918 did not challenge the Romanians politically or resist learning Romanian; the Hungarians did both. Hungarians never gave up their political right to rule Transylvania, and for them the sign of an educated person was fluent knowledge of Magyar. Thus before 1918 a Romanian in Transylvania who wished to improve his economic or social status had to learn Magyar. Anyone willing and financially able to do so was upwardly mobile, and the Hungarians readily accepted Magyarized Serbs, Slovaks, or Romanians into the elite.[30] After 1918 Hungarians did not easily accept political control from Bucharest or the need to learn what they considered an inferior language. Romanians and Hungarians therefore clashed politically and linguistically, while Germans avoided confrontation in both areas. And today Germans in the West are much less hostile in their assessment of RSR nationality policies.[31]

The territorial revisions and the drastic reduction in the German and Jewish populations during and after World War II raised the proportion of Romanians in the total population to 85 percent by 1956.[32] That figure has risen steadily ever since, just as the proportions and absolute numbers of the minority groups have declined. Indeed, only the Romanians, the Hungarians, and the small number of Turks concentrated in Constanța have shown a steady increase in the postwar era. The overall decline in minorities is particularly striking in a county-by-county breakdown of the changes between 1966 and 1977. The Romanian population increased in every county but one,[33] and the minority groups decreased everywhere (except for the Hungarians, Turks, and Gypsies).[34] Of the three exceptions, the Turkish population rose only in Constanța and Bucharest, but the Gypsies showed a widespread increase. In the latter case however, much of the growth may be mainly statistical: more reliable counting plus a greater willingness on the part of the Gypsies to define themselves as such to the census taker.[35] It would seem, therefore, that time is simplifying the complexity of ethnic relations in the RSR, and only one large group remains to be dealt with: the Hungarians. Yet even this group is shrinking compared to the Romanians: Hungarians showed large increases only in three counties—Covasna, Harghita, and Mureș, the Székely concentration—and in every county including these three the Romanian population rose more than the Hungarian both absolutely and proportionately.[36]

Education, Occupation, Urbanization. As might be expected from the history of ethnic settlement in southeastern Europe, the Romanians occupy an intermediate position among RSR nationalities in level of education, employment in the nonagricultural sector, and urbanization. Indeed, most of the minority groups tend to be above the Romanian average except the Ukrainians, Yugoslavs, and Gypsies. The published volumes of the 1977 census did not break down the education figures by nationality, so we have only the 1966 data plus the totals for 1977 (see table 8-2).[37] All the nationalities (except the Jews) followed roughly the same pattern: 75-80 percent had only a primary education, 10-15 percent had finished secondary school, and about 2 percent had a higher education. Perhaps the most significant finding in table 8-2 is the vast improvement between 1966 and 1977. But important differences among the ethnic groups are visible. For example, the Hungarians tend to surpass the Romanians in every category except higher education, and the Germans are slightly higher than the Hungarians and show a special preference for middle-level professional and trade schools. The Gypsies were by far the lowest, followed by the Ukrainians and the other Slavs.

The figures on higher education are crucial to an understanding of Romanian-Hungarian relations in Transylvania. Before 1945 there was intense competition between the two groups in precisely this area. Hungarians in the nineteenth and twentieth century have regarded university education as the major path to higher status (rather than commerce, which was most often selected by the Germans) and government service was the usual goal after graduation. Romanians tended to emulate the Hungarians, and competition between the two groups centered on, first, access to higher education, and then access to the bureaucracy.[38] The small number of places in the former, and the politicization of the latter (before 1918 favoring the Hungarians, and later the Romanians) created a bitter legacy, which finally hurt the Hungarians when the larger group gained control of the admissions process.

Other factors, however, have been important in reducing the number of Hungarians entering higher education, including choices by the Hungarians themselves. Romanian higher education under the RCP has been oriented toward engineering and the applied sciences, with relatively few places for literature, art, theater, and other cultural fields in which there are special facilities for the minorities and consequently university classes in their own languages. Most Hungarians going to the university would have had to study technical specialities in Romanian,[39] and they might instead have chosen careers that did not require such intensive Romanianization, thus preempting their university study. In contrast, other Hungarians, realizing that command of Romanian was a prerequisite to upward mobility, have chosen to send their children to Romanian rather than Hungarian schools in the lower grades. Both alternatives increase the resentment of the Hungarian community since the first leads to lower status, and the second cuts across and weakens linguistic boundaries.[40]

Occupational patterns show greater variation among the nationalities, although the Romanians still are in an intermediate position (see table 8-3).

Table 8-2
Education Level by Nationality

Nationality	Primary (%)	General Schools, 7-10 Years (%)	Middle: Professional or Trade (%)	Middle: Technical and Specialized Schools (%)	Specialized Lycees (%)[a]	Lycees of General Culture and Humanities (%)	Higher Education (%)
1966							
Romanians	75.81	10.66	4.71	2.97	—	3.65	2.20
Hungarians	71.75	14.56	5.41	3.06	—	3.72	1.51
Germans	68.40	14.76	7.61	3.61	—	3.82	1.81
Gypsies	96.61	2.90	0.42	0.03	—	0.04	0.00
Ukrainians, Ruthenians	86.12	9.00	1.49	1.39	—	1.19	0.80
Serbs, Croats, Slovenes	81.09	9.71	3.78	1.88	—	2.37	1.17
Russians	82.31	8.71	1.75	1.62	—	2.89	2.71
Jews	40.41	12.73	5.59	7.23	—	16.45	17.59
Others	75.04	10.10	4.40	2.74	—	4.89	2.83
Undeclared	77.29	9.41	3.35	3.10	—	3.65	3.20
Total, RSR	75.31	11.06	4.80	2.98	—	3.68	2.16
1977							
Total RSR	48.3	27.3	10.2	3.5	1.9	5.2	3.6

Sources: *Recensămîntul populaţiei şi locuinţelor din 15 martie 1966,* vol. 1, *Resultate generale,* pt. 1, *Populaţie* (Bucharest: Direcţia centrală de statistică, 1969), p. 189; *Recensămîntul . . . 1977,* vol. 1, p. 622-623.

Note: Percentages are of population aged twelve and over.

[a] 1977 only.

Table 8-3
Nationalities by Occupational Category, 1966

Nationality	Workers (%)	Intellectuals/ Functionaries (%)	Cooperative Peasants (%)	Individual Peasants (%)	Artisans (%)			Others (%)	Unidentified (%)
					Cooperative	Private	Total		
Romanians	38.86	12.33	39.69	5.53	2.05	0.81	2.86	0.27	0.45
Hungarians	45.85	11.62	34.19	1.98	4.06	1.44	5.50	0.45	0.40
Germans	58.62	13.60	19.73	0.99	4.77	1.12	5.89	0.64	0.55
Gypsies	47.30	0.50	30.38	2.60	1.63	14.61	16.24	2.61	0.37
Ukrainians, Ruthenians	41.28	4.37	18.29	33.70	1.02	1.08	2.10	0.08	0.17
Serbs, Croats, Slovenes	31.96	9.02	43.61	10.35	3.92	0.46	4.38	0.29	0.40
Russians	59.87	9.53	25.80	0.59	2.25	0.70	2.95	0.65	0.61
Jews	29.01	59.45	0.33	0.17	5.57	1.89	7.46	1.73	1.86
Others	43.60	13.57	27.82	8.24	4.02	1.10	5.12	0.81	0.84
Undeclared	33.22	14.12	24.17	3.55	2.08	1.12	3.20	1.17	20.57
Total RSR	39.91	12.33	38.55	5.22	2.30	0.92	3.22	0.31	0.45

Source: Computed from data in Recensămîntul . . . 1966, vol. 1, p. 175.

Again, we have data by nationality only for 1966, and the Germans and Hungarians are more modern than the Romanians (in the Marxist sense, that is, less involved in agriculture) while the other groups lag behind. The Hungarians tend to lead the Romanians slightly in every category except that of intellectual or functionary; this of course is related to higher education and also to the politicized bureaucratic stratum, dominated by Hungarians before 1918 and even during much of the interwar period. In the 1920s and 1930s the Romanians made serious gains in state positions, for example, with the railroads as officials and workers, but the private sector was much harder to invade.[41] By 1966, however, the private sector had been eliminated, and the Romanians had come into their own. But they had by no means eliminated the smaller ethnic groups from the bureaucracy; almost all the nationalities had between 11 and 14 percent of their numbers in the intellectual and functionary category.

Data on the urbanization of the nationalities (see table 8-4) follow the pattern established by tables 8-2 and 8-3 on education and occupational category. Hungarians and Germans had higher levels of urbanization than the ethnic Romanians, and the Ukrainians, Yugoslavs, and Gypsies lagged behind the other groups. On urbanization, however, data for 1966 and 1977 show clearly that the comparative advantage of the first two groups over the Romanians is shrinking, while the others are falling further behind. Regardless of policy intent, and this

Table 8-4
Urbanization of Nationalities, 1966 and 1977
(percentage)

	1966			1977		
Nationality	*Urban*	*Suburban*	*Rural*	*Urban*	*Suburban*	*Rural*
Romanians	34.1	3.9	62.0	43.0	4.1	52.9
Hungarians	44.4	2.6	53.1	50.0	2.5	47.5
Germans	45.2	4.5	50.2	49.6	4.7	45.7
Gypsies	25.3	2.4	72.3	33.8	2.4	63.8
Ukrainians, Ruthenians	9.4	0.6	90.0	8.5	0.3	91.2
Serbs, Croats, Slovenes	26.6	0.2	73.1	32.2	0.2	67.6
Russians	33.7	2.7	63.7	34.7	0.6	64.7
Jews	98.1	0.1	1.8	98.4	–	1.6
Others	51.2	2.8	46.0	50.6	3.8	45.5
Undeclared	55.8	2.6	41.6	42.6	2.7	54.7
Total RSR	35.3	3.8	60.9	43.6	3.9	52.5

Sources: Recensămîntul . . . 1966, vol. 1, p. 175; Recensămîntul . . . 1977, vol. 1, pp. 614-621.

is difficult to define although the rhetoric is egalitarian, the outcome of development policies has been to urbanize the Romanians as a group faster than the minorities.

Before leaving these three tables, we must note the distinctive characteristics of two ethnic groups on opposite ends of the social spectrum: the Ukrainians and the Jews. Although over 40 percent of the Ukrainians are listed as workers, 90 percent live in rural areas, and they were the only group to increase that proportion between 1966 and 1977. Many of the worker Ukrainians must then be involved in the technical aspects of agriculture or village life, which would justify their occupational classification. Alternatively, they must be commuters, workers who maintain their rural residence but commute to the city for work, returning every night or less frequently to see their families.[42] The Ukrainians show no tendency to become more urbanized, so any who do move permanently into cities must drop their ethnic identity very quickly. A final contrast between the Ukrainians and the other ethnic groups is the concentration of Ukrainian peasants in the individual sector. Virtually the only noncollectivized land remaining in Romania is land unsuited to large-scale agriculture, usually because of its high altitude and mountainous terrain. This implies an isolated location, and indeed the Ukrainians reside for the most part in Suceava and Maramureş, two of the most remote counties along the northern border with the USSR, and in Tulcea, which contains the water wilderness of the Danube delta and also borders the USSR. Only in Maramureş, however, did they show a numerical increase from 1966 to 1977.[43]

The other anomalous group are the Jews, who simply do not fit the pattern of Romanian society. Their record of achieving higher education in 1966 was eight times the national average. In a largely agricultural and rural environment 60 percent of the Jews were intellectuals or functionaries, 30 percent workers, and less than 1 percent peasants. Finally, over 98 percent lived in urban areas. But again, time is simplifying the diversity of Romanian patterns: of the 800,000 Jews in the period between the two world wars, only half survived World War II, and over 90 percent of the survivors have emigrated. About 33,000 remain, 65 percent of them are over 60 years old.[44]

The Evolution of Ethnic Relations, 1945-1965

In 1918 the Romanians had found themselves disadvantaged in their own country, and the subsequent modernization process, particularly urbanization and mass literacy, heightened Romanian expectations as well as the fears of the smaller groups.[45] Ethnic friction had of course occurred during the nineteenth century,[46] but the period between the wars was perhaps the worst for ethnic relations in Transylvania as the triumphant Romanians "moved to redress ethnic inequities" by challenging the Hungarians in their "historic niche" as government officials or functionaries in state economic enterprises, and threatening the Germans' dominance in private industry, commerce and banking.[47] Not until after World War II was the power base of both groups finally eliminated, and the timing and nature of the process was quite different in each case.

The worst period for the Germans was 1945 to 1950. In addition to those killed during the war, about 100,000 were evacuated by the German Army. About 75,000 of those remaining were deported to the USSR, and 10,000 never returned. Most deportees were sent back in 1948 and 1949, although some were kept until 1951, and about half of those who returned went to Germany or Austria. The 1948 census, regarded by Germans in the West as fairly accurate, revealed a total German population of 343,913,[48] just over half the size of the community in 1930. The Romanian statute of February 1945 protecting minority rights did not cover the Germans, and in March 1945 they lost much of their agricultural property in the agrarian reform. The state nationalized other types of property in July 1948, and a month later the German church schools were taken over by the Romanian government. In 1949 the tide began to turn: a German antifascist committee was established, providing a new organization which could dissociate the German community from fascism, and in September 1950 individual Germans regained their Romanian citizenship.[49]

Unlike the Germans, the Hungarians regard the immediate postwar years as the most favorable period for them, although they also lost proportionately more property than the Romanians in the economic reforms of the 1940s. Petru Groza was prime minister from 1945 to 1952, and Hungarians in Transylvania believe that Groza's "nationality policy was much more tolerant than that of his successors and he was relatively popular among the minorities."[50] Western observers in Transylvania in the late 1940s came to similar conclusions.[51] There were indeed numerous reasons for Romanians (and ethnic Hungarians) to regard the RCP itself as the champion of Hungarians' rights. In the interwar period, after all, the party had endorsed the right of national minorities to secede from Greater Romania, and a disproportionate amount of party support had come from areas heavily populated by minorities.[52] Romanians associated communism with Hungarians. Had not the communist, Béla Kun, gained control of Budapest after World War I, to be deposed only by the invasion of the Romanian army? And were not many leaders and members of the RCP itself non-Romanians?[53] Events of the postwar era thus gave some hopes to Hungarians, although the 1948 educational reforms made the Romanian language mandatory and began the reinterpretation of history that has reached such extremes under Ceauşescu.[54]

Hungarians now see the beginning of the end in 1949 when Lásló Rajk, Minister of the Interior in Hungary, was convicted as a Titoist spy and executed. Rajk was a Székely from Transylvania who had returned regularly for visits. He had often met with the leaders of the Hungarian community in Romania, many of whom subsequently were arrested.[55] Then in 1951-52 the General Secretary of the Romanian Party, Gheorghe Gheorghiu-Dej, eliminated two of his major rivals, Ana Pauker and Vasile Luca, the latter a Hungarian. Groza was removed as Prime Minister in 1952 and given a titular position, and in that same year an autonomous region was created for the Székelys in southeastern Transylvania. The region became a showpiece of Communist nationality policy, and in January 1953 Gheorghiu-Dej declared the nationality problem solved.[56] Two-thirds of the Hungarians remained outside the autonomous region, however, and the measures taken against them—limited communications with Hungary, wage discrimination, Romanianization of administrative organs and other desirable occupations—have been detailed elsewhere.[57] Essentially, the Hungarians claim that the Romanians were using their political power to invade sectors previously controlled by Hungarians, and they also assert that the policy was two-tiered, tolerant public regulations accompanied by less tolerant secret instructions.[58] Romanians, of course, respond that the RCP was merely consolidating communist power and that its policies aimed at the elimination of inequality.

The Soviet invasion of Hungary in 1956 produced unrest among Hungarians in Romania, and in the late 1950s overt steps were taken to lessen their unity and autonomy and hence their potential as a threat to internal order. The two most notorious examples were the forced unification of the Hungarian and Romanian universities in Cluj (Ceauşescu presided at the unification session in 1959, and the Hungarians have never forgiven him),[59] and the border changes imposed on the Hungarian autonomous region in 1960, which drastically diluted the Hungarian majority. The Hungarians regard these years from 1949 to Ceauşescu's election as General Secretary in 1965 as an era of steady decline in their status. Even Romanian publications waste little space in defending Gheorghiu-Dej's nationality policies.[60]

The evolution of the other nationalities resembled that of the two largest groups. Each lost whatever economic power base it had possessed in the postwar economic reforms. Several became the objects of special distrust due to their association with an outside enemy (the Yugoslavs during the 1948 Titoist scare, the Jews in the anticosmopolitan period of 1952-53, and the Russians and Ukrainians during the Comecon dispute of the early 1960s). With minor exceptions, all have declined as a proportion of the total population and almost all (though not, of course, the Hungarians) have declined in absolute numbers. The post-1945 reduction in the German and Jewish groups has resulted largely from emigration, the Germans before 1950 and in the wake of Ostpolitik and Helsinki, the Jews in 1948-1952 and since 1958.[61] Small numbers of other groups may have left but, for the most part, they have been assimilated; they have redefined themselves, or seen their children define themselves, as Romanian.

In summary, since World War II the complexity of ethnic relations in the RSR has become somewhat simplified, but the simpler situation is no less perplexing for the Romanians. The largest group, the Hungarians, are growing in absolute numbers and have picked up substantial support from abroad. This threatens Ceauşescu's foreign policy as well as his domestic control. His unease about the potential Hungarian danger has been clear since he assumed power in 1965, and he has evolved a number of strategies to deal with their discontent. It is to these strategies and the affect of past inequalities that I now turn.

Ceauşescu's Strategies and the Dilemma of National Inequality

The policies of Nicolae Ceauşescu toward the nationalities reflect his political philosophy. This combines egalitarianism and elitism, idealism and pragmatism, in ways that have characterized communist leaders since Lenin. As an old revolutionary from the illegal prewar days, Ceauşescu has egalitarian tendencies; as a party organizer from the late 1940s, he also recognizes the need for an elite and effective organization to bring about the socialist development of Romania. His long-term goals are egalitarian, but he is sufficiently pragmatic to see the short-term need for the "performance principle" (to use Walter Connor's phrase once again). While Ceauşescu may alternate his distributive emphasis between equality and reward for performance, he is consistent in his view that all individuals are instruments to further the economic strategies of the RCP. He points out again and again in his speeches that it is the duty of all Romanian citizens, regardless of sex, occupation, or nationality, to contribute fully to the economy. Women must work full time outside the home but also accept the double burden of their special childbearing and rearing function. Intellectuals must not only do their own work but also educate and inspire other Romanians to improve their contribution to society. The double burden of the nationalities is to become bilingual so that they can participate in the fulfillment of Party and state goals. If they do so, he is quite willing to allow for their special economic and cultural needs—as long as the cost is not so high as to detract from his development funds. Just as the economic system has not yet been able to afford the facilities to eliminate women's double burden, so, Ceauşescu argues, the party cannot afford to reproduce all cultural and educational opportunities in minority languages.[62]

When Ceauşescu came to power in 1965, he consolidated and still maintains his total control of the Romanian political system by a combination of political strategies that includes nationalism, personnel manipulation, and populism. His appeals to Romanian nationalism and his resistance to Soviet pressures have broadened his support. Even the Hungarians and Germans rallied to the tricolor of the Romanian flag in the aftermath of the Soviet invasion of Czechoslovakia. But fears of the USSR evaporated quickly, replaced by disillusionment by the mid-1970s. The disillusionment was most rapid and intense among the minorities, where Romanian nationalism is not an effective means of achieving popularity.

Personnel manipulation has proven extremely effective in some respects. Ceauşescu promoted his protégés to positions of power and has kept control by circulating his subordinates at will, never leaving them in one place long enough to establish an independent base within the Party. He also assures minority representation within the Bucharest bureaucracies and in local offices. Membership in the RCP and its Central Committee, and also in the Grand National Assembly and the county and local People's Councils, reflects the ethnic proportions of the total population.[63] Such proportions, even in electoral bodies where candidates compete for office, are carefully controlled.

Romania, unlike most other East European states, does have multicandidate elections with two or more individuals running for the same seat. In elections to the Grand National Assembly, for example, about 50 percent of the seats are contested. Important political officials at the national or local level are not opposed, for it is important that those *individuals* be elected. But the rest of the seats demonstrate the broad, representative nature of the assembly, and so must be won by ordinary citizens from all occupational levels and categories. Since these people are running for their category, and it is not important to the Party which individual wins, we find women running against women, Hungarians against Hungarians, and machinists against machinists. The outcome for each category is thus determined in advance.[64]

Of course the ethnicity of an individual is no guide to policy tendencies; Stalin demonstrated that convincingly for all time. And those members of national minorities admitted to the RCP or promoted to positions of responsibility are carefully screened for loyalty to the Romanian polity. Therefore any Hungarians or Germans who rise to prominence in the RSR are regarded with suspicion by their ethnic colleagues, who wonder at their success. At the same time they are not fully trusted by their Romanian comrades, who fear that their loyalty cannot be complete. The criticism by Hungarians abroad and the betrayal of an insider like Károly Király (a former county first secretary who complained publicly and repeatedly about Ceauşescu's nationality policies[65]) must have intensified the Romanians' mistrust. The manipulation of minority personnel, like the appeal to Romanian nationalism, cannot be termed a complete success. Those appointed are mistrusted on all sides. But the policy does help to mobilize support among the less advantaged nationalities: the presence of Serbs, Ukrainians, and even Gypsies in high office demonstrates to these groups their potential for upward mobility in Romanian society.

Ceauşescu's third political strategy, his populist appeals for mass support, also has but limited success among the national minorities. The personality cult, for example, may indeed be appealing to certain strata in the Romanian political system, although it is hard for Western observers to accept its necessity.[66] But since the cult emphasizes Ceausescu as national leader, like nationalism it fails to attract the non-Romanian ethnic groups. Other populist strategies—the stress on legality and broad participation in decisionmaking—received more emphasis before 1975 than they do today. Although they are still repeated as slogans, and consultative meetings are held with various economic groups (particularly in times of crisis), the slogans are mouthed rather than implemented, while the consultative meetings serve as forums for the explanation of party policy and not as open discussions of problems and solutions. As the personality cult has flowered, the participatory forms of populism have waned. And even in its most democratic form, Romanian populism would be feared by the smaller nationalities that could be threatened by majority rule.

Another emphasis that might be considered populist has recurred in the late 1970s: Ceauşescu's egalitarianism. A number of laws threaten elite privileges, usually with the stated goal of reducing inequalities, protecting national treasures (artistic or architectural), or saving scarce supplies (paper or hard currency). Although these laws apply to all citizens, they are particularly resented by the Hungarians, who would prefer to keep what few remnants of past privileges remain to them—central urban apartments (or, in the villages, homes on the main street), inherited property such as furniture or jewelry, and the ability to pass on educational opportunities to their children—or to exchange hospitality in Romania for gifts or other help from visiting foreign relatives.[67] The Romanian elite is also hurt by such laws, but the Hungarians are disproportionately affected, and again the less advantaged ethnic groups remain largely untouched and therefore less alienated.

Ceauşescu's Nationality Policy

Ceauşescu's general strategies of political control have been rewarded by the quiescence of the Romanian population, but these strategies have been much less successful with the minorities, and least of all with the advantaged groups like the Hungarians. And he cannot afford to alienate these groups completely if he wishes to maximize economic growth. The essence of his policy toward the nationalities might be termed induced assimilation, that is, public commitment to tolerance and equality along with economic policies that reduce ethnic exclusivity and so weaken ethnic boundaries.[68] Regime rhetoric has demonstrated constant concern for the minority groups. Radio and television broadcosts always note the good neighborly relations and cooperation among the ethnic groups in the development of their common homeland. Ceauşescu's own speeches inevitably include references to the "cohabiting nationalities" as citizens of the RSR, making their full contribution to the building of socialism, and in his frequent visits outside of Bucharest Ceauşescu has given priority to areas of minority habitation.

If problems arise he does not hestitate to criticize past policies and promise immediate changes. In August 1968, for example, trying to ensure Hungarian support during the Czech crisis, Ceauşescu went to Transylvania—Braşov, Cluj, and then the Szekely county of Harghita. In Harghita he admitted that, although steps had been taken to develop the relatively backward county, "we must honestly say that not too much has been done." He then pointed out the important investments to be made there under the current five-year plan, "for there can be true equality of rights . . . if material conditions are not ensured." Shortly thereafter, special nationality councils were set up to deal with the specific problems of each minority, to stimulate creativity in the nationality languages and also to cultivate "socialist patriotism," or loyalty to the RSR.[69]

Whether Ceauşescu is keeping his promises to the nationality groups is difficult to determine. Not only are there the usual problems of measuring policy outcome but accurate statistics are not available.[70] This makes almost meaningless any comparison over time in numbers of students, classes, texts, or other publications, and feeds Hungarian suspicions. Romanian data do seem to indicate increases in the number of Hungarian students at all levels through 1978. Hungarians contend that the data are inaccurate and that, in any case, the educational facilities are not sufficient; they complain in particular about the reduction in the number of secondary schools after the 1976-77 academic year and the rise in the minimum number of pupils required for a section in a minority language. The Romanians respond that the consolidation simply aimed at efficiency, that the number of schools teaching in minority languages remained the same, and that the nationality sections even increased. Indeed, many measures (such as the reduction in frequency, length, and circulation of most RSR newspapers and journals) are justified by Romanians as economizing but perceived by Hungarians as persecution. Romanians argue that their own language publications are also affected, and this is true. Such changes, however, especially threaten the Hungarians, who feel endangered and isolated in a tiny outpost of their own culture.

The economic situation of the nationalities is just as difficult to analyze, and available data can be used to support radically different conclusions. No information on individual incomes by nationality is available, so we must compare county statistics in regions of Romanian and minority habitation. Table 8-5 shows clearly that, as late as 1969, the national minorities were concentrated in the more advanced areas of the RSR. In the decade from 1965 to 1975, the Hungarian counties certainly were not deprived economically (see table 8-6). All showed above-average growth in gross industrial production, and most were above average in investment and per capita sales. The three below average in the latter categories, Cluj, Bihor, and Mureş, had started out well above average, and so could have been expected to register lower growth rates. (Hungarians would not accept such an explanation.)

If we examine the 1976 to 1979 investment figures in the context of

Table 8-5
Economic and Sociocultural Rankings of Romanian and Nationality
Counties, 1969

	Economic Rankings			Sociocultural Rankings		
Group	Romanian Counties	Nationality Counties	Mixed Counties	Romanian Counties	Nationality Counties	Mixed Counties
I	1	3	2	0	6	1
II	4	3	1	2	2	2
III	5	3	2	3	2	2
IV	6	1	1	8	1	0
V	5	1	1	8	0	2

Notes:
    Nationality counties are those with over 25 percent minority population in the 1966
census; Arad, Braşov, Cluj, and Sibiu would drop into the mixed group after 1977, but
since the goal here is to examine the pre-1970 status of these groups, the 1966 census is
used. Other nationality counties are Bihor, Covasna, Harghita, Mureş, Satu Mare, Sălaj, and
Timiş. *Romanian counties* had over 98 percent Romanian population in 1966 (plus Suceava,
96.1): Argeş, Bacău, Botoşani, Brăila, Buzău, Dimboviţa, Dolj, Galaţi, Gorj, Ialomiţa, Iaşi,
Ilfov, Mehedinţi, Neamţ, Olt, Prahova, Suceava, Teleorman, Vaslui, Vîlcea, and Vrancea.
Mixed counties include Alba, Bistriţa-Năsăud, Caraş-Severin, Constanţa, Hunedoara, Maramureş, and Tulcea.
    Economic and sociocultural rankings are based on Vladimir Trebici, *Populaţia României
şi creşterea economică* (Bucharest: Ed. politică, 1971), esp. pp. 285-289. Group I is the
highest ranking, Group V the lowest. Trebici discusses at length the indicators used and his
reasons for choosing them. Economic indicators include per capita production (industrial,
agricultural, and construction), per capita fixed assets, percentage of active population in
nonagricultural occupations, number of industrial workers per 1,000 residents, and per
capita income from the socialist sector. Sociocultural indicators include percentage of
population living in urban areas, percentage of population over twelve with intermediate or
higher education, number of radios per 1,000 residents, number of residents per physician,
and infant mortality.

Ceauşescu's campaign to equalize territorial production throughout the RSR,
however, we can see cause for Hungarian alarm. None of the major Hungarian
counties listed in table 8-6 were above the RSR average. In fact Braşov and
Hunedoara were the only counties in Transylvania above the average (see table
8-7). The big recipients of investment were the port facilities along the Danube
and connected industries, the mineral resources of the Jiu Valley, and the
traditional industrial areas of Bucharest and the Prahova Valley, including
Braşov. (The Danube and the Jiu Valley are areas of mixed nationality but
not predominately Hungarian.) The economic picture does remain ambiguous
since the poorest Romanian counties ranked low along with the Hungarian
regions. But the future does not bode well for the Hungarian areas: ten counties
have been singled out for special efforts in economic and social development
in the 1981-1985 plan, only one of which (Maramureş) has a significant Hungarian population.[71]

Table 8-6
Economic Growth in Major Hungarian Counties, 1965-1975

County	Increase in Gross Industrial Output 1975/1965 (%)	Rise in Investment 1975/1965 (%)	Increase in Sales of Goods Per Capita 1975/1965 (%)	Hungarian Population Per 1977 Census (%)
Covasna	329.0	655.4	201.2	77.9
Harghita	301.9	306.5	204.5	84.5
Satu-Mare	362.2	368.9	206.5	38.2
Salaj	482.5	442.0	215.9	23.6
Cluj	327.9	250.7	188.8	23.4
Bihor	332.5	210.5	192.1	31.0
Mureş	283.2	147.8	178.8	43.7
Total RSR	323.0	292.0	196.7	7.7

Source: The Hungarian Nationality in Romania (Bucharest: Meridiane, 1976), pp. 12-13, 16-17.

Migration within the RSR has been a cause of serious concern for the Hungarian community whose members feared that the equalization of economic resources by territory would entice Hungarians away from Transylvania to areas where their small numbers would result in rapid assimilation. The aggregate figures released in the 1977 census do indicate a downward trend in the size of Hungarian communities outside of the major centers of concentration. Presumably these individuals are being assimilated into the Romanian population, but there is no way to distinguish between assimilation and migration back to the larger communities. Eighteen counties saw increases in their Hungarian inhabitants, half of these outside Transylvania. But the increases outside Transylvania ranged from 1 to 280, averaging 111, while increases in the Transylvania communities were much more sizable, raning from 540 up to 26,873, with a mean of 8,152. We cannot be sure that the small increases outside Transylvania do not hide still larger numbers assimilated, but it seems that not so many Hungarians are moving into Romanian areas as was feared. Hungarians retort that the Romanian census does not accurately reflect the numbers of Hungarians outside Transylvania or those being assimilated. There is really no response to this suspicion, but there also is no way to prove such an allegation. The most we can say is that the 1977 census in the aggregate figures released to the public does not reveal a significant dispersion of Hungarians from Transylvania to the rest of Romania, a situation that should (but will not) relieve Hungarian anxieties.

Table 8-7
Counties in Order of per Capita Investment, 1976-1979

RSR Average	RSR Average	RSR Average
1. Constanța (O)	11. Bacău	21. Alba (H, G)	31. Teleorman
2. Gorj	12. Argeș	22. Iași	32. Ilfov
(Bucharest)	13. Covasna (H)	23. Neamț	33. Vrancea
3. Galați	14. Timiș (H, G, O)	24. Bistrița-Năsăud (H)	34. Vaslui
4. Tulcea (O)	15. Dîmbovița	25. Buzău	35. Harghita (H)
5. Brașov (H, G)	16. Cluj (H)	26. Sibiu (H, G)	36. Maramureș (H, O)
6. Brăila	17. Vîlcea	27. Mureș (H, G)	37. Botoșani
7. Caraș-Severin (H, G, O)	18. Olt	28. Arad (H, G, O)	38. Suceava
8. Hunedoara (H)	19. Dolj	29. Mehedinți	39. Satu-Mare (H)
9. Ialomița	20. Sălaj (H)	30. Bihor (H)	
10. Prahova			

Sources: Anuarul Statistic 1977, 1978, 1979, 1980 (Bucharest: Direcția centrală de statistică). Counties are listed in descending order of per capita investment for four years, 1976-1979.

Note: Letters indicate concentrations of minority populations: H = Hungarian, G = German, O = Others.

Conclusions

Relations among the nationalities in Romania are becoming simultaneously less complex and more difficult. Of the three largest interwar minorities the Germans and Jews were decimated by the war and its aftermath, and by emigration in more recent years. This leaves only the Hungarians as a sizable group within the Romanian polity, and even they are declining relative to the Romanian population. Yet they are increasing in absolute numbers, and their discontent, intensified by past inequalities, has attracted support in the West among Hungarian emigrés and organizations promoting human rights (not, however, from the Hungarian government, which places good relations with Bucharest above the interests of potential impoverished immigrants).

During most of its rule the Romanian Communist Party has maintained a monopoly on political power and in rather a strange sense has followed an egalitarian nationality policy based on individual rights. First, the regime has tried to reduce regional and occupational inequalities among the nationalities. This has tended to hurt the historically advantaged minorities and the formerly privileged classes, and in Transylvania the two all too often coincided. But the egalitarian commitment has also helped less developed regions, which, except for the Székely region, are primarily Romanian in population. Second, the emphasis has been on individual and not group rights. Any group or organization not directly controlled by the RCP has been regarded as a threat. The nationality councils, editorial boards, universities, theaters—any economic or cultural organization—must be controlled by Romanians loyal to the Party or by members of minority groups who are considered reliable. Individual rights in the RSR or in any political system can become meaningless without organizational rights to protect them. And, as we saw before, ethnic minorities have a special need for group autonomy to protect their community of language and culture.[72]

The political monopoly of the RCP has restricted the choices of ethnic Romanians as well as those of the national minorities. However, the smaller groups cannot even identify with the Bucharest government to the extent of feeling national pride in the achievements of Romania as a small state in international politics. The nationalism that has served the Party as a bulwark against its own people does not support it in its relations with the minorities. In the same way, the egalitarian rhetoric that increases Ceauşescu's popularity with the Romanian masses is perceived by the Hungarians as deliberate persecution.

Thus far, Ceauşescu has been able to prevent any serious outbreaks of nationality unrest inside the RSR. A number of internal factors point to increased tension in the next decade, however. The post-1979 economic crisis has brought frustration, and even xenophobia, to many ethnic Romanians including Ceauşescu, and the minorities could be convenient scapegoats in the 1980s, as in the 1930s. Also, the increasing urbanization of all groups should intensify competition for scarce places within the elite. The Hungarians still regard elite status as their right and resent Romanian privileges, and they have outside sympathizers willing to support them in their cause. In addition, if ethnic bonds weaken, the resulting insecurity will strengthen Hungarian resentment and desperation in the near future. What makes the disintegration of ethnic boundaries much slower and more bitter between the Hungarians and Romanians than it is for the other ethnic minorities is the Hungarian perception of inequality: the Romanians are not their equals and to be assimilated by them is intolerable. Outside interference also plays a role here. Rather than encouraging emigration as an escape valve, as in the case of Germans and Jews, Hungarian communities abroad refuse to relinquish their claim to Transylvania and encourage Hungarians there to resist assimilation.

In the long run, the Romanians are in a strong position. Their claim to Translvania is substantiated by possession and ethnicity. Even time is on their side as the Hungarians become a smaller and smaller proportion of the RSR. During the 1980s, however, ethnic tensions should rise. Economic difficulties, both internal and international, are likely to exacerbate relations and whatever policies Ceaușescu selects will be perceived by the Hungarians as persecution. In 1946 Hugh Seton-Watson wrote: "Transylvania is a country of mixed nationalities and . . . it can have no peace until these nationalities are equally treated."[73] But nationalities need *special* treatment, not *equal* treatment. Ironically, it is equal treatment as defined by the Romanian Communist Party that is intensifying the friction in Romania today.

Notes

1. An excellent recent summary of the situation may be found in Mihnea Berindei, "Les minorités nationales en Roumanie," *L'Alternative* 3 (March-April 1980):37-40, and 4-5 (May-August 1980):36-42. Another brief but very thoughtful treatment is George Schöpflin, *The Hungarians of Rumania* (London: Minority Rights Group, No. 37, 1978). There is a rich travel literature (see note 28) on the nineteenth century, and work of high quality is now becoming available as a result of field research (mostly by anthropologists) in Romanian towns and villages during the early 1970s; see notes 29, 40, 42, and *Dialectical Anthropology* 1 (May and September 1976):239-285, 321-347.

2. The one exception is Hungarian higher education; see the discussion in the text below and table 8-2. For a more detailed treatment of these issues, see my "Nation and Nationality in Romania," in George W. Simmonds, ed., *Nationalism in the USSR and Eastern Europe* (Detroit, Mich.: University of Detroit Press, 1977), pp. 504-521.

3. See *Witnesses to Cultural Genocide* (New York: American Transylvania Federation, Inc., and Committee for Human Rights in Rumania, 1979).

4. For an extended discussion of this point, see Trond Gilberg, "Modernization, Human Rights, Nationalism: The Case of Romania," in George Klein and Milan J. Reban, eds., *The Politics of Ethnicity in Eastern Europe* (New York: Columbia University Press, 1981), pp. 185-211.

5. Kenneth Jowitt, *Revolutionary Breakthroughs and National Development: The Case of Romania, 1944-1965* (Berkeley: University of California Press, 1971) reflects these hopes. For the disillusionment see the essays in Daniel N. Nelson, ed., *Romania in the 1980s* (Boulder, Colo.: Westview Press, 1981).

6. For the Hungarian view, see *Witnesses to Cultural Genocide* (the "Memorandum" by György Lázár, pp. 88-144, is excellent; Lázár is the pseudonym of a Hungarian still in Transylvania), or the essays in Anne Fay Sanborn and Géza Wass de Czege, eds., *Transylvania and the Hungarian-Rumanian Problem* (Astor, Fl.: Danubian Press, 1979), or *Rumania's Violations of Helsinki Final Act Provisions* (New York: Committee for Human Rights in Rumania, 1980). The official Romanian version is summarized in *The Hungarian Nationality in Romania* (Bucharest: Meridiane, 1976), and Monica Barcan and Adalbert Millitz, *The German Nationality in Romania* (Bucharest: Meridiane, 1978); for Romanian emigré publications, see C. Michael-Titus, *In Search of a Hungarian Diaspora* (London: Panopticum Press, 1979); *Tricolorul* (Toronto), 7 (September 1981):3, or the introduction to Simon Telkes, *How To Become a Hungarian* (Rome: Edizioni Europa, 1977).

7. This chapter reexamines some of the predictions in my "Nation and Nationality" in light of the 1977 census.

8. The type of friction that Karl Deutsch predicted would accompany the modernization process; see his *Nationalism and Social Communication*, for example (Cambridge, Mass: MIT Press, 1966).

9. See Donna Bahry and Carol Nechemias, "Half-Full or Half-Empty? The Debate over Soviet Regional Equality," *Slavic Review* 40 (Fall 1981): 366-383, esp. 370, 383, and the sources cited there, for a survey of the difficulties in measuring inequality in the Soviet context.

10. Bahry and Nechemias, p. 371.

11. An excellent and brief introduction to nationalities in the USSR is Ralph S. Clem, "The Ethnic Dimension of the Soviet Union," I, II, in Jerry G. Pankhurst and Michael Paul Sacks, eds., *Contemporary Soviet Society* (New York: Praeger, 1980), pp. 11-62. The sources cited there provide a convenient summary of work in the field. Useful examples of current research appear in Jeremy R. Azrael, ed., *Soviet Nationality Policies and Practices* (New York: Praeger, 1978). For a thoughtful Soviet treatment of the topic, see M.I. Kulichenko, *Rastsvet i sblizhenie natsii v SSSR* (Moscow: Mysl', 1981), esp. ch. 1;

to put this in perspective, see Martha Brill Olcott, "Contemporary Soviet Theories of Nationalism," a paper delivered at the New England Political Science Association (Newark), November 1981.

12. Low investment in nationality counties, for example; see my "Nation and Nationality," p. 510 and p. 518, Table VIII.

13. For superb introduction to this entire issue, see Walter D. Connor, *Socialism, Politics, and Equality: Hierarchy and Change in Eastern Europe and the USSR* (New York: Columbia University Press, 1979), esp. p. 19.

14. On Romania in 1971, see Trond Gilberg, "Ceausescus 'Kleine Kultur-revolution' in Rumanien," *Osteuropa* 22 (October 1972): 717-728, and Kenneth Jowitt, "An Organizational Approach to the Study of Political Culture in Marxist-Leninist Systems," *American Political Science Review* 64 (1974):1171-1191. For a discussion of Ceauşescu's duality, see my "Idol or Leader? The Origins and Future of the Ceauşescu Cult," in Nelson, *Romania in the 1980s*, pp. 117-141.

15. Keith Hitchins describes this in his *Orthodoxy and Nationality: Andrei Saguna and the Rumanians of Transylvania, 1846-1873* (Cambridge, Mass.: Harvard University Press, 1977), p. 170.

16. *Witnesses to Cultural Genocide*, p. 98.

17. Hungarian estimates are usually about 15 percent; they believe Romanian figures are too low due to inaccuracy and intimidation.

18. Greater Romania *(România Mare)* was the Romanians' term for their state in the interwar period. Hungarians also reject the 1930 Romanian figures as too low.

19. For the Hungarian chronology, see Sanborn and de Czege, esp. pp. 26-28. The Hungarian language is "Magyar." The Székelys also speak Magyar, but they are historically distinct from the other Hungarians and form the only compact Magyar group in the present counties of Covasna and Harghita. I use the term "Hungarian" to include all groups; likewise, I use "Germans" to include the Banat Swabians and the Transylvanian Saxons.

20. Julia Nánay, "The Hungarian Minority in Rumania," in Sanborn and de Czege, pp. 203-255, esp. p. 210.

21. Nánay, p. 211.

22. Hitchins, *Orthodoxy and Nationality*, pp. 4, 23.

23. Nánay, p. 211.

24. For the Romanian version of history in English, see Andrei Oţetea, *The History of the Romanian People* (New York: Twayne, n.d., but c. 1973).

25. For a description of the celebrations, see Radio Free Europe, Situation Report/10 (July 22, 1980), pp. 2-5.

26. For a despairing and bitter critique of Romanian historiography, see Vlad Georgescu, *Politică şi istorie: Cazul comunistilor romani, 1944-1977* (Munich: Jon Dumitru-Verlag, 1981), esp. pp. 50, 65-67, 70, 72.

27. Sam Beck and Marilyn McArthur, "Romania: Ethnicity, Nationalism,

and Development," in Beck and John W. Cole, eds., *Ethnicity and Nationalism in Southeastern Europe* (Amsterdam: University of Amsterdam, Center for Anthropology-Sociology, Papers on European and Mediterranean Societies, 14, 1981), pp. 29-69, esp. p. 68, note 2, and the sources cited. This is an excellent discussion of the relation between class and ethnicity in Transylvanian history.

28. Travelers observations bring out the differences among the ethnic groups quite vividly and reveal the roots of current prejudices. Among the most interesting were Emily Gerard, *The Land beyond the Forest* (London: Blackwood, 1888), William James Tucker, *Life and Society in Eastern Europe* (London: Sampson Low, Marston, Searle, and Livingston, 1886), and Charles Boner, *Transylvania: Its Products and Its People* (London: Longmans, Green, Reader, and Dyer, 1875).

29. This contrast between Germans and Hungarians in roles and expectations is described most succinctly by Katherine Verdery in "The Fate of Ethnic Identity in Socialist Romania," a paper presented at the meetings of the American Association for Southeast European Studies, Columbus, Ohio, April 9-11, 1981, and elaborated in "The Decline of Corporate German Ethnicity in Romania," prepared for a conference organized by William G. Lockwood on "Ethnicity and Economic Development in Europe, East and West" (Ann Arbor, Michigan, October 1978). See also her dissertation, "Ethnic Stratification in the European Periphery," Stanford University, 1976, and *Transylvanian Villagers: Three Centuries of Political, Economic, and Ethnic Change* (Berkeley: University of California Press, 1983). Verdery's work on ethnicity is crucial to an understanding of current politics. On the Germans, see Marilyn McArthur, "The Politics of Identity: Transylvanian Saxons in Socialist Romania," University of Massachusetts, 1981, esp. pp. 95-97 on their use of language. McArthur's studies of another area of Transylvania complement Verdery's research very effectively.

30. A wicked satire has recently appeared on this magyarization: Simon Telkes, *How To Become a Hungarian*.

31. For example, Wolf Oschlies, *Die Deutschen in Rumänian, I: Nachbarn seit Jahrhunderten* (Cologne: Bundesinstitut für ostwissenschaftliche und internationale Studien, 15, 1980), esp. p. 34; Ernst Wagner, ed., *Quellen Zur Geschichte der Siebenbürger Sachsen 1191-1975* (Schriften zur Landeskunde Siebenbürgens, Bd. 1, Cologne: Böhlau, 1976), esp. p. 336; Theodor Schieder, ed., *Documents on the Expulsion of the Germans from Eastern-Central Europe, III, Rumania* (Bonn: Federal Ministry for Expellees, Refugees, and War Victims, 1961). The last is the definitive description of the German community in Romania from 1918 to 1952 and includes documents and eye-witness transcripts. See esp. p. 120.

32. On the Germans, see Schieder, *Documents*. The literature on Jews in Romania is too large to cite here; for an introduction see Stephen Fischer-Galati, "Fascism, Communism, and the Jewish Question in Romania," in Béla

Vago and George L. Mosse, eds., *Jews and Non-Jews in Eastern Europe 1918-1945* (New York: John Wiley and Sons, 1974), pp. 157-175, and the sources noted there.

33. The exception was Botoşani, in the northeast corner, cut off from its historical hinterland of northern Bucovina. Its high emigration rate offset a rather high birth rate (over twenty-four live births per thousand inhabitants). See I. Marinescu, "La population de la Roumanie," *Revue roumaine des sciences sociales* 24 (Janvier-Juin 1980):23-34, esp. 27, 30.

34. There were other minor exceptions in a few counties, but *if we accept the RSR census* there was always a proportional decrease compared to Romanians.

35. These possibilities were suggested to me by a Romanian involved in planning for the 1977 census. Work is now being done on the Gypsies in Romania; see Sam Beck and Nicolae Gheorghe, "The Emergence of a Gypsy Ethnic Identity in Romania," presented at the Symposium on the Social Anthropology of Europe of the International Union of Anthropological and Ethnological Sciences, Amsterdam, forthcoming in Jeremy Boissevain and Hans Vermeulen, eds., *The Political Economy of Ethnicity*.

36. Again, note that the Hungarians dispute these figures.

37. The reasons for this omission are not clear; given the changes visible in Table 8-4, we might conclude that the Romanians are closing the gap between themselves and the advantaged groups—that is, becoming more equal. If the others are falling further behind, as in Table 8-4, then charges of discrimination would be substantiated.

38. Verdery makes these points in *Transylvanian Villager* esp. ch. 4, and in passing in her other works.

39. For more on this, see my "Nation and Nationality," pp. 510-512.

40. The limited options available to Hungarians were brought home to me in discussions with Mitchell Ratner, who has studied the educational choices of teenagers in Transylvania; see his "Schools, Jobs, and Young People in Romania: An Anthropological Account," in *Studia Univ. Babes-Bolyai, Philosophia*, 26, no. 2 (1981):10-17, or "The Human Side of Urban Development: Two Ways of Growing up in Contemporary Romania," unpublished paper. On the Germans, see McArthur, p. 254.

41. See Verdery's and McArthur's discussions of the interwar period.

42. On commuters in Romania, see: William Moskoff, "Sex Discrimination, Commuting, and the Role of Women in Rumanian Development," *Slavic Review* 37 (September 1978):440-456; Verdery's dissertation; Sam Beck, "Transylvania: The Political Economy of a Frontier," diss. University of Massachusetts, 1979, esp. ch. 10; David A. Kideckel, "Agricultural Cooperativism and Social Process in a Romanian Commune," diss. University of Massachusetts, 1979, esp. chs. 6, 7 and conclusions; Tom Cheetham, "Cooperativization as a Strategy for Modernization: The Romanian Case," diss. Brown University,

1981, esp. chs. 7, 10; McArthur, pp. 174-183; and John W. Cole, "Family, Farm, and Factory: Rural Workers in Contemporary Romania," in Nelson, *Romania in the 1980s*, pp. 71-116.

43. For an assessment of the Ukrainians in Romania, see "Ukrainians Abroad: In Romania," in *Ukraine: A Concise Encyclopedia* (Toronto: University of Toronto Press, 1971), pp. 163-167, and "Ukraintsi v Rumunii," in Athanas M. Milanytch et al., eds., *Ukrainian Settlements Handbook* (New York: Ukrainian Center for Social Research, 1980), pp. 63-67, and the sources cited. A fascinating interview with Mykola Pavliuk, for many years a professor in Bucharest, was published in "Kul'turno-hromads'ke ta naukove zhyttia ukraintsiv u Rumunii," *Journal of Ukrainian Graduate Studies* 2 (Fall 1977):62-71.

44. These figures were given by Moses Rosen, Chief Rabbi of Romania, in a talk on November 2, 1981 at Harvard University.

45. For a comparative view of the process, see Robert Melson and Howard Wolpe, "Modernization and the Politics of Communalism: A Theoretical Perspective," *American Political Science Review* 64 (December 1970): 1115.

46. See Hitchins, *Orthodoxy and Nationality*, passim.

47. Verdery, "The Decline of Corporate German Ethnicity," p. 27, and *Transylvanian Villagers,* ch. 4, p. 55.

48. Schieder, *Documents*, pp. 77, 81, 82, 121.

49. Wagner, *Quellen*, p. 333.

50. *Witnesses to Cultural Genocide,* pp. 60, 93.

51. Reuben H. Markham, for example, in *Rumania under the Soviet Yoke* (Boston: Meador, 1949), ch. 29, esp. pp. 539, 548-553.

52. See my "Nation and Nationality," p. 506, and the sources cited.

53. See my "The Romanian Communist Party and Its Central Committee: Patterns of Growth and Change," *Southeastern Europe* 6, pt. 1 (1979):1-28.

54. In 1948 the major change was a pro-Slavic orientation imposed by the Soviets; see Michael J. Rura, *Reinterpretation of History as a Method of Furthering Communism in Rumania* (Washington, D.C.: Georgetown University Press, 1961). In Transylvania, the Hungarians saw a pro-Romanian bias; see *Witnesses to Cultural Genocide*, p. 62.

55. *Witnesses to Cultural Genocide,* pp. 95-96.

56. Ibid., p. 97. On the showpiece, see Robert L. Wolff, *The Balkans in Our Time* (New York: Norton, 1967), pp. 453-454.

57. *Witnesses to Cultural Genocide,* pp. 97-103.

58. Ibid., p. 98.

59. Ibid., pp. 67-69, and Sanborn and de Czege, pp. 256-257.

60. In a brief anthology of Romanian political thought on the national question, eighty pages cover the sixteenth century up to 1939, sixty pages are reserved for the Ceaușescu era, leaving six pages for the post-World War II reforms and two pages for Gheorghiu-Dej; *Naţiunea şi problema naţională* (Bucharest: Editura politica, 1975).

61. The Ukrainian *Encyclopedia* dates the harsh pressure from 1958; see p. 166. On the Germans, see Verdery, "The Fate of Ethnic Identity in Socialist Romania," and McArthur. Rabbi Moses Rosen discussed the Jewish patterns (see note 44). Recent data on emigration are given in U.S. Congress, House of Representatives, Committee on Ways and Means, Subcommittee on Trade, *Hearings on the Extension of MFN Status to Romania, Hungary, and the People's Republic of China*, 97th Congress, 2nd Session, July 12 and 13, 1982, esp. pp. 11-32.

62. See the discussion of equality versus performance earlier in this chapter. Ceauşescu's combined egalitarianism and elitism are discussed in my "Idol or Leader," his views on women in my "Women in Romanian Politics: Elena Ceauşescu, Pronatalism, and Affirmative Action," in Sharon Wolchik and Alfred Meyer, eds., *The Changing Status of Women in Eastern Europe* (forthcoming). For his arguments on the costs of nationality education, see my "Nation and Nationality," esp. p. 511.

63. See my "Nation and Nationality," pp. 509-510.

64. See my "Participatory Reforms and Political Development in Romania," in Jan F. Triska and Paul M. Cocks, eds., *Political Development in Eastern Europe* (New York: Praeger, 1977), pp. 217-37, and "Women in Romanian Politics."

65. For details on the Király case and texts of his letters, see the Hungarian sources in note 6. On minority officials and intellectuals, see McArthur, ch. 10.

66. On the cult, see my "Idol or Leader?"

67. Laws passed during the 1970s affected rents and access to living space, defined certain types of personal property as "national treasures" (including church archives, particularly threatening to Hungarian cultural history), tried to reduce the effect of family background on educational opportunity, reduced the number and circulation of books and journals, and forbade foreign visitors (even relatives) to stay in homes of Romanian citizens.

68. I first used the term "induced assimilation" in "Nation and Nationality." Beck and McArthur in "Romania" and Verdery deal extensively with the use of exclusivity to preserve boundaries.

69. *Scînteia*, August 27, 1968, pp. 5-6; August 28, 1968, pp. 1-3. On the nationality councils, see Ceauşescu's speech in *Scînteia*, October 25, 1968, pp. 1-3, and for the actual creation of the Councils, see *Scînteia*, November 16, 1968.

70. The sources cited in note 6 illustrate the contradictory data and conflicting views on these issues.

71. Marinescu, 30. The counties are Botoşani, Gorj, Ialomiţa, Maramureş, Mehedinţi, Suceava, Teleorman, Vaslui, Vilcea, Vrancea. For a discussion of the campaign to industrialize the entire territory of the RSR, and its

results through 1977, see Gheorghe Şerban, "Consideraţii privind dezvoltarea judeţelor RSR in perioada 1967-1977," *Revista de statistică* 28 (August 1979): 7-17.

72. "Democratic theory and ideology has shifted to include both individual and group rights." On this point and the importance of the state in ensuring "group access to societal rewards," see Ronald Cohen, "Ethnicity: Problem and Focus in Anthropology," *Annual Review of Anthropology* 7 (1978): 379-403, esp. 402.

73. Hugh Seton-Watson, *Nationalism and Communism: Essays, 1946-1963* (New York: Praeger, 1964), pp. 102-103.

9

Inequalities and the Politicization of the Polish Working Class

Jack Bielasiak

One of the most important features of the 1980 workers' movement in Poland was its emphasis on egalitarianism. The need for social equality and social justice was predominant in the list of demands issued by the striking workers of Gdansk and Szczecin. As a condition for the settlement of work stoppages, the strikers called for an improvement in the standard of living of industrial labor, for better treatment of the underprivileged sectors of Polish society, and for an eradication of the special privileges enjoyed by the political and administrative elite. The workers' demands for equality, however, went beyond economic security and social welfare guarantees.

Indeed, the most critical aspect of the growing activism in Polish shipyards and factories was the politicization of the labor movement, which sought to obtain not only socioeconomic equality but also political equality. The first demand of the Gdansk interfactory strike committee (MKS) was the acceptance by the government of "free trade unions independent of the Communist Party and of enterprises."[1] This call stemmed from a growing realization that the permanence of economic and social gains obtained during the summer of 1980 strikes could be assured only through rearrangements within the political system.[2] In addition to the establishment of independent, self-governing trade unions, the workers also demanded freedom of speech and an open media as a means of rectifying a closed political system that stifled workers' participation in factory and community affairs.

The end of economic and social inequality therefore became tied directly to the elimination of discrimination in political participation. This politicization of the Polish workers' movement had several complex causes that can be traced to the experience of industrial labor in the 1970 and 1976 workers' unrests and the inadequate long-term responses of the authorities to the former crises as well as to the increasing stratification and conspicuous power and privilege evident in Polish society during the 1970s.

The roots of the egalitarian spirit of the summer of 1980 lay in the increasing awareness on the part of the Polish population that the prior decade witnessed strong social and economic differences. Surveys of Polish citizens during the 1970s revealed their concern with inequitable wages and social injustices and pointed to a growing uneasiness about the expanding socioeconomic distance between the diverse social strata.[3] While the perception of inequality was justified by the increasing discrepancies in economic and social benefits, the sentiment of injustice was aggravated by the decline in the standard of living of the entire society in the late 1970s in comparison to the early years of the decade. The discontent of the working class was thus formed by inequalities that became more pronounced as the Polish economy had to retrench, a fact that also accentuated the relative temporal decline in the living conditions of the industrial workers. In turn, both growing inequality and relative deprivation can be traced to the original program of building a second Poland initiated by the Gierek regime after its accession to power in December 1970.

The strategy of the new Gierek team was based on the leadership's assessment of the 1970 workers' demonstrations, which were viewed as a direct result of economic dissatisfaction. In order to alleviate the social tensions evident in Polish society, the Gierek program sought to improve the living conditions of the population by initiating a policy of rapid economic growth. Economic development was to be attained through increased investments in industry and a higher standard of living through wage increments and a freeze on prices.[4] The strategy was in fact a materialist conception of socialism, seeking to establish support for the regime by improving the social welfare of the Polish people. Alongside this economic program the Gierek policy called for consolidation and centralization of political power as instruments in the implementation of the "second Poland's" modernization.[5] The concentration of political authority in the highest echelons of the Communist party was justified as necessary for the success of the economic drive, which in turn was to resolve the nation's problems and fulfill society's needs.

The combination of economic and political strategies pursued by the Gierek regime, however, had grave consequences for the stability of Poland. The materialist approach to the building of socialism called for incentives for the rising strata of technocrats and bureaucrats, thereby relegating egalitarian values of socialism into the background. Just as materialism penetrated the entire society, so the bureaucratic caste increasingly identified success with the accumulation of its own powers and privileges. As long as the economic miracle of the early 1970s sustained growth for all groups in society, the regime was able to obtain legitimacy by relying on improved economic welfare. Nonetheless the policy of both industrial and consumption growth could not be maintained in the face of domestic overinvestment and worldwide recession.[6] By the mid-1970s the initial Gierek strategy of greater material distribution throughout society had to be curtailed, and what had begun as a device to obtain popular support turned rapidly to a cause of societal dissatisfaction. Unable to maintain its commitments of material benefits to all, and in the face of strong resistance on the part of the bureaucracy against the curtailment of its new found privileges, the government began to neglect workers' interests as consumers. The regime's attempts to lower living standards of the working class by raising prices while continuing the privileges of the political and managerial elites led to the growing conviction that inequalities were expanding rapidly to the detriment of industrial workers. The perception was further enhanced by another consequence of Gierek's initial strategy of political centralization, which contributed significantly to the isolation of the party and government leadership from popular sentiments and prevented working class inputs into centers of decisionmaking. The consequences of this political failure are well known: attempts to restructure prices of consumer goods in June 1976 and July 1980 met immediately with the workers' protests. In both cases the actions of laborers were motivated by a sense of injustice, which found root in the view that the working class was bearing the burden of economic failure while the elite continued to enjoy its privileges. The rebellion in the factories, ship-yards, and mines of Poland began as an attempt to prevent this inequality and ended up as a movement for the restoration of economic equality and social justice.

An obvious linkage therefore exists between the emergence of a political working class movement at the end of the 1970s and the regime's economic and political policies that affected substantially the structure of inequality throughout the decade. The relation between governmental programs and the socioeconomic distribution in turn strongly affected the perceptions of the working class as to its position in Polish society. More important, the growing perception of social and economic inequality led to an increased dissatisfaction with the distribution of power in Polish society and then to a growing awareness of the need to change the political influence of diverse social strata. The pre-occupation with social and economic equality resulted specifically in a greater cognizance of the importance of political participation and of political influ-ence on communicy and work-place decisions. The culmination of this trend was the articulation by striking workers in 1980 of not only demands for the rectification of economic and social inequalities but also for the formation of independent trade unions. The demands of the workers' movement were thus a reflection of the economic, social, and political inequalities present in the Poland of the 1970s and the workers' perceptions of these maldistributions. The positions of the labor class in 1980 can therefore be understood only within the context of the economic resources available to different strata of the Polish population, the social opportunities present for the various groups, and their access to participation in policy formulation throughout the 1970s.

Economic Inequalities

Economic factors were most directly responsible for the sociopolitical dissatis-faction of the Polish working class at the end of the 1970s, with the July 1980 price increase unleashing widespread labor protests and strikes. In conditions of increasing scarcity and inflation, wages became an important determinant of material welfare that made social differences ever more visible. The government's wage and price policies became critical in affecting both individual living standards and intergroup income and consumption patterns. The latter were also influenced by access to special privileges of elite groups, an entree to goods and services that became especially valuable as shortages became more pronounced in the marketplace.

The temporal decline in the socioeconomic well-being of the workers served to reinforce their subjective assessment of inequalities in Polish society.[7] Working class perceptions particularly were affected by the rising expectations of Gierek's early economic miracle and the ensuant propaganda of success, which depicted a society experiencing great material advances. This image produced significant hopes among the population that remained unrealized as the economy began to show increasing problems. The decline in economic performance directly affected the living conditions of the Polish nation. Table 9-1 depicts this situation in terms of wages and living costs. A clear difference exists between the first half of the decade and the latter years, reflecting respectively the boom and bust cycles of the Polish economy. In the first five years of Gierek's rule, nominal wages far outstripped living costs, resulting in an average yearly increase in real earnings of 7.1 percent. In contrast, the next four years witnessed both an increase in costs of living and a decline in nominal wages. This last trend is a reflection of deliberate government policies aimed at

Table 9-1
Wages and Living Costs

Year	Nominal Wages	Living Costs	Real Wages
Percentage Change from Previous Year			
1971	5.5	−0.2	5.7
1972	6.4	0.0	6.4
1973	11.5	2.6	8.7
1974	13.8	6.8	6.6
1975	11.8	3.0	8.5
1976	8.8	4.7	3.9
1977	7.3	4.9	2.3
1978	5.8	8.7	−2.9
1979	8.8	6.7	2.0
Average Yearly Increase			
1970-1975	9.8	2.4	7.1
1976-1979	7.7	6.2	1.3

Source: Adopted from Wieseaw Krencik, "Tempo wzrostu a rozpietosc plac w latach 1970-1979," *Gospodarka Planowa* 4 (April 1980), p. 203, table 1.

halting the economic deterioration by curbing consumer demand, thus lowering wage increments. The result of the combination of lower pay and greater inflation was a marked decline in yearly average increase in real wages during the 1976-1979 period. It is the drop from 7.1 to 1.3 percent in the increase of real wages between the two halves of the decade that most reveals the rapid decline in the population's economic welfare. The falling standard in actual living conditions was exacerbated by the prior rising expectations produced by the second-Poland policy, resulting in subjective feelings of relative deprivation.

That the regime's failure to deliver continued prosperity strongly affected the perceptions of Polish citizens regarding living conditions is evident from public opinion surveys. As table 9-2 shows, public evaluation of material well-being declined substantially in the post-1976 period, with those judging the living situation as very difficult or rather difficult increasing from 43 percent of respondents in 1976 to 72 percent in 1980, while those describing the material supply situation as bad jumped from 36 percent to 91 percent in the 1974-1980 period. The negative economic assessment had an obvious impact on the overall evaluation of the previous year, with a substantial shift from a good to a bad response occurring after 1976, so that at no time during that entire period did a majority of Polish citizens assess the prior year as good.

Table 9-2
Public Evaluation of Living Standards
(percentage of responses)

	1974	1975	1976	1977	1978	1979	1980
My daily life is							
Very difficult			4			7	17
Rather difficult			39			43	55
None too difficult			45			43	25
Not difficult			12			7	3
Consumer supplies are							
Bad	36	48	52			57	78-91
The previous year was for our society							
Good	60	81	23	43	46	32	8
Neither good, nor bad	14	9	29	33	33	39	11
Bad	8	1	37	15	13	21	78
No opinion	18	9	11	9	8	8	3

Source: Osrodek Badania Opinii Publicznej i Studiow Programowych (OBOP), Survey no. 7 (198), March 1981.

More important for our purposes is that the subjective evaluation of living conditions was unequally distributed among different occupational and income strata of the Polish society. A survey of living conditions among a representative national sample revealed that while most individuals felt that, between 1970 and 1978, their family's economic standard had risen at least somewhat, it is the intelligentsia and the higher income groups that attained the largest gains while workers and low-income groups fared the worst.[8] In a similar survey of the 164 largest Polish enterprises (table 9-3) employees self-identified their living levels, with the vast majority of workers (65 percent) stating that their standard was at the minimum or basic levels and only 33 percent at the sufficiency or highest levels. In contrast, 47 percent of the intelligentsia in the same enterprises were at the lower levels while 49 percent identified themselves as living in the two highest categories.

Clearly while the worsening economic conditions negatively affected the majority of the Polish population, it is the working class and in particular the lower income groups within it that evaluated their situation in the most pessimistic terms. Feelings of relative deprivation among workers were translated into assessments that tended to view the impact of economic deterioration as most pronounced at the lower levels of society and least influential at the higher social categories. In large part such a subjective perception of the effects of material decline mirrored economic reality, for the availability of discretionary income was lower among workers than among the administrative elite. This effect was compounded significantly by the social benefits accruing to the elite but not available to the working class, giving the impression to the blue-collar strata of a widening gap between the privileged and working class sectors of Polish society.

Data for income distribution in the 1970s tend to support the perceptions of growing differentials in Polish society. Extensive analyses of wage structure and per capita household income revealed that inequality tended to follow the overall pattern of the Polish economy, with a more equal dispersion associated

Table 9-3
Self-Identification of Living Standards
(percentage of Responses)

	Workers	Intelligentsia
Minimal level	23.6	9.6
Basic level	41.0	37.0
Sufficiency level	26.5	36.6
High level	6.6	12.7

Source: Zbigniew Sufin, "Spoleczne uwarunkowania i konsekwencje kryzysu," *Nowe Drogi* 12 (December 1980): 71-72.

with the years of material prosperity.[9] The distribution of wages and salaries in the socialized sector thus became more equal for manual and nonmanual workers in the early 1970s, a trend that was once again reversed in mid-decade (table 9-4). Inequality of earnings grew in the subsequent period to the point that in 1978 it had once again reached the 1967 level.

Working class sensitivity to inequalities heightened notwithstanding a decline in the wage gap between manual and nonmanual workers, a difference amounting to 6 percent between the two groups' median income in 1967 and 3 percent in 1978.[10] Other factors tended to override this rapproachment between manual and nonmanual earnings, however. For example, the income of the technical-engineering stratum continued to be substantially above that of the blue-collar employees. Similarly, the dispersion of wages was higher among the manual workers than white-collar employees, a ratio amounting in 1978 to 3.2 and 2.9 respectively (table 9-4). In fact, one of the most striking aspects of income differentiation in the 1970s was that intrasectoral dispersion within branches of the economy increased while the relative difference between the economic sectors tended to decline. The consequence was that the increase in inequality at the end of the decade within the industry, construction, transportation, trade, and other sectors were more pronounced than for the economy as a whole.[11] The impact of these trends was to highlight the visibility of pay differentials, since the discrepancies were most acute in the work environment closest to the individual employee. Comparisons of income were thus made not between different branches of the economy but rather between the higher salaries of the administrative-technical personnel and the lower wages of blue-collar workers in the same economic sphere, whether industry, construction, or transport. It stands to reason that workers were more likely to resent high incomes within their own enterprises than in work areas of a different economic

Table 9-4
Distribution of Wages and Salaries

| | $P_{90} : P_{10}$ Ratio | | | Minimum Wage as Percentage of Average Wage |
	Total	Manual	Nonmanual	
1967	3.14	3.23	3.12	42
1970	2.98	3.31	2.98	40
1972	2.83	2.86	2.78	n.a.
1973	2.95	2.68	2.41	n.a.
1976	3.11	3.14	2.97	33
1978	3.13	3.22	2.93	34

Source: Adopted from Henryk Flakierski, "Economic Reform and Income Distribution in Poland: The Negative Evidence," *Cambridge Journal of Economics* 5 (1981): p. 139, Table 1.

endeavor. As a result, the greater inequality in intrasectors income increased the workers' sensitivity to wage inequalities. The acuteness of such sentiments is evident in a poll by Osrodek Badania Opinii Publiczej of January 1981, when 86 percent of respondents judged wage differences to be too high, while only 4 percent thought them to be as they should be and another 4 percent deemed them too small.[12]

The perceptions of inequality were further reinforced in that the dispersion of wages created particularly severe inequalities between the high and low extremes of income, which again were felt more by manual than nonmanual earners. The 1970s witnessed the emergence of a substantial stratum with high income, while at the other end of the scale a large group of households (21 percent) was at or below the social minimum.[13] The lowest income groups in Poland fared particularly badly, as is evident from the statistic measuring the minimum wage as a percentage of the average pay. Despite increases in the former, the gap between the two increased: in 1970 the minimum equaled 40 percent of the average earning, in 1978 it had declined to 34 percent (table 9-4). Furthermore, in the latter year, more than half of the employees in the socialized economy earned less than the average salary.[14]

Other evidence as well points to the growing inequality of society, reflected primarily in the growing gap between the extremes of income dispersion. For example, the ratio between the highest and lowest wages increased in the 1970s until it reached 11:1 in 1978. In conditions where all wages rose rapidly, this meant that the differences in absolute income became even greater during the decade. Because of the higher cost of living, it also signified that people with relatively lower incomes were placed under extreme hardship. Data on per capita household income demonstrates this difficulty very strongly. In large part due to demographic features, since large families tend to bring down the standard of living of even relatively high earners, in 1976 46 percent of the families with three children and 77 percent of the families with four children had a per capita income below the social minimum.[15] Given the fact that larger families tend to be found in greater proportion among the working class than white-collar strata, this meant that the living conditions of industrial labor lagged further behind the administrative elite, despite the closing in income that occurred between the manual and nonmanual employees.

It is not surprising that, given such circumstances, a strong sentiment are among workers favoring wage restructuring. In a survey of steelmill employees, the overwhelming preference among blue-collar workers was in favor of decreasing the salaries of highest earners or increasing the wages of lowest earners (table 9-5). Fifty-four percent of the unskilled workers and 63 percent of the skilled laborers held such a position, in contrast to 44 percent of the foremen and 31 percent of the production directors. Other opinion polls substantiated the view that a vast majority of the population focused on wages as a predominant factor responsible for discrepancies in the standard of living.

Table 9-5
Opinions of Wage Differences by Occupation
(percentage of responses)

	Production Directors	Technical Personnel	Foremen	Skilled Workers	Unskilled Workers
Increase wage differences	—	2.4	0.9	1.4	1.6
Retain wage differences	56.8	34.1	28.7	15.7	19.6
Regroup wage levels among occupations	11.7	14.6	25.7	17.9	22.9
Decrease high wages or increase low wages	15.6	14.6	19.8	27.8	34.4
Decrease highest wages and increase lowest wages	15.6	34.1	24.7	35.7	19.6
Opinions on range of income					
Increase range of wages	13.7	2.4	6.9	1.4	1.7
Decrease range of wages	19.6	24.4	21.6	42.1	36.7

Source: Adopted from Bogusław Błachnicki, *Pracownicy Przemysłu Wobec Egalitaryzmu* (Wrocław: Ossolineum, 1979), p. 111, table 24, and p. 99, table 18.

Already in 1975, 91 percent of respondents in a survey concerning social divisions felt that differences among people in Poland were due "strongly" to variations in earnings or wealth, while those attributing the cause of such differences to education amounted to 76 percent, 77 percent to differences in managerial and nonmanagerial positions, and 66 percent to divisions between manual and nonmanual workers.[16] Even in 1980, when the country was undergoing severe economic dislocations and social tensions, the *Polacy 80* survey based on a national sample found that a primary issue of concern centered around changes in wages: among the responses 70 percent said they definitively favored limiting the salaries of highest earners, while 49 percent had a similar response toward guaranteeing equal income to all citizens.[17]

The strong concern with the structure of wages expressed in all these polls demonstrates without doubt that the increasing inequalities in Poland throughout the 1970s translated into a major social problem. The growing income differentials affected most strongly the views of the majority of the Polish citizenry. Moreover, the perceptions of inequality were most acute among the working class and low-income groups. An OBOP poll conducted in early 1981, for example, noted that among several severe problems prevalent in the nation, equality of income distribution was mentioned by 42 percent of unskilled workers, 36 percent of skilled workers, 34 percent of white-collar employees without higher education, and 16 percent of white-collar employees with higher education.[18] In the wake of these sentiments, it is not surprising that blue-collar workers favored most consistently some remedial action regarding the structure of salaries and wages. This is clearly evident from data in

Table 9-5, where skilled (42 percent) and unskilled (37 percent) workers in a steelmill supported to a significantly greater extent a decrease in wage spread than did foremen (22 percent), technicians (24 percent), and directors (20 percent). A similar national sample in *Polacy 80* found that skilled and unskilled workers favored a wage increment only to low earners in a greater proportion than did clerical employees and specialists.[19]

The consistent support for wage reform evident among the Polish population during the second half of the 1970s found strong expression during the work stoppages of July and August 1980. The ability of the strikers to vent their frustrations with the inequality of Polish society provided the opportunity to press for the transformation of income distribution among the diverse social strata and income groups. It is in this manner that a direct linkage existed between the inequalities present in the prior period and the demands emanating from the striking factories and shipyards. Specifically the workers were concerned with the establishment of a more egalitarian social structure and sought to attain this goal by demanding restrictions on the privileges of the political and administrative elite and wage increments to the low-income groups, notably poor workers, large families and pensioners.[20]

Social Differences

Changes in the level and dispersion of income are insufficient measures of well-being in Polish society, for social benefits and privileges derived from elite status substantially affected the living standards of the diverse social groups in the 1970s. In fact, as in the case of earnings, social benefits became an especially critical influence on the perceptions of inequality during the growing scarcity environment of the late 1970s. In these circumstances, as shortages of consumer goods and social services became more pronounced, privileges increasingly became more visible and contributed intensely to feelings of discontent and social injustice among the working class. These sentiments were affected both by the failure of social benefits to compensate for inequality of income, fueling the desire for more equal distribution, and by the conspicious consumption of the privileged that created a moral indignation channeled into a resentment of Polish elites.

The importance of social benefits in socialist societies is derived from the position that social policy is to perform a redistributive function, serving as a corrective to earning differences by improving the living conditions of the poorer strata through the provision of social services. In view of such official pronouncements, the normal expectations of the population are likely to be that expenditures in the social consumption fund are to serve the promotion of a more egalitarian distribution of goods and services by providing better social security, education, health care, or housing to low-income groups.[21] Such expectations, however, were largely disappointed in the Poland of the 1970s.

In the first place, Gierek's economic program was unable to sustain throughout the decade a multifaceted growth in industrial investment, consumption and social welfare. In the initial boom years, the government was able to proceed with the building of the second Poland by providing significant fiscal inputs (financed in large part by Western credits) into industrial development and, as a means of stimulating productivity, into the wage fund and social services. However, as the economy began to deteriorate in the mid-1970s, shortfalls began to be evident and the policy of growth across all three investment areas had to be curtailed. In an attempt to salvage the economy, the emphasis on industrial growth created a squeeze on the wage fund and social benefits. One consequence was to defer wage equalization so that pay differentials would serve as incentives for productivity. At the same time as income inequalities increased in the second half of the 1970s, the resources available for social welfare provisions also declined, so that the latter benefits could not be employed to counterbalance the growing earnings' dispersion. This trend is clearly visible from budgetary data in table 9-6, which indicates that from 1974 on the percentage of government expenditures on social security, health and education declined. The one exception in social services to the downward slide is in the area of housing, which was under especially severe strains so that the regime could not curb its commitment to housing construction. In general, however, a decline in the total allocation of resources to social welfare is evident at this time.

Nonetheless, since investments for the entire economy were being downgraded, the share of personal income derived from social benefits did not decline but was fairly stable throughout this period. Both social transfers in cash and in kind benefits derived from participation in collective consumption services remained steady at around 9 and 11 percent, respectively, of each individual's per capita income (table 9-6). That the portion of total income derived from social benefits remained steady at about 20 percent must be placed in the context of a positive correlation between personal income and gains from social welfare provisions,[22] meaning that the latter could not be used as a policy regulator to equalize differences in salaries and wages.

The evidence on the relation between these two components of income therefore calls into question the alleged redistributive function of social benefits. Ivan Szelenyi argued some time ago that the opposite effect is prevalent in socialist economies and that inequalities are due largely to the administrative allocation of goods and services to the wealthier sectors of society.[23] The case of Poland under Gierek certainly supports that argument, for the data on collective consumption among social strata indicates a maldistribution in favor of the high income groups. In 1975 for instance, the per capita value of social benefits was 40 percent higher in the uppermost income bracket than in the lowest, and the correlation held throughout the earnings' scale so that the larger the income the better value obtained from social services.[24] This linkage was true in virtually all areas of social welfare, with the disparities being

Table 9-6
Social Benefits: Expenditures and per Capita Income

	Percentage of Budget Expenditures on				Percentage of Social Benefits in		Benefit Ratio: Highest to Lowest Per Capita
	Social Security	Health	Housing	Education	Income Transfer	Collective Consumption	
1970	4.4	7.1	15.6	7.5	9.0	10.8	134.9
1971	5.1	7.0	15.4	8.0	9.4	11.4	N.A.
1972	5.2	7.3	13.9	8.2	9.1	11.6	N.A.
1973	5.1	7.8	13.3	8.5	8.9	11.5	123.6
1974	4.8	7.1	12.3	7.4	8.9	10.7	113.8
1975	5.2	6.8	13.1	7.2	8.4	10.7	126.5
1976	4.3	6.7	14.2	7.0	8.6	11.1	127.0
1977	4.4	6.6	16.0	6.7	9.0	11.0	N.A.
1978	N.A.	6.4	17.4	6.4	9.6	11.1	188.0

Source: David S. Mason, "Policy Dilemmas and the Polish Leadership," *Journal of Politics,* forthcoming. p. 5, table 1, and p. 7, table 2, and Henryk Flakierski, "Economic Reform and Income Distribution: The Negative Evidence," *Cambridge Journal of Economics* 5 (1981), p. 155, table 4, and p. 156, table 10.

especially significant in such critical benefits as health, housing, social security, and education. Moreover, the empirical trend shows a definite increase in the inequality of social welfare distribution over time during the second half of Gierek's rule. For example the cash social benefits obtained by the highest income bracket in comparison to the lowest one were 14 percent higher in 1974, 27 percent in 1976 and 88 percent in 1978 (table 9-6). The poorer groups were thus falling much further behind their more affluent counterparts. At the same time, it should be remembered, wages too were becoming further dispersed among the social strata.

The inevitable conclusion from the distribution and trend of social provisions in Poland during the late 1970s is that welfare benefits could not serve as a means to equalize real incomes. On the contrary, the advantage obtained by higher income groups from social redistribution signified that the latter contributed significantly to the growing gap in living standards among households from diverse socioeconomic strata. Since both cash transfers and collective consumption favored the more affluent, state welfare policy in fact compounded the inequality of wages. The reallocation of social funds by the government thus shaped further the structure of inequality in Poland rather than offering relief to the poorer groups. As a result of the better benefits obtained by higher income and white-collar groups, social inequality was more significant with welfare provisions than without them. That the working class was well aware of the impact that social benefits had on Polish society is evident from the August 1980 demands that not only wage but also social welfare policies be changed in favor of the poor.

The inequality present in the distribution of income and welfare aggrevated considerably the differences in consumption among the social groups. In particular during the last years of the Gierek period a polarization in the standard of living occurred, when the amenities enjoyed as a result of higher earnings became much more visible and were further compounded by other privileges derived from positions of power. The consequence was the emergence of a conspicuous consumption style that advertised openly the privileged status of the political and administrative elite.[25] The initial impetus for this nouveau riche living came from the government's program, which sought to reward strategic elites for their contribution to Gierek's economic policy. The boom years of the early 1970s facilitated the perpetuation of such behavior and led to the internalization of values that took for granted privileged compensation for service to the state. Ultimately this meant that conspicuous consumption became the mark of a successful career in the party or state apparatus.[26]

The benefits derived from positions of power were multivaried and touched all areas of socioeconomic activity.[27] Besides the higher salaries already available to most officials, they supplemented that pay through various income increments. Administrative personnel, for example, enjoyed special tax exemptions, family allowances, and honoraria, as well as work bonuses that provided a greater share of enterprise earnings to managers than industrial workers. Perhaps the most flagrant attempt at the institutionalization of social privileges for the political elite was the pension decree of October 1972, which provided no limits on retirement benefits and extended their beneficiaries to members outside the immediate family. Other instances of abuse of power also prevailed in the areas of housing, education, services, and justice. For example, in a nation with one of the worst housing records in Europe, one of the preferred perks of the elite was private villas and vacation homes, when families of non-manual employees already had better access to more spacious and better equipped housing than families of manual laborers. In the educational field, the point system that was designed to give preferential entry into universities to working class and peasant origin applicants was offset by the practice of ministrial and rectoral reserved places that went to the privileged. The latter also enjoyed access to scarce resources in the form of yellow curtain shops, foreign travel, exclusive health and holiday centers, as well as immunity from certain legal requirements, for example the R-ki exempting holders from traffic regulations, or the bypassing of construction codes by the elite.

Numerous other examples of social privileges enjoyed by the political and administrative personnel can be cited; the important point, however, is that these benefits were the manifestation of power abuses that provided the elite with goods and services that would otherwise be unavailable to them. The privileges were obtained because of connections, gifts, misappropriation of public funds, and other practices that permeated and corrupted the entire society. The privilege of status and position performed a demonstration effect that influenced the aspirations of all population strata. The problem was that in conditions of economic deterioration, such privileges could not be duplicated for society as a whole. On the contrary as shortages became more pronounced from the mid-1970s on, the working class was asked to absorb them through a decline in real income. And it is precisely because the elite was unwilling to sacrifice any of its benefits that the privileges of the political and managerial groups became so glaring in the late 1970s. As scarcities developed and corruption of power increased, the sense of relative deprivation among the working class was bound to be affected by the contrast between their material shortages and the elite's conspicuous consumption. Under the circumstances, feelings of frustration and anger at the arbitrary privileges and economic abuses were likely to surface.

This was especially so in view of the decline in mobility prospects for individuals of working class or peasant background. The pattern of the 1970s meant a significant decrease in intergenerational advancement, so that the working class became ever more hereditary in composition.[28] This translated into pessimism about personal opportunity, particularly as the prospects for working class individuals to ascend to low-level management positions diminished considerably in the late Gierek years.[29] Of course the discontent at the lack of opportunity for rising above blue-collar status was felt most intensely among young workers, who accounted for a particularly large portion of the Polish workforce. The percentage of young workers (under thirty was 35 percent in 1976, and most significantly it was highest in the metal, steelwork, and transportation (ca. 40 percent in each) sectors[30] where activism was most militant in the summer of 1980. The fact that young workers were most likely to maintain their class position must be juxtaposed with the increasing level of education of that youth, which produced higher expectations. The aspirations for social mobility, however, were blocked by the growing ossification of the Polish social structure, which was felt by the vast majority of the Polish population. Their subjective assessment on the question of equality and social justice is evident from a national opinion poll conducted in 1980 (table 9-7). Eighty-five percent of the respondents judged that inequalities in Polish society were very large or rather large, while in regard to trends over the last ten years 67 percent saw an increase in inequality but only 6 percent a decrease. Most striking is the ranking of positive values: 90 percent mentioned equality and justice, above law and order (82 percent), freedom of expression (71 percent) or information on authorities (61 percent), Clearly then, the frustrations born in

Table 9-7
Social Inequality and Injustice in
Society's Consciousness
(percent of responses)

Ranking of positive social values	
Equality and justice	90
Law and order	82
Freedom of expression	71
Information on authorities	61
Greater pay for skilled	26
Social inequalities are	
Very large	55
Rather large	30
Rather small	6
Very small	4
No opinion	5
Over the past ten years inequalities	
Increased	67
Decreased	6
No opinion	27

Source: Osrodek Badania Opinii Publiczej i Studiow Programowych (OBOP), Survey no. 27 (189), December 1980.

mobility blockage were uppermost in the minds of the working class—85 percent of that social group declaring the existence of inequalities.

The combination of social immobility and the demonstration of conspicuous consumption by the elite strata in the late 1970s proved to be an explosive problem. Increasingly cut off from advancement in the social structure, the working class realized it could never enjoy the social privileges available to the political-administrative apparatus. Rather, with the growing economic problems, industrial labor was faced increasingly with an environment of material scarcity. The authorities warned of further austerity measures and demanded the absorption of shortages by blue-collar workers.[31] In the face of the lack of individual opportunity, of blatant abuse of power by the political elite, and of shrinking economic benefits, the workers' only recourse appeared to be collective action to reverse the trend of events. The militant aspect of that action was forced upon the laboring class by the lack of political channels to express their discontent and seek redress.

Political Representation

Popular perceptions of the inadequacy of representative and participatory institutions were grounded in the development strategy initiated by Gierek in the post-December 1970 reevaluation of regime-society relations. A concentration of political authority within the party and government organizations was accomplished through a series of reforms in the early 1970s, in effect providing the Gierek leadership with undisputed control over national politics.[32] One of the fundamental steps in this process was an extensive administrative reform between 1973 and 1975 that effectively limited the political capabilities of the local and regional administrative units in favor of central party authorities, assuring greater responsiveness on the part of regional bureaucracies to Warsaw directives. A similar step involved the party organizations of the 164 largest enterprises, which were placed directly under the supervision of the Central Committee staff. While the proclaimed goal was to facilitate the exchange of information between industrial workers and the leadership to prevent renewed outbursts of labor discontent, the practical effect was to facilitate direct control of the major enterprises by the central party authorities. These administrative measures were enhanced by an expansion of the regime's supervision over the activities of public and state institutions. A major step in that direction was taken through the extension of the *nomenklatura* list to cover a wide range of social, educational, economic, and political positions to better control all aspects of people's lives.[33] Other efforts involved the restraint of public organizations by centralizing their operation under the strict guidance of the party. Of particular relevance to the working class was the creation of the Ministry of Labor, Wages, and Social Affairs, leading to a considerable concentration of policy formulation over issues of employment, wages, and work conditions. The shift signified a major devolution of the prerogatives of the trade unions in individual enterprises, further alienating blue-collar workers from institutions that were to function as representatives of working class interests.

The accumulation of power by the regime must be contrasted with the rhetoric of participation emanating from the authorities.[34] As a response to the growing assertiveness of the workers, as evident by the December 1970 and June 1976 unrest, the Gierek leadership sought to create the impression that the political center was paying attention to the interests of industrial labor by providing new channels for popular inputs into policy deliberations. The aim was to increase the workers' sense of political participation by exhorting such virtues of social democracy as leadership-mass consultations, the proletarian representativeness of social institutions, and workers' self-management. In reality these participatory mechanisms afforded only pro forma participation opportunities to the working class, while the content of policy deliberations continued to be determined by the party elite. While the government's emphasis on mass participation consisted primarily of gestures, it nonetheless introduced greater participatory expectations among the blue-collar stratum. It is in the wake of the gap between the premise of political involvement and the reality of workers' influence on decisionmaking that political inequalities in the polity and the work place emerged as a critical issue in the consciousness of the workers.

Evidence of differences in the political activism of the various social strata touches upon both political and economic participatory institutions. For example one of the major efforts of the Gierek administration involved an alteration of the Polish United Workers' Party's (PUWP's) membership in favor of industrial workers.[35] The action had as its basis an affirmative action program that sought to include a greater number of manual laborers in the Communist organization, in the hope of fostering working class support for the Party's policies. On the surface, the change in recruitment emphasis had a visible effect on the social composition of the ruling organization. After a prolonged period of stability in membership, with workers making up 40 percent of the total and white-collar groups about 44 percent, the trend was reversed in 1976 (table 9-8). From then on, the blue-collar component in the Party increased steadily, so that by 1979 the workers accounted for 46.2 percent of the PUWP members while the white-collar share had decreased to 33 percent. What appears to be at first a major shift favoring working class involvement in party politics is mitigated by other developments that testify to the continued underrepresentation of industrial labor in the PUWP and the Party's failure to provide the workers with political and economic opportunities.

In the first place the recruitment pattern reflected a continued disproportionate selection of members from white-collar groups, accounting for much

Table 9-8
Social Composition of the PUWP
(percentage)

	Workers	White Collar	Peasants	Others
1970	40.3	42.3	11.5	5.9
1971	39.7	43.6	10.6	6.1
1972	39.6	43.9	10.1	6.4
1973	39.4	44.0	10.2	6.4
1975	40.8	43.2	9.5	6.4
1976	44.9	38.8	9.3	7.0
1977	45.6	34.3	9.3	10.8
1978	45.7		9.4	
1979	46.2	33.0	9.4	11.4

Source: "Portret Partii," *Zycie Partii* 2 (1980) and *Rocznik Statystyczny,* annual.

higher saturation levels of the latter in comparison to the working class. At the end of the 1970s about 17 percent of all manual laborers were in the ranks of the PUWP, but the equivalent figure for the technocratic elite was close to 40 percent and for the professional strata above 50 percent.[36] This disparity in the share of the various social groups belonging to the PUWP was a reflection of the leadership's continued need to concentrate on infusing the Party with well-educated and skilled personnel capable of managing the modern society. The economic program of the Gierek regime placed a special demand on qualified professionals, thereby accounting for the permanance of high saturation of party membership by the white-collar stratum as compared with the working class. Another aspect limiting the effectiveness of workers' involvement n the PUWP was the much higher attrition rate of blue-collar members than their white-collar equivalents. The demands of activism, study, and responsibility were much more difficult to satisfy for the industrial laborer than the administrative employee, resulting in a greater reluctance to be active among workers than the nonmanual groups. The consequence was that many more workers resigned or were purged from party rolls than members of other social groups. To compensate for this different retention rate, workers made up a disproportionately higher percentage of new recruits. In effect the working class membership of the PUWP was subject to a revolving door phenomenon that signified lower stability in party affiliation, therefore limiting the influence of workers in party affairs. Of course this high membership turnover was in itself a reflection of the industrial labor's dissatisfaction with the Party's representation of blue-collar interests. The differences in saturation and attrition levels between the manual and nonmanual sections of the Party also had the effect of diminishing the mobility opportunities of the industrial workforce vis-à-vis the other strata. The stress on education and expertise as a requirement of Gierek's economic maneuver favored the white-collar population, who were then able to use party membership and political activism for social and economic advancement. In contrast, the lesser qualifications of working-class members considerably diminished their opportunity for upward occupational mobility in the late 1970s. Whereas party activism served previously as a stepping stone to managerial and administrative positions for some working class individuals, in the Gierek period the blue-collar employees found these positions increasingly closed off. The attraction of party membership thus declined, helping to account for the high attrition rate among workers. As a result of all these factors the party organization not only failed to represent labor's interests but ceased to function as a vehicle for individual workers' advancement.

The ineffectiveness of political participation as a channel for working class interests became especially evident in June 1976, when the government's attempted price increase met with the immediate opposition of the industrial labor force. These events clearly demonstrated that the regime's efforts to strengthen socialist democracy in order to be in tune with the opinions and demands of the workers were doomed once again to failure, as the consultations between leaders and laborers degenerated into routine forms that reflected bureaucratic views rather than the opinions of the workers or even the Party *aktif* cognizant of the labor's discontent. The government failure to gauge worker sentiments only strengthened the masses' perception that official political involvement could not be used to advance their interests. The consequence was a general decline between 1975 and 1978, evident from a public opinion survey, of citizens' participation in a variety of sociopolitical organizations, including production conferences, trade unions and workers' councils.[37]

Despite the downturn in political activism, the Gierek leadership paid little attention to a genuine reinvigoration of participatory and representative organs in the polity and the workplace. Instead it chose to revitalize the system through economic tinkering in the form of a new economic maneuver that left untouched the political arrangements and succeeded only in further alienating the workforce from the political authorities.

The perpetuation and even intensification of political inequalities in the late 1970s is especially visible at the enterprise level, where sociopolitical and economic activity varied substantially among the various sections of the workforce. The extent of workers' participation in factory organizations and policy discussions was substantially lower than that of other strata in the enterprise hierarchy. For example, a survey of thirty workers' self-government conferences in the mining industry showed that, of those taking part in discussion of issues, 22 percent were blue-collar and 78 percent were white-collar employees.[38] The impact of workers' opinions on policy content is thus likely to be less significant than that of the administrative and technical personnel, a conclusion supported by evidence concerning the scope of participation. An examination of workforce activities by occupational groups in the 164 largest enterprises revealed that in 1979 the engineering-technical strata overwhelmingly dominated all forms of activity not only in production but also in sociopolitical and workers' self-management institutions (table 9-9), despite an apparent willingness by the majority of the workers' to be active in decisions affecting work conditions.[39] Moreover, in the critical area of preparation for self-management conferences and meetings of trade union and political organizations the workers were also substantially underrepresented: only 13 percent of industrial employees took such action, as opposed to 24 percent of office workers and 38 percent of the technical personnel. Similar proportions were evident in regard to the fulfillment of elected functions in those sociopolitical organs, signifying that executive and administrative roles were also dominated by the white-collar employees. In the face of these findings, there is no doubt that workers' participation in enterprise activities was essentially nominal.

The inequalities in enterprise activism among the occupational strata severely limited the working class' ability to use participation in sociopolitical organizations as a channel for the presentation and defense of their interests. The result was that industrial workers attached little value to participatory opportunities in both the work place and the community, and instead increasingly perceived trade unions, self-management organs and party organizations as vehicles of management control. The lack of socialist democracy and the consequent differentiation in political influence was especially felt by the working class in the context of the growing socioeconomic inequalities and economic failures of the late 1970s, contributing further to the alienation of the blue-collar workforce and the intensification of social tensions in the industrial setting.

Table 9-9
Political Activism by Occupation
(percentage)

Enterprise Activities	Engineering Technical	Workers	Office Employees
Issue presentation to superiors	66.7	36.6	35.0
Issue presentation to sociopolitical organs	56.0	N.A.	35.7
Participation with comment at meetings	54.4	33.1	24.6
Preparation of materials for meetings	37.7	12.8	24.5
Election to sociopolitical organs	47.8	27.6	34.7

Source: Zbigniew Sufin, "Społeczne uwarunkowania i konsekwencje kryzysu," *Nowe Drogi* 12 (December 1980): 76.

The aggravation of relations between enterprise authorities and the workers was in large part due to the economic downturn in the second half of the Gierek decade. A principal consequence of the crisis was to strengthen the regime's reliance on a technocratic solution to the problems of industry, involving increased material incentives to management as an attempt to foster productivity. On the one hand this increased labor's dependence on administrative performance as a source of bonuses and social welfare, leading to substantial differences over distribution policies. On the other hand it transformed further the trade-union and self-management organs into vehicles for the stimulation of production, to the determinent of the representative functions of these organizations.[40] Instead of acting in defense of workers' interests, the latter's domination by white-collar personnel effectively turned the unions and councils into tools of management.

The workers' inability to foster their interests was aggravated at the same time by the bureaucracy's growing determination to safeguard the socioeconomic privileges attained during the first part of Gierek's rule. Precisely because of the growing economic difficulties, the Party and state cadres perceived the protection of their privileged position as their primary interest. In practice this involved a defense of the status quo that resisted any institutional transformations opening up the political process and providing the blue-collar stratum with a more significant voice in the determination of enterprise policies. Of course this attitude was reinforced by the centralized structure and practices of the Gierek regime, which also opposed a devolution of political power from the *apparat* to the masses. In these circumstances the workers' claims for improvements in their economic and social well-being remained unheeded and the aspirations of the manual workforce as well as its frustrations remained isolated from the official system of political and industrial relations. The working class' inability to express their interests through the official arrangements, much less to influence the content of economic and political decisions by means of political participation, forced them to develop alternative forms of activism to insure the satisfaction of their demands.[41] The alternatives increasingly involved actions outside the official framework, consisting for example of collective demonstrations in the form of work stoppages. These informal methods of representing workers' interests vis-à-vis management and political authorities widened the gap between the official system of workers' representation and industrial labor, instead channeling the workers' activism into more radical attempts to influence enterprise policies. The culmination of these efforts was the formation, from 1977 on, of a movement seeking to establish independent trade unions free of the Party's tutelage. This movement burst into the forefront of Polish politics in the wake of the summer 1980 strikes—a spontaneous expression of workers' discontent with the government's economic policies.

Inequalities, Politicization, Solidarity

The activism of the Polish working class in 1980 was rooted in the linkage between governmental policies, economic decline, and the resultant inequalities in society. The Gierek regime's inability to sustain a program of economic growth throughout the 1970s curtailed increased material compensation for all social groups. The ensuing retrenchment contributed to a disproportionate relative deprivation of the working class, which suffered a rapid decline in income growth at a time when the privileges of the political and managerial elites were maintained. As a consequence the inequalities in income and social welfare benefits became more pronounced and, in turn, strongly affected workers' perceptions. The conspicuous consumption advertising the privileged status of the elite was contrasted with the worsening living standards of manual labor. By the late 1970s the workers' subjective assessment of socioeconomic inequalities between the diverse social strata increased significantly, making the issue of social differences the most critical problem in the consciousness of the masses.

The perceptions of an inequitable socioeconomic distribution among social groups was aggravated by a growing rigidity of the social structure. In this context the mobility prospects for the average worker declined significantly and contributed to the view that industrial labor was permanently cut off from the privileges of the elite, instead facing increasing material scarcity. The lack of upward mobility for the working class made their awareness of inequalities and common aspirations for advancement more pronounced. In the face of entrenched privilege and power, the only resource for the alleviation of blue-collar frustrations appeared to be collective efforts for the redress of workers' grievances.

The politicization of the Polish working class stemmed from its failure to obtain economic and social justice through the official representative channels. The unresponsiveness of enterprise and social institutions to the demands of industrial workers increased their consciousness of the maldistribution of political power in Polish society. Inequalities in political influence of the different social strata became more critical in the face of shrinking economic resources, as the domination of enterprise organizations by white-collar employees precluded redress of the unequal income and welfare benefits. The failure to resolve the redistributive issue led to the accentuation of social tensions among the manual and nonmanual groups, a conflict that could not be alleviated to the satisfaction of the working class because of the inequities in political participation. The reality of workers' lack of influence in the industrial and community settings resulted in the rejection of the representative structures by the labor class, who sought instead to alter the distribution of political power in society by extrasystemic actions. These efforts took the form of informal collective pressures for the satisfaction of blue-collar demands that strengthened alternative mechanisms of interest representation and simultaneously mobilized the workforce to challenge the official structures of power.

The solidarity of the working class in the summer of 1980 was in turn the product of the workers' experience toward the end of Gierek's rule, and especially of the socioeconomic and political inequalities of the previous decade. The egalitarian, antihierarchical nature of the labor movement was immediately evident in the organization of the striking workers and in presentation of their grievances to the government.[42] The demands for socioeconomic justice and political equality formulated in the striking factories and shipyards were primarily a reflection of labor's frustrations in the 1970s. The original demands of the interfactory strike committee (MKS) in Gdansk and Szczecin, and the points of agreement between the MKS and the government in the August 31 accords are ample evidence of the workers' desire to rectify the social imbalances in Poland.[43] Moreover during the process of negotiations with the authorities and the mobilization of increased popular support, the movement's goals expanded from an attack upon the socioeconomic and political structures to the formulation of an egalitarian sociopolitical program.

The goal of equality was most evident in the call for economic redistribution emanating from the shipyards of the Baltic coast. The long-term dissatisfaction with income distribution was reflected in the attempt to rationalize the wage system by providing increments to all workers but channeling a greater proportional share to the poorer labor strata. The concern and solidarity with the poorest elements of Polish society were also visible in demands for improvements in the social welfare system: the establishment of a social minimum, allowances to large families, and increased aid to pensioners were all part of the Gdansk agreements. The resentment of conspicuous consumption by the power elite found a prominent place in the workers' grievances through their demands for the abolishment of special privileges of the political and administrative apparatus. Together all these issues formed the most numerous set of demands and by means of economic improvements for the working class, redistribution of social welfare benefits, and the limitation of privileges, sought to create a more egalitarian and just society.

At the same time the experience of industrial labor with existing structures of political participation and representation made the striking workes well aware of the need for institutional change as a guarantee of the socioeconomic gains. The previous inability of blue-collar workers to use tradeunion, self-management, and party structures to present their interests meant that alternative forms of representation had to be created. Without such new institutions the workers were condemned to extrasystemic, illegal actions as the only device for the formulation of their demands. The need for more permanent and acceptable mechanisms of representation gave rise to the most radical demand of the movement: the creation of independent, self-governing trade unions that would be concerned exclusively with the defense of workers' interests. The organization of a trade union outside the existing sociopolitical structure was meant to remove it from the influence of the white-collar stratum, providing instead a genuine voice to the working class. In turn the functioning of an independent organization as the true representative of labor depended on the availability of adequate information and the possibility of free expression. Trade unionism thus required the advocacy of civil liberties and a pluralism of ideas, turning the nascent workers' movement into a social force for economic and political reform. The previous experiences of the working class had made it well aware that economic changes could be guaranteed only through the democratization of the work place.

Notes

1. *The New York Times*, August 29, 1980. For an account of the negotiating process see Jadwiga Staniszkis, "The Evolution of Forms of Working-Class Protest in Poland: Sociological Reflections on the Gdansk-Szczecin Case, August 1980," *Soviet Studies* 33 (April 1981):204-231, and Andrzej Tymowski, *The Strike in Gdansk, August 14-31, 1980,* (New Haven, Conn.: Don't Hold Back, 1981).

2. Jack Bielasiak, "The Evolution of Crises in Poland," in Jack Bielasiak and Maurice Simon, eds., *Contemporary Polish Politics: Edge of the Abyss* (New York: Praeger, 1983), and Alex Pravda, "Poland 1980: From 'Premature Consumerism' to Labour Solidarity," *Soviet Studies* 34 (April 1982):167-199.

3. Stefan Nowak, "Values and Attitudes of the Polish People," *Scientific American* 245 (July 1981):45-53, and Jacek Kurczewski, "W Oczach Opinii Publicznej," *Kultura*, March 1, 1981.

4. Zbigniew Fallenbuchl, "The Polish Economy in the 1970s," in U.S. Congress Joint Economic Committee, *East European Economies Post-Helsinki* (Washington, D.C.: U.S. Government Printing Office, 1977).

5. Jack Bielasiak, "The Party: Permanent Crisis," in Abraham Brumberg, ed., *Poland: Genesis of a Revolution* (New York: Random House, 1981).

6. David Mason, "Policy Dilemmas and the Polish Leadership," *Journal of Politics*, forthcoming.

7. Jan Malanowski, *Polscy Robotnicy* (Warsaw: Książkai Wiedza, 1981), pp. 42-56, 111-158.

8. Lidia Beskid, "Potrzeby Ludnosci w Swietle Badan Społecznych," *Nowe Drogi* 6 (June 180):42-43. See also Lidia Beskid, "Warunki zycia klasy robotniczej," in Augustyn Wajda, ed., *Klasa Robotnicza w Społeczenstwie Socjalistycznym* (Warsaw: Ksiazka i Wiedza, 1979), and Mieczyslaw Kabaj, "Efektywuus c wzrostu plac," *Nowe Drogi* 2 (February 1980):128-142.

9. Wieslaw Krencik, "Tempo wzrostu a rozpietosc plac," *Gospodarka*

Planowa 4 (April 1980):202-211; Henryk Flakierski, "Economic Reform and Income Distribution in Poland: The Negative Evidence," *Cambridge Journal of Economics* 5 (1981):137-158; Maksymillian Pohorille, "Questions of Income Distribution in Poland," *Economic and Industrial Democracy* 3 (1982):159-176; and Jan Danecki, "Assumptions of Perspective Policy of Income Distribution in Poland," in the Polish Sociological Association, *Social Structure* (Wroclaw: Ossolinskich, 1978), pp. 53-78.

10. Flakierski, "Economic Reform and Income Distribution in Poland," p. 138.

11. Ibid., pp. 138-142.

12. Osrodek Badania Opinii Publicznej i Studiow Programowych, Survey no. 1 (192), January 1981.

13. Pohorille, "Questions of Income Distribution in Poland," pp. 164-165.

14. Flakierski, "Economic Reform and Income Distribution in Poland," p. 144.

15. Ibid., pp. 144-148, and Pohorille, "Questions of Income Distribution in Poland," pp. 164-165.

16. Nowak, "Values and Attitudes of the Polish People," p. 50. See also Stefan Nowak, "System Wartosci Społeczenstwa Polskiego," *Studia Sociologiczne* 4 (1979):155-173.

17. *Polacy 80: Wyniki Badan Ankietowych* (Warsaw: Polska Akademia Nauk, 1981), p. 106.

18. Osrodek Badania Opinii Publicznej i Studiow Programowych, Survey no. 10 (201), March 1981.

19. *Polacy 1980*, p. 82.

20. Staniszkis, "The Evolution of Forms of Working-Class Protest in Poland," and Tymowski, *The Strike in Gdansk.*

21. Waclaw Szubert, "Przedmiot, geneza i zakres socjalistycznej polityki społecznej," Antoni Kantecki and Jolanta Supinska, "Społeczne problemy konsumpcji," and Michal Winiewski, "Fundusze spozycia społecznego," all in Antoni Rajkiewicz, ed. *Polityka Społeczna* (Warsaw: PWE, 1979).

22. Pohorille, "Questions of Income Distribution in Poland," p. 169.

23. Ivan Szelenyi, "Social Inequalities in State Socialist Redistributive Economics," *International Journal of Comparative Sociology* 19 (1978):63-87. See also chapter 2, by Dan Nelson, in this volume.

24. Pohorille, "Questions of Income Distribution in Poland," p. 168, and Flakierski, "Economic Reform and Income Distribution in Poland," pp. 154-155.

25. Nowak, "Values and Attitudes of the Polish People," p. 51, and Aleksander Smolar, "Dystribucja Dobr Społecznych i Rozklad Systemu," *Aneks* 26 (1981):24-35.

26. Barbara A. Misztal and Bronislaw Misztal, "Transformations of Political

Elites in Poland," paper presented at the Annual Meeting of the Midwest Political Science Association, Milwaukee, April 1982, p. 10.

27. The discussion of privileges is based on Krzysztof Czabanski, "Przywileję," pt. 1, *Tygodnik Solidarnosc* 34, November 20, 1981, and pt. II *Tygodnik Solidarnosc* 35, November 27, 1981, and Smolar, "Dystribucja Dobr Społecznych i Rozklad Systemu," pp. 14-37.

28. Walter D. Connor, "Social Change and Stability in Eastern Europe," *Problems of Communism* (November-December 1977), pp. 16-32. See also Jan Bluszkowski, "Procesy ujednolicanja polozenia społecznego klasy robotniczej i inteligencji w społeczenstwie socjalistycznym," in Wajda, ed., *Klasa Robotnicza w Społeczenstwie Socjalistycznym,* pp. 135-164.

29. Jean Woodall, "New Social Factors in the Unrest in Poland," *Government and Opposition* 16 (January 1981):47-48.

30. Leszek Gilejko, "Postawy społecznopolityczne klasy robotniczej i ich uwarunkowania," in Wajda, ed., *Klasa Robotnicza w Społeczenstwie Socjalistycznym,* p. 270.

31. See the Central Committee Report to the Eighth Congress of the Polish United Workers' Party, *Trybuna Ludu* February 12, 1980. For a discussion of this issue, see Jack Bielasiak, "Polish Politics: The Permanence of Crisis," paper presented at the Annual Meeting of the American Political Science Association, Washington, D.C., August 1980, pp. 24-31.

32. Bielasiak, "The Party: Permanent Crisis," in Brumberg, ed., *Poland: Genesis of a Revolution.*

33. See the annex to Thomas Lowitt, "Y a-t-il des Etats en Europe de l'Est," *Revue Francaise de Sociologie* 2 (1979):450-465.

34. Jack Bielasiak, "Workers and Mass Participation in 'Socialist Democracy,'" in Jan F. Triska and Charles Gati, eds., *Blue-Collar Workers in Eastern Europe* (London: Allen and Unwin, 1981), pp. 88-107, and Jack Bielasiak, "Party Leadership and Mass Participation in Developed Socialism," in James Seroka and Maurice Simon, eds., *Developed Socialism* (Boulder, Colo.: Westview Press, 1982).

35. Bielasiak, "Workers and Mass Participation," in Triska and Gati, eds., *Blue-Collar Workers in Eastern Europe,* pp. 88-93.

36. Alex Pravda, "Political Attitudes and Activity," p. 52, and George Kolankiewicz, "Poland 1980: The Working Class under 'Anomic socialism'," p. 150, both in Triska and Gati, eds., *Blue-Collar Workers in Eastern Europe.*

37. Krzysztof Ostrowski and Zbigniew Sufin, "Aktywnosc społeczne w swietle badan," *Nowe Drogi* 11 (1979):161-163.

38. Roman Stefanowski, "Workers' councils 1956-1977," Radio Free Europe Research, Background Report no. 160, August 9, 1977. For analyses of workers' activism see Stefan Gajda, Janusz Kubasiewicz, and Kiejstut Roman Szymanski, "Społeczno-polityczna i produkcyjna aktywnosc zalog kluczowych zakladow pracy," pp. 95-118; Krzysztof Ostrowski, "Aktywnosc polityczna

robotnikow," pp. 119-134, and Waldemar Stelmach, "Udzial robotnikow w procesach zarzadania socjalistycznymi zakladami pracy," pp. 307-328, all in Wajda, ed., *Klasa Robotnicza w Spoleczenstwie Socjalistycznym.*

39. Adam Sarapata, "Polish Automobile Workers and Automation," in Jan Forslin, Adam Sarapata, and Arthur Whitehill, eds., *Automation and Industrial Workers*, vol. 1 (Oxford: Pergamon Press, 1979), p. 126.

40. Woodall, "New Social Factors in the Unrest in Poland," pp. 48-53.

41. Pravda, "Poland 1980" pp. 176-177.

42. Staniszkis, "The Evolution of Forms of Working-Class Protest in Poland." For a thorough examination of the workers' movement position toward egalitarianism, see David S. Mason, "Solidarity and Socialism," in Bielasiak and Simon, eds., *Contemporary Polish Politics: Edge of the Abyss.*

43. *Protokoly Purozumien Gdansk, Szczecin, Jastrzebie i Statut NSZZ "Solidarnosc"* (Warsaw: KAW, 1980).

10 Regional Inequalities in Czechoslovakia

Sharon L. Wolchik

Inequalities between men and women and among members of different classes in Czechoslovakia have led to political conflict at times and continue to have important implications for politics and policymaking at present.[1] There is little doubt, however, that the most politically significant social cleavages have been those based on ethnicity. The nature of ethnic conflict and the ethnic composition of the country have changed somewhat since the institution of a communist political system. Nevertheless, ethnic relations continue to be of concern to policymakers, and communist leaders have not been spared the difficult task of attempting to defuse the political problems that arise from ethnic tensions and inequality.

As numerous scholars have noted, conflict between the two main ethnic groups in contemporary Czechoslovakia, the Czechs and the Slovaks, predates the establishment of the current political system.[2] Members of these two nationalities share certain traits, including languages so closely related as to be mutually intelligible. These similarities, however, have proved far less significant for Czech–Slovak relations than the differences between the two groups that resulted from very different political histories and different levels of economic development.

Brought together in a common political state for the first time in 1918, Czechs and Slovaks entered the unified state with radically different experiences. The Czechs, who lived in the most industrially advanced area of the Hapsburg Empire, also had had the possibility of developing a national movement led by a Czech-speaking intelligentsia and the opportunity of participating in limited self-government under Austrian administration.[3] For the most part literate, they also had developed a relatively large urban middle class prior to the creation of the Czechoslovak Republic. The Slovaks, under Hungarian rule for over 1,000 years, experienced far less favorable conditions for national development. Under intense pressure to assimilate to the dominant Magyar culture, unable to establish Slovak language schools, and extremely limited in their ability to form Slovak national organizations, the Slovaks also inhabited an area that remained one of the least developed and most backward areas of the Austro-Hungarian Empire. As the result of these factors, Slovakia entered the new state with high illiteracy rates and a predominantly rural population.[4]

The Czechoslovak state established in 1918 did relatively little to remedy these differences. Efforts were made to develop Slovakia industrially and to improve the educational levels of Slovaks, but, with the exception of the latter

249

goal, met with little success. Thus, although the number of educated Slovaks increased markedly during this period and the number of Slovaks employed in industry also increased,[5] economic developments continued to be more favorable in the Czech Lands than in Slovakia, and elite efforts to improve Slovakia's position did little to close the gap between the two halves of the country.[6] Further, because policies with respect to Slovakia were decided upon in Prague and carried out largely by bureaucrats and teachers from the Czech Lands, they were often seen by Slovaks as further evidence of their unequal status in the Republic. Slovak dissatisfaction with the position of Slovakia within the unified state was one of the forces that helped to undermine the Czecho-slovak Republic during the interwar period;[7] it also led many Slovaks, including certain members of the new Slovak intelligentsia, to see the Slovak state set up in 1939 under Nazi tutelage as the realization of Slovak national aims.[8]

During the period between the two world wars, conflict between Czechs and Slovaks was compounded by that which arose from the other minorities in the state, most notably the Sudeten Germans, Hungarians, and Ukrainians, or Ruthenians. The forced transfer of the Sudeten Germans and Hungarians, and the loss of the Subcarpathian Ruthene to the Soviet Union at the end of World War II simplified the ethnic picture in Czechoslovakia,[9] but it did not eliminate the major source of ethnic conflict, that between Czechs and Slovaks.

The institution of a new political system in Czechoslovakia after World War II revived Slovak hopes for equality within a Czechoslovak state. Although the Košice government program adopted in 1945 as the basis of government of the newly liberated state did not explicitly mention federation, it did give wider guarantees to Slovak rights than had existed in Czechoslovakia during the interwar period.[10] Slovak hopes for equality in the new order were disappointed, however, for the communist leadership that came to power in 1948 soon embarked on centralist policies similar to those which had been adopted by the interwar governments. Slovak institutions, such as the Slovak National Council and Board of Commissioners, originally established as organs of self-government, were subordinated to the central government and functioned primarily to implement policies made in Prague. Slovak autonomy was further curtailed, and Slovak aspirations for recognition of their claims to cultural equality dashed, during the purge trials of the 1950s, when many native Slovak communist leaders were imprisoned or executed on charges of bourgeois nationalism.[11]

Slovak intellectuals and leaders only began openly to press their demands for greater equality in the 1960s during the period of innovation and experimentation that led up to the Prague Spring, and it was during this period that ethnic relations and the relative status of Czechs and Slovaks became once again central topics of political discussion and debate.[12] It was also in this context that Slovak intellectuals began openly discussing remaining inequalities between the Czech Lands and Slovakia. Although much of the discussion during this period centered on the legal and political aspects of Czech–Slovak relations, particularly on the question of federalization, economic issues, including Slovakia's relative level of economic development, were also important topics of debate. Certain economists and planners questioned the extent to which earlier programs designed to equalize the two parts of the country had succeeded. Acknowledging the efforts made to compensate for Slovakia's lower level of development prior to the institution of a communist system and the success of these efforts in industrializing the region, they nonetheless argued that the approach adopted by the centralized government was inadequate.[13]

As Victor Pavlenda, a Slovak economist who played an important role in the discussions during the reform period, noted in a book originally written in 1966 but published only in 1968, considerable differences remained in the level of economic development between the two regions. Pavlenda also discussed the impact of Slovakia's unequal status for the everyday lives of Slovaks. Noting that the leadership's goal was to equalize the living conditions of all citizens in Czechoslovakia, he noted that Slovaks typically had lower average wages than Czechs, worse housing , and fewer consumer goods. He also noted continued inequalities in health care and education between the two regions.[14] Countering claims that the federal government in the proposed federation should retain control of most economic planning, Pavlenda argued that only political autonomy and Slovak control over economic decisions would lead to the rapid elimination of existing inequalities.[15]

On October 27, 1968 the Czechoslovak National Assembly approved a law making Czechoslovakia a federal state.[16] The federal system adopted represented a compromise between the numerous proposals and viewpoints concerning the division of authority among federal and republic governments. Somewhat more centralistic in its formulation than many Slovaks desired,[17] the federal system was also enacted in political conditions far different from those envisioned by many of its supporters, who also supported the political reform ended by the Warsaw Pact intervention in Czechoslovakia in August 1968. Nonetheless, with this step, Slovak aspirations for an equal place in the Czechoslovak state were formally at least, satisfied.

Opinion varies widely about the actual meaning of this change for the status of Czechs and Slovaks. Czech and Slovak analysts tend, as may be expected, to emphasize the positive impact federalization has had in Slovakia, as well as the continued improvement in relations among Czechs and Slovaks that has allegedly followed the change.[18] Western analysts, on the other hand, have more frequently depicted federalization as largely window dressing. Pointing to the changes that increased the power of the federal government vis-à-vis the republics after federalization was enacted as well as the fact that the Communist party did not adopt a truly federal structure, such analysts argue that power remains largely centralized in Prague and Slovak autonomy a goal for the future.[19]

Despite the interest that federalization aroused at the time it was discussed and enacted, there has been little systematic evaluation of its results by Western scholars. This chapter is an attempt to examine this issue by focusing on the status of Czechs and Slovaks since 1968. Part of a larger study of Czech and Slovak relations, it does not evaluate the actual decisionmaking power of central versus republic governmental bodies or look at the extent to which the day-to-day operation of the political system approximates its description in the new constitution. Nor does it examine the impact of federalization on the ways in which Czechs and Slovaks perceive each other. Rather, it seeks to answer two more modest questions. First, to what extent has the position of Slovakia improved compared to the Czech Lands since the institution of a communist state in terms of levels of development and standard of living? Have communist leaders been successful, that is, in closing the persistent gap between Czechs and Slovaks? Secondly, what impact has federalization had on the actual status of Czechs and Slovaks? Have there been any marked changes in the relative position of members of these nationalities since 1968? If so, are these changes part of a larger process of equalization that began much earlier or do they indeed represent a significant improvement in the status of Slovaks dating from the time the federal system was enacted?

Measuring Equality: Approach and Limitations

Efforts to assess the relative status of members of different ethnic groups are subject to many of the controversies concerning how best to evaluate data concerning aspects of social and economic change. Several scholars have noted problems with the types of data available. One's judgment concerning the extent to which communist leaders have been successful in equalizing the status of members of various groups can, in fact, depend a good deal on the indicators chosen for examination.[20] The approach used in this chapter is based on a composite of indicators used by Czech and Slovak analysts in their discussions of social change in that country and others that appear most relevant to assessing the actual level of well-being of citizens in the Czech Lands and Slovakia.

In the pages to follow, I analyze the relative position of Slovakia and the Czech Lands in terms of levels of urbanization (measured by the proportion of inhabitants in each area living in cities over 20,000); of the labor force employed in industry and agriculture; and the share of national income (*národní duchod*) produced in each region. I also examine investment patterns (as indicated by total capital investment). As noted earlier, the ultimate goal of efforts to equalize conditions in the Czech Lands and Slovakia has been to neutralize the potential political effects of existing economic and social differences. Although the indicators listed may be of most concern to economic planners and other policymakers, the typical Slovak or Czech is far more concerned with what these indicators mean for the standard of living. Such perceptions concerning relative levels of material well-being pose the most serious potential political consequences. I thus also examine several indicators of material well-being, including infant mortality rates (as measured by the number of infants per 1,000 live births who die before one year of age); the number of students of higher education per 1,000 population between the ages of twenty and twenty-nine; and the average wage in the socialized sector of the national economy excluding agriculture. Finally, I examine the ownership of consumer durables, including washing machines, refrigerators, radios, televisions, and personal automobiles, in each part of the country.[21]

Ideally I would be most interested in comparing the status of Czechs and Slovaks. The data I have used are limited, however, insofar as they are available only for the two territorial areas of the state, the Czech Lands and Slovakia, rather than for individual nationality groups. In the Czech Lands, use of this information does not constitute a major problem, since most residents are Czech. In Slovakia a larger proportion of the population is not ethnically Slovak, however, but Hungarian or Ukrainian (Ruthenian). In 1970, for example, Czechs accounted for 94.5 percent of the inhabitants of the Czech Lands, while Slovaks constituted 85.5 percent of the inhabitants of Slovakia. Hungarians comprised 12.2 percent of the population in Slovakia and Ukrainians (Ruthenians) and Russians, 0.9 percent[22] The data presented for Slovakia, then, include information not only about Slovaks but about Hungarians and members of other ethnic groups. This limitation is not as serious as it may at first appear, however, for Czech and Slovak discussions of the issue tend to be couched far more frequently in terms of the relative positions of the two territorial units rather than of members of particular ethnic groups. Similarly, while it is the Czech–Slovak ethnic identification and the national aspirations of members of these national groups that have formed the basis of political conflict in the post–World War II state as well as the Czechoslovak Republic, this conflict has been expressed in territorial terms. Finally, even in Slovakia, Slovaks are by far the single largest ethnic group and thus most influenced by the trends discussed for the territory as a whole.

Trends in Levels of Development and Material Well-Being

Capital Investment per Capita

As the information presented in table 10-1 indicates, efforts to overcome the legacy of Slovakia's economic backwardness have been reflected in a level of capital investment per capita that has been higher in Slovakia than in the Czech Lands throughout the post–World War II period. Differences between the two areas appear to have been highest in early communist period, as the rate of investment per capita in Slovakia in 1950 was 1.2 times that in the Czech Lands. By the mid-1950s, however, Slovakia's edge decreased somewhat to 1.1 times the investment per capita in Bohemia and Moravia, a ratio that has remained

Table 10-1
Capital Investment Per Capita[a]
(selected years and five-year averages)

	CSSR	Czech Lands	Slovakia	Ratio: Slovakia/ Czech Lands
1950	15.4 Kcs	14.5	17.8	1.23
1955–1958[b]	27.0	26.4	28.8	1.09
1959–1963	40.4	39.9	41.4	1.04
1964–1968	47.1	45.9	49.8	1.08
1969–1973	66.1	64.8	68.9	1.06
1974–1978	88.4	87.4	92.8	1.06
1970	94.0	92.6	98.9	1.07
1980	95.4	93.5	101.1	1.08

Sources: From investment information in Federální statistický úřad, *Statistická ročenka ČSSR,* 1970, pp. 24–25; 44–45; 58–59; 1977, pp. 24–25; 42–43; 58–59; 1981, pp. 22–23; 40–41; 56–57 and population information in Státní úřad statistický republiky Československvenske, *Statistická ročenka republiky Československke* 1959, p. 54; 1960, p. 57; Ústřední komise lidové kontroly a statistiky, *Statistická ročenka ČSSR,* 1965, p. 84; 1966, p. 74; Státní statistický, úřad ČSSR, *Statistická ročenka ČSSR,* 1968, p. 70; Federální statistický, úřad, *Statistická ročenka ČSSR,* 1972, p. 101; 1977, p. 91; 1981, p. 107.

[a]standardized to 1967 prices

[b]1955–1958.

virtually unchanged throughout the 1960s and 1970s. Given this pattern, it is evident that federalization has not had an impact, one way or another, on relative investment levels in the two halves of the country, at least if we consider total investments.[23]

Composition of the Labor Force

One of the clearest changes in the relative position of Slovakia and the Czech Lands has occurred in the composition of the labor force, as measured by the proportion of the labor force engaged in agriculture or industry and construction. At the start of the communist period, the Czech Lands were considerably more industrialized than Slovakia. As tables 10-2 and 10-3 indicates, there has been a substantial equalization of the two regions in this respect, as reflected in the distribution of workers and employees in various sectors of the national economy.

If we look at employment in industry and construction, we find that approximately one-half as large a proportion of the labor force was employed

Table 10-2

Percentage of the Labor Force in Industry and Construction

(selected years and five-year averages)

	CSSR	Czech Lands	Slovakia	Ratio: Slovakia/ Czech Lands
1948	29.6	39.0	21.3	.55
1950	36.3	40.5	25.2	.62
1954–1958	40.4	45.0	27.5	.61
1959–1963	45.4	49.7	35.8	.73
1964–1968	46.6	49.0	39.4	.80
1969–1973	46.9	48.8	42.0	.86
1974–1978	48.0	49.4	44.5	.90
1979	47.9	45.2	45.2	.92
1980	46.5	45.1	45.1	.92

Sources: From information in Státní statistický úřad, *Statistická ročenka ČSSR*, 1968, pp. 22–23, 44–45, 62–63; Federální statistický úřad, *Statistická ročenka ČSSR*, 1969, pp. 22–23, 42–43, 58–59; 1970, pp. 22–23, 42–43, 58–49; 1977, pp. 20–21, 40–41, 56–57; 1981, pp. 22–23, 40–41, 56–57.

Note: Total includes women on maternity leave and extended maternity leave.

Table 10-3

Percentage of the Labor Force in Agriculture

(selected years and five-year averages)

	CSSR	Czech Lands	Slovakia	Ratio: Slovakia/ Czech Lands
1948	40.4	32.9	60.2	1.83
1950	36.9	30.6	53.5	1.75
1954–1958	31.0	25.0	46.9	1.88
1959–1963	23.1	19.4	33.6	1.73
1964–1968	18.9	16.4	26.2	1.60
1969–1073	16.8	13.9	21.6	1.55
1974–1978	13.9	12.1	17.2	1.42
1970	12.8	11.5	15.7	1.37
1980	12.7	11.4	15.5	1.36

Sources: From information in Státní statistický úřad, *Statistická ročenka ČSSR*, 1968, pp. 22–23, 44–45, 62–63; Federální statistický úřad, *Statistická ročenka ČSSR*, 1969, pp. 22–23, 42–43, 58–59; 1970, pp. 22–23, 42–43, 58–59; 1977, pp. 20–21, 40–41, 56–57; 1981, pp. 22–23, 40–41, 56–57.

in these areas in Slovakia as in the Czech Lands in 1948. Although a somewhat higher proportion of the labor force continues to be employed in industry and construction in the Czech Lands than in Slovakia, differences between the two regions decreased greatly in the past thirty years and were minimal by 1980. The largest part of this change occurred before federalization and reflects a slow but continuous process of change. At the same time, it is interesting that it was only in 1966 that the proportion of the labor force employed in these two areas in Slovakia surpassed that in the Czech Lands in 1948.[24] Differences between the two areas continued to decline after 1968, but at a slower annual rate.

There has also been a substantial change in the proportion of the labor force in each region employed in agriculture. As table 10-3 illustrates, over 60 percent of Slovakia's labor force, compared to approximately 33 percent of that in the Czech Lands, was engaged in agriculture in 1948. By 1980 this proportion had dropped markedly in both parts of the country. While proportionately more people are still employed in agriculture in Slovakia than in the Czech Lands, the difference between the two regions has decreased slowly but steadily throughout the post-World War II period. Whereas 1.83 times as many people in Slovakia as in the Czech Lands were working in agriculture in 1948, by 1980 this ratio was 1.36. In contrast to the trends in employment in industry and construction, however, the difference between the two areas in terms of the percentage of the labor force in agriculture decreased more rapidly from 1969 to 1980.[25] Despite this progress, however, approximately one-third more of the labor force remains in agriculture in Slovakia than in the Czech Lands.

Urbanization

In addition to the changes in the composition of the labor force in Slovakia the region has also become more urbanized (see table 10-4). As comparison of the proportion of total inhabitants living in cities with over 20,000 population in Slovakia and the Czech Lands indicates, differences between the two regions have decreased substantially in the past three decades. Whereas approximately four-tenths as many people lived in cities of this size in Slovakia as in the Czech Lands in 1950, by 1980, this ratio was 0.7. Although the urban population increased somewhat in Slovakia prior to 1968, much of the increase in population in cities of this size occurred between 1970 and 1980. In 1968 for example, the proportion of inhabitants in Slovakia living in cities over 20,000 was nearly 10 percentage points lower than it was in the Czech Lands in 1950.[26] Despite the more rapid increase in urbanization in Slovakia in the decade between 1970 and 1980, the proportion of inhabitants in Slovakia living in cities of this size

Table 10–4
Proportion of Total Population Living in Cities over 20,000
(selected years)

	CSSR	Czech Lands	Slovakia	Ratio: Slovakia/ Czech Lands
1950	23.6	28.2	11.5	.41
1955	24.9	28.9	14.7	.51
1961	25.3	30.4	13.6	.45
1964	27.6	32.5	16.3	.50
1968	29.2	34.1	18.3	.54
1970	31.1	35.7	21.0	.59
1980	40.0	44.0	31.8	.72

Sources: From information in Státní statistický úřad republiky Československé, *Statistická ročenka republiky Československé*, 1957, p. 37; 1959, p. 59; Státní statistický úřad Československé socialistické republiky, *Statistická ročenka ČSSR*, 1960, p. 58; Ústřední komise lidové kontroly a statistiky, *Statistická ročenka ČSSR*, 1966, p. 80; Federální statistický úřad, *Statistická ročenka ČSSR*, 1972, p. 84; 1981, p. 94.

in 1980 was approximately equal to the proportion of people in the Czech Lands in cities of comparable size in the early 1960s.[27]

National Income Produced

To what extent have the slightly higher levels of investment in Slovakia and the changes in the composition in the labor force affected production in Slovakia? In assessing the levels of development of the two regions in the country, Czech and Slovak analysts most frequently point to relative shares of national income produced (defined as the newly created values embodied in all material goods produced in a given year in the productive branches of the national economy).[28] If we look at this measure, standardized by the population in each part of the country, we see that there has been some improvement of Slovakia's relative position between 1960 and 1980. In table 10-5 one finds that the gap between the two regions closed more rapidly in the second decade of the period for which data are available than for the period between 1960 and 1968. Without comparable data for earlier time periods, however, it is not possible to draw firm conclusions concerning the relative amount of change before and after 1968.[29]

To what extent have these changes in levels of development had an impact on the lives of citizens of Slovakia and the Czech Lands? In the section to

Table 10-5
National Income Produced per Capita
(selected years and five-year averages)

	Slovakia/Czech Lands
1960	.74
1963–1968	.74
1969–1973	.79
1974–1978	.83
1979	.85
1980	.85

Sources: From information on national income in Federální statistický úřad, *Statistická ročenka ČSSR,* 1969, pp. 151, 160; 1970, pp. 151, 153; 1974, pp. 167, 169; 1977, pp. 133, 135; 1981, pp. 148, 151 and population in Ústřední komise lidové kontroly a statistiký, *Statistická ročenka ČSSR,* 1965, p. 84 and 1966, p. 74; Státní statistický úřad, *Statistická ročenka ČSSR,* 1968, p. 90; Federální statistický úřad, *Statistická ročenka ČSSR,* 1972, p. 101; 1977, p. 91; 1981, p. 107.

follow, I examine this impact by looking at educational access, incomes, infant mortality rates, and ownership of consumer durables.

Educational Access

The single area in which Slovakia has gained most in relation to the Czech Lands in the past three decades has been access to education. As table 10-6 illustrates, the proportion of students in higher education per 1,000 population between the ages of twenty and twenty-nine increased greatly in Slovakia since 1950 and has been higher in Slovakia than in the Czech Lands during several periods. The proportion of students in higher education per 1,000 population between the ages of twenty and twenty-nine in Slovakia already approximated the rate in the Czech Lands by 1956 and remained at this level until the mid-1960s, when it surpassed the Czech level. The difference between the two regions continued to increase, in Slovakia's favor, throughout the late 1960s and early 1970s, reaching a peak in 1973 when the proportion of students in Slovakia was six-tenths higher than in the Czech Lands.[30]

At first sight this area appears to be one in which federalization has had a noticeable effect, for differences between the two regions increased after 1968. However, the higher proportion of students in Slovakia during the late 1960s and early 1970s in fact appears more directly related to another phenomenon: the different impact the end of the reform period in the 1960s had in each part of the country. Less involved, by most accounts, in supporting the democratizing aspects of the reform than the Czechs, the Slovaks suffered fewer reprisals and purges once the reform period was forcibly stopped.[31] The magnitude of these differences in the educational realm is evident in the fact

Table 10-6

Total Students in Higher Education per 1,000 Population 20-29 Years of Age

(selected years and five-year averages)

	CSSR	Czech Lands	Slovakia	Ratio: Slovakia/ Czech Lands
1950	21.6	23.0	18.1	.79
1954-1958[a]	40.3	40.8	38.9	.95
1959-1963[b]	63.2	62.1	65.1	1.04
1964-1968	68.7	64.4	79.4	1.24
1969-1973	54.6	47.4	71.6	1.52
1974-1978	64.6	58.5	77.0	1.33
1979	76.2	72.2	83.3	1.15
1980	80.6	77.4	86.2	1.11

Sources: Information on students in higher education taken from Státní statistický úřad, *Statistická ročenka ČSSR,* 1968, pp. 42–43, 60–61, 78–79; Federální statistický úřad, *Statistická ročenka ČSSR,* 1977, pp. 38–39; 54–55; 70–71; 1981, pp. 38–39; 54–55. Data on population between the ages of 20–29 based on information in Státní úřad statistický republiky Československé, *Statistická ročenka republiky Československé,* 1959, pp. 55–58; 1960, p. 57; Ústřední úřad státní kontroly a statistiky, *Statistická ročenka ČSSR,* 1961, p. 75; Ústřední komise lidové kontroly a statistiky, *Statistická ročenka ČSSR,* 1963, p. 67; 1964, p. 117; 1965, p. 84; 1966, p. 75; Státní statistický úřad, *Statistická ročenka ČSSR,* 1967, p. 75; 1968, p. 91; Federální statistický úřad, *Statistická ročenka ČSSR,* 1969, p. 85; 1970, p. 85; 1972, p. 102; 1974, p. 101; 1977, p. 96; 1979, p. 101; 1981, p. 112.

[a] 1954-1958

[b] 1959, 1960-1963.

that there was a decrease in the absolute numbers of students in higher education in the Czech Lands after 1968, a decrease that lasted until 1974; during this period the number of total students in higher education decreased from 86,049 in 1968 to 72,731 in 1972. Only in 1975 did the number of students exceed the number receiving higher education in 1968. In Slovakia, by contrast, the total number of students decreased by 600 between 1968 and 1969, but then increased steadily throughout this period to 54,685 in 1974.[32] By the end of the 1970s the impact of these differing trends had decreased substantially. While differences between the Czech Lands and Slovakia decreased once again in the last decade, the proportion of students in higher education per 1,000 population from twenty to twenty-nine years of age remains a tenth higher in Slovakia than in the Czech Lands at present.[33]

Infant Mortality

Results in the area of health are not as favorable as they are in education, despite a substantial improvement in absolute levels of infant mortality in Slovakia. As table 10-7 suggests, infant mortality rates differed greatly in the Czech Lands

Table 10-7
Infant Mortality per 1,000 Live Births
(selected years and five-year averages)

	CSSR	Czech Lands	Slovakia	*Ratio:* *Slovakia/* *Czech Lands*
1948	83.5	71.5	109.5	1.53
1950	77.7	64.2	103.5	1.61
1954-1958	26.5	26.7	43.9	1.64
1959-1963	21.4	20.2	28.1	1.39
1964-1968	23.2	21.6	25.9	1.19
1969-1973	22.0	20.2	25.2	1.24
1974-1978	20.2	18.7	22.9	1.22
1980	18.4	16.8	20.9	1.24

Sources: From information in Federální statistický úřad, *Statistická ročenka ČSSR,* 1965, pp.22–23; 1969, pp. 22–23, 42–43, 58–59; 1977, pp. 20–21, 40–41, 56–57; 1981, pp. 20–21, 40–41, 56–57.

and Slovakia at the beginning of the postwar period. Although mortality rates were high in both parts of the country immediately after World War II and reflect the impact of the war on maternal health, in Slovakia approximately half again as many infants per 1,000 live births died before reaching one year as in the Czech Lands. The proportion of infants who die decreased rapidly in both parts of the country between 1950 and 1980. The decrease was particularly great in Slovakia during the 1950s, when mortality rates decreased from 103.3 per 1,000 live births in 1950 to 28.6 by 1960. Although infant mortality continued to decrease between 1960 and 1980 in Slovakia, the rate of decrease diminished, and the ratio of such mortality in Slovakia to that in the Czech Lands thus decreased very little. As the five-year averages in table 10-7 illustrate, the difference between the two regions on this indicator in fact increased on several occasions in the past twenty years and was greater in 1980 than in 1961. Federalization, then, appears to have had minimal influence on relative levels of health care, at least as reflected in infant mortality rates.[34]

Income

Adequate information to assess the degree to which incomes differ in the Czech Lands and Slovakia is difficult to obtain. As Table 10-8 indicates, average monthly wages in the socialized sector of the economy excluding agriculture have been very similar in both regions since 1948. Average monthly wages in industry are also virtually the same in the Czech Lands and Slovakia.[35] However,

Table 10-8

Average Monthly Wage in the Socialized Sector of the National Economy (Excluding Agricultural Cooperatives)

(selected years and five-year averages)

	CSSR	Czech Lands	Slovakia	Ratio: Slovakia/ Czech Lands
1948	823 Kcs.	834 Kcs.	764 Kcs.	.92
1950	948	970	854	.88
1953	1,097	1,111	1,036	.93
1954–1958[a]	1,255	1,267	1,139	.90
1959–1963	1,381	1,392	1,341	.96
1964–1968	1,570	1,578	1,543	.98
1969–1973	2,016	2,024	1,990	.98
1974–1978	2,373	2,386	2,342	.98
1979	2.579	2,592	2,549	.98
1980	2,642	2,656	2,611	.98

Sources: Federální statistický úřad, *Statistická ročenka ČSSR,* 1970 pp. 40–41, 58–59, 22–23; 1977, pp. 20–21, 40–41, 56–57; 1981, pp. 22–23, 40–41, 56–57.

[a]1955, 1957, 1958.

because of differences in the structure of the labor force, particularly the larger proportion of people working in agriculture in Slovakia who are not included in the average monthly wage information, these data may not accurately portray actual differences in individual incomes.

Available information concerning total income of the population in each region suggests that incomes are still somewhat lower in Slovakia but that the difference is decreasing over time. Thus the total income of the population standardized by population in Slovakia was 0.73 that in the Czech Lands in 1969. By 1976 this ratio had increased to 0.88 and by 1980 to 0.89.[36] Unfortunately, lack of comparable information for the period prior to 1969 prevents us from evaluating the extent to which trends in this area have changed since 1968. However, the information that is available indicates that there has been an improvement in this respect since federalization.

Consumer Durables

Relative trends in the ownership of consumer durables also illustrate the improvement in the standard of living in Slovakia in the past three decades. Whether one looks at ownership of electric washing machines, refrigerators, automobiles, radios, or televisions, differences between the Czech Lands and Slovakia have decreased since the first date for which information is available (see table 10-9). Only in the case of two of the consumer durables examined (radios and refrigerators), however, have differences been completely eliminated. Trends in the decrease of difference between the two regions before and after 1968 differ according to object. In the case of radios, washing machines, and televisions, the rate of change has been either relatively the same in the periods before or after this year, or greater in the earlier period. However, the data in table 10-9 do provide some support for the popular perception in the Czech Lands that Slovakia has experienced a faster improvement in the standard of living since 1968, for differences in the ownership of refrigerators and personal automobiles have declined more rapidly after 1968.[37] While the picture is mixed then, in terms of the rate of improvement after 1968, it has also been in the post-1968 period that the number of homes equipped with televisions and electric washing machines per 100 homes has equaled or exceeded 100 in Slovakia.[38]

Conclusion

The picture is mixed in terms of how successful communist leaders have been in overcoming differences between Slovakia and the Czech Lands. Compared to the situation before the institution of a communist system, Slovakia clearly has made a good deal of progress. Its relative position vis-à-vis the Czech Lands has also improved. In all except two of the areas examined, Slovakia still ranks behind the Czech Lands, but differences have decreased over time in most areas.

The composition of the labor force in the two regions is more similar now than at the beginning of the communist period, as are levels of urbanization. These changes are reflected in a decrease in differences between the two regions in national income produced per capita, although Slovakia still produced less per capita than the Czech Lands in 1980. This difference persisted despite a level of capital investment per capita which has been somewhat higher in Slovakia than in the Czech Lands throughout the period examined. However, differences between the two regions in the latter respect have been and remain relatively small.

If we look at indicators related to individuals' standards of living, the picture is in general similar, with the exception of educational access and ownership of certain consumer goods. Slovakia's proportion of students in higher education per 1,000 population between twenty and twenty-nine exceeds that of the Czech Lands and is the clearest area of success in equalization. Results are less favorable in the other areas investigated (income, infant mortality, and the ownership of personal automobiles, televisions, and washing machines), but in each, although differences persist, they have declined over time.

In most cases the change in governmental structure that occurred in 1968 appears to have had relatively little impact on differences between the two

Table 10-9
Consumer Durables: Number of Population per One Object
(selected years and five-year averages)

	CSSR	Czech Lands	Slovakia	Ratio: Slovakia/ Czech Lands
Electric washing machines				
1953	19.0	16.0	41.0	2.56
1955–1958	9.3	7.8	17.5	2.22
1959–1963	6.0	5.2	8.2	1.57
1964–1968	4.6	4.2	6.0	1.43
1969–1973	3.4	3.0	4.6	1.53
1974–1978	2.8	2.2	3.8	1.73
1979	2.0	2.0	3.0	1.50
1980	2.0	2.0	3.0	1.50
Refrigerators				
1953	156.0	139.0	226.0	1.63
1955–1958	86.0	76.0	125.3	1.66
1959–1963	25.2	22.4	37	1.64
1964–1968	9.6	8.6	13.2	1.54
1969–1973	5.2	4.6	6.4	1.39
1974–1978	3.8	3.4	4.2	1.24
1979	3.0	3.0	3.0	1.00
1980	3.0	3.0	3.0	1.00
Radios				
1953	5.0	4.0	7.0	1.75
1955–1958	4.3	4.0	5.3	1.33
1959–1963	4.4	3.4	4.0	1.20
1964–1968	3.0	2.6	3.0	1.20
1969–1973	2.0	2.0	2.6	1.30
1974–1978	2.0	2.0	2.0	1.00
1979	2.0	2.0	2.0	1.00
1980	2.0	2.0	2.0	1.00
Televisions				
1955–1958	134.8	97.8	7,675.0	39.11
1959–1963	13.6	11.0	31.2	2.67
1964–1968	5.8	5.2	8.6	1.65
1969–1973	4.0	3.6	5.4	1.52
1974–1978	3.0	2.6	3.8	1.46
1979	3.0	2.0	3.0	1.50
1980	3.0	2.0	3.0	1.50
Personal Automobiles				
1962	40.0	31.0	103.0	3.32
1964–1968	23.0	23.6	68.6	2.87
1969–1973	5.8	13.6	26.0	1.89
1974–1978	9.2	8.2	13.2	1.61
1979	8.0	7.0	10.0	1.43
1980	7.0	6.0	10.0	1.67

Sources; From information in Státní úřad statistický, *Statistická ročenka ČSSR*, 1960, p. 379; Ústřední úřad státní kontroly a statistiky, *Statistická ročenka ČSSR*, 1961, p. 394; 1965, p. 414; Federální statistický úřad, *Statistická ročenka ČSSR*, 1970, p. 456; 1977, p. 521; 1981, p. 538.

regions of the country. On most indicators the trend toward equalization continued steadily throughout the post-World War II period (infant mortality, levels of urbanization, labor force composition). Differences between Slovakia and the Czech Lands in these areas continued to decrease after 1968, but as part of a general trend begun considerably earlier. In the case of others, most notably average wages in the socialized sector of the national economy excluding agriculture and ownership of certain consumer durables, such as washing machines, radios, and televisions, much of the decrease in differences between the two regions occurred early in the communist period. Additional data on total income of the population in the Czech Lands and Slovakia indicate that there has been an improvement in this area in Slovakia since 1969, but it is difficult ot tell how this compares to the rate of change before 1968.

The clearest changes after 1968 have occurred in the area of educational access, but these changes appear to be due largely to the different course of the reform period in the Czech Lands and Slovakia rather than to the change to the federal structure itself. The faster increase in ownership of personal automobiles in Slovakia than in the Czech Lands after 1968 suggests that the standard of living in Slovakia may indeed have improved more rapidly after federalization, but this trend is contradicted by those in other aspects of ownership of consumer durables. In sum, there is little evidence so far that federalization has fulfilled the expectations of those Slovaks who saw it as necessary for eliminating remaining inequalities between the two regions. Further, the differences that have decreased more rapidly since 1968 may have done so due largely to other factors, such as the change in the political climate or the cumulative impact of changes begun earlier. On the other hand, while one cannot say that federalization has led, at least so far, to a noticeable reduction in remaining inequalities between the two regions, neither has it stopped the trend toward equalization already evident before it was put into effect.

What do these findings tell us about communist systems and socioeconomic inequalities? And what are their implications for political stability and policy-making in Czechoslovakia?

We must begin by considering how we ought to judge overall results. As Bahry and Nechemias have asked, is the cup half empty or half full? As these and other scholars have noted, one's answer to this question may depend on one's choice of indicators. It also may depend on the choice of time frame and reference group. Despite continued differences between the Czech Lands and Slovakia, the striking aspect of the data examined is the extent to which the gap between the two halves of the country has decreased. Compared to the situation in Czechoslovakia prior to the communist period and the continued differences among various regions of other socialist states, such as the Soviet Union and Yugoslavia, the results achieved in Czechoslovakia seem quite favorable. So, too, does the trend toward equalization if one compares it to the continued inequality which exists in Czechoslovakia along other social cleavages, most notably, between men and women.

But an important issue in assessing the political implications of social inequalities, is how affected groups view the situation. Do inhabitants of Slovakia judge their standard of living by comparing it to that of their parents or by looking at comparable groups in the Czech Lands? As the events in Poland in 1980-81 indicate, younger generations in communist states now appear to take for granted the material progress that their parents witnessed in the early post-World War II period. Far from being grateful to the communist regime for the progress achieved compared to the situation in 1945 or 1948, they are more concerned with how their standard of living compares to the immediate past and how it measures up to their expectations for the future. Although the situation in Czechoslovakia is obviously quite different, particularly in terms of opportunities for expressing dissatisfaction, than the situation existing in Poland prior to the imposition of martial law, it may well be that Slovaks are less impressed with the narrowing of the differences compared to those which existed in 1948 or even 1960 than they are with the (to be sure smaller) continued differences which exist today.

A related question is also important in assessing the political implications of these findings, and that is, how much equalization is enough? As Slovak claims made during the reform period in the late 1960s indicate, many Slovaks remained dissatisfied with their status in the Czechoslovak state despite the obvious progress that had occurred in the previous two decades. To what extent are Slovaks satisfied by the progress that has occurred since that time? To paraphrase the earlier question, does it matter if the cup is half full or nine-tenths full? What impact do various levels of reduction in the gap between the two regions have on popular perceptions and relations between inhabitants of the two areas?

A final question important in assessing the political implications of current regional differences in Czechoslovakia is the extent to which symbolic advantages may compensate for continued inequalities in the material sphere. Whatever the realities of how power is exercised and the actual competence of federal and republic governments, has federalization led Slovaks to see themselves as having an improved status in the state? And does this formal recognition of their claims to equality outweigh or compensate for continued differences in levels of economic development and standard of living?

Unfortunately, information is not available on how current differences are perceived by individuals in Slovakia and the Czech Lands at either the mass or elite level.[39] Nor are there any systematic data on how changes in the relative position of each region has influenced levels of tension or antagonism between Czechs and Slovaks.

Translation of social inequalities into the political arena also depends on a number of other factors the assessment of which is beyond the scope of this chapter. In addition to individuals' perceptions of their own status and that of members of other groups, such factors include the opportunities available for expressing political demands or dissatisfaction and the resources available to leaders of particular groups and, in unusual political times, mass publics, to press their claims. The extent to which regional disparities became political issues also appears to depend on the general political climate and the strategy of ethnic elites.

Currently opportunities for mass expression of dissatisfaction over regional differences or any other issue are clearly quite limited in Czechoslovakia. Possibilities for open debate among intellectuals over the extent and possible remedies for remaining inequalities are also severely restricted, compared to the situation in 1968. Still such issues are discussed to some degree among specialists, particularly those concerned with regional or territorial planning.[40] Furthermore, with the establishment of a federal system, consideration of the regional impact appears to have become institutionalized to some degree as one of the factors that must be taken into account in policymaking. Whether Slovak elites will use the federal mechanism to press for a reduction in regional disparities and whether the remaining differences between the Czech Lands and Slovakia will once again become acute political issues in Czechoslovakia are open questions, however.

Notes

1. For discussions of class inequalities see Walter D. Connor, *Socialism, Politics and Equality* (New York: Columbia University Press, 1979); David Lane, *The End of Inequality?* (Middlesex, England: Penguin Books, 1971) and *The Socialist Industrial State* (London: George Allen and Unwin, 1976); and Jaroslav Krejci, *Social Change and Stratification in Postwar Czechoslovakia* (New York: Columbia University Press, 1972). See Alena Heitlinger, *Women and State Socialism* (Montreal: McGill-Queen's University Press, 1979); Hilda Scott, *Does Socialism Liberate Women* (Boston: Beacon Press, 1973); and Sharon L. Wolchik, "Politics, Ideology, and Equality: The Status of Women in Eastern Europe," Ph.D. dissertation, the University of Michigan, Ann Arbor, 1977, for evaluations of differences between men and women and their implications.

2. See, for example, Peter A. Toma, "The Czechoslovak Question under Communism," *East European Quarterly* 3 (1969): 15; Josef Korbel, *Twentieth Century Czechoslovakia: The Meanings of Its History* (New York: Columbia University Press, 1977).

3. See Peter Brock and H. Gordon Skilling, eds., *The Czech Renascence of the Nineteenth Century* (Toronto: University of Toronto Press, 1970) and Bruce M. Garver, *The Young Czech Party 1874-1901 and the Emergence of a Multi-party System* (New Haven, Conn.: Yale University Press, 1978), for discussions of the status of the Czech Lands under Austrian administration and the development of Czech political life.

4. H. Gordon Skilling, in the introductory chapter of his *Czechoslovakia's Interrupted Revolution* (Princeton, N.J.: Princeton University Press, 1976), pp. 1-14, provides an excellent brief summary of differences between the two regions prior to the establishment of a communist system, as well as bibliographic references to other works on the topic. See Zora P. Pryor, "Czechoslovak Economic Development in the Interwar Period," in Victor S. Mamatey and Radomír Luža, eds., *A History of the Czechoslovak Republic, 1918-1948* (Princeton, N.J.: Princeton University Press, 1973), pp. 210-212 for a brief but informative summary of the economic and social differences between the two parts of the country prior to 1918. Pryor notes (p. 210) that illiteracy rates in Slovakia and Ruthenia were ten times higher than those in the Czech Lands in 1910.

5. See Owen Verne Johnson, "Sociocultural and National Development in Slovakia, 1918-1938: Education and Its Impact," Ph.D. dissertation, the University of Michigan, Ann Arbor, 1979, for a detailed analysis of the development of the Slovak intelligentsia in the interwar period.

6. As in later periods, the extent to which Slovakia benefited under the Czechoslovak Republic is a disputed issue. See Eugen Steiner, *The Slovak Dilemma* (Cambridge, England: Cambridge University Press, 1973), pp. 27-33, for a brief analysis of differing popular views; see Pryor, "Czechoslovak Economic Development in the Interwar Period," pp. 210-215 for information documenting the stagnation of Slovak industry and faster development in the Czech Lands during the latter part of the pre-World War II period.

7. Of course, other nationality issues also contributed greatly to the eventual demise of the Czechoslovak Republic, most predominantly the question of the Sudeten Germans. See J.W. Bruegel, *Czechoslovakia before Munich* (Cambridge, England: Cambridge University Press, 1973) for an analysis of this problem.

8. The issue of the Slovak state and Slovak actions during this period are also the subject of great dispute, by scholars as well as Czechs and Slovaks. See Dorothea H. El Mallakh, *The Slovak Autonomy Movement, 1935-1959: A Study in Unrelenting Nationalism* (Boulder, Colo.: East European Quarterly, 1979) and Steiner, *The Slovak Dilemma,* pp.34-59 for discussions of this period. See Stanislav J. Kirschbaum, "Le nationalisme minoritaire: le cas de la Tchecoslovaquie," *Canadian Journal of Political Science* 11, no. 2 (June 1974): 248-268 for a more analytical analysis of the development of Slovak nationalism in several different periods.

9. See Toma, "The Czechoslovak Question under Communism," pp.16-17 for information concerning the nationality composition of Czechoslovakia in 1948 and from 1950 to 1965; Vladimir V. Kusin, in *Political Groupings in the Czechoslovak Reform Movement* (New York: Columbia University Press, 1972), pp. 152, notes that minority nationalities (national groups other than Czechs and Slovaks) accounted for 36 percent of the population in interwar Czechoslovakia;

by 1968 this proportion had dropped to 6 percent. See ibid. pp. 143-161, for a discussion of the minority nationalities in the recent past and p. 152 for a discussion of inconsistencies in official figures concerning the numbers of particular minority national groups.

10. See *Košický vládní program* (Prague: Nakladatelstvı Svoboda, 1974).

11. See Galia Golan, *The Czechoslovak Reform Movement: Communism in Crisis, 1962-1968* (Cambridge, England: Cambridge University Press, 1971); Skilling, *Czechoslovakia's Interrupted Revolution,* pp. 451-489; Steiner, *The Slovak Dilemma,* pp. 93-111 for analyses.

12. Skilling, *Czechoslovakia's Interrupted Revolution,* pp. 451-459 and Appendix C provides the best summary of Slovak actions and the debates over federalism during the reform period. See also Steiner, *The Slovak Dilemma,* pp. 122-216.

13. See Skilling, *Czechoslovakia's Interrupted Revolution,* pp. 451-459, and Steiner, *The Slovak Dilemma,* pp. 133-138, for information on these debates. Sillling notes (p. 462) that Slovak leaders and experts were by no means united in their views concerning the optimum division of power between the federal and republic governments or their evaluations of Slovakia's progress during the previous period.

14. Victor Pavlenda, *Ekonomické základy socialistického riešenia národnostnej otázky v ČSSR* (Bratislava: Vydavatel'stvo politickej literatury, 1968).

15. See Skilling, *Czechoslovakia's Interrupted Revolution,* pp. 465-470, and Steiner, *The Slovak Dilemma,* pp. 131-132.

16. Though approved on this date, the federation actually went into effect only in January 1969.

17. Skilling, p. 873.

18. See, for example, Viliam Plevza, *Národnostná politika KSČ a česko/slovenské vztahy* (Bratislava: Práca, 1979), particularly pp. 374-377. Plevza also provides a detailed account of the debates leading up to federalization and information concerning the changes made after it was adopted.

19. See, for example, Kusin, *Political Groupings in the Czechoslovak Reform Movement,* p. 146.

20. See Donna Bahry, "Measuring Communist Priorities: Budgets, Investments, and the Problem of Equivalence," *Comparative Political Studies* 13, no. 3 (October 1980): 267-293 and the replies by Valerie Bunce, "Measuring Communist Priorities: A Reply to Bahry," pp. 293-298 and William A. Welsh, "On Understanding Budgets and Public Expenditures in Eastern Europe," pp. 299-312 in the same issue. See also Donna Bahry and Carol Nechemias, "Half-full or Half-empty?" The Debate over Soviet Regional Equality," *Slavic Review* 40, no 3 (Fall 1981): 366-383. See Ellen Jones and Fred W. Grupp, "Measuring Nationality Trends in the Soviet Union: A Research Note," *Slavic Review* 41, no. 1 (Spring 1982): 112-122 for a discussion of the impact of looking at various age groups in making comparisons.

21. As in other investigations of equality of social groups (c.f. John M. Echols, "Racial and Ethnic Inequality: The Comparative Impact of Socialism,"

Comparative Political Studies, 13, no. 4 (January 1981): 403-444; Connor; and Lane, *The End of Inequality?*). I have not attempted to create a composite index of social status or well-being. Rather, I examine each dimension separately, with the expectation that there may well be a good deal of variation in the extent of equalization for different indicators.

22. *Vývoj společnosti ČSSR podle výsledku sčítání lidu, domů a bytů 1970* (Prague: Federální statisticky úřad, 1971), p. 254. As noted earlier, Kusin, *Political Groupings in the Czechoslovak Reform Movement,* p. 146, discusses the variation in official statistics on nationality composition in Czechoslovakia. This variation appears to be greatest in the case of the Ukrainian or Ruthenian minority in Slovakia.

23. It is possible that the change of governmental structure in 1968 has been reflected in changes in the pattern of particular aspects of total investment, that is, in social or cultural areas or industrial development. Echols, "Racial and Ethnic Inequality," and "Politics, Budgets, and Regional Equality in Communist and Capitalist Systems," *Comparative Political Studies* 8, no. 3 (October 1975): 259-292; and Jack Bielesiak, "Policy Choices and Regional Equality among the Soviet Republics," *American Political Science Review* 74, no. 2 (June 1980): 394-405 have argued that there is a difference in how well communist leaders do in promoting equality among regions on social and cultural as opposed to economic variables. Unfortunately, because of changes in categories, it is not possible to compare changes in the individual items of total investment in Czechoslovakia before and after 1968.

24. Slightly over 39 percent of the labor force was in industry and construction in the Czech Lands in 1948. Slovakia achieved this level (39.2 percent) in 1966. From information in Federální statistický úřad, *Statistická ročenka ČSSR,* 1970, pp. 22-23, 42-43, 58-59.

25. The average annual rate of decrease for the two periods was 1.2 per year between 1948 and 1968 and 2.36 between 1969 and 1980. From information in sources listed in Table 10-3.

26. In the Czech Lands, 28.3 percent of inhabitants lived in cities of this size in 1950; 18.3 percent of the population in Slovakia lived in cities of this size in 1968. From information in Federální statistický úřad, *Statistická ročenka ČSSR,* 1969, p. 86.

27. Levels of urbanization in both halves of the country are somewhat low in comparison to those found in other developed countries. See Jiři Musil, *Urbánizace v socialistických zemích* (Prague: Nakladatelství Svoboda, 1977) for a comparative study of urbanization in socialist state.

28. These are defined in Czechoslovakia as industry, construction, agriculture, forestry, freight transport, communications for branches of material production, supply, trade and public catering, purchasing and other branches of material production. Federální statistický úřad, *Statistická ročenka ČSSR,* 1977, p. 119.

29. See Radoslav Selucký, *Ekonomické vyrovnávání Slovenska s českymi kraji* (Prague: Nakladatelstvi Svoboda, 1960) for information on the earlier period.

30. This proportion was 46.4 per 1,000 population between twenty and twenty-nine years of age in the Czech Lands in 1973 and 73.8 in Slovakia. From information in sources listed in Table 10-6.

31. See Skilling, *Czechoslovakia's Interrupted Revolution,* pp. 241-248 for a discussion of the difference course of the reform period in the Czech Lands and Slovakia.

32. Federální statistický úřad, *Statistická ročenka ČSSR,* 1977, pp. 38-39, 54-55, 70-71.

33. Results are very similar if we look only at full-time students. The main difference is that it took longer for the number of such students to reach pre-1969 levels in the Czech Lands than it did the number of all students (including night and correspondence students).

34. One finds continued differences as well in another indicator of health care, provision of hospital beds. However, the differences that persist between the two regions on this indicator may well be explained by the different age structures in the two areas, particularly by the fact that a larger proportion of the total population is over sixty years of age in the Czech Lands.

35. Based on information contained in the sources listed in Table 10-8. Average monthly wages in industry in Slovakia were 0.95 those in the Czech Lands in 1955 and 0.96 in 1980.

36. Jan Šindelka, in "Národnostní vztahy a sociální struktura socialisma v ČSSR," in Pavel Machonin a kolektiv, *Sociální struktura socialistické společnosti* (Prague: Nakladatelství Svoboda, 1967), p. 626, states that the income per one inhabitant was 21.7 percent lower in Slovakia than in the Czech Lands in 1960, but it is not clear how this figure was derived.

37. Conclusions are similar if we look at the number of households per 100 households that have particular objects. For example, in 1965 5 per 100 households in Slovakia, compared to 12 per 100 in the Czech Lands had personal automobiles; by 1970 the figures were 13 and 20, and by 1980 33 and 45. Federální statistický úřad, *Statistická ročenka ČSSR,* 1981, p. 538.

38. This occurred in 1980 for televisions and 1978 for washing machines (ibid.).

39. There is some evidence on mutual perceptions and evaluations of nationality relations made public during the reform period. See Skilling, *Czechoslovakia's Interrupted Revolution,* pp. 534-535 for the results of a poll that found very different evaluations of the seriousness of the nationality problem among Slovaks and Czechs in that period.

40. Examples of these discussions may be found in the publications of Terplan and Urbion, the territorial planning institutes in Prague and Bratislava.

Conclusion: Resource Distribution and Political Futures in Communist States

Daniel N. Nelson

Among all contemporary political systems, those governed by Communist parties are most identified with egalitarian values.[1] Contributors to this volume have, on many occasions, pointed to such a theoretical and rhetorical commitment:

> Socialism aims at equality. It emphasizes the common humanity and thus equal worth of human beings. . . (Susan Woodward)

> for revolutionary movements or organizations, legitimacy turns on expectations for socioeconomic and political "progress," usually seen as greater equality. . . . Marxism . . . emphasizes such equality in the presumed intimacy between party and proletariat. (Daniel N. Nelson)

> Communist regimes come to power with a strong ideological impetus to promote equality in the political, economic, social, and cultural realms." (Cal Clark)

With equal frequency they have pointed out the continued and in some cases expanding socioeconomic and political inequalities prevalent in communist states. That authors have focused upon such a paradox suggests no indictment unique to Communist party systems or socialist economies per se; instead, we have sought to identify and to explain the antecedents and consequences of such inequalities for Communist party rule.

Neither the antecedents nor the consequences of inequalities can be, Valerie Bunce argued, disentangled from international inequalities—a political economy of dependency relationships with which Eastern Europe is all too familiar. Linked inextricably to the regional hegemon in the USSR, the client states of Eastern Europe bear mounting costs of international and domestic inequalities. Any escape from inequality of power and resources, however, is unlikely to be led by party leadership in communist states. In Chapter 2 it was suggested that the political control by a Communist party rests on the continuance of inequalities insofar as the combination of participation and resources is unavailable to many segments of society; through such inequities, access to power is denied to non-sanctioned individuals and groups. Inequalities are in fact utilitarian for Communist party rule, performing a gatekeeping function to guard policymaking from unwanted inputs.

271

Inequalities in communist systems originate and persist, then, in a political milieu. The antecedents of a maldistribution of socioeconomic or political resources are themselves political. It follows that policymaking and implementation regarding resources distribution in communist states will reflect contradictions imposed by international dependencies and domestic political control. The USSR's welfare ideology and style therefore limit the methods and parameters of public activity directed towards equality. A collective dependency welfare ideology dictated by the Soviets' need to mobilize and direct public energies while pacifying and subordinating the public, argues John Robertson, has contributed to halting and erratic progress toward subsistence support by the state. In both East and West, concludes Robertson, "greater equality will have to come at the political expense of those unable, unwilling and/or unlikely to assume these costs." From cross-national findings presented by Cal Clark it is apparent that such costs have not been assumed in communist states; their general record is "about as inegalitarian on regional affluence and economic structure as comparable noncommunist ones." Following the dictates of a strategy to combine growth with "equity in reducing disparities in living conditions," most communist states (Clark notes that Yugoslavia is an exception) opt for allocations of public services that ameliorate continuing inequalities of wealth. Caught in a web of international dependency and domestic political insecurity, communist regimes are unable and unwilling to bite the bullet of inequalities. In comparative terms, their performance does not reflect their rhetoric.

Case studies have enabled us to understand in much more detail the antecedents of specific dimensions of inequality. Interesting parallels emerge from case studies regarding, for example, the role of central leadership in variations of interregional/provincial appropriations and investments. Donna Bahry finds that the expectation of higher per capita appropriations from Moscow due to Politburo representation of a union republic was not supported; nor were other hypotheses concerning the effect of republic leadership composition or change in republic leadership supported. David Lampton, analyzing interprovincial inequalities in China, likewise concludes that central policy choices are the key explanatory variables in determining provincial performance. The implications appear to be that communist systems respond not to the pressures of inequalities from below, but rather to intrabureaucratic interests. The political choices of party leaders are critical to the performance of communist systems regarding inequalities—choices that local leaders and conditions affect but do not determine. But as Robertson found in a comparative perspective, and Lampton and Bahry reinforce in specific cases, the values and ideological commitments of party elites allow little latitude in the distribution of resources. Both Lampton and Bahry, moreover, emphasize the role played by the sheer complexity of policymaking, a condition that constrains policy innovation to combat inequalities. The USSR has performed relatively well in mitigating interrepublic inequality for social expenditures, but the good performance on that dimension of inequality is rather fortuitous in Bahry's estimation; compromises made to resolve competing demands for funds result in a de facto equalization of appropriations.

Inequalities based specifically on ethnicity and language originated, of course, long before communist regimes. But as both Mary Ellen Fischer and Sharon Wolchik found, resource and paticipatory inequalities between or among nationalities have not been eliminated. The advance made in living standards and opportunities for Slovaks has been considerable since World War II, but Czech Lands remain advantaged on several important indicators, and federalism since 1968 represents no guarantee to Slovaks of political equality. Hungarians in Romania may be receiving more equal treatment in the Ceauşescu era, argues Mary Ellen Fischer, but Hungarians in Romania perceive that policy as decreasing their group and organizational rights. Thus the political import of ethnic inequality in communist systems has less to do with residual material gaps between nationalities than perceptions about the speed, direction, and intention of change. Evaluations by members of ethnic minorities of their status (in political or socioeconomic terms), rather than quantifiable differences, may be the most important antecedent of such inequalities in communist systems. Communist regimes have failed to alter the subjective orientation of minority nationalities they rule; inequalities among ethnic or linguistic groups remain politically volatile less because of what people have than because of how they feel as citizens of a particular Communist party state dominated by another nationality.

Socioeconomic gaps among Yugoslav republics unlike the Soviet and Czechoslovak cases, are increasing. Most indicators cited by Susan Woodward suggest that conditions are not favorable for a reversal of this trend during the 1980s. Concessions to political equality among Yugoslav republics and social strata (self-management, the market, and federalism) help diffuse threats to stability arising from discontent, but also worsen societal inequality. The political impotence felt by Hungarians or suspected by Slovaks, in Romania and Czechoslovakia respectively, may be less pronounced than various nationalities in Yugoslavia, but socioeconomic inequality is more evident. The linkage between different dimensions of inequality is thus dramatic in Yugoslavia, where managing one form has exacerbated another; antecedents of inequalities can be other inequalities.

Poland's experiences during the 1970s and early 1980s reiterate the importance of policy choices made by national political leaders as antecedents to inequalities. As Jack Bielasiak described trends during the Gierek decade, the economic planning of that Polish regime led to glaring material inequalities. Those most negatively affected (manual workers) were the same people for whom political expression was most limited via official channels. Left with no alternative to air their considerable grievances, workers took the route of collective militant action in the late summer of 1980.

From comparative analyses and case studies, it is reasonable to conclude that inequalities in communist systems have political origins. Although this generalization oversimplifies country-specific nuances, the contributors seem in agreement that policies may by Communist party leaders frequently exacerbate socioeconomic or political gaps among occupational strata, nationalities, or other population segments. In some cases actual performance in alleviating certain material inequities among regions or nationalities has been quite positive over time (as in Czechoslovakia and the USSR), whereas the subjective evaluations by citizens may continue to question the motives of a party leadership and to be dissatisfied with the pace of change. And, while authors have identified considerable variation among communist states concerning their progress toward equality on certain dimensions (classes more unequal in Poland than circa 1970; nationalities materially much more equal now than several decades ago in Czechoslovakia), they speak with some unanimity about the connection between Communist party rule and inequalities. Most blatantly in Poland, party elites benefited from inequalities, improving their material lives while enjoying privileges and access unavailable to others. In China the political survival of Deng Xiaoping and moderates depends on economic growth, which Lampton foresees as being related to increasing inequalities. Notwithstanding their relatively good record, the Soviet leadership may distribute resources equally only due to the political necessity of compromise. Putting their immediate political fortunes first, post-Tito Yugoslav leadership emphasizes political equality at the expense of widening socioeconomic gaps among regions and strata. Romanian Communist party elites meanwhile fashion policies that utilize the rhetoric of individual equality but deny to national minorities any organizational outlet by which they could protect their community.

The politics of inequalities in communist systems are thus as much in their origins as in their consequences. Why egalitarianism is not achieved and only partially pursued in Communist party states cannot be understood separately from (1) the relationship of East Europe to the regional hegemon, Moscow, (2) the function of inequalities in making policymaking influence inaccessible to minorities, women, workers, and other segments of society, (3) the welfare ideology that dictates that social security and public assistance are mobilization tools, and (4) a policy preference for increasing social services rather than undertaking a substantive redistribution of wealth. At the nation-state level, it is apparent that political factors are correlates of performance by communist systems in combating inequalities; policies in such regimes, it should surprise no one to find, arise from compromises among competing elites and bureaucracies, from calculations by party leaders of their own political fortunes, and from little more than self-aggrandizement (as appears to have been the case in Poland). These considerations do not mean that Communist party states will necessarily perform poorly versus inequalities; rather, they suggest that, no matter what such governments do to lessen differences of access to socioeconomic or political goods, egalitarian values may play no role whatsoever in the policymaking process. Indeed, substantial evidence has been presented here that progress against some dimensions of inequality may be the product of political compromise and that communist leaders are quite willing to accept inequalities that benefit their political position.

Systemic consequences of inequalities are varied and debatable. Not all dimensions of inequality have the same systemwide effect and not all communist states are similarly vulnerable. Nevertheless, contributors to this book have been uniform in their suspicion (albeit expressed with varying degrees of assurance and intensity) that the presence of inequalities is related negatively to the stability of Communist party rule.

Inherent to socioeconomic and political cleavages are feelings of relative deprivation and conflictual interactions between haves and have nots, between rulers and ruled, between elites and masses, and between majority and minorities. Most of all, inequalities imply conflict. Factories need not be idled by massive strikes to know that Polish workers constitute a stratum deeply alienated from party authority; acts of violence by Croatians or Albanians are only the most visible signs of ethnic conflict in Yugoslavia. Conflict, of course, occurs daily in much less evident forms as those who are denied material or partcipatory equality (or perceive such a denial) seek access to power; that a competition for resources will go on, means that ruling Communist parties must invest enormous sums of cadre time and money to convince citizens that the system listens and responds even while they repress any suggestion that the party's interests are those of only the haves and the elites.

But the party cannot disassociate itself from social strains engendered by inequalities. "In the final analysis", on Polish sociologist has written "it all comes down to the question [of] the legitimacy of the existing system:[2]

> With a centralized system of decision-making and supervision of [policy execution] . . . any, even small, deterioration of living standards brings into sharp relief the problem of methods of leader recruitment. Doubt is cast on the leaders' legitimacy and the question is revived as to whose interests are really represented by people in authority".[3]

Systemic performance, gauged by the extent to which principles of egalitarianism are implemented, thus becomes a formidable threat to the legitimacy of party rule. Criteria by which equity is measured vary among the cases discussed in this volume because the most politicized dimension of inequality is not uniform. Nevertheless Communist parties can be and are indicted by their populations for failures to produce—or to produce fast enough—the equity and justice to which the party commits itself. That domestic inequities are related to the influence of a regional hegemon or that socioeconomic and political gaps are not without utility for the party's control may deepen citizen alienation rather than explain away such inequalities. In systems where the party-state is highly obtrusive, planning and implementing the allocation of resources throughout the society and economy, the party leadership cannot sidestep the issue of inequity. Having sensitized the populations to egalitarian values over two decades (Cuba), almost four (in the case of Eastern Europe and China), or nearly seven decades (the Soviet case), the party's excuse for dictatorship of the proletariat can no longer be ignored when inconvenient. Struggling for continued growth in an era of worldwide economic malaise, ruling Communist parties in China, Romania, and Poland (among others) would no doubt prefer not to be reminded that a redistributive intent was thought to be inherent to socialism.

At the party's doorstep, will therefore be placed the impatience of Slovaks, the mistrust of Hungarians in Romania, the alienation of workers in Poland and the frustration of less developed provinces in Deng's China. Women, intellectuals, the aged, or any stratum or group believing that they are likewise unequal in material or participatory senses will also attribute to the party-state and its leaders their inability to achieve parity with comparison groups. As the attribution of inequities to the party continues, the political future of these regimes can be seen as more costly, more conflictual or both.

If ruling Communist parties do respond to inequalities, directing policy towards a fundamental redistribution of wealth, their political futures will involve significant human and material commitments. Such costs of redistributing socioeconomic and political goods would become apparent as more cadres are designated for developmental efforts in poor regions in combination with disproportionately large central investments to those locales. But the same response to egalitarianism also entails conflict; the redistribution of resources, particularly during times when growth is curtailed or absent, involves taking from some strata, regions, or groups for reinvestment elsewhere. Within the party and in society generally, the privileged resist such policies fearing that their political control will dissipate as others, heretofore denied access to power, are given the means by which to present demands upon the system.

Were the same regimes to avoid such short-term costs and conflicts by paying no more than lip service to the egalitarian values that first rationalized the party's hegemony, the long-term consequences may be more severe. The emphasis on growth seen in economic plans of most communist systems usually implies the concentration of wealth rather than its diffusion. Maximizing the party's mobilization capabilities likewise implies a concentration of cadres in certain key locales and industries. But the costs of such policy directions are likely to include a mounting alienation of citizens from party, as the gap between egalitarian expectations and system performance becomes more evident. Tangible effects of such alienation might appear first at the workplace as productivity falls and quality fails to improve. Ultimately the kinds of inequalities discussed in this book would make it much more difficult for a Communist regime to obtain the willing obedience of its citizens. As legitimacy, derived at best from system performance in postrevolutionary Communist party states, dissipates, overt conflict with the party may escalate—Poland being an extreme example. Seen as uncommitted to assuring the dignity of all citizens, the party loses whatever commitment there had been to quiescent citizenship.

Communist systems need not follow such a worst-case scenario. Inequalities imply, however, a political future in which ruling Communist parties face more, not less, difficulty in the maintenance of their position of hegemony without harsh coercion. Innovative and farsighted leadership, fortuitous international situations and combination of other variables may enable Communist parties to manage the conflicts and to absorb the costs of inequalities. Indeed, these regimes may have no choice in taking this rocky path, given (aside from China) the international inequalities imposed by their linkage to the USSR, the relationship between inequalities and political control, and a closely associated welfare ideology. Ironically political organizations that had origins in egalitarian values find their legitimacy doubted (or altogether absent) *because* of inequalities.

Notes

1. See Renata Siemienska's restatement of this ideological commitment in her paper "Mass-Authority Relations in the Polish Crisis: Anatomy of Social Consciousness", prepared for the APSA meeting, Denver, Co., September 2-5, 1982.
2. ibid., p. 2.
3. I.

Index

About the Contributors

Donna Bahry is assistant professor of politics at New York University. She holds the Ph.D. degree from the University of Illinois at Urbana-Champaign, and is the author of articles published in *Comparative Political Studies* and the *Slavic Review.*

Jack Bielasiak obtained the Ph.D. at Cornell University. Presently he is an associate professor of political science at the Russian-East European Institute at Indiana University. His articles on Soviet, Polish and comparative communist politics have been in the *American Political Science Review, Studies in Comparative Communism* and a wide variety of other edited works and journals. He has edited *Poland Today* (1981) and is now completing a book entitled *Poland: The Politics of Crisis.*

Valerie Bunce received the Ph.D. from the University of Michigan and is currently an associate professor of political science at Northwestern University. Her work has appeared in the *American Political Science Review, Comparative Political Studies* and other journals. Her book entitled *Do Leaders Make a Difference?* was published in 1981.

Cal Clark received the Ph.D. from the University of Illinois and he is now associate professor of political science at the University of Wyoming. He is co-author of *Comparative Politics of Foreign Policy and Trade: The Communist Balkans in International Politics* and *Development's Influence on Yugoslav Political Values* and is coeditor of *Dependency Reversal: Potentials in the Modern World System.* He has contributed to many journals including the *American Political Science Review, Comparative Political Studies, East Central European Quarterly* and *International Studies Quarterly.*

Mary Ellen Fischer, associate professor of government, Skidmore College, received the Ph.D. from Harvard University. A recipient of IREX, Fulbright, and ACLS grants for research in Romania, she has published articles on Romanian politics in *Balkanistica, Southeastern Europe,* and several books. Her contribution to this book was completed with support from the Russian Research Center, Harvard University, and the National Council for Soviet and East European Research.

David M. Lampton received the Ph.D. from Stanford University, did postdoctoral work at the University of Michigan, and since 1974 has been at The Ohio State University, where he is an associate professor in the Department of Political Science. Dr. Lampton's work has appeared in *The American Political*

Science Review, Foreign Policy, The China Quarterly, Problems of Communism, Studies in Comparative Communism, and *The Western Political Quarterly.* Professor Lampton is the author of *The Politics of Medicine in China.*

John D. Robertson obtained the Ph.D. degree from the University of Illinois. He is currently an assistant professor of political science at Texas A&M University. His research has appeared in *The American Economist, Comparative Social Research, Comparative Political Studies* and in edited volumes concerning Soviet politics.

Sharon Wolchik received the Ph.D. at the University of Michigan and is now an assistant professor of international affairs and political science and a member of the Institute for Sino-Soviet Studies at the George Washington University. She is coauthor of *Domestic and Foreign Policy in Eastern Europe in the 1980's* and has published articles on women in politics and social change in Eastern Europe in *Comparative Political Studies, Women & Politics, Studies in Comparative Communism,* and *Slavic Review.* She is currently working on a study of specialists' and professionals' influence on policy-making in Eastern Europe.

Susan Woodward holds the Ph.D. degree from Princeton University and is an assistant professor of political science at Yale University. Her articles on Yugoslav politics have appeared in journals such as *World Politics* and many edited volumes. In 1975–1976, she was a visiting fellow at the Center of International Studies at Princeton University, and in 1981–1982 she was research associate at the Harvard University Russian Research Center. Her research has included fieldwork in Yugoslavia.

About the Editor

Daniel N. Nelson received the Ph.D. degree at The Johns Hopkins University in 1975 and he is presently an associate professor of political science at the University of Kentucky. He is the author of *Democratic Centralism* and editor of and contributor to *Soviet Allies, Local Politics in Communist Countries, Romania in the 1980s* and *Communist Legislatures in Comparative Perspective.* His articles have appeared in *World Politics, Comparative Politics, Journal of Politics, Slavic Review, Soviet Studies, Problems of Communism,* and other journals and edited books.